'Forever their names are wri

This book is dedicated to the men and women of the Polish Air Force. They asked for nothing but to see their country free. They fought with bravery, courage, honour and loyalty alongside their allies in the Second World War.

The author will donate fifty percent of her royalties to the Polish Air Force Memorial Committee to support its work commemorating the achievements of the Polish Air Force and in honour of the fallen for the benefit of future generations.

'Mother I must go, you will see, your grandchildren will read about my actions in books.'

Stefan Wójtowicz's last words to his mother before leaving Poland in September 1939.

CONTENTS

FOREWORD

It may appear strange to begin with an apology, yet I feel I must. With regret, I cannot write about every one of the 17,000 Polish men and women of the Polish Air Force (PAF) who made their way to Great Britain to continue the fight for freedom in the Second World War. These men and women deserve to have their stories told because they are all heroes. They flew, fought, and bled alongside our Royal Air Force (RAF) to keep the Nazi evil from Great Britain's shores while their own country was ripped apart. My book has been written as a tribute to each one of the 17,000 unsung heroes.

I hope those with little knowledge of the Polish Air Force's contribution during the Second World War will come to appreciate the huge debt we owe them for our freedom.

This book has been the result of over thirty years of research to learn more about the Polish pilots of the Second World War. During that time I have traced and interviewed the pilots and their families to ensure that this book is filled with their own words. This book is my way of sharing their stories with others in an accessible way.

The interviews cover many aspects of the Polish Air Force in the Second World War. They cover air force training in Poland, the Polish campaign, fighting in France and evacuation to England by various routes. There are insights into the training of Polish pilots in Great Britain, the RAF fighter and bombers squadrons, and the women ferry pilots. The experiences of Polish prisoners of war (POW) in Stalag Luft III and the impact of war on the pilots' families in Poland also feature in the book.

On the Polish Air Force standard on one side are written the very apt words, *'Love demands Sacrifice'*.

It has been a great personal honour for me to interview many Polish men and women ex-combatants and their families while researching this book. I am grateful for the trust given by each person who took me into their confidence.

To listen in awe to the stories of their lives during the dark days of the Second World War has been an honour. Each story holds a special place in my heart. I am a better person for knowing them. Writing this book has not been easy in parts — not the work, but researching and writing about the cruelty inflicted on the Polish nation. I have shed many tears in sadness while sitting with those I have interviewed, and my tears stain the many letters sent from Poland. Yet, I have felt uplifted by the spirit of a nation of people who never gave up fighting during the occupation despite the terrible atrocities inflicted upon them by the Nazis and Soviets.

The human spirit can never be defeated by such evil, for it resides in a higher place than this.

PREFACE
The Polish Air Force Fights On

The roar of German aircraft filled the sky over Poland in the early hours of the 1 September 1939. One and a half million German ground troops waited under cover of darkness, ready for what would become a rapid and brutal invasion.

After the First World War, when Poland gained independence on 11 November 1918 from the Austro-Hungarian and German Empires, and after the Bolshevik conflict of 1919-1920, Poland was not in a position to spend large amounts of money on her armed forces. The country was ill-equipped to do battle with the organised, well-armed German military. Poland had delayed full mobilisation until 30 August 1939 on the advice of British and French authorities, but the delay did nothing to prevent Hitler from attacking. Instead, it put Poland at a disadvantage. Two-thirds of Poland's troops had yet to reach the front line when the first sound of German gunfire boomed across the sea near Gdańsk (later Danzig), signalling the beginning of the invasion.

The Polish Air Force responded in aircraft that was mainly obsolete. The courageous pilots flew into battle against overwhelming odds with little fuel and ammunition held in reserve. The Polish Air Force had approximately 350 aircraft, including 27 PZL-7 fighters and 175 PZL-11 fighters. These two-gun monoplanes were slower than the German fighters but more manoeuvrable.

To preserve as much of its air assets, the Polish Air Force had moved approximately 1,000 airmen and ground crew to secret airfields in late August 1939. In comparison, the Luftwaffe had approximately 2,000 aircraft and more held in reserve.

Poland June 1939 — Group of cadets and their instructor Corporal Pilot Antoni Widawski at Dęblin training school. Photo: author's own collection.

The Luftwaffe airmen took off in poor visibility during the early morning on 1 September 1939. They attacked with one aim — to crush Poland. Most of Poland's people were sleeping peacefully, unaware of the destruction and cruelty many in the country would face.

Captain Krasnodębski took to the sky that morning as commander of the Warsaw No.111 Kościuszko Squadron.

> *'We were flying from dawn to night in order to combat continuous enemy raids, trying to prevent unrestrained bombardment and the strafing of defenceless people in towns and cities. The battles were fierce and very hard and uneven as the German planes were faster with superior firepower and more numerous. Despite these discrepancies we won many battles but unfortunately suffered severe losses. During one action I attacked a Dornier which crashed in flames killing all the crew. Satisfied with our success the flight proudly cruised awhile over the burning aircraft.'*

The Polish fighter pilots destroyed seven enemy aircraft during their many sorties that morning. Later that afternoon, the Luftwaffe flew towards the Polish capital Warsaw. The Polish airmen of No. 111

Kościuszko Squadron and No. 112 Wing Squadron, both part of No. 111/1 Fighter Flight Squadron Wing, flew to attack the German bombers and their fighter escort. They destroyed a further eight enemy aircraft.

By 2 September 1939, many civilians lay dead; their blood soaking into the earth of the country they held dear. Warsaw was burning, along with towns and cities all over the country. The following day, Neville Chamberlain announced that Great Britain had declared war on Germany.

In Poland, thirty-five-year-old Captain Krasnodębski flew in combat on 3 September 1939 and faced his enemy head on. Tracer bullets from a German Messerschmitt Me110 aircraft hit the Captain's aircraft. Suddenly, Captain Krasnodębski's aircraft became engulfed in flames, forcing him to bale out. His parachute opened but, as he floated through the smoke, the Messerschmitt Me110 returned to finish him off. In those moments, Captain Krasnodębski's thoughts drifted to his colleague, who had baled out of his aircraft the previous day and had been shot dead while suspended in his parachute. Captain Krasnodębski heard bullets and prepared to die.

The bullets came from guns fired by twenty-seven-year-old Lieutenant Arsen Cebrzyński of No. 111 Kościuszko Squadron. With deadly intent in his heart, Lieutenant Cebrzyński fired and hit the German fighter, sending the enemy aircraft and its two airmen crashing to earth. Captain Krasnodębski landed safely with bruises and minor burns. While the Captain recovered, Captain Gustaw Sidorowicz, then Captain Wojciech Januszewicz led No. 111 Kościuszko Squadron.

The Polish Air Force flew in many military operations against overwhelming odds during September 1939. By 8 September 1939, the Polish Air Force was in a desperate position — there were men to fly the aircraft but little ammunition, fuel, or spare aircraft parts.

Soviet aircraft attacked the Polish airfield near Buczacz a week later. In a secret agreement, Hitler had enticed Stalin into the war in exchange for a share of Poland and other European countries. During the first two and half weeks of September, the Polish Air Force lost 114 aircraft and fifty airmen. They fought valiantly against the German attack from the north and west, and Soviets approaching from the east.

The September campaign in Poland was one of the most fiercely fought battles in the Second World War. The Polish Air Force destroyed 126 enemy aircraft over Poland. The Polish anti-aircraft artillery destroyed 150 enemy aircraft. A further 279 enemy aircraft were so damaged, they were unable to take to the sky. Polish forces took out of action a total of 555 enemy aircraft before they were forced to withdraw. Poland's defence lasted for just thirty-five days, but it took the Germans many more months to recover.

By 17 September 1939, the day the Soviets invaded Poland, most of the Polish Air Force had received orders to withdraw to Romania. The plan was to regroup in Romania and await reinforcements. With heavy hearts the pilots obeyed. Captain Krasnodębski said goodbye to his wife Wanda. Lieutenant Cebrzyński took one last look at his young wife Jadwiga and their son Jacek. He wondered if they would survive under the bloody boot of Nazi and Soviet power.

Many of those in the Polish Air Force had no time to bid farewell to their families. The pilots left Poland to continue the fight from foreign shores.

Sergeant Stefan Wójtowicz was fortunate enough to say goodbye to his family before journeying to Romania. The tall, attractive Sergeant had been awarded his eagle wings in June 1939, the same month of his twentieth birthday. When he visited his family for the last time in mid-September 1939, his mother cried and begged him not to go.

'Mother I must go, you will see, your grandchildren will read about my actions in books.'

On 25 September 1939, the Luftwaffe began to bomb Warsaw. Over 500 tons of high explosive rained down upon the city. Many men, women, and children lay dead among the rubble. Smoke and the smell of death filled the air, but the people refused to surrender.

Romania abandoned the pre-war plan to assist Poland and declared neutrality. To appease Hitler, the Romanian authorities corralled the Polish airmen into internment camps. Some Polish pilots escaped the camps, others received help from sympathetic Romanians.

Corporal Eugeniusz Szaposznikow was twenty-three years old and filled with hate. He had flown over thirty sorties in Poland with No. 111 Kościuszko Squadron and was itching to continue the fight from France. He hatched a plan with two other pilots to escape from the Romanian internment camp. They cut through the wire fence and ran as fast as their legs would carry them while bullets fired by Romanian guards whizzed past. They made it to a river and escaped.

Pilots made their way to France by travelling over land through Yugoslavia and northern Italy. Some paid bribes to escape by air and sea from the Black Sea ports of Constanța and Balchik; others moved through the straights of Syria. Polish pilots streamed out of Poland and Romania by any available route. All hope for continuing the fight now depended on the pilots reaching French soil.

In France, the French Air Force welcomed the Polish pilots and ground crew. A total of 135 Polish pilots posted in various squadrons achieved sixty-seven kills. For every Polish pilot in the air, more were waiting on the ground without an aircraft to fly. As each day passed, the Polish airmen grew more and more frustrated and consumed with the desire to avenge their homeland.

France in spring 1940 — Cadet Officer Kazimierz Karaszewski (centre) waiting to join French air squadrons. The other two pilots were later killed during bomber operations from Great Britain. Photo: Permission of Kazimierz Karaszewski

On 17 June 1940, the news that everyone was dreading came — Marshal Pétain had announced the surrender of France. General Sikorski, the Polish Commander in Chief, gave the order for all Polish units in France to evacuate to Great Britain by any means possible. With the exception of one Polish Air Force squadron, which continued in Africa, the Polish forces made their way across the English Channel to continue the fight alongside their British Allies.

France 1939 — Witold Urbanowicz (centre wearing armband) with some of the fifty cadets he helped to evacuate from Poland to Romania and France. Photo: Permission of Kazimierz Karaszewski.

The first Polish airmen and ground crew landed in England in late 1939. Posted to RAF Eastchurch, the Polish pilots received medical assessments on arrival, followed by English lessons and instruction on the RAF rules and regulations. There seemed to be many tedious parades but no RAF flight training.

The Polish airmen became frustrated. They wanted answers to their questions: *When will flight training take place? We are fighter pilots and what we do best is fight the enemy. How can we kill the enemy in the air when we are kept on the ground?*

After weeks of waiting, the Polish airmen's uniforms arrived. All hope that they were to fly in combat soon vanished. More time passed. The Polish airmen became more vocal in their feelings of anger. Tensions mounted and arguments flared between Polish and British officers. The language barrier only added to the tension.

Many of the Polish airmen had tasted the sweetness of revenge during combat in Poland and France. They knew what it was like to face the enemy and the pleasure of shooting them down. Many of the men in the Polish Air Force had flown for years, developing excellent flying skills. In Poland, they had pitched their meagre resources against the well-armed German troops, but the British did not trust their expertise. Some senior figures in the RAF only saw the Polish defeat. After all, the Polish Air Force had lasted only a few weeks in September 1939.

Finally, in the spring of 1940, the RAF sent a selection of Polish airmen for flight training. After the fall of France in June 1940, the bulk of arriving Polish airmen and ground crew were sent to Blackpool. Poland moved her Government-in-Exile from France to England. On 5 August the Anglo-Polish Agreement was signed. In the agreement, the Polish Air Force kept its independent sovereignty. The distribution of personnel for training was in the hands of the Inspectorate General. The British commanded the operations, but the tactical side of some operations remained in Polish hands.

On 2 August 1940 No. 303 Polish Fighter Squadron was formed at RAF Northolt in South Ruislip, Middlesex under No. 11 Group. Many of the Polish pilots chosen for the squadron had fought together in Poland with No. 111 Kościuszko Squadron under Major Krasnodębski.

R/T training in the air began on 10 August, formation flying on 12th and patrol flying on 24th. Soon the Polish Eagles of Kościuszko Squadron would bloody their wing tips in the Battle of Britain.

INTRODUCTION
to No.303 Kościuszko Squadron at RAF Northolt

The name given to No. 303 Tadeusz Kościuszko Squadron (City of Warsaw) followed a long Polish Air Force tradition. The formal name of the squadron was No. 303 (Polish) Squadron but after Wing Commander Krasnodębski intervened, *'the English authorities agreed to the adoption for the Wing/Squadron, the name Kościuszko.'*

The squadron was named after Tadeusz Bonaventura Kościuszko, the leader of the Polish resistance of 1794. Tadeusz Kościuszko was born in 1746 in a small village now in Belarus. He trained in the Corps of Cadets in Warsaw at the age of twenty. He is a national hero in America for his work as a military engineer during the American war for independence, and in Poland for fighting against Russian and Prussian forces. In 1794, he led the Kościuszko Uprising against the partition of Poland. The defeat of the uprising put an end to Polish independence for the next 123 years.

The 7th Kościuszko Squadron formed in 1919 when a group of American volunteers joined the 3rd Fighter Squadron at Lwów. American and Polish pilots flew together in the Polish-Bolshevik war of 1919-1920 under the command of Cedric Fauntleroy and later, Merian Cooper. After the war, the 7th Kościuszko Squadron joined the 1st Polish Air Regiment as No.111 Kościuszko Squadron.

In late July 1940, Squadron Leader Ronald Kellett arrived at RAF Northolt in South Ruislip, Middlesex to command a Czechoslovakian Squadron. He was less than pleased to find he was to lead a Polish squadron rather than an RAF squadron. He discussed the inevitable barriers faced by the Polish squadron with British Air Officer Commanding (AOC) RAF Fighter Command, Hugh Dowding. He aired his concerns — how could the Polish and British fight together without a common language? Could the Polish pilots receive and follow orders given in English over the transmitter during combat? AOC Hugh Dowding listened to Squadron Leader Kellett's concerns. He was also wary of forming a Polish squadron. During August 1940, he returned many times to RAF Northolt with Air Vice-Marshal Keith Park to keep a close eye on the squadron's progress.

RAF Northolt's Station Commander, Group Captain Stanley Vincent introduced some excellent camouflage. He had the hangars painted to look like the houses in nearby South Ruislip. Windows with curtains and flowerpots were added for extra detail. He camouflaged the mess and the stores as buildings. The two runways at RAF Northolt were painted a murky green-blue to look like a river. It was usual for pilots flying to the airfield for the first time to experience a dose of apprehension when landing on what looked like river close to houses.

The first Polish squadron, No. 302 Polish Squadron, had been formed on 13 July 1940 at RAF Leconfield in Yorkshire. Less than a month later, the RAF formed a second squadron, known as No. 303 Kościuszko Polish Squadron. Northolt was also home to No. 1 RAF Squadron, No. 1 Royal Canadian Squadron, and No. 257 Squadron until No. 257 Squadron left for Debden on 15 August 1940. A flight from No. 264 Squadron arrived on 12 August, No. 229 Squadron arrived on 9 September 1940 and on the 18 September, a lone Spitfire flew in from No. 92 Squadron.

On 2 August 1940, the Polish pilots posted to No. 303 Kościuszko Squadron began to arrive at RAF Northolt, along with the Polish ground crew. Some wore the dark blue battledress and berets that they had worn in France. They were divided into three flights - 'A' and 'B' Flight were airmen and the ground crew were 'C' Flight. The pilots had accrued over 400 flying hours during their time in Poland.

For each senior RAF officer in the Squadron, there was a Polish equivalent serving alongside. Squadron Leader Zdzisław Krasnodębski was the Polish Commanding Officer. He and Squadron Leader Kellett could go up with either flight. Flight Lieutenant John Kent commanded 'A' Flight with Flying Officer Witold Urbanowicz as second in command.

Flight Lieutenant Athol Forbes commanded 'B' Flight with Flying Officer Wacław Łapkowski as his second in command.

Squadron Leader Kellett and General Ujejski of the Polish Air Force agreed that more Polish pilots could be recruited from Blackpool if needed.

At the formation of No. 303 Kościuszko Squadron, twenty-eight of the thirty-six pilots were Polish. Squadron Leader Ronald Kellett and Flight Lieutenant Athol Forbes were English, and Flight Lieutenant John Kent was Canadian. Sergeant Jozef František and Sergeant Jozef Kania were Czechoslovakian pilots who had fled to Poland and fought with the Polish Air Force. They are included in the collective term 'Polish pilots' used throughout this book. Three more Polish pilots arrived in September 1940.

Reuben Hotel, London 1941 — Squadron Leader Kellett, Flight Lieutenant John Kent and Flight Lieutenant Athol Forbes receiving their Virtuti Militari.
Photo: Permission of Ronald Kellett.

Flight training began on 3 August 1940. The Polish pilots spoke little English, but most spoke fluent French, as did Flight Lieutenant Forbes and Squadron Leader Kellett. Obvious language difficulties arose on both sides during the early stages at RAF Northolt. The interpreter Pilot Officer Walters assisted where he could.

Pilots attended English classes on site which included basic English words to use over the radio transmitter. Some pilots travelled to Uxbridge for more comprehensive Radio Transmitter (R/T) training. Later, the Polish pilots often forgot all the English words during the excitement of battle. It did not seem to make any difference to their fighting skill.

On 10 August 1940, D. A. Upton relieved the acting Adjutant Pilot Officer Hadwin. Others to arrive were the Polish Adjutant, Captain W. Zyborski, Captain J. Giejsztowt (Fighter control operations room) and Chief Mechanic Flying Officer Wiókiewicz (Engineer). The Polish Medical Officer, Pilot Officer, Dr. Wodecki, arrived on 22 August 1940 along with just over a hundred ground crew.

The Polish Air Force squadrons in Poland had been smaller than RAF squadrons, but slightly larger than a flight. That was not the only difference. Many of the Polish airmen entered the RAF with a lower rank than they had gained in Poland. This allowed the Air Ministry to pay the pilots the wage for the lower rank. Many Polish airmen were not happy with their lower ranks, and it was a view echoed by the RAF airmen. Many of them agreed when someone said, *'They are going to be flying with us and many will die with us, they should be treated equally.'*

RAF Northolt — Pilots of No. 303 Kościuszko Squadron relaxing between sorties. Photo: Permission of Henneberg family.

Except for a few early mishaps, the Polish pilots settled into their training flights from RAF Northolt. When flying in Poland, the pilots opened up the throttle by pulling it back, but the throttle of a British Hawker Hurricane was pushed forward. Unlike the Polish aircraft, a Hurricane had a retractable undercarriage, and there were a few early incidents where the aircraft landed on its belly. Everything was back to front at first, but the Polish airmen soon got the hang of things.

The uniform for No. 303 Kościuszko Squadron was the usual RAF uniform, but with subtle differences. The uniforms had Polish buttons on them, Polish badges, and a Polish flash at the top of the jacket sleeves. The Polish badge on the cap bore the emblem of an aviation eagle with Hussars' wings, as designed by Antoni Gruberski. The Polish silver eagle — its wings open in flight, and its beak holding a green laurel — was presented to the Polish airmen who took part in combat. 'The Field Pilot's badge,' as it was known, was awarded to Squadron Leader Kellett, Flight Lieutenant Forbes, Flight Lieutenant Kent, Sergeant František, and Sergeant Kania.

The Polish Air Force flag was flown with the RAF flag at Northolt and all other RAF stations with Polish squadrons. The pilots had the squadron's personal insignia painted on their Hurricanes. Later, they added a tally of their kills near to the insignia. The usual RAF markings remained.

From 1942, No. 303 Kościuszko Squadron had the Polish red and white chequered insignia painted on the aircraft they flew. It had first been painted on Polish Air Force aircraft in 1920.

The guns on the squadron's Hurricanes were set to fire straight ahead at 200 yards. This required high-accuracy shooting, but could prove deadly at close range. The Hurricane's maximum speed was about 320mph. The eight-gun Browning machine guns (four on each wing) were covered in cloth to stop condensation jamming up the gun. The guns fired 300 rounds of ammunition in bursts lasting fourteen seconds. AOC Hugh Dowding insisted that the cockpit was armour-plated with bulletproof glass for protection.

The training flights gave the squadron a taste for battle. The pilots became more impatient with the endless training. All the training in the world was worthless unless it used where it mattered — in combat.

Soon the legend of No. 303 Kościuszko Squadron flew as an eagle upon the wing.

On 30 August 1940, six Hurricanes from No. 303 Kościuszko Squadron were making dummy attacks on British aircraft during a training exercise. Flying Officer Ludwick Paszkiewicz sighted German aircraft. Against orders, he broke formation and flew to intercept the enemy.

'When he was almost head on, he saw me and went into a steep dive. I followed and as he pulled out, I fired from directly behind, a burst at 250 yards at the fuselage. Overtaking him, I fired a long burst at 100 to 20 yards at the starboard engine from underneath. The engine stopped and burst into flames.'

Flying Officer Paszkiewicz was elated. It was the moment the Polish pilots had been waiting for since landing in England. It was proof they had the flying skills. It was also a chance to avenge for the slaughter in Poland during September 1939 and fight against the ongoing destruction of their homeland.

On landing, Flying Officer Paszkiewicz was reprimanded for breaking formation without permission. Then he was congratulated on his kill. That night, Squadron Leader Kellett made a telephone call to Fighter Command and No. 303 Kościuszko Squadron, which had been at 'readiness for action' since 17 August 1940, became operational on the 31 August 1940.

Sources: Polish Air Force Association.Combat Reports from The National Archives, Kew Air 50/117, Operational Report Diaries from RAF Northolt. Interviews: Eugeniusz (Gen) Szaposznikow, Aug 1986; Flight Lieutenant Jan Kowalski, 1986; Wing Commander Ronald Kellett, Jun 1986. Mr. Dennis Arthur Britton, 1978.

PART I

PILOT BIOGRAPHIES & MEMOIRS
The Eagles of No. 303 Kościuszko Squadron

During the Battle of Britain, thirty-six pilots of No.303 Kościuszko Squadron flew from RAF Northolt. Twenty-eight of the Polish pilots arrived at the airfield to join the newly formed squadron during August 1940. A further three Polish pilots were transferred from No. 302 Polish Squadron in late September 1940.

When they left their families in Poland to face the occupation, the Polish pilots had no way of knowing what the future held for their loved ones. This sacrifice boiled as molten hatred in the hearts of the pilots and fuelled their relentless fight against the enemy across Poland and France. Many found their way to England after the surrender of France, by which time their young faces were etched with the intimate experience of war but their determination to continue the fight showed no sign of waning.

The following biographies and memoirs of the thirty-six founder members of the No. 303 Kościuszko Squadron have been prepared using the words of the pilots and their families as recorded in official reports, interviews, and letters. The dates of their key battle moments can be cross-referenced with the detailed Combat Reports found in Part III of this book.

Where it has not been possible to trace living relatives or obtain official records, the pilot biography is brief.

The listed names are the founder pilots of No. 303 Kościuszko Squadron who 'flew high upon the wing' during the Battle of Britain:

1. Sergeant Tadeusz Andruszków
2. Sergeant Marian Bełc
3. Sergeant Michał Brzezowski
4. Flying Officer Arsen Cebrzyński
5. Pilot Officer Jan Daszewski
6. Pilot Officer Mirosław Ferić
7. Flight Lieutenant Athol Forbes
8. Sergeant Josef František
9. Sergeant Paweł Gallus
10. Flying Officer Bogdan Grzeszczak
11. Flying Officer Zdzisław Henneberg
12. Flying Officer Wojciech Januszewicz
13. Sergeant Jozef Kania
14. Sergeant Stanisław Karubin
15. Squadron Leader Ronald Kellett
16. Flight Lieutenant John Kent
17. Sergeant Jan Kowalski
18. Squadron Leader Zdzisław Krasnodębski
19. Flying Officer Wacław Łapkowski
20. Pilot Officer Witold Łokuciewski
21. Pilot Officer Bogusław Mierzwa
22. Sergeant Jan Palak
23. Pilot Officer Jerzy Palusiński
24. Flying Officer Ludwick Paszkiewicz
25. Sergeant Edward Paterek
26. Flying Officer Marian Pisarek
27. Pilot Officer Jerzy Radomski
28. Sergeant Jan Rogowski
29. Sergeant Antoni Siudak
30. Sergeant Eugeniusz Szaposznikow
31. Flying Officer Witold Urbanowicz*

32. Sergeant Mirosław Wojciechowski
33. Sergeant Stefan Wójtowicz
34. Sergeant Kazimierz Wünsche
35. Flying Officer Walerian Żak
36. Pilot Officer Jan Zumbach

Biographies for the following Polish pilots are not included:

1. Sergeant K. Krawczyński arrived 2 August 1940 but was posted sick on 18 August 1940.

2. Flying Officer K. Łukaszewicz arrived in July 1940 then was posted to No. 501 Squadron at RAF Gravesend. During a sortie on 12 August 1940, he was shot down by a Messerschmitt Me109 and killed.

3. Flying Officer S. Pietraszkiewicz arrived 21 August 1940 and was posted to No. 307 Squadron on 10 September 1940.

4. Sergeant Leon Switon was posted from No. 54 RAF Squadron to No. 303 Kościuszko Squadron 'B' Flight on 16 August 1940. Soon after, he was posted sick then became a flying instructor at the Polish Flying School at RAF Hucknall.

*Flying Officer Witold Urbanowicz became Acting Polish Squadron Leader of No. 303 Kościuszko Squadron after Squadron Leader Zdzisław Krasnodębski was shot down and badly burnt on 6 September 1940.

Note on ranks: The RAF awarded ranks to the Polish pilots that differed from their Polish Air Force ranks. The RAF gave a Major in the Polish Air Force the rank of Squadron Leader. A pilot with the Polish rank of Lieutenant became a Flying Officer. A Second Lieutenant became a Pilot Officer in the RAF, and a Sergeant was the same in both air forces. Throughout the war, the RAF awarded higher ranks to the Polish pilots on merit. See the Glossary for more detail. Each pilot's rank changes in the biographies and Wing sections to reflect their promotions.

Note on types of sorties: Sorties were given code names such as 'Circus,' where fighters escorted bombers over the English Channel into France to protect them from enemy fighters.

The 'Rhubarb' involved a small number of fighter aircraft, usually attacking in pairs, and flying low under radar detection. The purpose was to carry out one quick surprise attack on enemy airfields and other nearby enemy targets such as barracks, hangers, gun posts, various airfield defences, and goods trains.

The 'Ramrod' was similar to a Circus sortie. Fighters escorting or meeting up with bombers over France were used to draw enemy fighters away from attacking RAF bombers.

Further descriptions of the types of sorties can be found in the Glossary.

Note on using a pilot's own words: The interviews and memoirs quoted throughout the book are as they were originally written by the pilots. Only minor corrections have been made where it aids clarification.

Name: **Tadeusz Andruszków**
Squadron: No. 303 Kościuszko Squadron
Decorations: Krzyż Walecznych (KW) Cross of Valour

Tadeusz Andruszków was born on 18 November 1920 in Lwów, Poland. He trained at the Polish Air Force Training School for Non-Commissioned Officers in Bydgoszcz and qualified as a pilot shortly before the outbreak of war. He served with the No. 162 Fighter Squadron in defence of Poland.

After the German occupation of Poland, Tadeusz Andruszków was ordered to Romania. He entered an internment camp on arrival but later escaped to France. Keeping one step ahead of the Germans after the fall of France, he made his way to England and was given refresher pilot training.

Sergeant Andruszków joined No. 303 Kościuszko Squadron at RAF Northolt on 21 August 1940. He destroyed a Dornier Do17 with another pilot (a shared kill) on 15 September 1940. He destroyed a Heinkel He 111 eleven days later — the day before he died.

On 27 September 1940 at around 09.30 hours, the young Sergeant was shot down and killed. His Hurricane crashed on land near Holywych Farm in Cowden, Kent. He was nineteen years old.

Sergeant Andruszków is laid to rest at Northwood Cemetery in grave 208, section H.

See Combat Reports for the following dates:
- 15 Sep 1940
- 26 Sep 1940
- 27 Sep 1940

Sources: Pilot information from the Polish Air Force Association, Combat Reports from The National Archives, Kew Air 50/117, Operational Report Diaries from RAF Northolt.

Name: **Marian Bełc**
Squadron: No. 303 Kościuszko Squadron
                        No. 58 Operational Training Unit
Decorations: Virtuti Militari (VM) - 5th Class
                        KW Cross of Valour - three Bars
                        Distinguished Flying Cross (DFC) - two Bars

Marian Bełc was born on 27 January 1914 in Poland. He flew in defence of Poland during the September campaign of 1939, destroying at least one enemy aircraft. After an internment in Romania, he escaped to France, then to England. He was posted to No. 303 Kościuszko Squadron at RAF Northolt on 2 August 1940.

Marian Bełc flew on many sorties with No. 303 Kościuszko Squadron during the Battle of Britain. He destroyed seven enemy aircraft.

On 15 May 1941, six Spitfires took off from RAF Northolt at 11.20 hours on a Rhubarb sortie. Marian Bełc and Pilot Officer Drobiński attacked a German Junkers JU52 bomber as it taxied along an aerodrome at St. Inglevert, France. Over the coast during the return flight, Marian Bełc attacked enemy shipping and an E-Boat.

In April 1942, he was posted to No. 58 Operational Training Unit, RAF Grangemouth in Scotland.

Marian Bełc lost his life in a flying accident on 27 August 1942. During a low approach at Baladown in Gloucestershire, the Master training aircraft Bełc was flying lost height and crashed, killing him and the trainee pilot on impact. He was twenty-eight years old.

Shortly after his arrival in England, Marian Bełc fell in love and married a Scottish girl Audrey Stephenson. They had a son Marian Edward, who was ten months old when his father died.

Three months after Marian Bełc's death, Audrey took Marian Edward to receive his father's DFC. The medal was pinned to the young boy's coat.

Audrey helped Marion Edward remember his father by telling him stories and showing him the few photographs she had of the short time she had spent with her husband.

Sgt Marian Bełc is laid to rest at Northwood Cemetery in Grave 267, Section H.

See Combat Reports for the following dates:
- 26 Sep 1940
- 27 Sep 1940
- 30 Sep 1940
- 5 Oct 1940
- 7 Oct 1940

See Wing section for the following dates:
- 28 Jun 1941

Sources: Pilot information from the Polish Air Force Association, Combat Reports from The National Archives, Kew Air 50/117, Operational Report Diaries from RAF Northolt.

Name: **Michał Brzezowski**
Squadron: No. 303 Kościuszko Squadron
Decorations: KW Cross of Valour

Michał Brzezowski was born in Dawidgrodek, Poland on 26 February 1920. In 1936, he trained at the Polish Air Force Training School for Non-Commissioned Officers in Bydgoszcz and qualified as a pilot in 1939. He flew in defence of Poland with No. 151 Fighter Squadron until he was ordered to Romania.

In France, he flew with Groupe de Chasse, defending the Bloch aircraft Factory in the City of Châteauroux (these flights were known as Chimney Flights). He flew with other Polish pilots, Lieutenant Arsen Cebrzyński and Corporal Eugeniusz Szaposznikow. On one occasion Michał Brzezowski's aircraft was hit, but he made a successful forced landing in a field in France.

He was evacuated to England after the fall of France. He joined No. 303 Kościuszko Squadron on the 21 August 1940, where he was reunited with Arsen Cebrzyński and Eugeniusz Szaposznikow. On 11 September he destroyed two Heinkel He111s. Four days later, on the 15 September, he was shot down in combat over Gravesend. His Hurricane was last seen diving towards the Thames Estuary.

Sergeant Michał Brzezowski's young body was never found. He was twenty years old.

See Combat Reports for the following dates:
- 11 Sep 1940
- 15 Sep 1940

Sources: Pilot information from the Polish Air Force Association, Combat Reports from The National Archives, Air 50/117, Operational Report Diaries from RAF Northolt. Interview with Flight Lieutenant Eugeniusz (Gen) Szaposznikow, Aug 1986.

Name: **Arsen Cebrzyński**
Squadron: No. 303 Kościuszko Squadron
Decorations: Virtuti Militari 5th Class
                KW Cross of Valour two bars
                Croix de Guerre

Arsen Cebrzyński was born on 8 March 1912 in Batumi, Georgia. His father was a Polish doctor and his mother was a qualified pilot. During the Revolution (the collective term used in Poland for First World War followed by Polish-Bolshevik war of 1919–1920), Arsen Cebrzyński and his brother Wiktor spent a short period of time in an orphanage while their parents were fighting. Later, the boys went to live with their grandparents, who were responsible for most of the boys' upbringing.

During the latter part of the war, the boys' father died and their mother remarried. Their mother's second husband Stanisław Karpińksi was a pilot who, years later, became a General and the last Commander In Chief of the Polish Air Force in Great Britain. Arsen Cebrzyński and his brother returned to live with their mother and stepfather seven years after the end of the First World War.

By 1929, the brothers had joined the Rawicz Flying School near Poznań. They qualified in 1931 and trained together at Dęblin Officers' School from 1931 until 1934. Arsen became a fighter pilot attached to No. 111 Kościuszko Squadron serving under Captain Zdzisław Krasnodębski (who later became Arsen's Commanding Officer in Great Britain). Wiktor went on to train as a bomber pilot and flew as an observer with the Polish Air Force.

In 1937, Arsen Cebrzyński fell in love and married an actress Jadwiga in Warsaw. A year later their son Jacek was born.

After Germany's invasion of Poland on 1 September 1939, Arsen Cebrzyński flew in defence of Poland. During one air encounter, he saved the life of Captain Krasnodębski, who was under attack by a German Messerschmitt Me109. He had baled out of his badly damaged aircraft, but as his parachute opened, the enemy fighter flew into attack. Arsen Cebrzyński intercepted and shot down the Messerschmitt.

On 7 September 1939 Jadwiga Cebrzyński said her farewell to her husband with a sense of foreboding. He was returning to his squadron to prepare for evacuation to Romania.

'When my husband Arsen came to say goodbye to us I knew he would never return. I had the same feeling when my father left who was a Doctor and was organising on the battle front medical care for the injured. I never saw my dear husband or father alive again.'

Later that month, Arsen Cebrzyński travelled with other pilots to Romania, then to France. In France he flew in combat with Groupe de Chasse 11/6 with other Polish pilots; among them Lieutenant Henneberg, Sergeant Brzezowski, and Corporal Szaposznikow. Later, they all flew together with No. 303 Kościuszko Squadron.

Leading his flight in a Bloch MB152 aircraft, Arsen Cebrzyński destroyed one enemy aircraft. He shared in another kill with Lieutenant Henneberg.

On another occasion, Arsen Cebrzyński's aircraft came under heavy fire. Although his aircraft was riddled with bullets, he managed to land without injury.

After the fall of France, he travelled to England and completed the RAF's refresher training before taking up his posting with No. 303 Kościuszko Squadron on 21 August 1940.

'Our boys could not wait when on English soil to repay, if only partially, for the wrong done to the Fatherland during and over the years of occupation. All reports and memories are only part of what atrocities were really committed all over Poland during those times. Even we, in Poland, did not know about the [horrors] which took place. When news reached us of what was happening, it was

impossible to comprehend how a nation of such high culture of the Germans was capable of such extermination and destruction of other European Nations.' Jadwiga Cebrzyńska

While on a sortie during the Battle of Britain, Arsen Cebrzyński's Hurricane was hit and crashed in flames on farmland in Sandhill in Pembury, Kent. The local farmer Mr. Kendall rushed to help but could do nothing for the twenty-eight-year-old pilot. Arsen Cebrzyński had been thrown from his aircraft and sustained fatal injuries. It was the 11 September 1940.

Arsen Cebrzyński's grave at Northwood Cemetery. He was shot down and killed on 11 September 1940. Photo permission: Carl Boyle.

Early in the war, Jadwiga Cebrzyńska had received travel papers for herself and her two-year-old son Jacek to travel west but would not leave her ill mother. She spent most of the war years in Warsaw with her young son but moved after their house was destroyed in the bombing.

Jadwiga took part in the Warsaw Uprising in 1944 while attached to Lieutenant Andrzej Company in the inner city area. She was deported on 5 October 1944 to a camp deep within Germany and was liberated along with the rest of the camp by a Canadian division on 13 April 1945. Months in the camp had taken its toll on Jadwiga, who faced further devastating news when she finally discovered that her husband had died so soon after arriving in England.

She travelled to London in 1947 to collect her late husband's personal effects and to visit his resting place at Northwood Cemetery. In London she became very ill and spent a long time in a hospital convalescing. Jadwiga visited the grave of her husband and took the time to pay her respects to his friends from No. 303 Kościuszko Squadron who were also laid to rest in the cemetery.

Arsen Cebrzyński's brother Wiktor was a navigator flying in Wellington bombers with No. 300 Squadron. On 19 June 1941, he was shot down during a Bomber Command operation targeting Bremen. He and another man from the Wellington survived the night, but were captured upon landing and sent to Stalag Luft III as prisoners of war. Wiktor and many others were liberated from the camp after the war ended. He was tragically killed in an accident soon after arriving back in England.

Back in Poland, Jadwiga resumed her acting career to support herself and Jacek. She never remarried but kept the memory of her husband alive for their son by telling him stories and sharing photographs

Jacek Cebrzyński became a pilot, got married had and named his son Arsen in memory of his father. Arsen became a doctor, had a family and carried his grandfather's name with pride.

Flying Officer Arsen Cebrzyński is laid to rest in Grave 187, Section H at Northwood Cemetery.

See Combat Reports for the following dates: 11 September 1940

Sources: Pilot information from the Polish Air Force Association, Combat Reports from The National Archives, Air 50/117, Operational Report Diaries from RAF Northolt. Interview with Jadwiga Cebrzyńska on 26 November 1987, Wanda Krasnodębska on 22 Jul 1987, Flight Lieutenant Jan Kowalski 1986, and Flight Lieutenant Eugeniusz (Gen) Szaposznikow, Aug 1986. Profile photo: Jadwiga Cebrzyńska.

Name: **Jan Daszewski**
Squadron: No. 303 Kościuszko Squadron
Decorations: Virtuti Militari 5th Class
                 KW Cross of Valour - three Bars

Jan Daszewski, known as Joe to his friends, was born on 5 April 1915 in Poland. Flying in defence of Poland in September 1939, he shot down an enemy aircraft with No. 112 Fighter Squadron. After evacuating to Romania, he made his way to France and moved on to England after France fell to the Germans. He was posted with the rank of Pilot Officer to No. 303 Kościuszko Squadron on 2 August 1940.

During a sortie on 7 September 1940, he destroyed an enemy Dornier aircraft, but the celebration of his first kill was cut short when his Hurricane was hit by enemy fire. He managed to bale out, despite suffering from severe injuries. At first, the people on the ground mistook him for German, but he was able to convey that he was Polish fighting with the RAF. He was taken to Waldershire Hospital in Kent for treatment. It took many months for him to recover from the severe wounds to his body and burns to his face.

Jan Daszewski returned to No. 303 Kościuszko Squadron in the spring of 1941 to fly with the No. 1 Polish Fighter Wing. On 20 April 1941, an Me109 attacked him while he was flying over France with six Spitfires. When he tried to fire back, he discovered that four of his guns had frozen. His aircraft was hit by a shell in the fuselage but he managed to land safely.

At 09.41 hours on 4 April 1942, No. 303, No. 316 and No. 317 Polish Squadrons from No. 1 Polish Fighter Wing took off from RAF Northolt on a Circus operation, escorting Boston bombers over France. Their target was the St. Omer railway. German Focke-Wulfs FW109s attacked the Polish fighters that were defending the RAF bombers. Three enemy fighters were destroyed and two others were damaged. The Germans were not the only casualties of the day — Jan Daszewski's Spitfire was lost over the English Channel. It was the day before his twenty-seventh birthday.

See Combat Reports for the following dates: 7 Sep 1940
See Wing section for the following dates: 4 April 1942

Sources: Pilot information from the Polish Air Force Association, Combat Reports from The National Archives, Air 50/117, Operational Report Diaries from RAF Northolt. Interview with Flight Lieutenant Jan Kowalski, 1986. Interview and consultations with Squadron Leader Gandi Drobiński, 1986 onwards.

Name: **Mirosław Ferić**
Squadron: No. 303 Kościuszko Squadron
Decorations: Virtuti Militari 5th Class
KW Cross of Valour
DFC

'This pilot has displayed great coolness in operations, setting a fine example to the rest of his section. He has personally accounted for 6 enemy aircraft and probably another one.'

DFC Citation as recommended by Squadron Leader Kellett 23/9/1940

Mirosław Ferić, known as Mika to his family, was born on 17 June 1915 in Tawnik, Yugoslavia. His father was from Yugoslavia, and his mother from Poland. In 1919, Mirosław Ferić moved to Ostrow in Poland with his siblings and his mother, who was a teacher.

After completing his grammar school education in June 1933, Mirosław Ferić was accepted into the Polish Air Force Officers' School at Dęblin. His mother was not happy that he had wanted to become a pilot, but Milosław's childhood dream of flying had never diminished. His dream had come true when he qualified as Second Lieutenant at Dęblin in 1938.

In the September campaign of 1939, Mirosław Ferić flew with No. 111 Kościuszko Squadron in defence of Warsaw and shot down at least one enemy aircraft. During the campaign, his aircraft was hit and badly damaged, forcing him to bale out or perish.

Mirosław Ferić was evacuated to Romania then made his way to France, where he was attached to L'Armee de L'Air until the fall of France. He made his way to England and was posted to No. 303 Kościuszko Squadron on 2 August 1940.

On 2 September 1940, Mirosław Ferić's Hurricane began to leak oil while flying on a sortie. Moments later, smoke poured forth and his aircraft became hard to control. He managed to land in a field in Kent.

During the Battle of Britain, Mirosław Ferić started a squadron diary, which he had intended for his family back in Poland. The diary grew over time, with many pilots adding some words. King George VI and Sir Winston Churchill were invited to add their signatures. It became a diary for the entire squadron and a place for pilots to write about fallen friends.

During 1940, Mirosław Ferić fell in love with an English woman and became the proud father of their son, Michael (later known as Philip) in October 1941.

Mirosław Ferić was taken ill in November 1941 and was admitted to a hospital to convalesce. He returned to No. 303 Kościuszko Squadron at RAF Northolt in February 1942.

On 14 February 1942, he took his Spitfire up for a practice flight. At approximately 3,000 feet, the wing of his aircraft broke off and ripped away a part of the tail. The aircraft spiralled out of control. The force and speed of the descent made it impossible for Mirosław Ferić to bale out successfully.

Many at RAF Northolt and the local people watching from the ground, witnessed the terrible sight. The Spitfire and its twenty-seven-year-old pilot plummeted into the ground a few hundred yards from where the Polish War Memorial now stands.

Mirosław Ferić's diary, continued throughout the Second World War in his memory, expanded into many volumes. It is kept at the Polish Institute and Sikorski Museum in London.

Throughout the war, the Ferić family in Poland did not hear from Mirosław. Parcels arrived for the Ferić family from Portugal, leading them to believe he was still alive. Zwonimir Ferić wrote how the family discovered the truth about the parcels:

'In the war in 1939, my mother and our family in Poland were deported by the Germans from central Poland with only hand luggage. We settled in Warsaw where again we lost everything in the Warsaw Uprising. This is why we have no memorabilia of my brother. We had no news from my brother since he left Poland. My brother Mirosław realised that any contact with the West could provoke sanctions (arrest camps) by the Germans. As we learned later, parcels with coffee, which we received from Portugal until the end of the war, were not a sign of life from my brother.'

The packages came from a scheme, which arranged for goods to be sent to family members in Poland from Portugal. The Polish pilots paid into the scheme, and even after the pilot died, the parcels were sent. With no other news available, the parcels gave families hope that their loved ones were still alive. The Ferić family was devastated when in May 1945 they found out the truth from the RAF Commission in the Polonia Hotel in Warsaw.

Shortly after learning of the tragic death of Mirosław Ferić, the family learned of Philip, the son Mirosław had fathered in England. For many years, the family could not make contact with Philip Ferić. In 1987, forty-two years after the war had ended, Mirosław Ferić's brother Zwonimir, wrote about his nephew.

> *'Today he is a mature man. We do not know what he knows of his father, we do not know what he does, if he already has his own family. This is very distressing and sad, unfortunately, we do not know anything about him.'*

In recent years, Philip Ferić has attended the annual memorial service held at the Polish War Memorial, South Ruislip in September. He has been given the honour of laying a wreath in memory of the fallen pilots of No. 303 Kościuszko Squadron.

Flying Officer Mirosław Ferić is laid to rest at Northwood Cemetery in Grave 232, Section C. He was twenty-seven years old.

See Combat Reports for the following dates:
- 31 Aug 1940
- 2 Sep 1940
- 6 Sep 1940
- 15 Sep 1940
- 27 Sep 1940
- 5 Oct 1940

Sources: Pilot information from the Polish Air Force Association, Combat Reports from The National Archives (TNA), Air 50/117, Operational Report Diaries from RAF Northolt. DFC approved 16 October 1940. Citation by kind permission of Cabinet Office Licence No PSI C2006010220. TNA Ref Air/2. Interviews: Zwonimir Ferić (brother), September 1987; Dennis Arthur Britton, 1978; Flight Lieutenant Jan Kowalski, 1986; Flight Lieutenant Gen Szaposznikow, Aug 1986.

Name: **Athol Forbes**
Squadron: No. 303 Kościuszko Squadron
No. 66 Squadron
No. 165 Wing
Decorations: Virtuti Militari 5th Class
DFC
OBE

Athol Forbes was born 4 April 1912 in Hanover Square, London to Scottish parents. He spent his early childhood in France, then returned to England to continue his education.

He joined the School of Army Co-Operation for a short period of time then he joined the Royal Air Force in 1935 to learn how to fly. Athol Forbes married in 1938.

On 4 August 1940, Athol Forbes was posted to RAF Northolt as Flight Lieutenant with No. 303 Kościuszko Squadron. He flew many sorties with the squadron during the Battle of Britain and destroyed seven aircraft.

He spoke fluent French, as did most of the Polish and Czech pilots, and learned to speak Polish in a short period of time.

'I carry great respect and true affection for the Polish airmen of 303. I was very proud of my time spent with them. Had it not been for some of the pilots of 303 I would not have survived the Battle of Britain. They were gallant and quite fearless when flying to the aid of others in danger. I got on well with them all they certainly knew how to enjoy themselves when down The Orchard Pub and were popular with the ladies. I spent many an hour chatting with Josef František about Czechoslovakia. The ground crew worked tirelessly and nothing was too much trouble. It was a great honour

for me when I was awarded the Polish medal, the Virtuti Militari by General Sikorski at the Reubens Hotel in London.'

In October 1940, Athol Forbes left Northolt for a posting to No. 66 Squadron in West Malling. He flew with No. 66 Squadron until 1942, then spent the next three years in Burma serving as Wing Commander then Group Captain, and a year as acting Air Commander. He later received an OBE for service in Burma.

While fighting the Japanese, Athol Forbes sustained a wound to his back, which troubled him all his life. After the war, Athol Forbes remained with the RAF until 1948.

In his civilian life, Athol Forbes joined Thomas Delane Plastic Division for a few years, after which he worked overseas as a manager of forklift trucks at Lance Bros. To celebrate his fortieth birthday his family arranged for him to fly a Meteor Jet.

For many years, Athol Forbes attended RAF reunions and enjoyed meeting up with old friends. He kept in contact with Johnny Kent and Jan Zumbach along with other pilots and ground crew of No. 303 Kościuszko Squadron. Athol and his wife attended many musical evenings in London at the Sikorski Institute (now known as the Polish Institute and Sikorski). He took great pleasure in his family and enjoyed spending more time with his children and grandchildren during his retirement

Group Captain Athol Forbes passed away in 1981. In a moonlit ceremony, his ashes were scattered by his family at the Polish War Memorial. It had been Athol Forbes' wish to be with the Polish airmen he had respected so much.

'Had some of the pilots of 303 not saved my life I would not have lived and enjoyed a long life. I owe them my life.'

See Combat Reports for the following dates:
- 5 Sep 1940
- 6 Sep 1940
- 7 Sep 1940
- 11 Sep 1940
- 26 Sep 1940
- 27 Sep 1940

Sources: Pilot information from the Polish Air Force Association, Combat Reports from The National Archives (TNA), Air 50/117, Operational Report Diaries from RAF Northolt. Personal papers of Athol Forbes. Interview with Mrs A. Forbes, 1986. DFC approved October 1940. Profile Photo: Mrs A. Forbes.

Name: **Josef František**
Squadron: No. 303 Kościuszko Squadron
Decorations: Virtuti Militari 5th Class
                 KW Cross of Valour - three bars
                 Croix de Guerre
                 Military Cross (Czechoslovakian)
                 Distinguished Flying Medal (DFM) and bar

Josef František was born 7 October 1912 in Czechoslovakia. After completing his training in 1934, he joined the Czechoslovakian Air Force as a mechanic, then as a pilot.

When the German army marched into Czechoslovakia in March 1939, Josef František openly protested alongside others against the Germans presence and was arrested. Managing to escape, he stole a plane and machine-gunned German troops on his flight to Poland.

Once in Poland Josef František dropped his rank from Lieutenant to Corporal and joined the Polish Air Force to help defend Poland.

During combat, his PZL fighter was shot down and he was once more taken prisoner by the Germans. Not content to await whatever fate the Germans had in store, he soon escaped and made his way to Romania, then France.

In France, Josef František shot down enemy aircraft while flying an old aircraft with a machine-gun strapped on.

He arrived in England after the fall of France and was stationed with other Czechoslovakian pilots. Although he had many friends in the Czech Air Force, he preferred to fly with the Polish airmen and put in a request to join a Polish squadron. His request was granted and he was sent to RAF Northolt to join No. 303 Kościuszko Squadron at its formation on 2 August 1940.

Josef František was an excellent fighter pilot but found it hard to obey orders when in combat, preferring to hunt for the enemy on his own. To Josef František, rules were made to be manipulated. Often he would catch up and shoot down a battered enemy aircraft struggling back across the English Channel towards France.

As with all the Polish pilots, Josef František had a burning hatred for the enemy after witnessing the death and destruction they had caused. Josef František was often restless on the ground. All he wanted to do was to take to the sky to kill the enemy in the rage of battle.

Josef František became the top Fighter Ace in the Battle of Britain by destroying seventeen enemy aircraft in many successful sorties with No. 303 Kościuszko Squadron.

While trying to land his aircraft, Josef František lost his life in a mysterious flying accident. It was the 8 October 1940 — the day after his twenty-eighth birthday.

Three days after Josef František's death, the squadron moved from frontline duties to RAF Leconfield for a much-needed rest.

Josef František is laid to rest in Northwood Cemetery, Grave No. 246.

See Combat Reports for the following dates:
- 2 Sep 1940
- 3 Sep 1940
- 5 Sep 1940
- 6 Sep 1940
- 9 Sep 1940
- 11 Sep 1940
- 15 Sep 1940
- 26 Sep 1940
- 30 Sep 1940
- 8 Oct 1940

Sources: Pilot information from the Polish Air Force Association, Combat Reports from The National Archives (TNA), Air 50/117, Operational Report Diaries from RAF Northolt. Interviews Mrs A Forbes, 1986; Wing Commander Ronald Kellett; Flight Lieutenant Jan Kowalski 1986; and Flight Lieutenant Eugeniusz (Gen) Szaposznikow, Aug 1986. DFM approved 1 October 1940. Profile Photo: Polish Institute and Sikorski Museum.

Name:	Paweł Gallus
Squadron:	No. 303 Kościuszko Squadron
	No. 302 Squadron
	No. 309 Squadron
	No. 316 Squadron
	No. 317 Squadron
Decorations:	Virtuti Militari 5th Class
	KW Cross of Valour and bar
	DFC

Paweł Gallus was born 28 April 1920 in Szcawina in Poland. From 1936, he trained at Bydgoszcz and qualified as a pilot in 1939.

He flew in defence of Poland with No. 112 Fighter Squadron during the September campaign of 1939 and evacuated to Romania, where he was interned. After escaping, Paweł Gallus made his way to France with other Polish airmen. He flew in defence of the French Bloch aircraft factory until the fall of France.

Paweł Gallus landed on British soil in June 1940 and was posted to No. 303 Kościuszko Squadron at its formation on 2 August 1940. His posting with the squadron was a short one. After a flying accident in training, he was posted to No. 5 Operational Training Unit at RAF Aston Down, but moved again on 27 September 1940 to No. 3 Squadron at RAF Turnhouse, near Edinburgh.

In March 1941, Paweł Gallus was flying with No. 316 Polish Squadron at Pembury. By October 1941, he had completed night fighter training before a posting in Exeter with No. 317 Polish Squadron. In April 1942, he returned to No. 316 Polish Squadron.

While flying on a sortie with No. 316 Polish Squadron on 6 July 1943, Paweł Gallus and other pilots attacked four Me109s over Amiens, France. He shot down an Me109, and Wing Commander Gabszewicz shot down another.

In August 1943, a new posting took Paweł Gallus to Air Traffic Control. In April the following year, he joined No. 302 Polish Squadron on operations until February 1945. At the time the war ended, Paweł Gallus was serving with No. 309 Polish Squadron.

Paweł Gallus left the Polish Air Force with the rank of Warrant Officer in 1948. He got married and started a family in Northamptonshire.

Sources: Pilot information from the Polish Air Force Association, Combat Reports from The National Archives (TNA), Air 50/117, Operational Report Diaries from RAF Northolt. Interviews: Flight Lieutenant Jan Kowalski, 1986; Squadron Leader Gandi Drobiński, interview and consultation, 1986 onwards. DFC approved 1945.

Name: **Bogdan Grzeszczak**
Squadron: No. 303 Kościuszko Squadron
Decorations: KW Cross of Valour - two bars

Bogdan Grzeszczak was born 10 August 1908 in Poland. He was serving in the Polish Air Force when war broke out and flew in defence of Poland. He travelled to Romania in September 1939, and after a brief stay at an internment camp, he escaped to France. After the surrender of France, he journeyed to England for refresher flight training. He joined No. 303 Kościuszko Squadron on its formation on 2 August 1940 but left in Spring 1941 to become an instructor at No. 58 Operational Training Unit at RAF Grangemouth, Scotland.

On 28 August 1941, Bogdan Grzeszczak died in a tragic flying accident while practising dogfights. His Master aircraft went into a steep dive after avoiding another aircraft. Unable to pull out of the dive, Bogdan Grzeszczak's aircraft crashed with both pilots inside. The force of the impact threw Bogdan Grzeszczak from the aircraft into a lake. He died shortly after. He was thirty-three years old.

Flying Officer Bogdan Grzeszczak is laid to rest in Northwood Cemetery Grave 179, Section H.

See Combat Reports for the following dates:
- 26 Sep 1940
- 27 Sep 1940

Sources: Pilot information from the Polish Air Force Association, Combat Reports from The National Archives (TNA), Air 50/117, Operational Report Diaries from RAF Northolt. Interviews: Squadron Leader Gandi Drobiński, 1986 onwards. Profile Photo: Gen Szaposznikow.

Name: **Zdzisław Henneberg**
Squadron: No. 303 Kościuszko Squadron
Decorations: Virtuti Militari 5th Class
                       KW Cross of Valour and bar
                       Croix de Guerre
                       DFC

'This Officer has taken part in active operations since the formation of this squadron as a section leader and as acting Flight Commander. He has shown initiative and tenacity in pressing home attacks. He has accounted for the following enemy aircraft: 4 Me109s, 1 Dor, 1 Hei 111. Probably a further 2.'

Squadron Leader Kellett's recommendation for the DFC

'Strongly recommended, he has proved himself an Officer of great gallantry and determination and modesty.'

Group Captain Vincent's recommendation dated 23 Sep1940.

Zdzisław Henneberg, known as Dzidek, was born on 5 May 1911 in Warsaw, Poland. He trained at Dęblin Officers' School from 1929. After qualifying, he trained to become one of the school's instructors.

Zdzisław Henneberg 1922. Photo: Permission of Henneberg family/author's collection

In 1938, he married Krystyna Dydynska, who was seven years his senior. Sadly for the couple, there was too little time to start a family during the brief months they had together before the outbreak of war.

Zdzisław Henneberg flew in defence of his hometown, Warsaw until he was evacuated to Romania. He escaped to France, where he led a flight of nine aircraft in defence of the Bloch aircraft factory.

After the fall of France, Zdzisław Henneberg led his flight across the English Channel to England. He and two other pilots were the only three Polish airmen who flew to England from France. They landed in a field in Sussex and was later sent for training. Zdzisław Henneberg was posted to No. 303 Kościuszko Squadron on 2 August 1940.

He flew many sorties during the Battle of Britain and continued to fly with the squadron. Zdzisław Henneberg became Squadron Leader of No. 303 Kościuszko Squadron in February 1941, the same month he received a wonderful surprise. His wife Krystyna could not bear their separation any longer and left Poland illegally. Somehow, she made her way through war-torn Europe with only a few meagre possessions and reunited with her much-loved husband. They enjoyed two happy months together before tragedy struck.

On 12 April 1941, a flight of six Spitfires led by Squadron Leader Henneberg took off from RAF Northolt and split up in pairs over the Crecy area. Squadron Leader Henneberg and his No.2, Flight Lieutenant Kustrzyński attacked an unidentified airfield and other ground targets. Squadron Leader Henneberg's aircraft was hit and on the way back to England, was forced to ditch into the English Channel. He was seen on the surface in his Mae West, raising one arm. The nearest coast, Dungeness was a twelve-mile swim.

Pilots of No. 302 Polish Squadron flew in search of him, but were unable to locate him in the rough seas and failing light. Reluctant to give up hope on his close friend, Acting Squadron Leader Wacław Łapkowski continued the search with Pilot Officer Strzembosz the next day. A cannon shell hit Wacław Łapkowski's aircraft forcing him to land the damaged aircraft. He was taken to a hospital to treat an injury to his hand and a severe head injury.

Squadron Leader Zdzisław Henneberg drowned in the English Channel on 12 April 1941, a month before his thirtieth birthday. His body was never recovered.

The Second World War was a devastating time for Zdzisław Henneberg's family. His parents Anna and Adolph were killed. In 1942, Adam Henneberg was fighting with the AK Home Army (Armia Krajowa) when he received news of his brother's death over a concealed radio. Adam was murdered in Auschwitz later in the war. Hanna Henneberg had trained as a pilot but worked as an artist. Sadly, she died in 1937. Only one brother, Wacław survived the war. He fought in Monte Cassino, Italy and was later captured and interned in a Lithuanian camp.

Poland 1911 — Adam, Wacław holding Zdzisław, and Hanna Henneberg. Photo Permission of Zofia Rozycka/author's collection.

Zdzisław Henneberg's loss came as a shattering blow to his widow Krystyna. She remained in England but never remarried and passed away at ninety-two years old.

See Combat Reports for the following dates:
- 31 Aug 1940
- 2 Sep 1940
- 3 Sep 1940
- 7 Sep 1940
- 9 Sep 1940
- 11 Sep 1940
- 15 Sep 1940
- 27 Sep 1940
- 5 Oct 1940

Sources: Pilot information from the Polish Air Force Association, Combat Reports from The National Archives (TNA), Air 50/117, Operational Report Diaries from RAF Northolt. DFC Approved 16 October 1940 Ref TNA Air/2. DFC Citation by kind permission of the Cabinet Office: Licence PSI No C2006010220. Interviews: Wing Commander Ronald Kellett, Jun 1986. Flight Lieutenant Eugeniusz (Gen) Szaposznikow Aug 1986. Professor Maciej Henneberg, 7 Jan 1988; Zofia Rozycka, Nov 1987. Profile Photo: Gen Szaposznikow.

Name: **Wojciech Januszewicz**
Squadron: No. 303 Kościuszko Squadron
Decoration: Virtuti Militari 5th Class
KW Cross of Valour

Wojciech Januszewicz was born on 30 April 1911 in Poland. He was a qualified pilot with the Polish Air Force when the Germans invaded Poland in September 1939. He destroyed at least three enemy aircraft before receiving orders to evacuate Romania. He escaped from Romania to France, where he led a flight of Polish airmen from Meaux.

Wojciech Januszewicz arrived in Blackpool after the fall of France and, after refresher flight training, joined No. 303 Kościuszko Squadron on 2nd August 1940.

On 6 September 1940, after coming under heavy fire he crash-landed at Lenham in Kent but was unhurt. On 26 September his Hurricane was badly shot up, but he managed to land in a field safely. Wojciech Januszewicz was not so fortunate on his third enforced landing on 5 October 1940.

On Wing patrol, twelve aircraft from No. 303 Kościuszko Squadron took off to meet No. 1 Royal Canadian Squadron. Approximately 150 enemy aircraft flying north near Rochester attacked from the clouds above. Enemy fire riddled Wojciech Januszewicz's Hurricane with bullets, and he dropped out of the sky. His aircraft crashed to the ground in Stowting, Kent and flipped over, becoming engulfed in flames. Many local people watched in horror but were unable to do anything to help. Wojciech Januszewicz was twenty-nine years old.

Flying Officer Wojciech Januszewicz is laid to rest in Grave 231, Section H at Northwood Cemetery.

See Combat Reports for the following dates:
- 6 Sep 1940
- 26 Sep 1940
- 5 Oct 1940

Sources: Pilot information from the Polish Air Force Association, Combat Reports from The National Archives (TNA), Air 50/117, Operational Report Diaries from RAF Northolt. Interviews: Interviews Wing Commander Ronald Kellett, Jun 1986; and Flight Lieutenant Jan Kowalski, 1986. Photo: Gen Szaposznikow.

Name: **Josef Kania**
Squadron: No. 303 Kościuszko Squadron
                 No. 315 Squadron
Decorations: KW Cross of Valour

Josef Kania was born 26 January 1920 in Czechoslovakia. He trained as a pilot in the Czech Air Force and qualified shortly before the outbreak of war.

After the German military forces had invaded his country, he fled to Poland and flew with the Polish Air Force. He travelled to Romania with the Polish pilots in September and escaped to France to continue the fight.

After the fall of France, Josef Kania made his way to England. He arrived in July 1940 and after refresher flight training was posted to No. 303 Kościuszko Squadron on 21 August 1940. He joined the newly formed No. 315 Polish Squadron in January 1941, but his posting was a short one. By April 1941, he was posted to the ferry pilots' school in Kemble, Gloucestershire, presumably to train pilots. In early 1942, he was posted to the Anti-Aircraft Co-Operation Unit, where he served for two years.

Josef Kania left the Polish Air Force in 1946 as a Warrant Officer and remained in England.

Sources: Pilot information from the Polish Air Force Association, Combat Reports from The National Archives (TNA), Air 50/117, Operational Report Diaries from RAF Northolt. Interviews: Interviews Wing Commander Ronald Kellett, Jun 1986 ; and Flight Lieutenant Jan Kowalski, 1986.

Name: **Stanisław Karubin**
Squadron: No. 303 Kościuszko Squadron
Decoration: Virtuti Militari 5th Class
               KW Cross of Valour - three bars
               DFM

'This pilot has shown conspicuous gallantry in the face of the enemy and up to 6 September 1940, when he was wounded had shot down 3 Me109s and 1 He111. Sgt Karubin refused sick leave when he was discharged from hospital and rejoined his squadron.

On the 30th September when his flight pursued a force of Dor17s escorted by Me109s across the Channel he shot down an Me109. Again on 5 October he shot down another Me109 when his squadron was engaging a large enemy formation thus making a total of 6 enemy aircraft shot down.

In every op in which he had been engaged both before and after being wounded, Sgt Karubin had shown great courage and initiative and his keenness has been an inspiration to the others of his squadron.'

Leigh Mallory. Air Vice-Marshal Commanding No 12 Group RAF
Recommended by Hugh Dowding 14 November 1940

Stanisław Karubin was born 29 October 1915 in Niemayki, Poland. He trained at Dęblin Officers' Flying School with his friend Eugeniusz (Gen) Szaposznikow, who he would later fly with No. 303 Kościuszko Squadron. Stanisław Karubin qualified as a pilot on 6 April 1935 and married his first love Janina on Boxing Day 1938.

When the Nazis invaded Poland, Stanisław Karubin flew with No. 111 Kościuszko Squadron in defence of Poland until ordered to Romania along with many other Polish pilots and ground crew. To escape Romania he obtained false travel papers using the name 'Myszka', which means 'little mouse'. He found this name amusing and had chosen it as he was short in height and had a slight build. During his journey, he sent his wife a Christmas card with news that he was well and would soon be in France.

He arrived in England in early summer of 1940 and was posted to No. 303 Kościuszko Squadron on 2 August 1940. On one of his sorties during the Battle of Britain, Stanisław Karubin was shot down and was admitted to a hospital to treat the burns he sustained during the crash. He rejoined the squadron soon after.

Gen Szaposznikow recalls his friend's fun character. He was always cheerful, full of optimism and made it his mission to try to get in any photograph. His positivity filled the letters he wrote to Janina.

He sent a few letters to her during 1940 and early 1941 full of confidence that he would one day return to a free Poland to be with his family. On the reverse side of the letters, Gen Szaposznikow wrote messages of hope for his own family.

Northolt 1940 — Sergeant Kazimierz Wünsche, Sergeant Stanisław Karubin and Sergeant Eugeniusz (Gen) Szaposznikow. Photo: Permission of Gen Szaposznikow.

On that fateful day, 12 August 1941, Stanisław Karubin took one look at the misty sky and decided it was a bad day to fly. He took to the air, but during the training exercise in Eskdale Cumberland, his aircraft crashed into the side of Mount Norm Crag. Twenty-five-year-old Stanisław Karubin was killed instantly.

In Poland, Janina received the news of her husband's loss from the British Embassy. She could not believe the sad news. At Stanisław's funeral, someone claiming to be his brother-in-law asked for personal possessions. Everything was handed over except the military decorations and papers, which the authorities later passed to Janina. Janina believes that whoever collected the personal possessions did so with good intentions. He may have become a victim of war and unable to return them to her.

Janina remained in Poland and never remarried. She never recovered from the loss of her beloved husband and never came to terms with the shattered hopes they had shared about starting a family.

Sergeant Stanisław Karubin is laid to rest in Castledown Cemetery, near Sunderland in Grave 722, Section 1.

See Combat Reports for the following dates:
- 6 Sep 1940
- 30 Sep 1940
- 5 Oct 1940

Sources: Pilot information from the Polish Air Force Association, Combat Reports from The National Archives (TNA), Air 50/117, Operational Report Diaries from RAF Northolt. DFM Citation by Kind permission of Cabinet Office Licence PSI No C2006010220 TNA Kew Air/2. Interviews. Janina Karubin, Feb 1988; Wing Commander Ronald Kellett, Jun 1986; Flight Lieutenant Eugeniusz (Gen) Szaposznikow, Jul 1986. DFM approved 13 January 1941. Profile Photo: Permission of the Polish Institute and Sikorski Museum.

Name: **Ronald Kellett**
Squadron: No. 249 Squadron
No. 616 Squadron
No. 303 Kościuszko Squadron
No. 71 Eagle Squadron
No. 615 Squadron
Decorations: Virtuti Militari
DFC and bar
Distinguished Service Order (DSO)

Ronald Kellett was born 1909 in Eldon, County Durham. Following the interview, transcribed below, Ronald Kellett emphasised that the story of No. 303 Kościuszko Squadron is the story of the Polish pilots.

Before the outbreak of the Second World War, I worked as a Stockbroker for Laurence Prust. I joined the Auxiliary Air Force in 1933 and learned how to fly. It is a most wonderful experience to soar as a bird, high upon the wing.

I was called up just before the outbreak of war. In 1939, as a Flight Lieutenant, I was posted to No. 616 Squadron. Another posting followed to No. 249 Squadron, which patrolled the Yorkshire coast. Very occasionally we encountered the enemy.

Late July 1940, a posting came for RAF Northolt as a Squadron Leader of a soon to be numbered Polish Squadron.

At first, I was quite annoyed at having to lead a Polish squadron; I felt the Polish pilots might be a hindrance more than help to the RAF. I believed the Polish mechanics would not have the skills to work on our aircraft. At first, whenever I spoke to any of them in French, they seemed to almost ignore my instructions. As time passed, I was pleased to admit how wrong I was about the Poles.

During the Battle of Britain, my eyes were opened to their outstanding flying skills and bravery. In the air they could sight the enemy when it was but a mere speck in the sky; their eyesight was as an eagle. In combat, the pilots of No. 303 Squadron would not hesitate to give their life to save a pilot in distress. Many a time I witnessed this as they would circle around, not leaving until they were sure the danger had passed.

My life and the lives of my two Flight Lieutenants are owed to some of the pilots of No. 303 Squadron.

My three musketeers, — as I called them — Sergeants Stanisław Karubin, Gen Szaposznikow, and Kaz Wünsche had flown to my aid on many a sortie, risking their lives to protect me. I do not believe any other squadron had better maintenance or NCOs than No. 303. As the weeks passed at RAF Northolt, we all got to know each other well. The atmosphere between the British, Polish and Czech was very friendly. I did, however, often clash with Flying Officer Witold Urbanowicz. Personality wise, we did not always see eye to eye; he was excellent as a pilot and I respected him.

Throughout the Battle of Britain, many evenings were spent singing, playing various instruments, and socialising in the mess. Group Captain Stanley Vincent would often join in and a good time was had by all. On other free evenings, we often travelled back and forth to The Orchard Public House in Ruislip —up to twelve of us at a time would squash into my old Rolls-Royce. We were always made welcome at The Orchard and the drinks would flow. We had many good times there.

One of my narrow escapes while flying with No. 303 was on 6th September 1940. After a fierce battle with some Messerschmitts, my Hurricane was badly damaged; I decided to bale out. Unfortunately, I found myself trapped in my aircraft or rather what was left of it. 'Oh bugger I thought'. With no option, I had to land and rather quick. Biggin Hill was the nearest airfield. I tried to land as best as I could. I flew my Hurricane in at 150mph taking the whole of the runway. I finished up by going through the boundary fence and landing on the road. I was able to use the flaps of my aircraft, as it was nose heavy. One of my Hurricanes wings, the left wing, ran in low. As the brakes still worked, I had been able to swing my aircraft to the right as it hit the boundary fence. My

Hurricane had no rudders left or elevators and a hole in each wing large enough for a man to jump through. Men ran quickly to me, axing off my canopy and dragging me out as Biggin Hill was under heavy attack by the Luftwaffe. I was later taken to a hospital and felt fortunate my injuries were not too bad. Sadly, Squadron Leader Zdzisław Krasnodębski was not so fortunate. While in hospital, I had seen Zdzisław after he came out of the operating theatre. He had terrible injuries and was very badly burnt. I have never forgotten the state he was in, he bore his pain bravely. Seeing him like it upset me.

After leaving No. 303 Squadron, I became a Wing Leader at North Weald. Later, I led No. 71 Eagle Squadron into action for the first time. In 1942, there came a posting to the Air Ministry where I was in charge of fighter training. For a while, I edited 'Fighting Talk'. Later, I was Commanding Officer of No. 615 squadron, which was Royal Auxiliary Air Force until 1949. In civilian life, I resumed my position at Laurence Prust.

After the war, I attended many Air Force reunions where I always enjoyed meeting with old friends I had flown with. One of my proudest moments in the war was when I was awarded the Virtuti Militari.

As the years have passed since the war, I often see in my mind's eye the faces of the pilots of No. 303 who lost their lives. They were once so full of life and hope of returning to a free Poland; they remain forever young in one's memory. One day I hope to meet with them in a higher place than this.

Ronald Kellett lived for many years on a farm in Kent with his wife Daphne. They had five children and many grandchildren.

Wing Commander Ronald Kellett passed away in 1998 at eighty-nine years old.

See Combat Reports for the following dates:

- 31 August 1940
- 5 Sep 1940
- 6 Sep 1940
- 15 Sep 1940
- 26 Sept 1940
- 5 Oct 1940
- 6 Oct 1940

Sources: Interview Wing Commander Ronald Kellett, Jun 1986. DFC approved 1 October 1940. Distinguished Service Order (DSO) approved October 1940. Profile Photo: Ronald Kellett.

Circa 1980s, W/Cdr Ronald Kellett commissioned artist Graham Coton to paint three combat scenes in which W/Cdr Kellett was involved. The painting shown here is of combat over Southampton waters on 26 September 1940 involving No. 303 Kościuszko Squadron and the Luftwaffe. Reproduced with kind permission of W/Cdr Ronald Kellett's family.

Name: **John Kent**
Squadron: No. 92 Squadron
              No. 303 Kościuszko Squadron
Decorations: Virtuti Militari 5th Class
              DFC
              AFC Bar

John Alexander Kent, known to his friends as Johnny, was born 23 June 1914 in Canada. He was *struck by the flying bug* at an early age, relishing any opportunity to see aircraft in flight and devouring books about his fighter heroes.

At seventeen years old, he took lessons at the Winnipeg Flying School and knew he could fly at the end of his first lesson. On days when the weather delayed his morning flights, he visited other sections on the airfield. It was during these visits that he met many notable First World War pilots, including Roy Brown, who had shot down Baron Von Richthofen (The Red Baron).

When John Kent received his private pilot's licence at the age of just seventeen, he was the youngest licensed pilot in Canada. He obtained his commercial licence and a qualification to fly seaplanes. In 1933, he joined the RAF on a six-year Short Service Commission.

He returned on leave to his native Canada for a holiday in 1937. John Kent thought he would leave the RAF and become a pilot with Trans-Canadian Airlines. He attended an interview and returned to England with the promise of a position in twelve months time. On his return to England after two months in Canada, news of his new posting *drastically changed his plans and put paid to all ideas of becoming an airline pilot.*

John Kent could not have been more pleased with his posting to the Royal Aircraft Establishment in Farnborough as a Test Pilot on the Experimental Section's Instrument, Armament and Defence Flight. During his two-year posting, he carried out 300 collisions, including dangerous mid-air collisions into balloon cables. He was awarded the Air Force Cross in 1939 and qualified for a Non-Specialist Permanent Commission with the RAF.

In the autumn of 1939, John Kent reported to RAF Heston for duties on high altitude photographic reconnaissance. A short posting in Meaux in France followed, but he returned to England after the fall of France to spend four hectic days at No. 7 Operational Training Unit at Hawarden, North Wales to train on Hurricanes. He returned to Farnborough to find his next posting to No. 54 Squadron had changed. As a valuable test pilot, he was not to fly in operations. John Kent was not happy with the news but only had to wait a week to learn of his next posting

John Kent arrived at RAF Northolt in late July 1940 as a Flight Lieutenant in No. 303 Kościuszko Squadron. He felt annoyed at his posting to a foreign squadron that had yet to be formed.

'All I knew about the Polish Air Force was that it had only lasted about three days against the Luftwaffe and I had no reason to suppose that they would shine any more brightly operating from England.'

As the days and weeks passed John Kent witnessed the flying skills of the Polish airmen and was happy to admit he had been wrong to doubt them. He made many lasting friendships and earned the nickname 'Kentowski'. He admired that in the air, the Polish pilots risked their lives to protect other pilots in distress, and had, on more than one occasion, had his own life saved by the pilots of No. 303 Kościuszko Squadron. During one sortie, Flying Lieutenant Henneberg kept six Me109s off John Kent's tail. He was deeply upset when Squadron Leader Henneberg was killed in 1941.

During the Battle of Britain, John Kent flew many successful sorties. In October 1940, he and the squadron parted ways. He left to take up a post as Squadron Leader with No. 92 Squadron at RAF Biggin Hill. Before the pilots of No. 303 Kościuszko Squadron left for a much-needed rest at RAF Leconfield, they invited John Kent to write in the squadron diary started by Mirosław Ferić. He wrote:

'It is with genuine regret and sorrow that I terminate my association with the Squadron, the finest the RAF has seen.'

After another promotion to Wing Commander of a training unit at RAF Heston, John Kent returned to RAF Northolt to fly with No. 1 Polish Fighter Wing — the Northolt Wing. The Wing's sorties included targets of St Omer, Hazebrouck, and Boulogne. John Kent destroyed twelve enemy aircraft on various sorties throughout the war.

Other postings within John Kent's diverse career with the RAF included a six-month lecture tour in America and Canada. He was never quite sure if this *'was meant to be a reward or penance.'*

In 1942, he returned to England and was to command No. 313 Czechoslovakian Squadron. He then moved to the Middle East for a posting as Wing Commander. This was followed by a posting as Personal Staff Officer to Sir Sholto Douglas, Commander in Chief and Military Governor in the British Zone of Occupied Germany. When Sir Douglas handed over the reins to his successor, John Kent returned to England as the Chief Test Pilot at Farnborough.

In 1952, he took command of RAF Station Oldham, followed by RAF Tangmere, and a final unwanted administrative Staff Officer post at Headquarters No. 12 Group, Newton in Nottinghamshire. On 1 December 1956, his request to be placed on the Retired List was granted and he took up a new career in the aviation industry.

Few pilots could have had such a varied career in the RAF as John Kent. He never forgot those he flew with and felt the loss of the many friends who died during the war. He kept in touch with many of the Polish airmen he had flown with.

Group Captain John Kent married and had a family after the war. He passed away in 1985 at seventy-one years old.

See Combat Reports for the following dates:
- 3 Sep 1940
- 6 Sep 1940
- 7 Sep 1940
- 9 Sep 1940
- 15 Sep 1940
- 17 Sep 1940
- 23 Sep 1940

- 27 Sep 1940
- 1 Oct 1940
- 8 Oct 1940

See Wing section for the following dates:
- 8 Jul 1941

Sources: Pilot information from the Polish Air Force Association, Combat Reports from The National Archives (TNA), Air 50/117, Operational Report Diaries from RAF Northolt. Interviews Mrs A Forbes, 1986; Wing Commander Ronald Kellett, Jun 1986; Flight Lieutenant Jan Kowalski. Gen) Szaposznikow, Jul 1986; General Witold Urbanowicz, 1987. Quotes: 'One of the Few' by John Kent, Publisher William Kimber 1971; John Kent's entry in Mirosław Ferić's diary sourced from the Polish Institue and Sikorski Museum, London. DFC approved October 1940. Profile Photo: Ronald Kellett.

October 1940 (from left to right) P/O Mirosław Ferić, F/L John Kent, F/O Bogdan Grzeszczak, P/O Jerzy Radomski, P/O Jan Zumach, P/O Witold Łokuciewski, F/O Zdzisław Henneberg, Sgt Jan Rogowski, Sgt 'Gen' Szaposznikow. Photo: Permission of Gen Szaposznikow

Name: **Jan Kowalski**
Squadron: No. 303 Kościuszko Squadron
                 No. 315 Squadron
                 No. 317 Squadron
                 No. 145 Squadron
Decorations: Virtuti Militari 5th Class
                 KW Cross of Valour - three bars
                 DFC

Jan Kowalski was born 19th November 1916 in Mircze, a small village in Poland. In 1986, he wrote this memoir about his life.

From a small child, I used to climb high upon the bows of trees and dream of one day flying as a bird.

My dream became a reality when I began my flying apprenticeship (Youth Air Force Training), aged sixteen, at Bydgoszcz for three years. The first two years training at Bydgoszcz included learning to control and fly a glider. The first part of glider training was spent sitting in a frame followed by jumping around thirty metres in the air. The next step was to glide successfully down a slope. On my first attempt at gliding it was nearly dusk, I had just witnessed the previous apprentice crash into a tree and break his leg. This made me a little apprehensive but did not deter me, after gliding straight down thankfully I made a perfect landing. As I glided down it was so very quiet but for the whistling sound of the glider as it glided through the air. It was a marvellous experience — as near to a bird upon the wing as one could get.

More flight training followed during the next two years. During this time, I was taught how to strip an aircraft down, take it completely to bits find out how it all worked, then with great patience reassemble the aircraft. I found the mechanical side very interesting and had a great respect for the skills of mechanics especially when a mechanic would have to sometimes work at speed and I did not.

The third part of the year was mostly flying. At the end of the three-year course, some of the apprentices became pilots, others mechanics.

In 1935, I undertook further training at the 1st Training School in Warsaw. This was followed by reconnaissance training then aerobatics.

In 1936, I was in 112 Fighter Squadron, where I spent eighteen months. After which, I was sent on an instructor course at the Dęblin Officers' School, where I qualified as an instructor.

Before the outbreak of the Second World War, some of the pilots, ground crew and I were moved to an airfield in Krosno which is in the southern part of Poland.

I remember 1st September 1939 very clearly, for how could any Polish person ever forget.

I was asleep and suddenly awoken at 6.30 am by the sound of aircraft approaching. I knew that it was not our aircraft as none went up until after 8 am. Within seconds, the German aircraft were dropping bombs all around us. We quickly ran to the trenches that had only recently been dug out. Three rows of buildings, the mess, living quarters, and hangers were all hit. The hangers were burning but the bomb that dropped in the living quarters did not go off. After receiving orders I flew to collect my pupils from the training school. After receiving further orders my cadets and I moved east then south. We all flew in two-seated aircraft that were not good enough for combat in the Polish Air Force but were quite adequate for the needs of my pupils and I.

After landing safely in Romania we were given a little money and lived on bread and grapes. The Romanians gave us some petrol and those we encountered were very helpful to my group. We flew over the hills and landed in Bucharest, after which we were moved to the Black Sea. On our arrival, we were billeted in comfortable accommodation. Shortly after we boarded a ship with many other Polish airmen and mechanics; the ship sailed us to France.

In France, I was to continue instructing Polish airmen to fly. I trained them at an airfield near Normandy flying mainly two-engine aircraft. Later along with other Polish airmen, we were given orders to ferry aircraft to Bordeaux. After arriving in Bordeaux, the French took control of the aircraft: all the aircraft were well guarded by the French. I was given a tip-off by one of my pupils, also called Kowalski (he was half-Polish and half-French) that France was soon to surrender. Along with my pupils and other Polish airmen and their mechanics, we boarded one of the ships in the harbour, a Polish merchant ship. Many of the ships were British others Polish a British destroyer lay nearby. The ship we were on, sailed us into Falmouth in Cornwall. In Falmouth, a well-organised reception awaited our arrival.

After arriving in England, I was sent to Glasgow, Scotland then to Blackpool in England. A posting followed on 21 August 1940 to RAF Northolt in South Ruislip to No. 303 Polish Squadron. After flight training the squadron became fully operational on 31st August. In the squadron were many men I had known in my air force days in Poland.

While flying with 303 during the Battle of Britain, I was returning from a sortie. Over Southampton my Hurricane was hit by an Me 109 and badly damaged, the damage included the instrument panel. Flying north I sighted the barrage balloons and the Thames. I then followed the long stretch of water that was the marker towards Northolt.

After landing safely back at Northolt the bullets were removed from my hurricane, one of which I kept as a souvenir. I always carried it with me for luck. 303 Squadron flew many successful sorties in the Battle of Britain. Sadly I lost many friends, some so very young.

When 303 Squadron moved to Leconfield for a rest after the hectic days of the Battle of Britain many new pilots arrived. Some of the original pilots of 303 including myself prepared for night fighter training.

On one such late afternoon, 303 were on readiness. It was nearly dusk when our squadron was called to scramble for battle Convoy duties. 303 Squadron took off, once over the Convoy as we circled around at about the same time RAF Leconfield was being bombed, I remember it so clearly. On our return it was dark, the airfield had been lit up as well it could be from the lights of the lorries and cars. Landing safely among the many potholes, a bit tricky but I managed it I was wearing my lucky bullet that no doubt helped.

In 1941, I was promoted to Flying Officer and transferred to 315 Polish Squadron at Speke in Liverpool, during March and April mainly formation flying. A move followed to Anglesey with 315 Squadron for night flying. In the summer of 1941, I returned to Speke where our squadron flew Mark 1 Spitfires, a very beautiful aircraft.

In July 1941, 315 Squadron were posted to RAF Northolt which was like a home to many of us Poles; there was something special about RAF Northolt that could not be put into words. We were given Mark 2 Spitfires. I flew with The Polish Wing from Northolt being 306, 308 and 315 Squadrons. Other Polish squadrons flew with the Polish Wing including my old squadron 303. I flew with 315 Squadron on Circus ops flying over the Channel on Convoy duties, which I and others found very monotonous flying.

On 1st March 1942 with 315 Squadron, I was posted to Woodvale that was about seven miles north of Liverpool, many months were spent training there. In September of that year, I was posted back to RAF Northolt along with my squadron until November 1942.

Another posting followed to train Polish airmen for fighter combat. While training these pilots a request came through for the Africa Campaign, I volunteered straight away and was pleased to be accepted.

I was promoted to Flight Lieutenant. With fourteen other Polish airmen I was sent to Glasgow in Scotland, fifteen of us Poles boarded a ship that joined a long Convoy. Some of the ships in the Convoy sailed to Iran amongst them the ship we were on. When landing in Iran, there were other Polish airmen and American airmen of Polish decent. From Iran we travelled to Algeria by Dakota aircraft then to Tripoli. Some of the pilots flew to collect aircraft. I was attached to the 3rd flight of 145 Squadron. This flight 145, the Polish detachment, later became known as 'Skalski Circus' led by Squadron Leader Stanisław Skalski we destroyed twenty-five enemy aircraft losing only one pilot who was made a POW. Our makeshift aerodrome was a long stretch of beach. The sand was very hard due to the salt content that made a hard film over the sand. Other landing strips had wire mesh over the sand to help when landing. We had special filters fitted to our Spitfires. We were on readiness all day long, sitting for hours in our cockpits in full battle dress including our Mae Wests. The heat was stifling, burning hot we were most uncomfortable sitting, waiting. We were about twelve miles from the front line. When taking off we flew turning right then left looking out for the front line.

Often, I heard the sound of nearby guns firing. Flying over the sea and the Bay of Tunisia sighting many Convoys. The squadron flew until the end of the Africa Campaign.

After the Africa Campaign other Polish airmen and I that I had flown with, flew to Gibraltar. While in Gibraltar our Squadron learnt that General Sikorski was there, we all requested permission to fly back with him. Our request was refused. We were all completely devastated when we learnt of General Sikorski's and the others aboard the aircraft deaths, dying in a supposed flying accident. Had our request been granted, Squadron Leader Skalski, the other pilots and I in the Polish detachment of 145 Squadron would have been killed. With heavy hearts on General Sikorski's loss, we flew back to Britain aboard a Lancaster bomber.

On my return to Northolt, I was posted to Air Traffic Control. Later a posting came to 317 Polish Squadron. To prepare for the invasion our squadron moved to various airfields.

In May 1944, I took part with 317 Squadron attacks on the V1 installations; at first, we were all unsure of what exactly the target was. In July and August of 1944, many sorties were flown attacking the V1 installations. We were then posted to Lin on reconnaissance duties. Another posting followed to Antwerp. As winter approached 317 Squadron was moved to Ghent also in Holland. I remember New Year's day 1945 very clearly. Our squadron took off before sunrise and I saw a V2 going up. On our way back to base the Luftwaffe had attacked the aerodrome, a lot of damage had been done and sadly men had lost their lives.

Many of the aircraft on the ground had been destroyed; we had to land at a nearby airfield. Not a very pleasant way for some to begin the New Year; worse still for some, there was to be no New Year.

In May 1945 at war's end, I was posted back to England, returning to Blackpool. The Polish Air Force was then transferred to Dunholme Lodge in Lincolnshire. While at Dunholme Lodge, airmen were asked if any of them wanted to transfer to EASSU (this unit brought back German aircraft to Britain). I was one of those who transferred. It felt strange flying aircraft that I had once been doing my best to shoot down; aircraft that had once been flown by men that may have shot and killed friends of mine and many others who had flown in defence of freedom. I flew back many Junkers to various airfields including Brize Norton, Farnborough and Manston.

The Germans made them serviceable for us to fly. I flew with the Unit *to ferry aircraft back until June 1946. I was then posted to Air Traffic Control where I was made an Air Traffic Control Officer.*

In 1947, I left the Air Force. I would not return to live in Poland under Communist rule. When the war ended my heart was heavy with sadness for Poland and her people, for we had lost so much. We had not won the war; politicians had betrayed Poland and given her to the Soviets. England was to become my second home, for it was not the British people who betrayed Poland — they were always loyal. My wife had managed to escape from war-torn Poland and Europe to be reunited with me at war's end. My wife had bore witness to many terrible sights that haunted her all her life. Together we began a new life. At first, as was the case for many that had been in the forces, work was hard to find. My wife and I settled in Lincolnshire. At first I worked by mending broken furniture and doing a little carpentry. I also found I had a natural talent for upholstery. Joining a small family run business, I worked for a while in upholstery.

In 1955, my wife, our young daughter and I moved to Nottingham. Later two sons came along. I worked for Jessops, which belonged to the John Lewis chain, in the soft furnishing section. I worked for Jessops full time until 1971, then part time until 1974, after which I retired.

I returned to Poland briefly only twice over the years to visit my sick mother.

I often think of my time at RAF Northolt, home for so many fighter pilots and ground crew of the Polish Air Force. I have many fond memories of the people of South Ruislip throughout the wars years. Sometimes I was billeted with local families at Eastcote, Ruislip Gardens and Ruislip Manor where I was always treated well. At RAF Northolt, in the winter months the weather was often foggy. When not on ops we would drive slowly through the fog early evening to The Orchard Public House, enjoying a drink and the company of some of the local people; we were always made welcome. Many a late night the fog was so thick you could not see your hand in front of your face, let alone drive. We would leave the car and feel our way along the country lanes. It was quite a long walk but somehow we found our way back, ready for ops the next day.

I often attended PAF reunions, where others and I paid our respects at the Polish War Memorial to those lost. I also attended Battle of Britain reunions and a reunion held by the Americans at Alconbury.

A particularly enjoyable reunion was the '40th Battle of Britain' anniversary reunion held at RAF Northolt. Everything was so well organised for us, we went to visit the Ops room at Uxbridge, which I and others found most interesting. We attended a service at the Polish War Memorial at South Ruislip to pay our respects to those who paid the ultimate sacrifice, as is always done when attending reunions over the years.

In my retirement I enjoy gardening, I find growing plants from seed and watching their progress very rewarding. Mine is a cottage style garden and I spend many an hour out in the fresh air, pottering, feeding and watching the birds. I remember once when I soared as a bird high up on the wing my first flight in a glider in Poland aged seventeen.

Flight Lieutenant Jan Kowalski passed away in Nottingham in the year 2000.

See Combat Reports for the following dates:
- 26 Sep 1940
- 27 Sep 1940

Sources: Interview with Jan Kowalski, 1986.

1940 (from left to right) Sgt 'Gen' Szaposznikow, mechanic, Sgt Jan Rogowski (sitting), Sgt Marian Bełc, Sgt Jan Kowalski. Photo: Permission of Jan Kowalski/author's collection.

Name: **Zdzisław Krasnodębski**
Squadron: 303 Kościuszko Squadron
Decorations: Virtuti Miltari 5th Class
                 KW Cross of Valour

Zdzisław Krasnodębski was born 10 August 1904 near Łukow in Poland. His wife Wanda Krasnodębska has kindly given permission for his memoir, written after the Second World War to be reproduced in this book.

I started my Army service in 1920 during the war against the Bolsheviks. At sixteen years of age, I volunteered with 201 Warsaw Infantry Regiment. After my release from the army, and completion of the Lwów Cadet Corp. In 1925, I joined the Air Force Officers' School on a pilot's course.

Later my dreams were fully realised when I joined the famous 111 Kościuszko fighter squadron of the 1st Air Force regiment in Warsaw. American pilots formed this squadron as the 7th after the end of the war in 1918. They were stationed in France and decided to come to Poland to help Poland in the war against the Bolsheviks.

This was a gesture of gratitude, a repayment of a debt owed to Tadeusz Kościuszko for his actions on United States soil. They named the squadron 'Tadeusz Kościuszko' and designed the squadron's badge, which was painted on the aircraft's body. The badge depicted the American flag on the background of a four-cornered cap and two crossed sickles, and the headgear and weapon of peasants who so heroically fought at Raclawice under the command of Tadeusz Kościuszko. The American pilots had fought bravely under the Polish sky. All were decorated with the highest battle distinctions. After the end of the war, they returned to the United States except for three who are resting forever at the Defence of Lwów Cemetery.

Remembering the squadron's proud tradition, we always endeavoured to maintain the highest flying standards. Every year on Remembrance Day we would fly to Lwów in order to lay a wreath under the American colleague's memorial. During the Second World War the Memorial and the whole cemetery was barbarically destroyed in order to eradicate all that is Polish in the unquestionable Polish domain. But the heroic spirit of those who rest in the cemetery no force can destroy, for it will live forever and remain an example for future generations.

In 1936, I was nominated Leader of the 111th Kościuszko Squadron and two years later Commander of the 3rd Fighter Wing composed of 111th and 112th Squadrons.

In 1939, in anticipation of war, as Commander of the Fighter squadrons, I received orders for the transfer of the Fighter Wing to the provisional airfield at Zielonka near Warsaw. It was apparent that the main airfield at Okęcie was well known to the Germans, it would probably be the first place they would bomb.

On 1 September 1939 the unannounced war started. We were flying from dawn to night in order to combat continuous enemy raids trying to prevent unrestrained bombardment and strafing of defenceless towns and villages. The battles were fierce and very hard and uneven as the German planes were faster with superior firepower and more numerous. Despite these discrepancies we won many battles but unfortunately suffered severe losses. During one action, I attacked a Dornier which crashed in flames killing all the crew. Satisfied with our success the flight proudly cruised awhile over the burning aircraft.

On 3 September in the morning, alerted we started as usual. At about 3000m altitude we encountered a squadron of Messerschmitt 110s that we attacked. A fierce battle developed the sky was full of planes in combat. Tracer bullets were cutting through the blue-sky crisscrossing smoke poured forth from burning aircraft. However, the battle did not last long as the Germans recognised that in circular combat our aircraft were superior thanks to their high manoeuvrability. The Me110s started to retreat with our aircraft in hot pursuit. As I pursued one of the Me110s, unfortunately ,the distance increased and recognising the fruitlessness of further pursuit,

I began to head towards our airfield. Nearing the place where a short time ago our flight was in combat I spotted a lone Messerschmitt 110. Aware of the greater speed of the enemy's plane and realising I could not approach it from the rear within effective shooting range, I decided to attack frontally. We flew against each other face to face, with me at a favourable slightly higher altitude, I did not fire because having only two machine guns, I had to be much closer for an effective attack. The German pilot on the other hand with superior armament, four machine guns, and two guns commenced firing from a considerable distance. When I saw the tracer bullets, I flew my machine higher in order to avoid the fire area, at the same moment my aircraft was hit and burst into flames. Without giving it a second thought, I released my belt disconnected my earphones and jumped. Pulling the parachute's handle the chute opened, as I remained suspended in space. Looking downwards I saw my plane plunging towards the ground in a mass of flames and smoke, disintegrating on impact into a mass of tangled metal. I felt sad for my plane. After a while as my eyes scanned the sky, I saw an enemy plane turning in my direction.

Fear struck me as I remembered when yesterday one of my colleagues was fired upon whilst suspended by his parachute. I did not want to die but there was no possibility of saving myself. I was, I believed, condemned to wait idly for the inescapable heartless fate... I looked and saw one of our planes on full throttle closing in on the Jerry. The attack was a complete surprise to the Jerrys. After a few seconds without any attempt of defence, the German aircraft crashed in flames to the ground, taking both men with it whilst I safely floated down and landed under the guard of flying comrade Lt. Arsen Cebrzyński. My burns were attended to by the Wing's Doctor and I again was in charge of the Wing. Due to the continuous battles and complete lack of reinforcements our strength soon diminished and out of twenty-two aircraft only nine remained.

Later in September, when the Russians crossed the Polish border we flew our nine aircraft to Romania. From Romania we left for France by various routes in order to continue the struggle.

In France with my men, I organised the squadron, unfortunately, the lack of aircraft prevented the squadron's full equipment. Therefore, some squadrons were assigned for the defence of sensitive areas.

I with my squadron joined the French Wing in the Paris area. There were no alarm facilities organised to signal any oncoming enemy aircraft.

Planes were started up on ones own observations, e.g. often too late as when our airfield at Étampes was bombarded, we started to take off amongst bursting bombs.

After the defeat of France we left for England in order to continue the struggle for freedom.

In July 1940 in England whilst in Blackpool, I received orders to organise a Fighter Squadron with my Warsaw crews. This was with the objective to be ready for action as soon as possible. This being in order to assist English fighters, who heroically are worthy of the highest praise, who offered resistance to the German Luftwaffe during the then in progress Battle of Britain.

After the formation of the Fighter Squadron, we were stationed at Northolt airfield near London. We were allocated the number 303 and on my intervention, the English authorities agreed to the adoption for the Wing/Squadron the name Kościuszko. We also had the Kościuszko badge painted on the aircraft's body, after training on new equipment and the familiarisation with the operational system of action based on Radar observation.

On 31 August 1940 the 303 Squadron became officially operational and flew into action. Every day we flew brought triumphs but also defeats.

Such a day of misfortune was 6 September, when twelve Hurricanes were ordered up and later only five returned to base. On this day we started as usual on 'alert.' During this period, the Luftwaffe concentrated their main efforts against London in order to try to break the morale of the defenders. Therefore, we received orders to attack and disorganise the enemy bomber formation heading for London without regard to the presence and number of German fighters shadowing the operation. Directed over the R/T from the ground, we attacked a squadron of Dornier bombers. Just as I had one in my target visor I was hit. The glass from the instrument panel and burning petrol filled my cockpit as my Hurricane had no fire screens between the fuel tanks and pilot. I opened the cockpit, disconnected the belt and radio earphones, oxygen mask and jumped. I did not open my parachute straight away in order to avoid the battle area and, not as I did in Warsaw, become an easy target for the enemy. When at last I decided to open the parachute, I could not seem to locate the handle, which moved with the chute from the normal position when I jumped. The earth neared menacingly fast. At last I located the handle, pulled it and experienced a sharp pull and quietness prevailed. It was then that I felt severe pain in my burnt hands and legs. After a short while I heard aircraft approaching me, I thought history repeats itself but luck was with me as I recognised our Hurricanes. When I neared the ground, a new hazard developed when from nearby bushes soldiers from the Home Guard approached me with rifles ready to fire. Apparently, they were assuming I was a German parachutist, at that time they were feared in England in anticipation of an invasion from the air. My precarious position was made worse by the fact I was a foreigner to them, Polish uniform which they did not recognise and I did not speak English. I was only saved from a tragic end thanks to their English restraint. The delay of opening my parachute during baling out proved to be my salvation, as the stream of air extinguished the flames of my burning suit. Thereby I escaped the fate of one of the English pilots in a similar situation to mine; tragically he opened the parachute prematurely and the flames of his burning suit burnt the ends of his lines and he crashed to earth. From the place that I landed, I was taken to a nearby hospital then to the East Grinstead Hospital. As a patient, I was under the excellent care of the Surgeon Archie McIndoe and the devoted care of the lovely sister where my health was later restored. I became one of the founder members of what was to be later known as 'The Guinea Pig Club.'

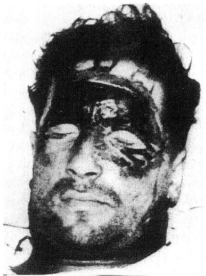

September 1940 Zdzisław Krasnodębski recovering from burns sustained in combat. Photo: Permission of Wanda Krasnodębska.

While in hospital I was decorated with the Virtuti Militari by General Sikorski, which was a great honour.

In the meantime while I recovered, 303 Squadron excelled in constantly winning famous victories. During the Battle of Britain, amongst all the squadrons, 303 destroyed the highest number of enemy aircraft in less than six weeks. The squadron gaining the admiration and recognition amongst our own and others, 303 squadron's fame spread worldwide.

After leaving hospital, I left for Canada with the Polish Military Mission; this was with the object of recruiting youngsters for the Polish Forces.

Later, I returned to England and I was appointed Commander of the Heston Fighter base.

During the continent's invasion, I was ordered to organise the 131 Wing, i.e. the Mobile Base of Polish squadrons. After the organisation of the Wing, I joined the Air Force Academy. After completion of the course, I was nominated Commander of the Polish Pilots School at Newton near Nottingham.

At the end of the war and the tragic for Poland, Yalta Agreement, I did not return to Poland for obvious reasons. I was reunited with my dear wife Wanda, who had managed to escape from Poland. Wanda had been a soldier of The Underground AK in Poland and fought in the Warsaw Uprising, witnessing many terrible sights.

During the war, Wanda Krasnodębska took part in various activities with the AK Home Army in Poland, including running secret messages from one resistance fighter unit to another. Despite the danger, she gave refuge to Polish men and women on the Nazi wanted list. If caught, the penalty usually resulted in torture, then deportation to the hell of a concentration camp, or a swift death by gunshot. Wanda was eventually caught by the Germans after the Warsaw Uprising in 1944 but managed to escape. The following year, the Soviets questioned her ,but she was released. Wanda felt it was unsafe to remain in Poland, and managed to escape with the help of the AK Home Army, who smuggled her through Czechoslovakia to British-occupied Germany. Here, Wanda and her husband were reunited in 1946. Back in England Zdzisław Krasnodębski remained with the Polish Air Force until it disbanded in 1947.

We did not wish to remain in England, consequently, my wife and I emigrated to South Africa. At Cape Town, I worked as a taxi driver and from time to time conducted tourists to the Cape of Good Hope, with hope of a better future. However, after a while not seeing any prospects for an improvement of my situation in South Africa, my wife and I left for Canada in 1951. Canada proved to be more hospitable to us.

See Combat Reports for the following dates:
- 6 Sep 1940

Sources: Interview with Mrs Wanda Krasnodębska, 22 Jul 1987, who kindly gave permission for inclusion of some her late husband's memoirs and photographs.

Remembering Zdzisław Krasnodębski

by Witold Urbanowicz

Witold Urbanowicz wrote the following before Poland's Independence in 1989. He asked for it be included in this book about his friend **Zdzisław Krasnodębski**. The following was written by General Witold Urbanowicz in 1986:

The stormy past of Polish airmen forms their own legend — even an abstract. The present is their actual problem — how to live through their life's autumn in order not to waste remaining energy but conserve it for the approaching winter. The belief of having achieved something gives us satisfaction, maturity and solemn wisdom of advancing old age. I do not know what life is, less what death is at all about. Learning of the death of any of the Polish pilots in exile, I am consumed by sadness and nostalgia. I recall the memory of years gone by, remembering their life's achievements and failures. It is hard for me to believe that they are gone.

I met Zdzisław Krasnodębski for the first time in 1932 when assigned to the 1st Air Force Regiment in Warsaw. I remember Lt. Zdzisław Krasnodębski when on a sunny morning he stood with other Fighter pilots in front of the Okęcie hangers. Short and slim good looking man with a childlike face. A moment later Krasnodębski fastened his parachute, entered the cabin of the Fighter PZL-7 and started vertically from the hangers. I was fascinated by his start, as an observer with the Wing on night bombers I dreamed of the Fighter Air Force. Later on I met Krasnodębski at the Officers' Mess we had a talk. I learnt that he finished the Cadet Corp at Llów, whereas I the one in Modlin. This bound us together. For me Krasnodębski was an authority older than I was by a few years, he had also served longer in the Air Force. Krasnodębski had a low but pleasant voice, was self-disciplined, intelligent with a good sense of humour but serious in matters of duty. His style of command was based on friendly relations with his subordinates. Humorous and very understanding, he was neither automation nor a 'walking regulations manual'.

His squadron personnel was also friendly disposed towards their Commander. The only exception was Warrant Officer Kazimierz Mozel the mechanic's supervisor who opposed him, Mozel having been with The Kościuszko Squadron since the Polish-Bolshevik war. He considered himself the King of the squadron. Krasnodębski was also called 'King' apparently named so from the moment General Rayski asked him, how he felt in the new PZL-7 aircraft. Krasnodębski answered, 'Like a King'.

When Warrant Officer Mozel complained Krasnodębski hurried him for aircraft to be ready for early morning. Krasnodębski pacified Mozel with the words.

'Chief, do not worry the King won't prick the eye of the King.'

Krasnodębski often played poker and bridge at the Officers' Mess, sometimes until early morning but he was always first at the hanger even before W/O Mozel.

Krasnodębski was married but I followed the sport of being single. We met frequently at dances, drunk, sung, conversed; in short we enjoyed ourselves. We were young and full of optimism. Krasnodębski's favourite Tango was the Lwów Tango.

When he would join in with singing the Lwów Tango his wife Wanda would utter the words, 'Zdzisiu, perhaps you have had too much to drink.'

On one particular day in 1936, Krasnodębski assembled his squadron at the hangers and addressed them as follows. 'Please gentleman, our squadron was honoured to have been chosen to undertake a combat mission. The day after tomorrow we are flying to Sarny in Polesie and there we will defend the construction of defence positions against Bolshevik's Air Reconnaissance.' Krasnodębski issued appropriate orders to the chief of mechanics, to me he allocated the supervision of readiness of the squadron for action.

We started from Okęcie at dawn, our MG's loaded with live ammunition. The airfield at Sarny was located at a forest's border, it was small and uneven but the landing was accomplished without damage to our aircraft. Krasnodębski was very pleased and W/O Mozel maintained that this was his success. He said, 'The machines are serviced like shining threads, therefore the successful landings.'

On the same day the squadron was alerted by phone, from an observation post on the Polish-Russian border. We started with Krasnodębski as a pair. Soon after we spotted a Russian reconnaissance aircraft at about 1000m altitude that manoeuvred between the clouds. He must have spotted us because he turned towards Russia. We attacked him but did not fire, our orders were to force the Bolsheviks to leave Polish airspace. We cruised for another half an hour along the Polish-Russian border. After landing, I noticed a strange message written with chalk on a blackboard. A telephone message from the Observation post.

'Polish fighter attacked Russian aircraft who immediately turned to the east,' and under the message was written, 'The King chased the Bolshevik's cat away.'

Near the runway, we erected a large tent which served as our HQ, dining room, resting place for the crews, and ammunition store. Conditions were battle-like. Krasnodębski as Commander displayed many talents caring for the Kościuszko Squadron's true continuation of battle tradition from the time of The Polish-Russian war. In those conditions I became to know him very well, we often talked a lot together.

He dreamed about plans for the future to be Wing Commander and I take over from him the Kościuszko squadron. Krasnodębski was a born fighter pilot, an outstanding teacher and organiser on the ground and in the air, a formidable tactician. As a 'gentlemen' he gained his crew's trust obedience as well as their confidence. His righteous character positively influenced his subordinates. He was not a paper tiger, not a regulations man. Even in those limited social circumstances at Sarny, he was still able to organise for his squadron cultural recreation. Often at the pub called 'Night Club', he would enjoy singing the 'Llów Tango'. In the meantime, the Bolsheviks flew over Polesie's defence position, 'This is intolerable,' said Krasnodębski to me. 'If you see a Bolshevik who refuses to obey your order to retreat open fire.'

On the day of the alert duty with Lt. Nałecz we hurried to the east. A moment later we spotted a Bolshevik aircraft. He flew cheekily to the west completely ignoring our warning (wing movement). I was sure the Bolshevik did not see me when I came near to him, I observed the guns opening fire against us. I ducked the plane with Lt. Nałecz and we proceeded to attack the Bolsheviks, firing in short bursts. I was not sure whether the plane caught fire or accelerated, leaving a trail of engine smoke behind him. He disappeared in the clouds and we lost sight of him. After we landed Krasnodębski said to me, 'a telephone call from Observation post reported the Bolshevik aircraft crashed on the moor.' I described exactly what happened. Only I was not quite sure if I was right firing at the Bolshevik.

'Don't worry,' Krasnodębski assured me. 'He fired at you first. Were you to shower him with flowers?'

We received no further news about the aircraft; this was strictly secret. Even Krasnodębski ordered that no one from the squadron was to say anything to strangers. The more so bearing in mind that many 'strangers' were cruising around Sarny. The Russian spy network was well developed. On the same evening, we celebrated 'the chase of the Bolshevik cat'. During the drinks, we contemplated who is worse Hitler or Stalin. 'These two criminals will accommodate themselves, as did the Russian Tsar with Germany in respect of occupying Poland,' said Krasnodębski.

We did not foresee that only three years later Hitler would come to an understanding with Stalin and both would attack Poland. I listened with pleasure to the rational comments from Krasnodębski.

On one particular day he said to me —

'Tomorrow you will fly to Warsaw, deliver the plane for an overhaul and will settle some business at The Regiment. On this occasion you will have a look at our hanger and see if everything is in order. If you find it necessary, press a few buttons on someone.

Yes, I pressed some buttons for oxidised MGs of our planes. After a talk with the gunsmith, I learned Major Kosiński from training squadron, who seldom flew kept the gunsmith busy with his own private affairs.

I tightened the screw on the gunsmith cancelling his travels to Warsaw. Then Kosiński tightened the screw on me even better; I was fired from the Regiment and transferred to Dęblin Training School. There parted our paths for quite a long time. I was cross with Krasnodębski for doing nothing to prevent my exclusion from the Fighter Air Force. Krasnodębski explained that there was nothing he could do in my case. To add to my scorn he added that, such as myself are required in training. 'After all the war is getting nearer and our Air Force needs to be extended,' he said. 'What war?' I asked, not satisfied.

After the 1939 campaign we met again in France. He was a distinguished veteran as the Commander of the Fighter Wing, he flew/ fought in the defence of Warsaw. Shot down, Krasnodębski saved himself by parachute. I also fought on in a training fighter aircraft in the defence of Dęblin but this was not recognised. Pawlikowski was in command of the Pursuit Brigade in defence of Warsaw during the September Campaign he did not accept me into the Fighter Squadron in France. Krasnodębski remained in France with his Kościuszko squadron crews, whilst I left for England.

After the collapse of France, Krasnodębski with other Polish pilots arrived in England. At that time I was already with an English Fighter Squadron 145, I had two victories in the air with the squadron.

One day the squadron Adjutant said to me, 'You are requested to report immediately to the Air Ministry.' I had no clue as to the reason. At once I went by duty car to London. At the Air Ministry I spoke to some Vice Marshal, he informed me of my transfer to the Northolt airfield. On the evening of that day at the Officers' Mess, I met many of the Polish fighter pilots and amongst them 'reigned' Krasnodębski.

'What are you doing here?' asked Krasnodębski. I informed him I was transferred to Northolt.

He told me, 'The Polish Fighter Squadron 303 are stationed here.' I was completely surprised by the situation because I did not know the Polish squadron was already organised.

'Don't you know about it?' Krasnodębski asked. I replied, 'That the Air Ministry and not the Polish Inspectorate sent me.' Krasnodębski told me he had 'especially asked for me at the Polish Inspectorate.' It was possible that the Polish Inspectorate did not grant this request, therefore the misunderstanding.

During the night I had a rather long talk with Krasnodębski. An Englishman Squadron Leader Kellett was attached to the squadron, he did not speak Polish but knew a little French, most Polish airmen spoke French.

The following day I met Squadron Leader Kellett, we did not like each other, from the first moment an 'anti-love' syndrome developed between us.

The 303 Squadron was composed of pilots from the Kościuszko Squadron in Warsaw, which had fought so gallantly in the defence of our capital Warsaw in 1939. Krasnodębski was not only the Polish Commander of 303 Squadron but also its inspiration authority, colleague and friend. He organised and trained the squadron in the air and on the ground.

The Northolt Station Commander Group Captain Stanley Vincent, a man of high culture became a friend of the 303 crews; he highly valued and loved Poles.

In one of the first battle sorties of 303 Squadron, Krasnodębski was shot down by the Germans and saved himself by parachute. The German who *attacked him I attacked and shot down. Only after landing I learnt that the one who saved himself by parachute was my leader Krasnodębski. The same day in the evening I visited him at the hospital near London, his face was burnt and bandaged and his hands badly burnt. Krasnodębski said to me, 'Assume Command of the 303 Wing and lead it to honour and glory for the Fatherland and the King. Convey my greetings to the squadron.'*

I left the hospital with a heavy heart. Maybe I had a premonition that Krasnodębski will never fly again as a Fighter pilot. He was the mainstay of the Polish Fighter Air Force. I did not foresee after the war he would choose to remain in exile. Never could I imagine him to live outside Poland the more the role of the immigrant.

After many years, I buried my hurt that Krasnodębski did not prevent my transfer from Warsaw to Dęblin. That he did not select me to join the list of Fighter pilots in France. Also that he omitted me at the very beginning of the 303 Squadron organisation in England.

Krasnodębski was very loyal towards his colleagues and subordinates but in those situations, he always did his best 'for the cause'. It was obvious during the organisation with Col. Pawlkowski of the Fighter Polish Air Force in the west, he could choose in the first place fighter pilots who had combat experience in the September Campaign in Poland. In consequence, Krasnodębski benefited me by his honest approach to the Polish cause. At Dęblin as an Instructor at the Fighter School, I had gained wide experience in air combat. Apart from that, I trained along with other pilots, young fighter pilots who joined me from Dęblin to the west. Some of them were later Commanders of Fighter Squadrons and Wings in the battles against the Germans. Who knows, through this 'training' Krasnodębski may have saved my life? Perhaps I could have been shot down by the Germans in Poland or France, as was the fate of so many brilliant Polish fighter pilots.

Krasnodębski did not have many triumphs in the air; his success was on the ground, in training and upbringing of young Officers whose Commander he was. The most important thing, with his outstanding righteous character, was he gave an explicit example to Air Force Officers, including older and higher rank than himself.

After prolonged treatment in the hospital, Krasnsodębski did not fly again. His arms were severely burnt to such a degree that he had difficulties in holding a cigarette. His face also suffered but more affected was his mind. He visited the 303 Squadron, watching starts and landings of pilots. This was not the same Krasnodębski, the smiling and full of action-spirited man.

As Commander of the 303 Squadron Krasnodębski was awarded the Virtuti Militari, which he received while in hospital, General Sikorski personally presented him with this honour.

In 1941, with Krasnodębski we embarked on the voyage to Canada. He and I were attached to the 'General Dutch Mission' whose task was to enlist volunteers from the American and Canadian Polonia for Polish Armed Forces. During those days, we were flown together all over America. The themes of our speeches were the German and Russian crimes inflicted on the Polish nation.

Krasnodębski was excellent and in those subjects relating to Germany and Russia, he proved very objective. He stressed that for the crimes against the Polish Nation; responsible were the Nazi and Communist Parties. At that time 'certain circles' with President Roosevelt on top, maintained that Soviet Russia was 'a democracy' which intended to establish peace all over the World. Krasnodębski managed to convince these admirers of Stalin that they were mistaken and shortly will come to realise it themselves.

Krasnodębski held the Polish flag highly and had no hesitation in stating his position.

One day while we were in Los Angeles, Arthur Rubinstein's secretary phoned us up at the hotel, conveying an invitation from Rubinstein to participate in a party at his home. Krasnodębski said to me. 'We should not accept an invitation of this nature, Rubinstein himself should have called us.'

We did not go to the party. A few days later during a reception at Jan Kiepura, Rubinstein was there and asked Krasnodębski, why he did not accept his invitation. Krasnodębski replied.

'We represent the Polish Air Force which is fighting so that other countries including the United States may sleep in peace.'

'Yes it was a mistake on my part,' answered Rubinstein extending his hand to Krasnodębski.

After returning from Canada in 1942, Krasnodębski joined the Cabinet of the Supreme Commander of Polish Forces, the Department of Co-Operation with Poland. I on the other side flew to Washington as Deputy Air Attaché. From there I managed to land in China, where with so-called 'Flying Tigers' I fought against the Japanese.

In 1944, I returned from China and again met Krasnodębski on London cobbles. It was already apparent that the Allies will lose the war and that the victor will be Russia. In the main, President Roosevelt and his advisors handed Russia countries, for which Russia did not even ask. The Polish question was already decided and Russia would again occupy it.

In conversation with Krasnodębski, we dreamed about the future. He was more pessimistic than I was, perhaps he had more experience in life as he was a few years older than I. He was convinced that 'we will never return to Poland alive.'

I somehow counted on a revolution in Russia, with the Russian nation freeing itself from the totalitarian dictatorship.

'Perhaps but not in our lifetime.' Krasnodębski tried to convince me.

Waiting for the allies' invasion of the European continent, we attended together confidential meetings of the so-called 'Young Officers Group'.

Our intention was to retrieve tired Officers from the battlefields and transferring them to Head Office for a rest. This was not an easy job; Officers in various positions of the Command Staff did not even want to think about this revolutionary idea.

I was nominated Air Force Attaché in Washington. Krasnodębski remained in London. Before my departure, we conversed for hours. About what, mainly the future and fate of after war Poland. In this mode, we considered our own involvement in the event.

After the end of war, the fighting soldiers deserved a rest. But things happened differently.

Brutal politicians, who acted under Russian dictate at an inopportune time in the wrong period, abandoned the Polish soldier. The Polish nation was again put under Russian dominance. The Iron Curtain closed. Again the Polish soldier marched through fields and forests battling for a day to day survival in foreign lands. Often ill-disposed to the 'Wandering Soldier'.

Krasnodębski settled in Canada, I in America the rest of the Kościuszko Squadron of 303 dispersed over the whole world. Only a few survived. Like wilted leaves they fall to the ground, landing, again winter will come and then the spring.

In August 1980, I received two letters from a friend. To one was *attached a photo of a famous former pilot with a tired from age face. On his chest a string of Medals, one a Virtuti Militari which he received after the war at a time he could not sit in the cockpit of an aircraft. The second letter was even sadder, the death of Zdzisław Krasnodębski. He died in his sleep on the 3 July of that year. His body was cremated and ashes deposited at the Veterans' Cemetery in Toronto.'*

Name: **Wacław Łapkowski**
Squadron: No. 303 Kościuszko Squadron
Decorations: Virtuti Militari 5th Class
                       KW Cross of Valour - three bars

Wacław Łapkowski, known to his family as Watek, was born on 6 November 1913 in Dyneburg, Lithuania. His father Ambrozy, an Officer in the Polish Army, was killed by the Russians during a battle in 1920. His mother never remarried but devoted her time to raising her son.

Wacław Łapkowski followed his childhood dreams to become a pilot and attended The Cadet Corp at Chełm in 1927. The following transcription is of a certificate Wacław Łapkowski received at Dęblin Officers' School, where he qualified as a pilot in 1934.

CERTIFICATE

Rank, Surname and Christian name: 2nd Lt Observer Łapkowski Wacław Unit: 1st Air Force Regiment. Born 6.11.1913 Dyneburg Iatw.

Completed 2 months Preliminary Pilots Course from 17.9.34 to 14.11.34 on Aircraft RWD 8 with Walter Junior 110 KM Engine. Completed 13 flights with double control in time 1123 and 67 flights Solo in time, including 21 flights as follows — 'Skobli' left 3. 'Skobli' right 4. 'Skobli' doubles 4. Spirals 4. Field landings 2. Emergency landings 2. Landing with propeller stopped 1.

Distance flight from Dęblin to Warsaw return.

Final Course results: very good.
Opinion: Very talented student. Learns quickly and steadily.
Start and Landings: mastered completely.
In the air: very good.
Orientation: very good student with high self-confidence that sometimes leads to excesses.

Date: Dęblin, 14 November 1934

Commanding Officer of Officers' Pilots School: Major Pilot Beseljak
Commander of Officers' Air Force Training Centre: Lt Col Pilot Eng. Wieden.

During the September Campaign in Poland 1939. Wacław Łapkowski flew in defence of Poland with No.111 Fighter Squadron, flying a PZL-11. He destroyed at least one enemy aircraft.

Extract from a collage of Łapkowski family photographs. Wacław Łapkowski, aged 17 years old (bottom right), and his parents.
Photo: Permission of Witold Pietraiewicz/author's collection.

On 17 September Wacław Łapkowski followed orders and evacuated to Romania, where he was interned. He escaped and made his way to the Polish Consulate in Bucharest, where he was issued with false papers and a passport describing him as a Polytechnic Student. The Germans encouraged the Romanian authorities to report anyone bearing a passport of a Polish airman, so false papers were vital to allow free travel.

During October 1939, Wacław Łapkowski travelled to Belgrade, Greece, then to France. Along with other Polish airmen and ground crew, he arrived in Paris on 11 October 1939. He left the country after the fall of France to continue the fight in Great Britain.

Wacław Łapkowski was posted to No. 303 Kościuszko Squadron on 2nd August 1940 after his refresher training. While on a sortie during the Battle of Britain, Wacław Łapkowski was badly injured and forced to bale out of his burning Hurricane. He wrote a letter to his cousin Zygmunt Pietrasiewicz, who later flew with Bomber Command in England (see Appendix 4). The translated letter reads:

1 December 1940
Torquay

My Dear,

Through unusual ways I received your letter. It was difficult to communicate with you, the more I was pleased to receive your letter that was wandering for so long all over the World. During the first half of September I was shot down, and up to now have been in various hospitals. In the mentioned battle I downed one JU 88 and damaged another. But I was attacked by a Messerschmitt 109 whose guns cut me to pieces. I had to jump from the burning machine with great difficulty. On this occasion I got burnt and unpleasantly broke my arm near the joint. Now I am nearly all right. Possibly, I will join my squadron in about two to three weeks.

Please, write to me how you are as the news from your letter is already not actual [up to date]. I am waiting for your reply, hugging you cordially and sending kind greetings.

Write to me how you are and what you are doing.

W

After recovering, Wacław Łapkowski rejoined No. 303 Kościuszko Squadron in January 1941. On 22 January, he had another narrow escape while on a sortie flying from RAF Northolt.

The following is a translated account written by Wacław Łapkowski. His rapid, short sentences create an evocative sense of fast-paced action:

'We received orders to attack with MG-fire on low altitude Military Objects in the north-east part of occupied France. Preferred objects: Enemy airfields and eventual other Military targets. The only proviso: 'No attacks which could harm civilian French population.'

Six of us called to execute this task. To fly possibly in pairs. On the set day we were waiting for good weather conditions. In the afternoon the weather was right for us. Clouds low over the English Channel and France according to Met-report.

Start: 3 pairs already 80 in the air-direction France. English coast under us Hurricane pairs flying now in wafer formation. Pairs choosing their course, we disperse. I am setting compass and assume height underneath clouds. With me, is flying one of the 2nd Lts, my old comrade from the same squadron when fighting in Poland. Now and again we are both on a mission, a 'German Party'. We are nearing the French coast we hide in the clouds, I navigate by instruments, slowly minutes pass. The clock's hands indicate it is time to lower altitude below clouds and look for targets. We descend, clouds are thinning out, after a while we are below them on height of about 200 feet. I am trying to orient myself, looking for a target. Will I find one? This problem occupies my mind completely.

There it is. I see an Airfield, two planes are taking position to start, they are old acquaintances Me 109s.

I am in a favourable position, I veer to the right attacking from the rear. Behind me the second Hurricane is attacking. Instantly, I prepare plan for next attack. On my line on the other end of the Airfield, I see AA gun positions. Somewhat to the left at the verge of the airfield a small forest, surely there must be something. For reflexes are no time, they are not on the visor. I press the button for a series of bursts then a second then a third. One plane leaned on its wing, the other stopped, I knew my No. 2 would finish the job.

The ground is nearing, I level out attacking the AA gun position. I saw heads at the MGs but they ducked. I fire a series, level out over the gun positions.

A light turn to the left, I scrutinize the forest, on the right edge barracks, on the left several Me 109s hidden. One of them stood with a provocatively shining black Swastika on its body. I am aiming at that cross firing. My plane nears the treetops, I want to fire as long as possible; suddenly before my propeller there are some wires. For any reaction it is too late, a strong pull on the aircraft, an intense flash. I level out close to the treetops. I turn my head backwards, from the forest which I flew over, smoke is rising. I now realise that what I hit was a high voltage power line on metal constructed poles.

My No. 2 attacked after me with his MGs, completing the destruction of the 2 Me 109s. Then the AA defence opened up. One round hit his plane a bullet-proof glass panel. His replies in short, attack after attack. During the attack he fired until the last moment, colliding with grazing with the tip of his wing the sandbank of the AA MGs. This reply seems to be sufficient; one AA position out of action. The aircraft's wing slightly damaged. In sequence, followed the attack on the barracks in the forest, a few series. This attack finished as well.

Course 280. Over the sea my No. 2 wants to stay with me, but this proves to be difficult because of gunfire.

On my plane from the wings and steering hangs about 25 yards of torn cable that bangs and pulls against the wings and steering. It is difficult to control my plane. Flying on low altitude is impossible. The steering of the aircraft is limited. If I were attacked, I could not even turn to fight, my ammunition was also short. Therefore, I decided to enter the clouds, I am gaining height. From the left, AA guns are starting to fire, good that rounds are exploding behind me; this gun fire is with me until I am hiding in the clouds.

I am already on 500 feet under the clouds. On my flight line I see a trio, they are not Me 109s, that means I am near the coast, they may have been alerted. On my right there are as well some machines all is in order. I am entering clouds, navigating by instruments is more and more difficult. The hanging cables are wanting to have more of a say in controlling the plane than I, a battle develops between us. Obviously, I am losing.

I am falling out of the clouds and hiding in them again. To keep the proper course is impossible. In the end victory is on my side, I manage to penetrate the thick clouds. I am correcting my course again.

I am alone. Over me is the blue sky and the sun. I am returning to the top of the clouds. I am analysing the time, I must be near the coast. High time, as my engine temperature is rising, this because of the damaged radiator. I am descending into the clouds, the sun disappears, and the engine rattles through the thinning clouds. At last, I can see the sharp outline of the English coast. I am home. Hurricanes have passed the test.'

On 12 April 1941, Wacław Łapkowski's good friend, Squadron Leader Zdzisław Henneberg was shot down while returning from a sortie. He was last seen in the cold, choppy waters of the English Channel, believed to be alive.

The next day, Wacław Łapkowski and Pilot Officer Strzembosz flew in search of Squadron Leader Henneberg. During the search, they were attacked by ten Me109s. With their aircraft badly shot up they managed to land safely. Wacław Łapkowski was taken to a hospital for treatment for a head injury and a minor hand injury. After a short recovery, he returned to No. 303 Kościuszko Squadron as Squadron Leader.

On 2 July 1941, Wacław Łapkowski was leading the Polish Fighter Wing on a sortie to escort Blenheim bombers over France and target the power station at Lille. From height, over forty enemy fighters attacked the Wing. Wacław Łapkowski's Spitfire was hit and disappeared. When he did not return to base, the initial view was that he had been in a mid-air collision with another pilot who had not returned. Sergeant Gorecki, the other pilot, was rescued from the English Channel three days later and able to confirm that there had not been a collision.

Some time later, the body of Wacław Łapkowski was found washed up on the coast of Belgium. He was twenty-seven years old.

Squadron Leader Wacław Łapkowski is laid to rest in Grave 224, Lombardsidje Communal Cemetery, Belgium.

Wacław Łapkowski's cousin, Witold Pietrasiewicz, remembers how the family in Poland learned about the death:

'In my family I was the first to know about Wacław's death, through my brother who was also a pilot in bombers in England. I received the news as early as 1945.

When in 1946 my mother and aunt Łapkowski visited me from the Wilno region, I did not at first mention to my aunt about her son Wacław's death. The poor soul lived in hope. For about two years we prepared her for the tragic news.

Auntie Łapkowski always maintained. "Watek surely is not alive".

At last my brother from England informed her by letter dated 7 April 1948 of his death. Part of the letter reads:

My Dear Auntie,
What I want to say to you now, you as a loving mother must already know
of the fate of your son who will never return. There is nothing more left for
me but to express my most sincere sympathy and condolences about the loss
of your beloved son. Mother, receive this hurtful news with the pride of a
Polish mother. A mother whose son gave his life for truth and justice, for
which he always fought. The name of your son is written in golden letters
in the History of Fighting Poland and in the history of the Squadron he
led into battle as its Commander. Major Wacław Łapkowski Commander
of 303 T.Kościuszko Fighter Squadron failed to return from Air Battle
over France on the 2nd July 1941 and was declared lost by the Air Force
Command.'

Witold Pietrasiewicz remembered what a tragedy this was for all the
family.

'After the letter was read aloud we all started to cry. We all felt so sad his
body had been washed up in Belgium where he is laid to rest with no one of
his family at his grave. After my cousin Wacław left Poland in September
1939, my aunt — his mother — never received any communication
from him.

While cousin Watek flew defending freedom, as did many other Polish
airmen far from home, many of our relatives also fought on in Poland.
In cousin Wacław and my family, one of our uncles, an Officer, was
murdered by the Russians at Katyń. All our family on our mother's side
were members of the AK (Army Krajowa) in the Wilno region. Some that
were captured by the Germans escaped the death sentence only to be sent
to the hell of Auschwitz, others shot. I myself had a lucky escape although
two members of my family were not so fortunate.

In June 1944 partisan members of the 24th Braslawska Brigade of the
Wilno region of which I was a member, found ourselves after the arrival
of the Russians, brutally disarmed at Kardunce. On 15 July numbering
a thousand, we were marched for many miles, the Russian guards shot
those that tried to escape. After a month, nearly six hundred of us were
interned at Opsa at Ruperdach. After this we were taken to a Railway
Station Czarny Brod, where a go between from Wilno told us we were
to be deported to Russia. Over fifteen thousand AK Polish soldiers had
already been deported to Russia from the Wilno region. Knowing what

we had to do after the tip off and with few Russian guards in evidence at that time we waited our chance. When near a forest with our leader we made our escape. Around eighteen hundred did not get away, they were shortly after deported to Russia. Before winter arrived the Russians rounded up as many Home Army AK soldiers as they could and deported them. I managed to make it safely home to Wilno before winter took hold, where I went into hiding to avoid the Russians. I hide in the home of my father and Watek's uncle. From 6 December 1944, the home was searched many times during the nights and over the following weeks. On 15 January 1945, my father and one of my brothers were taken from their farm by the Russians and imprisoned. My father spent six years and six months in prison and my brother later eleven years in a deportation camp being very badly beaten and maltreated all because they would not give me up. Always I carry the guilt, because of my being with the partisans my father and brother suffered. Many relatives on both sides of my cousin Wacław and my family fought, three others were in the Polish Air Force in England.

After the Second World War ended, Auntie Łapkowski's health was bad, broken by life, her husband killed by the Bolsheviks during the invasion of Poland in 1920, then her son lost. She had no one apart from her sister, my mother and me. She lived with us until her death in 1952. On her grave I have placed a photo of her and my cousin Wacław — a symbol of his memory with his name, rank, when he was killed and where he is laid to rest in Belgium.

I had always wanted to visit the grave of my dear cousin Watek but with the communists in control it would have been impossible to leave Poland to do so; also the cost if it were possible would have been so high. On his grave, are written the words carved in stone Squadron Leader Wacław Łapkowski lays my dear cousin Watek.'

On the day Squadron Leader Wacław Łapkowski was shot down and killed, a DFC recommendation was made, *'DFC for conspicuous gallantry and success in leading his squadron. He has personally destroyed at least 5 enemy aircraft.'*

The award was not proceeded with because of Squadron Leader Wacław Łapkowski's death on the same day. This award would have been a treasure beyond price to his grieving mother and family.

See Combat Reports for the following dates: 5 Sep 1940.
See Wing section for the following dates: 2 July 1941.

Wacław Łapkowski's nominal grave. Nominal graves were bought by the family of the airmen who were lost during the Second World War and never found or were not laid to rest in Poland. Wacław Łapkowski's mother is buried in the grave. Photo: Permission of Łapkowski family/author's collection.

Sources: Personal papers of Wacław Łapkowski. Interview Witold Pietrasiewicz, 15 Nov 1987. DFC Citation as follows by kind permission of the Cabinet Office Licence -Licence PSI No C2006010220. The National Archives, Kew Ref Air/2. Profile Photo: Łapkowski family.

Name: **Witold Łokuciewski**
Squadron: No. 303 Kościuszko Squadron
Decorations: Virtuti Militari 5th Class
KW Cross of Valour and bar
DFC

Witold Łokuciewski was born on 1 February 1917 in Russia. He joined the Polish Air Force in 1936 and graduated from Dęblin Officers' School in 1938. He and two fellow Dęblin cadets, Mirosław Feric and Jan Zumbach, earned the nickname 'The Three Musketeers', which continued when they flew together in No. 303 Kościuszko Squadron.

When Germany invaded Poland, Witold Łokuciewski flew with No.112 Fighter Squadron, destroying at least one enemy aircraft.

He travelled to Romania and was among the last Polish airmen to leave Romanian camps to travel to France, arriving in October 1939.

Like so many Polish pilots, he left France for England and, after refresher training, was posted to No. 303 Kościuszko Squadron on 2nd August 1940. Witold Łokuciewski, known to his friends as Tolo, destroyed eight enemy aircraft before he was shot down.

During a sortie on 13 March 1942 with No. 303 Kościuszko Squadron, Witold Łokuciewski's Spitfire was hit. With the aircraft's cockpit full of smoke and damaged controls, he had no option but to bale out to save himself. As he hit the ground, he passed out. The Germans took him to a nearby hospital in France, where he received treatment for his injured leg.

As a prisoner of war, Witold Łokuciewski was taken to Stalag Luft III, where he met many other airmen, among them some of his Polish friends. He managed to escape from the POW camp but was recaptured soon after. During the famous 'Great Escape' from Stalag Luft III, Witold Łokuciewski's name was on the list of those to escape through the tunnel. He was waiting for his turn to enter the tunnel when the alarm sounded. Had he gone down the tunnel, he may have met the same terrible fate that befell the fifty escapees that were murdered by the Gestapo.

Witold Łokuciewski returned to No. 303 Kościuszko Squadron after the POW camp was liberated at the end of the Second World War. He remained with the squadron until it was disbanded in 1946.

Shortly after the outbreak of war, Russian soldier's took Witold's father, a headmaster, from his home and was never seen again. Like so many, he probably perished in the long, freezing march to the Russian Labour camps deep within Russia.

Witold Łokuciewski's brother-in-law also suffered at the hands of the Russians — he was one of the 4,000 Polish men whose bodies were discovered following the massacre in 1940 at the infamous Katyń forest in Russia. Many more bodies were never found.

Faced with such loss, Witold Łokuciewski's mother was desperate for her son to come home and wrote to him in 1946, begging him to return to Poland. After a lot of soul-searching, he returned to Poland for family reasons.

Back in Poland, Witold Łokuciewski found work hard to come by. In the early 1950s, he did various low-paid work to put food on the table, something that became more important when he married Wanda and started a family.

In 1956, Witold Łokuciewski rejoined the Polish Air Force after much deliberation. He became Polish Naval Military Attaché in London from 1969 until 1972. This post upset many Polish war veterans who knew him. Many who lived in exile did so because they refused to return to live in a Poland under communist rule and saw Witold's post as a betrayal. Some of those who had previously chatted with Witold Łokuciewski at reunions in England never spoke to him again because of the post he had taken. This action deeply upset Witold Łokuciewski. Other ex-combatants remained, as they had always been, his friends.

Flight Lieutenant Witold Łokuciewski passed away in 1990 in Poland at seventy-three years old.

See Combat Reports for the following dates:

- 2 Sep 1940
- 7 Sep 1940
- 11 Sep 1940
- 15 Sep 1940

Sources: Pilot information from the Polish Air Force Association, Combat Reports from The National Archives (TNA), Air 50/117, Operational Report Diaries from RAF Northolt. Interview: Flight Lieutenant Bernard Buchwald, 1986. DFC approved 2 July 1941. Profile Photo: Gen Szaposznikow.

Name: **Bogusław Mierzwa**
Squadron: No. 303 Kościuszko Squadron
Decorations: KW Cross of Valour

Bogusław Mierzwa was born 14 March 1918 in Warsaw. His father was a financial civil servant working for the railways. Bogusław had two brothers and a sister.

He attended Prince Jozef Poniatowski Grammar School where he won first prize in History. He was presented with the book, 'The History of England,' which captured his imagination and inspired his aspiration that *maybe one day I will visit England.'*

In 1936, Bogusław Mierzwa commenced training with the Polish Army, then attended the Dęblin Officers' School the following year to train as a pilot. He qualified and was due to become a Second Lieutenant, but Germany invaded Poland and he entered the war at the lower rank of Cadet Officer.

He flew in defence of Poland under Captian Pilot Juliusz Frey with 14th Fighter Command until the order came to evacuate to Romania. Before leaving, Bogusław Mierzwa wrote an emotional letter to his parents, thanking them for his upbringing. This letter managed to find its way to his parents and was the only form of farewell he was able to send.

After leaving Romania, Bogusław Mierzwa made his way to France, then England. He joined No. 303 Kościuszko Squadron at RAF Northolt on 21 August 1940.

On the 16 April 1941, he flew on a sortie with No. 303 and No. 601 Polish Squadrons, escorting bombers over France to target a fighter airfield at Berck-sur-Mer. On the return flight, a squadron of

Messerschmitt fighters attacked, hitting Bogusław Mierzwa's aircraft and that of another pilot. His Spitfire was badly damaged and crash-landed close to the seafront at Dungeness. He was dead before people arrived to help. He was twenty-three years old.

While in England, Bogusław Mierzwa had not written to his family in Poland. Many pilots were afraid that their letters would put their families at risk of reprisal. If any news came through, it was often news of the pilot's death. In 1943, Bogusław Mierzwa's father received the news of his son's death but chose not to tell his wife. It wasn't the first time he had faced such tragic news. In Autumn 1940, Bogusław's brother, Ludwick was killed, and in the spring of 1941, his other brother, Mieczysław died. Both were murdered in Oswiecim Auschwitz. How could Bogusław Mierzwa's father tell his wife all three of her sons were dead? The tragedy did not end there — Bogusław Mierzwa's father lost his life in 1944 while fighting for Poland in the Warsaw Uprising. Only Bogusław Mierzwa's mother and sister survived the war.

1918, Poland — Bogusław Mierzwa as a baby with his mother.
Photo: Permission of Mierzwa family/author's collection.

For over forty years, Bogusław's mother and sister knew little of his time in England, only that he had flown with No. 303 Kościuszko Squadron. After learning that someone was trying to located the families of the Polish pilots, she wrote an emotional letter:

'You mention that you are in possession of details relating to my brother while in England, and have met some who flew with him and knew him. We know nothing of his life when far away, only that he died. For the sake of family love, anything is very important, relevant and interesting. I would be grateful to you if, during your spare moments, you could share with me those details of how he fought and how he died. Presumably, he did not live long enough to receive Polish or British decorations.'

In 1989, it was an honour for the author of this book to send many details and documents to Bogusław Mierzwa's sister along with his medals.

Pilot Officer Bogusław Mierzwa is laid to rest at Northwood Cemetery in Grave 290, Section H.

Sources: Pilot information from the Polish Air Force Association, Combat Reports from The National Archives (TNA), Air 50/117, Operational Report Diaries from RAF Northolt. Interviews Mirosława Radomska; Flight Lieutenant Jan Kowalski, 1986, Squadron Leader Gandi Drobiński,1988 onwards. Profile Photo: Mierzwa family.

Name: **Jan Palak**
Squadrons: No. 302 Squadron
                  No. 303 Kościuszko Squadron
Decorations: Virtuti Militari 5th Class
                  KW Cross of Valour and bar
                  DSO (twice)
                  DFC
                  Air Crew Europe Star

Jan Palak, born on 12 February 1911 in a small village near Lublin in Poland, was the eldest of six children. As a young child at play he often pretended to be an aeroplane, running around with arms outstretched and imagining he was soaring up high.

Leaving home as a young man, he worked in an aircraft factory, until he was accepted into The Dęblin Officers' School where he trained to be a fighter pilot.

When Poland was invaded in September 1939, Jan Palak flew in defence of Warsaw with No. 111 and No. 112 Fighter Squadrons.

After receiving orders to evacuate, he made his way by various routes to France. After the fall of France, he found himself in Blackpool with many other Polish airmen. After training, Jan Palak was posted with the rank of Sergeant to No. 302 Polish Squadron at RAF Leconfield.

He destroyed an Me109 while flying with No. 302 Squadron during the Battle of Britain. On 29 September he was posted to No. 303 Kościuszko Squadron at RAF Northolt, where he continued to fly sorties. In January 1942, he was posted for a short time to No. 58 Operational Training Unit, RAF Grangemouth. By September 1942, Jan Palak had rejoined No. 303 Kościuszko Squadron at RAF Kirton-in-Lindsey, Lincolnshire as a Warrant Officer.

'During 1943, King George VI and Queen Elizabeth along with the two Princesses, their Royal Highnesses Princess Elizabeth, and Princess Margaret visited the Polish pilots. I had the honour of presenting a bouquet of red roses to Her Majesty the Queen. Suddenly, seemingly from nowhere Princess Elizabeth rushed towards me, clasping my hand and asking me to show her inside the cockpit of the Spitfire. I dutifully obliged, explaining many details of the aircraft to her Royal Highness Princess Elizabeth, who seemed most interested.'

From late 1943 until Easter 1944, Jan Palak was in the operational room at RAF Northolt. In mid-1944, he rejoined his first squadron, No. 302 Polish Squadron.

Jan Palak refused to accept a higher rank, remaining as a Warrant Officer. He enjoyed training the young airmen and helping them to gain confidence. Many of those he trained looked on him as a father figure.

After the war ended, Jan Palak met and fell in love with Stefanie, a Polish girl in England. They married in 1946 and had two sons and a daughter. With a giggle, Stefanie remembers the first time they met:

'When I first met Jan, I looked him up and down, noticing his worn out shoes. I thought to myself he needs looking after and I am the woman to do so.'

In 1947, Jan Palak joined the RAF as a test pilot. He left the RAF in 1960. The family moved to Somerset after he left the RAF in 1960. He worked for the chocolate company, Cadbury until his retirement.

Jan Palak was a quiet and private man and enjoyed restoring antique clocks during his retirement. He found it very relaxing.

He had settled into life in England, but there was always an open wound, festering beneath the surface.

'The betrayal of Poland meant my husband Jan could never return to live is his beloved country when the war ended. He never attended reunions and rarely spoke about the war finding it very painful to recount the memories of so many friends lost. His one dream, as for so many from the Polish Air Force dreams, was to one day return when Poland was free and to fly to a free Poland.'

Warrant Officer Jan Palak passed away a few days before his seventy-sixth birthday.

See Combat Reports for the following date: 5 Oct 1940.

Sources: Interview Mrs S Palak, Mar 1987. Shortly before Jan Palak passed away he had agreed to be interviewed. I am indebted to Mrs Palak for continuing with the arrangement and welcoming me into her home at such a sad time. However, *we did meet, did we not, Jan!*

Name: **Jerzy Palusiński**
Squadron: No. 303 Kościuszko Squadron
No. 306 Squadron
No. 308 Squadron
No. 316 Squadron
Decorations: Virtuti Militari 5th Class

Jerzy Palusiński was born 13 August 1912 in Poland. He left Poland in September 1939 and travelled to Romania, then France. After the fall of France, he travelled to England, arriving in the summer of 1940.

Jerzy Palusiński was posted to No. 303 Kościuszko Squadron on 21 August 1940 as a Pilot Officer and remained with the squadron until early 1942. He transferred to No. 308 Polish Squadron then to No. 306 Polish Squadron before returning to No. 303 Kościuszko Squadron to fly many sorties as Flight Lieutenant.

In September, Jerzy Palusiński moved to No. 316 Polish Squadron for a posting in the operational room. He then moved to Admin and Special Duties, where he stayed until the end of the war.

Jerzy Palusiński stayed with the Polish Air Force until 1947, spending his final sixteen months of service at Headquarters No. 84 Group. He remained in England, got married and became a pig farmer.

Flight Lieutenant Jerzy Palusiński passed away in 1984 at seventy-two years old.

Sources: Operational Report Diaries from RAF Northolt.

Name: **Ludwick Paszkiewicz**
Squadron: No. 303 Kościuszko Squadron
Decorations: Virtuti Militari 5th Class
                       KW Cross of Valour
                       DFC

'F/O Ludwick Paszkiewicz. Has commanded a flight since the formation of the squadron and has contributed very largely to the success of its operations by his intelligent and daring leadership. He has personally accounted for 6 enemy aircraft.'

DFC Citation by Squadron Leader Ronald Kellett 23/9/1940.

Ludwick Paszkiewicz was born 21 October 1907 in the Lublin area of Poland. After his training in the Polish Air Force, he qualified as a pilot in 1932.

Shortly before Germany invaded Poland in September 1939, Ludwick Paszkiewicz was on a course in France, training to fly French aircraft. He was not in Poland in September 1939 to fly against the Germans but was joined in France by many Polish airmen to continue the fight. He flew with Groupe de Chase III. After the fall of France, he evacuated to England and joined No. 303 Kościuszko Squadron at its formation on 2 August 1940.

On 30 August 1940, Ludwick Paszkiewicz broke formation during a training exercise to intercept an enemy aircraft. He shot down the enemy fighter and returned to RAF Northolt celebrating his success with a victory roll over the airfield. Despite receiving a reprimand for disobeying orders, his demonstration of skill in combat was pivotal for No. 303 Kościuszko Squadron. The following day the squadron was officially made operational. The Eagles of No. 303 Kościuszko Squadron had struck, and continued to strike the enemy with deadly accuracy throughout the war.

On 27th September 1940, less than a month after his first kill, Ludwick Paszkiewicz's was shot down and killed. The thirty-two-year-old pilot's Hurricane crashed in flames near Crowhurst Farm, Borough Green in Kent.

Flying Officer Ludwick Paszkiewicz is laid to rest in Grave 224, Section H at Northwood Cemetery.

See Combat Reports for the following dates:
- 30 Aug 1940
- 2 Sep 1940
- 7 Sep 1940
- 11 Sep 1940
- 15 Sep 1940
- 26 Sep 1940
- 27 Sep 1940

Sources: Pilot information from the Polish Air Force Association, Combat Reports from The National Archives (TNA), Air 50/117, Operational Report Diaries from RAF Northolt. Interview Wing Commander Ronald Kellett, Jun 1986. DFC approved 16 October 1940. Citation by kind permission of the Cabinet Office - Licence PSI No C2006010220. TNA Ref Air/2. Profile Photo: Jan Kowalski.

Name: **Edward Paterek**
Squadron: No. 302 Squadron
                   No. 303 Kościuszko Squadron
                   No. 315 Squadron
Decorations: KW Cross of Valour

Edward Paterek was born 30 May 1910 in Poland. In September 1939, he was evacuated to Romania, France, and finally to England in 1940.

After refresher flight training, he was posted to RAF Leconfield to join No. 302 Polish Squadron at its formation in July 1940. Edward Paterek destroyed two enemy aircraft while flying on sorties with the squadron.

He was posted to No. 303 Kościuszko Squadron at RAF Northolt on 23 September 1940 and remained there until he was posted to No. 315 Polish Squadron at its formation in 1941.

During a training flight on 28 March 1941, Edward Paterek's Hurricane was in a mid-air collision with another aircraft. He was killed when his aircraft crashed into the sea.

Sergeant Edward Paterek was thirty years old when he lost his life, and his body was never found.

Sources: Operational Report Diaries from RAF Northolt.

Name: **Marian Pisarek**
Squadron: No. 303 Kościuszko Squadron
               No. 308 Squadron
               No. 315 Squadron
Decorations: Virtuti Militari Silver Cross and Gold Cross
               KW Cross of Valour three Bars
               DFC

Marian Pisarek was born on 3 February 1912 near Warsaw, Poland. He began his training with the Polish Air Force in 1935. When Poland was invaded, he flew with No. 141 Squadron and destroyed at least one enemy aircraft. After receiving orders to evacuate from Poland, he made his way to Romania, then to France.

After arriving in England and undertaking refresher flight training, he was posted to No. 303 Kościuszko Squadron on 21 August 1940. He remained with the squadron until he joined No. 315 Polish Squadron for a short posting in early 1941. In March of that year, he was posted to No. 308 Polish Squadron and flew many sorties.

Marian Pisarek was promoted to Squadron Leader of No. 308 Polish Squadron in June 1941 and shot down his eleventh kill four months later. In December 1941, he was sent to No. 11 Group Headquarters.

He returned to RAF Northolt on 24 April 1942, succeeding Wing Commander Rolski as Wing Commander. The following morning he led the Wing of twenty-four Spitfires on a Ramrod operation. The Wing had a very successful sortie destroying five Focke-Wulf FW190s, with two damaged.

Four days later, Marian Pisarek led the Wing of twenty-three Spitfires from RAF Northolt and twelve Spitfires from the Heston Wing. The Wing split up over Hardelot in France, with some of the Wing attacking the enemy. On the return flight, Marian Pisarek aircraft's was hit by Focke-Wulf fighter and went down somewhere over the English Channel. He was thirty years old.

See Combat Reports for the following dates:
- 7 Sep 1940
- 15 Sep 1940
- 5 Oct 1940
- 7 Oct 1940

See Wing section for the following dates:
- 21 Sep 1941
- 29 Apr 1942

Sources: Pilot information from the Polish Air Force Association, Combat Reports from The National Archives (TNA), Air 50/117, Operational Report Diaries from RAF Northolt. Interview Flight Lieutenant Jan Kowalski, 1986. DFC approved 16 August 1941.

Name: **Jerzy Radomski**
Squadron: No. 303 Kościuszko Squadron
                 No. 316 Squadron
                 No. 72 Squadron
                 No. 222 Squadron
Decorations: Virtuti Militari 5th Class
                 KW Cross of Valour - three Bars
                 Croix de Guerre with palm

Jerzy Radomski was born on 18 July 1915 in Czernichów. His father was a lawyer. At eighteen years old he was able to fulfil his childhood dream of becoming a pilot by joining the Polish Air Force and training at the Dęblin Officers' School.

When Germany invaded Poland on 1 September 1939, Jerzy Radomski took off in his PZL-7 fighter in defence of Warsaw. In one encounter, he shot down an enemy aircraft but not before a bullet hit him just above his heart, bouncing off his Polish silver eagle.

'I could not believe it, I felt at that point that the eagle would always protect me. From that day onwards I always had it with me when I flew.'

In another battle against the Germans, Jerzy Radomski's PZL-7 was hit, forcing him to bale out of the damaged aircraft. His aircraft crashed to the ground, but Jerzy Radomski managed to open his parachute and float down to safety. He landed a little shaken, but unhurt.

After receiving orders to evacuate from Poland, Jerzy travelled to Romania but was interned on arrival. He managed to escape and make his way to France, then after the fall of France, he went to England.

On 21 August 1940, Jerzy Radomski was posted as a Pilot Officer to No. 303 Kościuszko Squadron. He recalls one part of the radio transmitter training at Uxbridge.

'We were given bicycles and portable radio receivers and told to cycle around while flying orders were transmitted to us in English. This was with the idea of us Polish pilots getting used to hearing orders in English from a radio transmitter. We all learned the orders parrot fashion. Once we all learned this we were all so impatient to get up into the air. Every day we waited to become operational was like torture to us all.'

While flying with No. 303 Kościuszko Squadron, Jerzy Radomski's Hurricane was badly hit.

'I thought about baling out but one of my friends had baled out a few days earlier and was never found in the Channel. Sticking with my aircraft I landed just short of the sea in Dungeness. My aircraft was smouldering so I got out quickly, as I did so people approached me in a very unfriendly and strange manner. They started poking me with sticks. They must have thought I was German, as my English was very basic. I was horrified to learn I had landed in a Minefield. It was late evening before everything was checked out fully; too late to return to RAF Northolt. It was decided I should stay in Clapham overnight and travel back to South Ruislip in the morning. As I lay on my bed in the lodging house in London relaxing, suddenly a German raid took place. The whole house began to shake; I was just about to leap out of bed when the ceiling collapsed from the nearby bomb blast. The house next door but one received a direct hit. I hoped that the people of the house had not been inside; all around was burning. When I finally returned to Northolt, the next night I had a premonition I would survive the war.'

After the Battle of Britain, Jerzy Radomski flew on various sorties with Polish squadrons and with British squadrons. He also spent time serving at Operational training units.

In 1943, he was promoted to the rank of Flight Lieutenant with No. 303 Kościuszko Squadron. The following year, he met and fell in love with Helena. It was love at first sight for Helena too:

'As soon I saw him, I knew I would marry him.'

Helena had joined the Polish WAAFs after escaping a Russian labour camp and making her way to England with her sister.

'In 1940, the KGB sent me and my sister to Kazakhstan, in Russia. We endured two horrendous years, living in filthy conditions doing slave labour. We lived every day with the threat of being taken out and shot. In September 1942 we escaped with the help of a Polish serviceman who hid us until we were taken to Persia. In Autumn 1943, we managed to get to Palestine, then England, where we arrived in the spring of 1944.'

Jerzy Radomski and Helena married on Boxing Day 1944 in Weston Super Mare. Their son Andrzej was born in 1947.

During the war years, Jerzy Radomski flew 108 operational sorties. After the war ended, he and Helena lived for many years at South Ruislip near to RAF Northolt. Jerzy Radomski joined the RAF in 1951.

In 1953, he took part in the Royal Fly Pass in Hampshire. Jerzy Radomski was the only Polish airman to take part. He served with the RAF until 1972.

In 1976, twenty-nine-year-old Andrzej was training to be a doctor but fell ill while taking his final exams. Sadly, he passed away before receiving the news that he had passed his exams. Jerzy Radomski died two years after his son. He was sixty-three years old.

See Combat Reports for the following date: 30 Sep 1940

Sources: Interview Mrs Helena Radomska, 1986.

Name: **Jan Rogowski**
Squadron: No. 303 Kościuszko Squadron
                     No. 74 Squadron
                     No. 306 Squadron
                     No. 315 Squadron
Decoration: Virtuti Militari 5th Class
                     KW Cross of Valour

Jan Rogowski was born on 3 January 1920 in Poland. He joined the Polish Air Force in 1937 and qualified as a pilot just before the outbreak of the Second World War. After receiving the order for evacuation, he made his way to Romania, France, and then England.

Jan Rogowski was posted as a Sergeant to No. 303 Kościuszko Squadron at its formation on 2 August 1940. He remained with the squadron until early 1941, when he was posted to No. 74 Squadron at RAF Biggin Hill. During sorties flown from RAF Biggin Hill, he destroyed an Me109 during combat.

He attended instructor courses and in April 1942, then was posted to No. 58 Operational Training Unit to help train young airmen. Another posting followed at RAF Northolt to fly operations with No. 306 Polish Squadron, then from April 1943, he was flying sorties with No. 315 Polish Squadron as a Flight Sergeant.

On 28 May 1943, four enemy Me109s attacked No. 1 Polish Fighter Wing during operations over St Omer and Hazebrouk in France. Jan Rogowski was flying over the English Channel during the attack and was killed when bullets from the Me109s hit his Spitfire.

Jan Rogowski was the last of the founder members of No. 303

Kościuszko Squadron to lose his life while flying from Great Britain. He was twenty-three years old.

Flight Sergeant Jan Rogowski is laid to rest at Pihen-lés-Guînes War Cemetery in France in Grave No. 2, Plot 1, Section C.

See Combat Reports for the following dates:
- 2 Sep 1940
- 6 Sep 1940

Sources: Pilot information from the Polish Air Force Association, Combat Reports from The National Archives (TNA), Air 50/117, Operational Report Diaries from RAF Northolt.

Name: **Antoni Siudak**
Squadron: No. 302 Squadron
                 No. 303 Kościuszko Squadron
Decorations: Virtuti Militari 5th Class

Antoni Siudak was born 1 April 1909 in Imbramowice Poland to a farming family with six children. He was in the police force for a short period of time, then trained to be a pilot at Bydgoszcz. Before the outbreak of the Second World War, he was an Instructor at Dęblin Officers' School.

Antoni Siudak flew in defence of Poland during the September Campaign, then travelled to Romania after receiving the order for evacuation. He managed to escape the internment camp in Romania and make his way to France, where he was attached to No.145 Squadron based at Lyon Bron.

After the fall of France, he made his way to England to continue the fight. He received refresher flight training and, in late July 1940, was posted as a Sergeant to No. 302 Polish Squadron at RAF Leconfield.

On 23 September 1940, he moved to RAF Northolt for a posting with No. 303 Kościuszko Squadron and destroyed two enemy aircraft during his short time with the squadron.

Two weeks after joining the squadron, Antoni Siudak lost his life when a lone German bomber dropped bombs on RAF Northolt. The Junkers Ju88 had been following the squadron between the clouds while the squadron was on a morning patrol duty. While the Hurricanes landed, the enemy bomber attacked and killed three people. Antoni Siudak was killed when his Hurricane was hit by a bomb. This was the only occasion during the war that bombing at RAF Northolt led to the loss of a pilot's life. Antoni Siudak was thirty-one years old.

One of Antoni Siudak brothers managed to escape to England, where he settled after the war.

Sergeant Antoni Siudak is laid to rest Northwood Cemetery in Grave 225, Section H.

See Combat Reports for the following dates:
- 5 Oct 1940
- 6 Oct 1940

The Post Office at South Ruislip circa 1930s: On 6 October 1940 Sergeant Antoni Siudak was killed by a bomb dropped on RAF Northolt. The bomb blast shattered the windows of the South Ruislip Post Office located half a mile away. Photo: author's collection.

Sources: Pilot information from the Polish Air Force Association. Interviews: Tadeusz Siudak. Wing Commander Ronald Kellett, Jun 1986.

Name: **Eugeniusz 'Gen' Szaposznikow**
Squadron: No. 303 Kościuszko Squadron
Decorations: Virtuti Militari - 5th Class
                  KW Cross of Valour - three Bars
                  DFM

'Sgt Szaposznikow has taken part in numerous engagements and proved himself to be a pilot of exceptional skill and great daring. He has destroyed 6 enemy aircraft and probably another in the past month. Flying as No 3 in the leading section he had not only fearlessly attacked greater superior numbers, by his coolness and quickness of decision has frequently saved his leaders and companions. It may be truly said that his score is but part of his merit in recognition of his gallantry. Aircraft destroyed 3 Me 109s, 2 Me 110s, 1 Dor 215 plus 1 Me 109 prob.'

DFM Recommended by Squadron Leader R. Kellett 2nd October 1940.

'This Polish Sgt has shown great gallantry. His coolness and quick judgement have on several occasions when he has been flying a No 3 saved his Leader and fellow pilots. He has shot done 6 enemy aircraft even in this he is outstanding in courage and dash. I strongly recommend him for the immediate award of the DFM.'

AVM Keith Park
DFM Recommended by Hugh Dowding.

I was born on 17 July 1916 in Warsaw, Poland. My father brought me up as my mother died when I was six years old. Since a young child, I had always been fascinated by aeroplanes. Like so many children I dreamt of one day flying one.

When I became of age, I joined the Dęblin Flying School as a young eaglet eager to earn my wings. My first few months of training included flying gliders, which I found a marvellous experience. Later training, included flying in a two-seated PWS with an instructor, we often practised aerobatics. My first solo flight was in dense cloud and bad weather, but it did not deter me, I simply loved it

After qualifying in 1936, I was posted to 111 Kościuszko Squadron which was a Warsaw-based squadron flying at that time mainly PZ-11s. Shortly before Germany invaded Poland, No 111 Squadron moved nearly twenty miles away to a makeshift airfield.

When the Germans invaded, most of us in 111 Squadron spent all day in the cockpit so we could take off quickly. Our aircraft were vastly outnumbered. The squadron I was in took off many times during a day. I flew over thirty sorties in three weeks. Having no radar we never had any advance warning of where the German aircraft were. The German's aircraft were faster, better armed, and they had the advantage of height over us. When it was realised we could no longer defend Poland, and were running out of fuel, aircraft, and spare parts we were ordered to fly to Romania. The Russian had by now started to invade Poland from the east.

When we landed in Romania, much to our surprise we were interned in camps. After spending a couple of weeks in a camp, two others pilot and I decided we were going to escape. Over several days we secretly prepared a hole in the wire fence, we cut through the barbed wire whenever we got the chance. Finally, one afternoon we made our escape, as we did so the guards opened fire. We got through the hole in the fence very quickly indeed not wishing to catch any bullets. We ran quickly towards a river. Around the edge of the river was a thicket of canes. Breaking a cane each we submerged ourselves under the water using the canes to breathe through. The guards jabbed their bayonets through the canes trying to find us. After a while they gave up and left, we were lucky the bayonets did not hit their targets — us. We hid there until it started to get dark, then soaking wet but alive, we crossed the river. We were not sure where we were. Travelling through the nights towards Bucharest, we hid during the day. After a couple of nights, we became very hungry, having eaten only a few potato shoots. We then decided to move in daylight and came across a small town. We knew we had to change into civilian clothes but had no money with us. We stood looking into a tailor's shop window. Suddenly the shop door opened and we were all pulled into the shop. The gentleman who had pulled us in was a Jewish tailor who spoke Polish. He gave us some much-welcomed food, informing us that the Polish Government was in exile in Bucharest. He later drove us in his old car to the city. As we arrived there, he told us to jump quickly from his car into a taxi which had come alongside us. We did as he asked it happened so quickly that we never got a chance to thank him for all his help as he drove off. The taxi driver drove us to the Polish Embassy.

From the Polish Embassy we were sent to the Black Sea coast and billeted in chalets. From there, it was arranged for us to take a Greek boat to Marseille. There were around two thousand of us Poles that boarded the ship. My two friends and I were given false identities that seemed to satisfy the authorities.

After arriving in Marseille in France in November 1939, we were sent to Istres, which was France's largest airbase. At Istres, we were then to have re-established the Polish Air Force in exile. The French could not afford to give us equipment. We were then drafted into the French Air Force. I was sent to Lyon for training, I was in No.11 Group, known as The Lafayette, flying Bloch 52s.

On my first combat, I destroyed a Hei 111. As in Poland, we were vastly outnumbered by the Luftwaffe aircraft. Later many of us that were sent from one airfield to another, finally ended up in Toulouse. From Toulouse we flew against the Italians, some us flew Devoitine 520s. These were superior to the Italian Fiat biplanes. Many of the French pilots, who were unfamiliar with the fuel tank system, flew towards Africa and ended up in the Mediterranean never to be seen again. Around the time of Dunkirk, I selected a brand new French plane, stealing petrol over several days which I took from the bombers at the airfield. I planned to make my escape when the time came and fly to Africa.

Before I was to leave, General Sikorski ordered that all Polish personnel were to be released from their squadrons in France so that they could go to Great Britain. The other two pilots who I had escaped with from Romania prepared to make our way to England. We went by lorry to a small port on the Spanish border, there we picked up the last Royal Navy ship to leave port.

After landing on the East Coast of Britain, we were sent to a camp in Scotland, where we were reorganised.

On 2nd August 1940, I was posted to RAF Northolt at South Ruislip to join a new squadron to be formed, No. 303 Squadron. Before becoming operational at Northolt, we Poles were all anxious to get into battle to blast the huns from the sky. After our combat experiences in Poland and in France, the wait seemed endless. But we had to follow British regulations that demanded a certain amount of flying hours in their aircraft.

On 31 August 1940 we became officially operational. Our chance at last in Britain to take revenge on the enemy, which we did with great pleasure. I had my guns on my Hurricane set straight ahead at 200 yards. Most of my attacks were at close range.

While with 303 during the Battle of Britain we would spend many free evenings in The Orchard Public House in Ruislip. My friends always called me Gen. They always made us feel so welcome at The Orchard, putting on a good spread for us, which we all appreciated. I spent many enjoyable evening there with my friends from 303. We used to have our drinks ready for us on the bar as soon as we arrived. When the flight I was in was not on duty until the afternoon, the night before up to ten of us would squash into an old Ford or Squadron Leader Kellett's old Rolls Royce; we were often packed as sardines in a tin but it was worth it. We were told to drink plenty of milk. We had a large milk churn set up on one side of the bar which we would have our whisky topped up with, thus we were often seen to be drinking milk. Often on free evenings spent at The Orchard, late evening into early morning we would be sleeping on the floor of The Orchard. Always before 7am the following morning we would be back at base ready for duty. You needed to have time to relax, as flying in the Battle of Britain was very hectic, and it was nice to have a few hours to chat with your friends socially. I lost many good friends in the Battle of Britain.

On 11 October 1940, No. 303 was posted to RAF Leconfield for a rest. While there we did some night flying, also trained other pilots. As Leconfield was a new station the airfield was of soft clay.

On one occasion at Leconfield the flight I was in was scrambled. As I started to open up the throttle to move off, the scramble was cancelled, and we all had to return to the dispersal point. I knew the Germans were in the vicinity as I sat in my Hurricane my mechanic stood nearby. As I looked up, I saw two Hei 111s flying to attack our aircraft on the ground. I quickly shouted contact to my mechanic but my engine would not fire *due to still being hot. The German bombers were heading straight towards us. I watched as their bomb bay doors opened and the bombs began to fall. They fired towards us, one of their bombs dropped in the distance, another dropped a few yards in front of me and another a few feet away from my aircraft's wing. I saw another hit the hangers behind me. At this time, I sensed a smell nearby and the thought crossed my mind the Germans were using gas. I closed my eyes tightly at the same time as I tried to get out of my Hurricane, I then heard a moaning sound under my aircraft. I released my harness and dropped from my Hurricane with my eyes still closed. As I landed I opened my eyes, I saw a perfect cross above me.*

I thought that is it I am in Heaven. Seconds later, I realised I was at the bottom of a bomb crater. The cross above me was my aircraft which had its undercarriage blown off. As I climbed out, I saw the poor mechanic under the wing, he had been shot through the chest. I pulled him out and tried desperately to help him but he was in a very poor way; he bore his pain very bravely. Sadly, he died later. There were many mechanics running around everywhere, trying to help where they could. One of the hangers was on fire. My Hurricane was a mess with bullet holes everywhere, in all one hundred and seventy, but not one hit my cockpit. Probably the soft clay on the station had deadened the force of the explosions and saved my life.

Later a posting came for me to Montrose on an instructor's course. Another posting followed to Newton in Nottingham where I spent nearly two years as an Instructor and became a Flying Officer.

I requested to return to 303 Squadron, my request was granted in December 1943.

Some of the ops with 303 included the D-Day invasion in 1944. As we flew overhead, I had a marvellous view of the invasion. There were tracers of various colours as the allied attacked the beaches. We were very superior in numbers against the German forces. On our D-Day flights we would have an early morning cooked breakfast at 3am, then take off, later returning to another cooked breakfast at 7am — very tasty.

We usually took off four times a day.

While with 303 Squadron I took part in the close escort for the Thousand Bomber Raid on Caen by Halifax and Lancaster bombers. Although the town was flattened, the Germans still held it.

In late 1944, while on a sortie with 303, my Spitfire was shot up over

Calais and the engine caught fire. After losing glycol coolant my engine stopped. Having sufficient altitude, my Spitfire managed to glide across the Channel. My aircraft landed in England with the engine on the beach and the remainder in the sea with the waves splashing over it. Luck was on my side that day.

On a series of sorties with 303 Squadron, the aircraft were fitted with long-range auxiliary drop tanks; this enabled us to strafe roads, railways military installations and airfields further afield than before. This low flying was a greater pressure than even flying in the Battle of Britain. We had to fly very low, often muck carts in fields would drop the sides exposing German machine guns firing at us. Many of my good friends I had flown with in 303 were lost on these operations.

In late 1944, I was made a Flight Lieutenant.

With 303 Squadron we were sent to scan Holland for the V2 launch sights. Also continuing our strafing duties until war ended.

In 1945, I married my long-time girlfriend Olive, who I first met in Nottingham in 1941. We later had one son. After war ended and the terrible situation for Poland, I choose not to return to a Poland under Communist rule. For two years in England, I trained Polish airmen until 1947 when I relinquished my commission.

Work as for so many that had been in the forces was not easy to find. One of my first jobs was sweeping the floor for a little money, this was followed by working for the gas board. Later my wife and I ran a mushroom farm. Later we ran a public house in Matlock for many years. My wife Olive learnt to speak Polish and for many years taught Polish Cookery.

After many years, we visited Poland, where often we visited the wife of my dear friend Stanisław Karubin, who had died in the war.

I attended some of the reunions held at RAF Northolt. At a Polish function in 1985, I was very proud to meet his Royal Highness Prince Charles and spent twenty very interesting minutes chatting with him.

In my retirement, I enjoy the company of my family. I have two lovely granddaughters. I enjoy making various wines and walking many miles with my Rottweiler dog Sultan, who is a very good listener.

Flight Lieutenant Gen Szaposznikow passed away on 8 July 1991 in Nottingham, England.

See Combat Reports for the following dates:
- 31 Aug 1940
- 7 Sep 1940
- 11 Sep 1940
- 23 Sep 1940
- 27 Sep 1940
- 7 Oct 1940

Sources: DFM Citation by kind permission of Cabinet Office Licence. Licence No PSI C 2006010220. The National Archives (TNA) Ref Air/2. Interview/Memoirs Gen Szaposznikow, Aug 1986. DFM approved 23 December 1940.

Name: **Witold Urbanowicz**
Squadron: No. 601 Squadron
                  No. 145 Squadron
                  No. 303 Kościuszko Squadron
                  14th Air Force America
Decorations: Virtuti Militari 5th Class
                  KW Cross of Valour - four bars
                  DFC and Bar
                  Air Medal China
                  Flying Cross
                  Air Medal America

'F/O Witold Urbanowicz. This Officer has shown himself an able courageous leader in command of a flight in the squadron. Previously he had destroyed 2 enemy aircraft and since joining this squadron he has accounted for at least a further 4 and prob 2 others.'

DFC Citation 23/9/1940.

Witold Urbanowicz was born 30 March 1908 in Poland. The Polish Air Force training he started in 1930 would stand him in good stead during the war years.

Three years before the Second World War broke out, Witold Urbanowicz was an instructor at the Dęblin Officers' School training cadets.

'When flying I felt like a bird and was at one with my plane.'

In the September campaign of 1939, Witold Urbanowicz flew in defence of Poland. In the squadron's first combat, the pilots encountered around one hundred German fighters and around sixty bombers. After the first sortie, they landed back having destroyed two enemy aircraft. Witold Urbanowicz and his flight flew twenty combat sorties, over thirty hours in the air flying PZL-7s and PZL-11s. The tactics Witold Urbanowicz usually used was to attack from high altitude, from the sun, and firing at a distance of 100 yards to target the bombers.

After receiving orders to evacuate to Romania, Witold Urbanowicz took with him the fifty cadets he had been training at Dęblin before the outbreak of war. After crossing the frontier on 17 September 1939 and making sure his cadets were safely in Romania, Witold Urbanowicz returned to Poland to continue the fight. On his arrival in Poland, he was arrested by the Russians but managed to escape the next evening. Crossing the frontier three days later, Witold Urbanowicz was reunited with his fifty cadets.

By sheer determination, Witold Urbanowicz managed to keep all his cadets together and helped them safely to Constanța in Romania. In Constanța, the cadets boarded a ship, and Witold Urbanowicz packed them safely in the ship's bunkers. After arriving in port, they boarded another ship to Marseille in France.

In January 1940, Witold Urbanowicz was on English soil in Eastchurch. After the initial refresher fighter training, he was posted to No. 601 Squadron at RAF Tangmere, then to No. 145 Squadron, where he shot down two enemy aircraft. He then joined No. 303 Kościuszko Squadron on 21 August 1940 as a Flying Officer.

On 6 September, Air Vice Marshal (AVM) Keith Park nominated Witold Urbanowicz to take over as Polish Commanding Officer of No. 303 Kościuszko Squadron while Squadron Leader Krasnodębski was recovering from burns he had sustained in combat.

Witold Urbanowicz used special tactics during the Battle of Britain to attack German bombers at a distance of no more than 200 yards away, and attack fighters from no further than 100 yards when possible.

'In the air I was always on the alert. I observed the space around me all the time. Generally speaking down on earth I do not like someone following me, especially someone unknown. Often in the air, I felt my opponent was aware he was being attacked by me. Usually, he manoeuvred his plane, sometimes senselessly in an attempt at ducking, at this precise moment I opened fire and made sure I was not attacked. Often I had been, then I would stop the *attack often at maximum speed withdrawing from the range of fire. During the Battle of Britain, I believe the language problems could have been avoided with 303 by attaching an Officer who spoke Polish to the ops room. After the Battle of Britain, this was carried out successfully. Most of the personnel of 303 Squadron got on very well together, although Squadron Leader Kellett and I never saw eye to eye.*

I contributed some of the success of 303 during the Battle of Britain to Group Captain Stanley Vincent, a remarkable man, a great friend of the Poles. I truly believe he did contribute to 303's splendid success in combating the Luftwaffe. He was a great administrator and a friend of flying and ground personnel.

Air Vice Marshal Keith Park often came to from Uxbridge to Northolt to speak to the personnel of 303 Squadron not only about air battles but about the life of the personnel at the airfield. He was a true friend of the Poles and a great enthusiast of 303 Squadron.'

In the summer of 1941, Witold Urbanowicz went to America and Canada with the object of recruiting those of Polish descent into the Polish Air Force. Before leaving for America, he helped to organise the No.1 Polish Fighter Wing at RAF Northolt.

In the summer of 1942, he returned to England but was back in America by December 1942 as Assistant Air Attaché at the Polish Embassy in Washington DC, where he met and fell in love with a Polish girl. They married in 1943.

By 1943, Witold Urbanowicz was a Group Captain. His request to General Chennault for a transfer to China had been approved, and he was flying with the 14th Air Force – the Flying Tigers. He destroyed eleven Japanese Zero fighters while flying a P-40 in China.

Witold Urbanowicz returned to England briefly in 1944 but was once again back in America by August 1944, this time as the Air Attaché to the Polish Embassy in Washington DC.

To most, Witold Urbanowicz was fearless and daring in the sky, but Witold recognised that he was able to control his fear.

'Was I afraid of the enemy in the air? Of course. I always started for combat with the sense of danger in the fight, but I was always controlled. I believed in my victory over the enemy. After landing I debriefed my pilots in a calm mood. I never reprimanded any of them. I discussed our combats informally.'

At the end of the war, like many Polish people, Witold Urbanowicz found the thought of living in Poland under communist rule intolerable. The Allies' betrayal of Poland had hurt him deeply, and his parting at the end of the war from the RAF added to the sense of betrayal.

'My parting with the RAF was a very unpleasant surprise. After the end of the war, the Air Ministry did not pay me my War Gratuity. In answer to my letter, I was told that I had not been in Great Britain at the moment the war ended. Because of this, the Gratuity is not due me. I replied that I had been during the Battle of Britain, and after the historic battle was over, I fought the German Luftwaffe. I received a laconic reply from the Air Ministry. "The case is closed." My English colleagues were disgusted with such a reply as was I.'

Witold Urbanowicz went to live in America but found that work was hard to find. At first, he had to settle for a desk job with American Airlines while he and his wife raised their son Witold. Later, he found he had a gift for writing about his war exploits, and his books were well received.

Finally, the day Witold Urbanowicz had dreamed of arrived in 1989 — Poland achieved independence. He could visit his homeland and inspire the next generation of pilots. He promoted to General and was invited to speak at the Dęblin Officers' School in Poland. The cadets listened in awe to his words of wisdom with the utmost respect for such a man.

In his twilight years, Witold Urbanowicz enjoyed time with his son and grandchildren. General Witold Urbanowicz died at eighty-eight years old.

See **Combat Reports** for the following dates:
- 6 Sep 1940
- 7 Sep 1940
- 15 Sep 1940
- 26 Sep 1940
- 27 Sep 1940
- 30 Sep 1940

Sources: Interview General Witold Urbanowicz, 1986; Bernard Buchwald, 1992. DFC Citation by kind permission of Cabinet Office. Licence PSI No C2006010220. The National Archives Air/2 DFC approved 16 October 1940.

Also see Witold Urbanowicz's memories of Zdzisław Krasnodębski (see Krasnodębski's profile) 1987.

Name: **Mirosław Wojciechowski**
Squadron: No. 303 Kościuszko Squadron
Decorations: Virtuti Militari 5th Class
                   KW Cross of Valour - three bars

Mirosław Wojciechowski was born 6 March 1917 Poland. He was in the Polish Air Force when Poland was invaded in September 1939 and flew with No. 142 Eskadra. After receiving orders to evacuate to Romania, he escaped and made his way to France, then England.

After refresher training, Mirosław Wojciechowski was posted as a Sergeant to No. 303 Kościuszko Squadron on 13 August 1940. He flew many sorties with the squadron.

While on a Circus operation on 23 June 1941, twelve Spitfires took off in the early evening from RAF Northolt. Mirosław Wojciechowski flew to the rescue of a Spitfire pilot that was under attack by two Me109s. He fired his guns at a distance of 100 yards, hitting one of the Me109s Both wings on the enemy aircraft broke off, and it exploded into flames. It was a successful sortie for the squadron; they returned to base having shot down four Messerschmitts with three probables.

Just over a week later, on 2 July 1941, Mirosław Wojciechowski was flying on a Circus operation with No. 303 Kościuszko Squadron, targeting the power station at Lille. An Me109 shot Mirosław Wojciechowski's Spitfire, causing heavy damage. He was severely hurt and had trouble flying his aircraft back to RAF Northolt. Against the odds, he landed at Martlesham, taxied his Spitfire to the perimeter and switched off his engine. He managed to pull himself from the aircraft and staggered about 300 yards before collapsing near to the sick quarters. The cockpit and wing of his aircraft were covered in blood. It was quite a while before he recovered from his injuries. On the same day, Mirosław Wojciechowski lost one of his close friends, Squadron Leader Wacław Łapkowski, who he had flown with since the Battle of Britain.

In late 1942, Mirosław Wojciechowski was posted on an instructor's course and returned to No. 303 Kościuszko Squadron in February 1943.

On 4th April 1943, Mirosław Wojciechowski received a posting to Elementary Flying Training School as an instructor with the rank of Warrant Officer.

When the war ended, Mirosław Wojciechowski fell in love and married an English girl Dorothy, who had served in the WAAFs. They remained in England and had a daughter and son.

Mirosław Wojciechowski remained in the RAF, where he served with No. 247 squadron flying various jets.

He lost his life in a tragic flying collision in October 1956. He was thirty-nine years old.

Warrant Officer Mirosław Wojciechowski is laid to rest in Middle Wallop Churchyard. He was buried with full military honours.

See Combat Reports for the following dates:
- 11 Sep 1940
- 15 Sep 1940
- 17 Sep 1940

Sources: Pilot information from the Polish Air Force Association, Combat Reports from The National Archives (TNA), Air 50/117, Operational Report Diaries from RAF Northolt. Interview: Flight Lieutenant Gen Szaposznikow.

Name: **Stefan Wójtowicz**
Squadron: No. 303 Kościuszko Squadron
Decorations: Virtuti Militari 5th Class

Stefan Wójtowicz was born 19 June 1919 in Wypnisze (Wypnicha) village in Lublin, Poland. He began his Air Force training in Bydgoszcz at the School for Non-Commissioned Officers in 1937. He obtained his pilot's qualifications in June 1939 at Krosno. In the September campaign, he flew in defence of Poland with No.111 Fighter Squadron.

On 18 September 1939, he received orders along with many other pilots and ground crew to evacuate to Romania. While in Romania, Stefan Wójtowicz wrote a letter to his family about how he felt about them and the fate of Poland. No further written correspondence ever followed during his lifetime.

Cadet Officer Stefan Wójtowicz with his sister Matylda (right) and his niece. Photo taken just before Germany invaded Poland in 1939. Photo: author's collection.

After reaching France, Stefan Wójtowicz flew with Captain Pilot Kazimierz Kuzian in defence of Nantes. When France fell, he made his way to England and was posted as a Sergeant to No. 303 Kościuszko Squadron at its formation on 2 August 1940.

While on a sortie on 11 September 1940, Stefan Wójtowicz fought a lone battle with six Messerschmitts and, according to witnesses, shot down two enemy Me109 aircraft. His Hurricane was severely damaged in the fight and crashed in flames on land at Hogtrough Hill, Westerham. Many local people, including children, witnessed his bravery but there was nothing they could do to help. Those who were working nearby in the fields ran to his aircraft and realised he was Polish by the tattered remains of the word 'Poland' on his uniform. He was twenty-one years old.

During the war, Stefan Wójtowicz's family in Poland believed he was alive, as parcels from him would often arrive from Lisbon. They were sent by an organisation delivering parcels that had been pre-paid for by Stefan Wójtowicz.

In July 1946, they found out the truth. One of Stefan's brothers was reading a book by Arkady Fielder on No. 303 Kościuszko Squadron, which described Stefan's death. The whole family was devastated.

In later years, some of Stefan Wójtowicz personal effects were sent to his family in Poland, including a letter written by Stefan on 29 August 1940. He wrote about his premonition that he would have an early death and had asked a friend to notify his family should it happen.

His sister, Matylda's memory of her brother Stefan is frozen in time:

'The picture I preserve in my memory of my brother Stefan, he was tall very attractive, always full of life and energy. Unusually joyful and friendly towards people and very much loved by his family. Stefan loved reading books, often he read sitting high up in a tree in our garden, this way avoiding pressure from his/our elder brothers to participate in domestic agricultural work. Only I knew where to find him when he was looked for but this was our secret. Our elder brothers often complained to our parents, yet they all favoured him, Stefan as the youngest amongst them. I adored my brother Stefan. When he left for flying school at Bydgoszcz, I was waiting with longing for him every holiday when he would bring his friends with him.

I remember intensive preparations before Stefan's arrival, of those most welcome guests. The house smelled with cleanliness and fresh house baking and there was happy talk and pleasantries. My happiness knew no bounds when my brother Stefan lifted me on his shoulders and we wandered across the lanes and fields.

Then the nightmare, The War. On a certain day, two motorcycles stopped at our house. It was my brother Stefan, his Commanding Officer and two friends. They stopped for a while to say goodbye. My mother pleaded with Stefan to stay (as always every mother wants to protect her child with a safety net and keep the child near to her). Stefan answered. - "Mother I must go, you will see, your grandchildren will read about my actions in books." These words my mother often repeated, and so it happened. For our family remained deep despair.

My memory of my brother does not fade, my memory preserves above all the beautiful frame of my brother Stefan, my adoration for him and his great sensitivity shown to me.'

Peter Finch, a young boy in the Summer of 1940, remembers the day of Stefan Wójtowicz's crash.

'I and some of my friends were swimming in a large water tower near Westerham Fire Station when one of our friends ran to tell us that the Hurricane pilot that had been killed that afternoon lay at the fire station. Later that day, curiosity got the better of two of my friends and I. We climbed up to look through the window in the fire station. The sight that met my eyes was terribly sad. A young pilot's badly burned body laid out. It really brought it home to me, the horror of war. My friends and I felt ashamed that we had looked upon the heroic young pilot. The sight has never left me, more than sixty years after I first saw it. I learned later that the pilot was Polish. Many local people who witnessed the dogfight believed the Polish pilot was killed instantly in the air and his aircraft suddenly plummeted to the ground. After the war, I found out the pilot's name was Stefan Wójtowicz. I often said a prayer for his sacrifice of life. I was honoured in 2010 to attend a memorial ceremony to Stefan on the 70th Anniversary of his loss and learn more about him and the many Polish airmen who flew in the Second World War.'

1940 — Stefan Wójtowicz with Ruth.
Photo: Permission of Wójtowicz family.

Shortly before his death, Stefan Wójtowicz became engaged to Ruth, an auxiliary nurse in a London Hospital. Ruth was devastated when Stefan was killed and never forgot him. Years later, two of Ruth's grandchildren were named in remembrance of her first love. Stephen and Stephanie are proud of their connection to the young heroic Polish pilot who gave his life for freedom.

Sergeant Stefan Wójtowicz is laid to rest in Northwood Cemetery Grave 209, Section H.

See Combat Reports for the following dates:
- 3 Sep 1940
- 7 Sep 1940
- 11 Sep 1940

Sources: Pilot information from the Polish Air Force Association, Combat Reports from The National Archives (TNA), Air 50/117, Operational Report Diaries from RAF Northolt. Interviews: Mrs Matylda Winiaska, Oct 1986; Mr Peter Finch, 2005 and Mr Bob Stevens, 2005 (both witnessed the dogfight that killed Stefan Wójtowicz in 1940). Profile photo: Wójtowicz family/author's collection.

Name: **Kazimierz Wünsche**
Squadron: No. 303 Kościuszko Squadron
No. 315 Squadron
Decorations: Virtuti Militari 5th Class
KW Cross of Valour and four bars
DFM
Various French medals
Knight's Cross - Flying Medical Service

Kazimierz Wünsche was born 5 June 1919 in Jaroslaw, Poland. In 1936, he joined the School for Non-Commissioned Officers in Bydgoszcz. He joined the Fighter High School in Grudziadz from April 1939 to June of that year then attended Dęblin Officers' School.

In the September campaign of 1939, Kazimierz Wünsche flew in defence of Poland with No. 111 Fighter Squadron and made his way to Romania on 17 September 1939. After escaping from the internment camp on 11 November 1939, he made his way to France to fly with Polish pilots in Lyon Bron and later with Groupe de Chasse II/8.

In June 1940, Kazimierz Wünsche boarded a boat at La Rochelle and sailed to Plymouth. He travelled to Blackpool for refresher flight training and was posted to No. 303 Kościuszko Squadron on 2 August 1940.

During a sortie on 9 September 1940, Kazimierz Wünsche came under attack from two Me109s. He baled out of his damaged aircraft, his skin burning from the flames. On the ground, he waited in agony until he was rescued and taken to Hove Hospital for treatment. His wife remembers:

'Two of his most treasured possessions from the war years were two letters sent to him when he was shot down and injured in the Battle

of Britain. These letters were sent to him while in hospital, written by school children wishing him a speedy recovery.'

He remained with No. 303 Kościuszko Squadron and flew many sorties until 1944. During this time, he was sometimes posted to train pilots.

In 1944, he was made a Flight Lieutenant and transferred to No. 315 Polish Squadron, where he remained until the end of the war.

In August 1945, Kazimierz Wünsche was sent on staff duties at RAF Coltishall and was released from duty the following year.

In 1946, Kazimierz Wünsche fell in love and married a Polish girl Irena, who had escaped Poland and joined the WAAFs in England.

Irena had taken part in the Warsaw Uprising in 1944 as a member of the AK Home Army in Poland. She was captured and taken to a POW camp where she was forced to live in terrible conditions. With the help of the AK Home Army, she managed to escape from the camp and make her way to England.

In 1947, Kazimierz Wünsche took his wife and two daughters to live in Poland. He was one of only two founder members of No. 303 Kościuszko Squadron to return to Poland to live. He rejoined the Polish Air Force in Dęblin and worked as an instructor until 1952.

In 1956, he took a job in a newly formed Flying Medical Assistance (ambulance), where he remained until he suffered a heart attack in 1970. Flight Lieutenant Kazimierz Wünsche passed away on 10 July 1980 at sixty-one years old.

See Combat Reports for the following dates:

- 31 Aug 1940
- 5 Sep 1940
- 6 Sep 1940
- 9 Sep 1940

Sources: Interview with Mrs Irena Wünsche, 24 Nov 1986. Profile Photo: Gen Szaposznikow.

Name:	**Walerian Żak**
Squadron:	No. 303 Kościuszko Squadron
	No. 308 Squadron
Decorations:	Virtuti Militari 5th Class
	KW Cross of Valour and Three Bars
	DFC

Walerian Żak was born 14th April 1911 in Poland. He flew in the defence of Poland during September 1939 until he was ordered to evacuate to Romania. From Romania, he travelled to France and then England. He joined No. 303 Kościuszko Squadron on 21 August 1940 as a Flying Officer.

While flying on a sortie on 27 September 1940, Walerian Żak's aircraft was damaged, but he survived by baling out. He spent many months recovering from his injuries, which included serious burns on his face.

In May 1941, he was posted back to No. 303 Kościuszko Squadron in the operations room. After regaining his full health, he was posted as an instructor to No. 58 Operational Training Unit at RAF Grangemouth in Scotland.

Walerian Żak was later given command of No. 308 Polish Squadron in May 1942 and was made Squadron Leader in March 1943. A few months later, he led the Wing at RAF Kirton-in-Lindsey, which was followed by a posting to No. 11 Group HQ in February 1944, and various training courses.

After the war, Walerian Żak married. He and his wife Jeanne settled in England. He passed away 14 March 1969 at fifty-seven years old. He is laid to rest in Northwood Cemetery, near to the resting place of the many Polish airmen who sacrificed their lives during the Second World War.

See Combat Reports for the following dates:
- 15 Sep 1940
- 26 Sep 1940

Sources: Pilot information from the Polish Air Force Association, Combat Reports from The National Archives (TNA), Air 50/117, Operational Report Diaries from RAF Northolt. Interview: Jan Kowalski, 1986. Walerian Żak's DFC was donated to the Imperial War Museum, London.

Name:	**Jan Zumbach**
Squadron:	No. 303 Kościuszko Squadron
Decorations:	Virtuti Miltari 5th Class
	KW Cross of Valour Three Bars.
	DFC

'This Officer has taken part in many operational flights and has proved himself a courageous and capable fighter pilot. He has destroyed 7 enemy aircraft and probably another 2.'

DFC recommendation by S/L R Kellett 23/9/194

Jan Zumbach, known to his friends as Johnny, was born 14 April 1915 in Poland. Jan was still young when his father died, so he was brought up by his mother. It is said that as a young man, Jan Zumbach forged his mother's signature so he could join the Polish Army.

In 1936, Jan Zumbach left the Polish Army and joined the Polish Air Force, where he qualified as a pilot in 1938. He flew with No. 111 Fighter Squadron, but in Spring 1939 he broke his leg and was unable to fly in combat when Germany invaded Poland in September1939. When ordered to evacuate, Jan Zumbach flew an aircraft to Romania.

In Romania, soldiers were instructed to impound any Polish aircraft. On landing, Jan Zumbach pretended he needed to taxi his aircraft to a safe area but took off again and landed a safe distance away. Like many other Polish airmen and ground crew, he made his way to Bucharest to collect money for food, and false papers stating he was a student. He then left Romania and made his way to France, where he was attached to a French squadron. France fell before the squadron became operational, so Jan Zumbach made his way to England.

Jan Zumbach was posted to No. 303 Kościuszko Squadron on 2nd August 1940 as a Pilot Officer and flew on many sorties.

On the 13 October 1941, Jan Zumbach was flying with No. 1 Polish Fighter Wing on a Circus operation to escort six Blenheim bombers. Before reaching the English Channel, he attacked two Me109s and shot one down. Bullets from three attacking Messerschmitts pierced the pressure pipe on Jan Zumbach's Spitfire, rendering its guns useless. Managing to avoid another attack, he flew back to RAF Northolt and landed safely.

In December 1941, Jan Zumbach was posted as an instructor to

No. 58 Operational Training Unit at RAF Grangemouth in Scotland. He was promoted to Flight Lieutenant in mid-March 1942 and returned to No. 303 Kościuszko Squadron, where he remained until the end of the year.

From December 1942 to April 1943, Jan Zumbach was a Liaison Officer for Polish airmen under No. 9 Group. He was then posted as Squadron Leader of the Polish Fighter Wing at RAF Kirton-in-Lindsey. In 1945, Jan Zumbach was an Operational Officer at No. 84 Group HQ.

After the war, Jan Zumbach refused to live in a Poland under communist rule. Instead, he was able to get a Swiss passport on the basis that his paternal grandparents were from Switzerland.

He continued to fly, and for a while had a lucrative career smuggling various items (but never drugs). He also flew in the Congo and Biafra conflicts.

He lived for many years in France, where he fell in love and married a young French woman Gisele. They later had a son Hubert.

Jan Zumbach kept in contact with many of those he flew with during the war. They described him as *a larger than life character, a loyal friend and he lived life to the full.*

Squadron Leader Jan Zumbach passed away in 1986 in France and is laid to rest in Warsaw, Poland.

See Combat Reports for the following dates:
- 3 Sep 1940
- 7 Sep 1940
- 9 Sep 1940
- 11 Sep 1940
- 15 Sep 1940
- 26 Sep 1940
- 27 Sep 1940

Sources: Pilot information from the Polish Air Force Association, Combat Reports from The National Archives (TNA), Air 50/117, Operational Report Diaries from RAF Northolt. Interviews: Wing Commander Ronald Kellett, Jun 1986; Mrs A Forbes, 1986; Flight Lieutenant Jan Kowalski, 1987; Squadron Leader Gandi Drobiński, 1987. DFC approved 16 October 1940. DFC Citation by kind permission of Cabinet Office. Licence PSI No C2006010220. TNA AIR/2.

26 September 1940 – HRH King George VI visits RAF Northolt. It's a proud day for pilots of No. 303 Kościuszko Squadron. Shaking hands with the King from right to left are P/O Mirosław Ferić, P/O Jan Zumbach, F/O Bogdan Grzeszczak, F/O Wojciech Januszewicz. S/L Ronald Kellett is stood beside King George and Witold Urbanowicz is standing behind him. Photo: Permission of Eugeniusz (Gen) Szaposznikow.

PART II

IN THEIR OWN WORDS
Other Pilots' Memoirs

Seventeen thousand Polish men and women served in the Polish Air Force, many of whom flew from Britain in the Second World War. The memoirs included here are written by Polish pilots in their own words, covering a wide range of the Polish Air Force activities — training in Poland; the September Campaign; evacuation and the continuing fight. They are the stories of a female Ferry Pilot; airmen under enemy fire, and prisoners of war. Ultimately, they are the stories of unrelenting resistance and cruel betrayal. The memoirs echo with the lasting sadness of men writing before Poland broke free of communist rule in 1989.

I am indebted to the following people:

Wing Commander Jan Biały is believed to be the oldest Polish airman that flew with the Polish Air Force in Bomber Command. His memoir is reproduced here by kind permission of his sister Mrs Halina Dyaczyńska. First interview 1986, with supplementary information between 1986-1988.

Flight Lieutenant Bernard Buchwald for writing his wartime memories and for allowing me to use extracts from his book OD WRONY DO SPITFIRE'a, including sections — In Captivity, II Dulag Luft and Stalag Luft III. Interview 1986. Permission to use extracts from his book granted 7 August 2006.

Flight Lieutenant Kazimierz Karaszewski served with No. 309 and No. 317 Polish Squadrons. Interview 19 May 1988 and concluded 20 February 1990.

Squadron Leader Franciśzek Kornicki served with No. 303, No. 308, No. 315, and No. 317 Polish Squadrons. His memoir describes his first sortie in July 1941. Interview August 1987.

Flight Lieutenant Jan Maliński served with No. 302 Fighter Squadron and No. 307 Night Fighter Squadron. He has kindly written his memoir and granted me permission to reproduce 'The Eagle Owls' and 'The Polish Night Fighter Song', for which he wrote the music. Interview 6 November 1987, and supplemental information 1987-1988.

First Officer Stefania Karpińska née Wojtulanis has kindly given a written interview dated 1 April 1989 about her time as a Woman Ferry Pilot.

Stanisław Sroka was a member of the Armia Krajowa (AK Home Army in Poland) and shares his knowledge about Special Operation Executive operations in Poland during the Second World War. He wrote the account at a time when details about these operations had not been released into the public domain.

Wing Commander Jan Biały

I was born on 16 June 1897 in Kraków, Poland. In 1918, I joined the Polish Army. Wishing to become a pilot in 1923, I commenced training in the Polish Air Force at Bydgoszcz. In 1928, I was transferred to 11th Fighter Regiment at Lidzie together with the Wing, then followed a transfer to 2nd Air Force Regiment at Kraków. In 1930, I had a terrible flying accident from which I was very fortunate to survive. It was believed I would never fly again. I was determined to keep my eagle wings. After many months in hospital where I received excellent care and with my determination not to be beaten, I recovered. Later rejoining my squadron, I was put in charge of training pilots ready for combat with the Wing. In 1938 I married.

When war broke out in Poland, I was Wing Commander of the Regiment (Squadrons) in Kraków. The Wing (Dywizjon Linowy) was equipped with PZL-23 Karaś bombers. This little known Wing flew in the September Campaign of 1939.

I kept the battle diary of the Wing. Unfortunately, before we were evacuated to Romania, I had no choice but to destroy the battle diary in case it fell into the wrong hands. I rewrote the diary in late 1939 as follows:

24 August 1939 Poland
At 16.00 hours the Regiment/Wing was put under alert. At the conference Commander Lieutenant Colonel Stanisław Nazarkiewicz ordered the mobilisation of combat units. In accordance with High Command orders, the 21st and 22nd Squadron forms the Light Bomber Wing, to the disposition of High Command (later incorporated into the Bomber Brigade). The 24th Squadron was put to the disposition of the Army 'Kraków' for distance reconnaissance.

27 August 1939
Rail transport arrives in the early morning hours at Radom. The airfield is situated at Radom's Racetrack. It proves unsuitable for the bombers. It would require amelioration [vast improvement] and the removal of vast amounts of hay. The airfield at Sadków is chosen for the aircraft's landing.

28 August 1939

Conditions of flying personnel — pilots and observers on active service trained quite well. Eighty percent are trained in night-flights on Karaś, all personnel trained in flights without visibility. Gunners on active service trained well and numbers insufficient being fifty percent of actual requirements.

Necessary completion with reserve observers and gunners. Reserve flying personnel training on average is poor, as many have not been flying Karaś bombers. The most serious deficiency is the lack of Gunners.

In the Wing (Dyon) is a surplus of flying personnel but needing additional training; after some time, they would be ready for combat duties. The Technical Personnel active service and reserve are quite good and in certain respects, reservists are better than active servicemen are. The spirit in the Wing is very good.

30 August 1939

During the early hours, the German observation aircraft are flying at high altitude over Radom and Sadków. In the afternoon, orders were received from Bomber Command to transfer the Wing to the Airfield at Wsola. In the evening, Radom and Wsola turned from being quiet to extremely busy. The reason being 'mobilisation' is proclaimed. One feels war is imminent.

31 August 1939

Airfield Wsola. Organisation of the airfield and Anti-Aircraft Defences. The 21st Squadron is placed north of the airfield, the aircraft are camouflaged in the Forest. The 32nd Squadron is on the west without camouflage at a distance at 100m.

1 September 1939

'WAR.' From early morning, Dornier 17 German bombers are flying in three and fifteen formations over our Airfields at high altitude. The Radom region seems to be the distribution point of incessant flights.

The same was repeated the following few days. The Brigade HQ is approached to organise a Fighter-trap in the region. The request is turned down the reason being a lack of necessary numbers of fighters.

In the morning, a liaison officer is sent to Bomber HQ. He arrives with Battle orders, an organisation detail map lists of German targets and secret orders from the Supreme Command.

The maps received of Polish and German territory were incomplete. Scales 1:100,000; 1:500,000; 1:300,000. The file of German target's airfields and army objects were never used. The orders and Battle Diaries etc. were all later destroyed on the Romanian border.

The secret Supreme Command order was already issued before the war, prohibiting categorically, the bombardment of inhabited areas and civilians. This order was not passed on to the Squadrons in view of the experience of German tactics employed in Poland.

In the evening, news was received from Radom and Sadków, the airfield was completely destroyed. Obviously, the Germans had detailed information of aircraft deployment. The transfer to Wsola was just in time.

3 September 1939

Bomber Brigade Command orders the survey of the region of Częstochowa, Lublin, Opole, Strzelec in regard to German Army movements, especially Panzer Units. The task is carried out by the crews of the 1st Squadron with Lieutenant Observer Kasprzyk and Sergeant Pilot Wójcik with bombs on board. The first battle flight. In the region Częstochowa and further Lubiniec, the crew meets anti-aircraft artillery and machine-gun fire German and Polish. Our units do not recognise our own planes firing at all aircraft. These incidents are repeated also during the following days, necessitating in informing our own AA Units of our own Bomber and even Observation Flights. The results of observations are heavy German Army and Panzer movements in the mentioned regions.

One of the first operational flights was carried out early morning by Cadet Officer Observer Stefan Gębicki, Sergeant Pilot Wacław Buczyłko, Corporal Gunner Teofil Gara. Due to fog, the observation task was impossible to complete. Sergeant Pilot Buczyłko decided to go further west and bombard a factory in Oława. This was surely the first bombardment of Germany during the war. In the afternoon, an order was received to observe the region Częstochowa. Owing to the long-range observation, the crew had permission to land at Łódź Airfield if unable to reach base. The crew: 2nd Lieutenant Rudolf Wilczak and Major Pilot Wojciech Uryzaj, he had volunteered to participate although he was the pilot of a Fokker, he did not return.

The Wing Commander received orders from Bomber Brigade to

bombard columns in the region of Radom — Pławno by three planes (Klucz) in ten-minute intervals. The reason to repel advancing columns. Altitude 1000-1500m bombs 50 or 100kg. Task performed from 1st Squadron — two trios, and from 2nd Squadron — three trios including one with four aircraft. They encounter heavy AA Flak and fighters over the target causing heavy losses. The result of the bombing was very good, after bombing started to gun Germans from low altitude. From the operation three aircraft from the 2nd Squadron failed to return, shot down among others was Commanding Officer of 2nd Squadron Captain Pilot Kazimierz Slowinski.

Command assumes under Lieutenant Observer Bolesław Nowicki. After return and refuelling, fixing of bombs, once again four trios bombard Panzer Columns moving from Radom to Gorzkowice and Przedbórz.

The results very good, despite AA flak and enemy fighters. Our losses shot down were two planes, one from 1st and 2nd Squadrons. The aircraft from the 2nd Squadron was shot down after completion of the bombardment during the additional task of observation in the Przedbórz, Włoszczow and Koniecpol regions.

The pilot of the aircraft of the 2nd Squadron was injured, the aircraft being badly damaged with the observer seriously wounded. The aircraft flew into land at the Kamien airfield, misjudged the approach. Realising at the last moment that he would land in the forest, the pilot accelerated but due to his low altitude crashed into the trees. The plane caught fire and the tanks exploded. The technical crew rescued the pilot and gunner from the burning plane but the observer they were unable to save due to the exploding tanks and ammunition. The wounded were taken to hospital at Radom.

All the Bomber-sorties encountered heavy defence. The question arose if it was not more effective to carry out bombing from low altitudes. This method was not employed due to the lack of delayed action detonators. In that entire day, eight bomber sorties were carried out. German losses were heavy; equally great were our losses. Five of our crews did not return from combat, one aircraft destroyed and burnt out on our own airfield.

Of the crews shot down escaping by parachute was Captain Observer Stefan Alberti and Sergeant Pilot Wacław Buczyłko with Captain Alberti escaping to Kielce, then through Stanisławów to Romania. About Sergeant Buczyłko nothing was known. The plane that burnt out on our airfield.

Of the crew, 2nd Lieutenant Wacław Grandys was badly burnt.

Despite heavy losses and heroic experiences, the morale of the Wing's crew was very good. The surviving crews waiting impatiently for an opportunity to avenge their dead colleagues; to avenge the destruction by the Germans on the villages and towns and the suffering of the civilian population.

The crews observed the burning of villages the destruction caused by the Germans, thus proceeded the feelings of hate against the invader and involuntarily created the intention to employ the same kind of methods against the Germans.

4 September 1939

Since dawn technical personnel prepare the aircraft for action. In the morning, nine Karaś aircraft are ready with bombs. No battle orders were received during the day but by order of the Bomber Brigade HQ two reconnaissance sorties were carried out. It was characteristic that observation flights showed that instead of the former travelling in compact formation, the order of distances of 100 to 200m is now employed, with units occupying small villages, towns and forests, if access allowed.

5 September 1939

Since dawn aircraft are prepared for action. Equipment is ready. Ten aircraft are out of action, two repairs are under way.

In the morning orders are received from Brigade HQ for two bombing and observation flights.

During the afternoon, the Wing receives orders for the preparation of transfer to the airfields Podlodow and Marianów. It is worth mentioning the selfless help given by civilians and the co-operation of the Telephone Exchange personnel at Radom who despite constant bombardments, efficiently carried out their duties. Ultimately, the 1st Squadron lands at Podlodem airfield and the 2nd Squadron safely at their new airfield Marianów. The road transport arrives at dawn at Moszczanki.

7 September 1939

Airfield Marianów. In the afternoon, the Brigade Commanding Officer's order received to bombard with the whole Wing the Panzer units north of Łódź. The enemy to be surveyed on three roads.

One in the direction of Ozorków, number two Piątek Kutno, and finally Stryków Łowicz.

The orders are immediately complied with. Three (Klucze) carries out the operation under my command being Major Dipl. Jan Biały. This is preceded by twenty minutes by a reconnaissance aircraft.

The meeting point Brzeziny was reached very efficiently in time. As radio contact was not established the participants were waiting for the observation aircraft to arrive. In the direction of Łódź, three Messerschmitts were sighted, who saw our close formation. They did not attack. When after forty minutes the observation plane did not arrive the Commanding Officer ordered each of the three to seek targets on their own and bombard them. The targets chosen were in the region Ozorków-Stryków. On the return flight whilst strafing the enemy, the Wing Commanding Officer's plane was attacked by two Messerschmitts in the Żyrardów region. One of the enemy fighters was shot down. German fighters north of Łódź shot down the observation aircraft that had proceeded the Wing during this operation.

8 September 1939

During the afternoon, two trios bombed German Panzer columns in the region of Sokołów. The column was detected during regrouping in a forest north of Sokołów. The enemy losses were heavy.

From the operation trio, one aircraft was forced to land due to being hit by the enemy perforating the plane engine. The plane was damaged and the crew did not return to base. On the return flights, our trio meets three Dornier aircraft flying in very loose formation. Our Karaś trio attacks one of the Dorniers, which does not want to accept the fight. The three German aircraft regroup and thanks to their superior speed, disappear.

In the afternoon, the Germans bombard the airfield at Marianów. This was rather a medium bombardment. The Germans located the airfield through agent's intelligence but from the air could not find it, therefore, they bombarded and burnt a village about one to two km from the airfield. On the nearby terrain, they dropped mine-bombs which exploded two to three minutes after the drop.

Severely felt is the absence of a mobile park as well with food and technical supplies. Aircraft repairs were performed by Blacksmith methods, with pipes etc as substituted materials. Communication with the Brigade's HQ was very troublesome. Reconnaissance information could not be instantly communicated, orders arrived late, the smooth operation, and procedure was constantly interrupted.

The Liaison aircraft RWD8 of the 2nd Squadron sent to Warsaw on the 7 September it did not return.

Only one Liaison aircraft remained which was constantly in use.

In the morning hours occurred an unfortunate incident at the Marianów airfield. Due to a pilot's error during landing, the plane from the Łódź Squadron crashed into the forest with the Commanding Officer Captain Skibiński and all.

10 September 1939

On this day, the operation of the Wing ceased during the Polish-German War in Poland. The summarily carried out were: sixteen bombing sorties and nineteen reconnaissance flight.

German losses to Panzer Columns very heavy. In the air, shot down one Messerschmitt, possibly another in the region of Radom. Confirmation could not be definitely obtained.

The German Armed Forces were completely modernised and prepared for modern warfare, whereas we were at the beginning of re-equipment, in the main using equipment from the First World War.

The Cavalry could not attack tanks and the Air Force had to be able to cope with the enemy. It must also be remembered that the general mobilisation was interrupted for political reasons.

Referring back to the Wing's (Dyon) fate after handing over of aircraft and equipment the road transport moved towards Romania.

16 September 1939

I received news at Horodenka that the Russians crossed the Polish borders, disarming Polish units and occupying our territory. After confirmations of this news and receipt of Polish Air Force HQ orders to evacuate to Romania. I crossed the Romanian border with the crews the following day. A new chapter of my Second World War experiences was to begin.

In Romania and France

After arriving at Tulcea in Romania, there was little time for meditation about Russia's breaking of international law, having signed with Poland a non-aggression pact.

At that time, it was most important to organise the dispersed Polish Armed Forces and to arrange their transfer to France for the continuation of the war against Germany in defence of our national rights.

At once in Romania and Hungary, organised authorities started to evacuate Polish soldiers to France. This was in order to reorganise the Polish Armed Forces for the fight against the brutal, unscrupulous German invader.

Instructions were received from France from General Władysław Sikorski, who was nominated General Commander of the Polish Armed Forces.

Most Romanians received us hospitably and helped as much as they could in reaching France. We had to act quickly as the Germans threatened to subjugate those countries. Disguised in civilian clothing, with false passports and identity cards, most of us were mainly pretending to be labourers looking for work abroad. They penetrated all borders on the way to France.

Together with other airmen, I was directed to a holiday resort a small harbour on the Black Sea 'Balchik,' where from we were to leave by ship.

After several days at the Port, a ship or rather a smuggler boat arrived to take us. This boat was used to smuggle anything worthwhile doing. The Captain was either Romanian or Greek; he knew his business well. The proof of this was his frequent changing of the flag on the open sea. All of us had to hide under the deck where wooden planks served as beds without mattresses or straw, this was rather beneficial as far as hygiene was concerned. The weather was hot despite being October; under the deck was very stuffy and on the boat was insufficient drinking water. All this was bearable as the voyage from the Balchik to Beyrouth lasted only a few days. During the passage, there was even a humorous moment. One of the airmen, I think he was a mechanic, bored by the heat jumped from the boat for refreshment. The cooling amateur was swimming well but on the boat alarm being raised 'Man overboard,' the vessel reduced speed and the good swimmer helped by a rope managed to climb up on deck, sufficiently cooled off.

Passing the Dardanelles, Turkish authorities searched the vessel but it was not really a search. Apparently, the Turks were informed of the ship's cargo. Our transport was booked as Transport of Labour.

After arriving in port, the French General Weygand approached the Polish transport commander with the request for information about the September Campaign. Because I spoke French well, I was delegated with two other Polish Air Force Officers to see the General. I reported on the

Campaign of the German bombardments of open towns, the murders and cruelty against the civilian population.

General Weygand mentioned that he had information from General Pétain, which the Germans acted in accord with international law. I realised then that his words were the result of German propaganda and in that spirit, I terminated the talk with the General.

After a short stay, we embarked on a French passenger ship which took us to Marseille where we were then transferred to nearby Salon, a French air base, which was to be our temporary home until the start of the formation of the Polish Army.

After several weeks at Salon, I was transferred in 1939 to the French air base Lyon where from, at the beginning of 1940, I was appointed the Commander of the Polish Airmen and Technical Personnel at the air base Rennes in Normandy. During that time, the General Commander of the Polish Forces, General Sikorski, promoted me to Lieutenant Colonel Pilot. These were the first scant promotions for the September Campaign and my selection amongst other deserving officers in the armed forces was a compensation for the troubles I endured with my Wing, and of the others in the armed forces in the difficult fulfilment of a soldier's duty.

At Rennes, I immediately started to organise the training of airmen and technical crews on two engine aircraft. Our pilots flew up to this time in only single engine planes. Therefore, training on two engine aircraft was a necessity. The basic rules were the same, but manoeuvring of two engine planes had to be mastered. As Chief of Pilotage, I nominated a reserve pilot, who in Poland flew as an airline pilot on two engine planes and had wide experience. A Captain Pilot, who before the war was mainly employed as a Staff Officer and as a pilot completed only the flying hours necessary for obtaining qualifications for Pilot Bonus Payments.

He approached me with a complaint, why was he not in charge of Pilotage according to his rank instead of somebody of inferior rank. I replied 'that in the Air Force, especially in Pilotage, not rank but know-how and experience with qualifications are playing a decisive role and that his complaint is baseless.' He wanted to appeal to the Air Force Commander, but I do not think he did so, being afraid of the consequent loss of prestige. During this period, a distinct antagonism developed between some young and older flying personnel, especially against the so-called 'Forest Grandads' (Lesni Dziatkowie) to whom, some attributed to *a high degree the catastrophic September Campaign. Critique is necessary, as it promotes progress, limiting regression but it is not always well founded. It is a fact that during mobilisation, old and young were called in, not always fit and able to be usefully employed on foreign soil, but there were also old ones who volunteered and performed exposed actions often better than the younger ones. I also could have been classified a 'Forest Grandad' and yet I had many opportunities to take an active part in the war, instead of choosing tranquil retirement. Fortunately, this temporary antagonism of some of the younger against the senior soon disappeared due to the rapid development of the war.*

France still lived in the clouds, believing that Germany would not attack her, calling the war 'Drôle de Guerre' (silly war). Reality proved different.

After the occupation of Poland and secured safety from the east and especially in the south, Germany felt free to attack France during the first quarter of 1940. The French defence line was broken during the first offensive. It should be remembered that France had nearly a year to prepare against the Germans. She was not surprised by German action, had time to reinforce her Army in addition to the held-in-high-esteem 'Maginot Line'. Instead the Army retreated without proper resistance, some French soldiers it seemed, did not want to fight, abandoning arms retreating in chaos. France lacked a leader of the kind of Clemenceau during the First World War. Marshal Pétain was already too weak, without will, blinded by Germany's might, to prevent defeat.

The situation of the Polish Army in France became critical. General Sikorski issued orders to retreat to the south of France and from there, evacuate to Great Britain by sea or via the French Colonies in the north of Africa. The agreement for the acceptance of the Polish Forces by Britain was signed by General Sikorski and the Premier of Great Britain Winston Churchill.

As Commander of the Flying and Technical Personnel Group at the French base Rennes, I ordered the transport to Marseille. As the Group was not numerous enough to occupy a special train, we used scheduled trains running to Marseille.

The Polish soldier faced a second defeat. In Poland we were defeated but not subjugated, we were still in a position to fight the German invader but not on Polish soil. The defeat of France must have resulted in severe depression for some Polish soldiers. France, a country that had all the means necessary to defeat the Germans with a well-equipped Army reinforced by the British Expedition Force was for us unbelievable.

Our journey by train to the south met with troubles caused by the disruption of the rail service. I remember such an interruption when we were forced to spend the night at a certain place and wait for transport the next day. I gave orders that the group was not allowed to disperse; Officers, NCOs and other ranks were to stay together. The place was a disused hall, without amenities beds etc. Some Officers asked for permission to spend the night in a hotel, I refused and we stayed together. This way we arrived in Marseille where at the station I met General Weygand, whom I had informed in Syria about the situation in Poland. I approached him asking for his opinion about the French-German Campaign. He replied coolly that the situation would soon turn to the better, which everything is in order. And he was right, as a few days after our conversation France signed 'unconditional surrender'. Did everything really turn to the better?

At Marseille, I received orders to leave for Salon, an airfield not far from Marseille to which Polish airmen from Romania were directed after their arrival in France.

At Salon, I met the same Major the Air Force Commander who received us the first time we arrived in Salon. From his behaviour and conversation, I deduced that he had serious accusations against Poland, as he attributed the outbreak of war and the French catastrophe to Poland. I did not react to his opinion, there was no point. However, I learnt that at the airfield were over ten, super-modern for those days, two engine aircraft, Potez. The number I do not remember but I think they were 57s.

Realising that those planes would fall into German hands, I proposed to the Base Commander the transport of those machines by my Group to the North African Base at Oran airfield in order to prevent their falling into German hands. The Commander agreed to the proposition but knowing our pilots were not conversant with this type of plane, he assigned several French pilot instructors to acquaint us with this type of aircraft. A formidable difficulty of the aircraft was their tendency to veer off uncontrollably during take off to the left or right, which at high speed of start caused damage to the undercarriage and often fire. The French instructors completed several flights with each of our pilots, paying special attention to the start procedure. We familiarised ourselves with the instruments and pilot cabin as well as the flight path to the Oran airfield. I set the assembly time at the airfield for seven o'clock with start at eight o'clock in order that we would get the meteorological forecast. As far as I can remember, we had crews for about fifteen aircraft, the start of a single aircraft was to take place at five-minute intervals.

The crews assembled punctually on the following day. Once again I gave instructions about the flight path, checked the crews and after receipt of the Met. forecast, I ordered to start engines at eight o'clock. During the engine start the Adjutant of the base Commander arrived running with instructions received from the French Air Force Commander, prohibiting any aircraft from leaving the airfield. A pity that the order did not arrive a few minutes later, we would have been in the air already. With regret, we left the airfield. Recalling our experience in Poland, contemplating how nice it could have been to have one Wing of those 'Potez' reconnaissance and light bombers at that time.

After again arriving in Marseille, we were loaded on a ship which transported us to North Africa, to Casablanca. After a few days, we sailed to Great Britain. The acceptance of Frenchmen aboard the ship was strictly forbidden. A number of French Officers and other ranks who intended to continue the fight against the Germans had to smuggle themselves secretly aboard dressed in Polish uniforms with Polish badges. Women and children were also barred from boarding the ship.

After a few days at sea, we disembarked at Glasgow in Scotland.

Service in the Polish Air Force in Great Britain

The Scottish people received us cordially and hospitably. We were linked with the Scottish through historical events. We know about them from history, when they fought for their freedom and retention of their separate identity. Equally, I believe they appreciated our struggle against foreign domination and restoration of independence. The news about Poland, the betrayal and invasion of Poland by the Germans were well known to them. They were aware of the circumstances under which the Germans overpowered Poland; therefore, the sympathy shown to us on every occasion was visibly demonstrated.

I remember when a Pole entered a bar and ordered a drink, he could never pay for it. Always the bill was paid in advance by a Scotsman.

I myself had an experience of their willingness to help us and make our stay in a foreign country more pleasant. One day I was sitting in a Glasgow park when a middle-aged woman approached me saying something I could not understand. My knowledge of English at the time was very poor; I tried to speak to her in French. She could not understand any of it and after a while, she offered me a £5 note, which was a lot of money then. Naturally, I refused to accept it but she insisted I should accept. Realising I would not take the money, she left. I could see on her face the look of regret and deep hurt. Later, I felt sorry I had refused and had probably offended her. I was sure she would have been pleased had I accepted.

It is said that Scotsmen are mean that they refuse to spend. During my short stay in Scotland, I was convinced of their hospitality and cordiality towards us Poles. I realised that their feelings were akin with ours from their days of fighting for freedom against the English, who in the end enforced their supremacy. Despite Scotland being part of Great Britain, of its history with common social economic and political interests, they preserved their own national identity. To call a Scotsman an Englishman is considered an insult. To call a Scotsman mean is perhaps derived from many being poorer than the English, with a lower standard of life.

After a short stay in Glasgow, I was ordered to join the RAF at Bramcote near Coventry and to organise a Bomber Wing with Polish flying personnel. At first, I was surprised and somewhat displeased, as after the September campaign, the collapse of France I wanted to rest in order to recuperate my moral and physical strength. On the other side, I came to the conclusion that to be elected for the organisation and command of a Bomber Wing on British soil was an elevation amongst colleagues of the same or even greater merit. The temporary depression disappeared and instantly I reported for duty at Bramcote.

I would like to mention that the organisation of the British Air Force was different from ours, especially of Battle units. Our Air Force was organised in Regiments of Bomber and Reconnaissance Wings, Fighter Wings, Support Wings for co-operation with the Army Units and Training Wings and training centres for additional Pilot and Administration Staff training. In the RAF, there were no regiments with various units but RAF Stations with one type of organisational tasks. On such Stations was one to three Wings.

In my opinion, this type of organisation was better for tactical reasons, better training facilities and easier administration, especially regarding technical supplies. On such stations, there were usually one to two hangars primitively built, in general for repairs. Battle aircraft were not kept in hangars but dispersed at airfield edges. I think this way of keeping aircraft without expensive hangars is more practical, cheaper and less exposed to bombardments. For our excuse, winters in Poland are much more severe than in Great Britain.

The Wing I was to organise 304 Bomber Wing/Squadron of 'Silesia'.

Its organisation started in August 1940. As Commander of the Wing, the Polish Air Force Inspectorate nominated myself, Lieutenant Colonel Dipl. Pilot Jan Biały, and Squadron Commanders Captain Observer Jan Buczmo, and Captain Pilot Jan Gazdzik. The Wings personnel consisted of flying and technical personnel of the 2nd Kraków Regiment, 6th Lwów Regiment and later reinforcements from the 4th Torun Regiment. The flying personnel had already battle experience from actions in Poland.

At first, 304 Bomber Wing was equipped with Fairey Battle single engine with retracting undercarriage, with a crew of three — a pilot, navigator and gunner — with two MGs and 750kg bomb load. These aircraft were similar to our Karaś. Nevertheless, additional training for pilots was necessary for mastering the undercarriage procedure. Pre-war aircraft did not have retractable undercarriages. Training was also necessary for 'blind flying' meaning by instruments only, use of instruments etc. After about six weeks of training at the end of October 1940, the crews were complete and trained for operational duties.

In November 1940, the Wing was re-equipped with Wellingtons, two engines with a crew of six being two pilots, navigator, radio operator and two gunners. The Wellington's armament: four to eight heavy MGs, bomb load about 4000kg. The aircraft was designed for long distance flights, especially at night and later for anti U-boat operations. The flying and technical personnel required also additional training on the new aircraft, especially night flights and the control of the two engines demanded special attention.

The additional personnel required were obtained from airmen reserve and volunteers from other army units and camps who managed to reach Great Britain from Russia. After their sufferings, they were given the opportunity to continue the fight for freedom against the Germans.

The flying personnel were composed of various ages, active and reserve *forces, of all professions. Differences and class distinctions soon disappeared; united by the common purpose of fighting for Poland, to repay the wrong and cruelty inflicted on the Polish nation by the Germans.*

At the end of the organisation period of the Wing, I was called to the Inspector of the Polish Air Force General Observer Ujejski.

General Ujejski informed me that according to British requests, I was to transfer command to Colonel Pilot Paweł Dudziński, and remain at the disposition of the Polish Air Force Inspectorate. This order surprised me and when I asked General Ujejski for the reason, I received an evasive reply. I could only assume that the British HQ demanded the change, as there were absolutely no objections against me.

Meditating later about the reasons, I thought that the English did not like my retention of Polish Army/Air Force procedures, such as morning assembly, report, gatherings, conferences etc. instead of adopting English Air Force customs and regulations, which of course I was not conversant with. I was convinced that in a time of war, time should not be wasted for assimilation of English internal procedures instead of battle training. I was of the opinion that we were all part of the RAF but also the Polish Air Force fighting for the same common goal. Whether the English had other reasons I never tried to find out. During the war, there are more serious problems to be considered than less important details.

The RAF and English snobbism of some and desire to impose in all aspects their own customs changed after our Battle Squadrons, at first the Fighter and later the Bomber Squadrons, achieved such successes.

According to orders, I transferred the Wing's command to Colonel Pilot Dudziński and reported to the Base Commander of the Polish Air Force at Blackpool.

After a few weeks rest, I asked the Inspectorate for any assignment connected with the war effort of the Air Force. Shortly after, I was transferred to Millom Station where British gunners and bombers were being trained. At such stations, there was a shortage of pilots for training flights. Willingly, I undertook piloting of two engine aircraft 'Botha,' which was a heavy metal constructed plane often suffering defects in the air. Accordingly, an order was issued that in such cases, the pilot should not try to land but the whole crew was to escape by parachute.

In performing the task of pilotage, I achieved rather good results. My name figured for a long time, on the table of best achievements in guiding the aircraft precisely on target.

On our uniforms, worn for differentiation, Polish ranks were worn on the uniform lapels and the English on the sleeves. In addition, we wore the label 'Poland' on the shoulders.

In the English and world press, many articles were published about Polish battle success. Humorous anecdotes were construed, for example, if an English pilot was unsuccessful in love the change of uniform with the label 'Poland' would solve his problem of the heart. Personally, I experienced preferential treatment in shops when everything out of the ordinary was done to satisfy me, in addition to superlatives expressed about the actions of Polish pilots.

After the Battle of Britain on some of the airfields, especially where Polish fighter wings were stationed, one being RAF Northolt, the hosts were Poles. The English held only mainly administration positions. All else connected with operational duties, except tactical positions, were in Polish hands. I was told that in some Officers' Messes, plaques were displayed with the inscription 'Spoken English'.

After six months at Millom as pilot 2nd Lieutenant, I was transferred to the British Command as Liaison Officer for the South Training Group, consisting of over ten Air Force stations for British flying personnel, navigators, bombers and gunners. On those stations were also Poles and my task was to keep liaison between them and the Polish and English Authorities. My obligation was that I was also to intervene in disputes and suggestions outside battle training as well as preparing relevant reports for inspection. For inspection of dispersed training stations, I had a 'Moth' liaison plane to fly as and when needed during my work with the South Group. Later when I was transferred to the North Group, I had a fighter plane 'Vibauld'

During my time, I was rather lucky. I remember a situation that was typical of weather changes in Great Britain. I was flying from an airfield in Scotland near Dumfries, the distance about 150 km. At the start, the weather was good, clouds about 1000m high. After meeting with the Polish personnel, I decided to return in the afternoon. When nearing Dumfries I noticed on the right a complete blanking out of the horizon. Anticipating the possibility of fog, I did not circle the airfield as is customary but landed straight away. Rolling the aircraft to the hangar, I found myself in such a thick fog that visibility was reduced to a few metres. I realised what would have happened had I left a few minutes later (unable to land, looking for a place for an emergency landing etc). Pilots flying in Great Britain, especially Scotland and Wales had to count with unforeseen changes in weather conditions.

Returning to frictions between different nationalities and disciplines, I remember a situation at one of the Air Force stations. I was called to deal with an incident involving a Polish and English NCO, both were trainees. The Pole was called a 'bastard' during a light-hearted but heated argument. The Pole reported the incident to the British Commanding Officer, a Colonel; he treated the matter very seriously and wanted to deal with it through a military court. When I arrived he asked me whether for us to be called 'bastard' is a personal insult. I replied yes, nobody is allowed to insult family dignity. I succeeded in solving the problem amicably, the English NCO apologised and they went for a drink. At the end, the Colonel explained that 'bastard' in England is not used as an insult but rather a light-hearted dig, but he agreed that feelings and customs of other nationals had to be honoured.

I had the opportunity to compare our lifestyle with the English of various classes. Through the wife of Marshal Champion de Crespigny, I was invited to join high-class people, who were socially approachable by persons of the same class. In their company, I noticed a great deal of snobbism and old fashioned customs (not justified as 'lower' classes had often-higher moral standards and intelligence). But on the other side, they did not show their class supremacy towards subordinates, often helping them in difficult circumstances, never insulting their personal pride, appreciating their work.

At the end, of 1942, I asked to be transferred to the 304 Bomber Wing (Squadron) for operational sorties, which I had organised during the second half of 1940.

At first, the Inspectorate did not agree but renewed requests succeeded and I was transferred to the 304 Bomber Wing as a pilot. I did not ask for more, pilot duties satisfied me completely.

When I arrived at the Wing I found many changes. The Wing had suffered heavy losses. Not many had finished the full term of operational flights of thirty sorties/operations. Only a few of the old guard remained the others were newly trained in Great Britain. Thirty operational flights do not seem much, but they are arduous, physically and morally trying, against heavy AA defence on long range flights. Taking into consideration that on every bomber operation five percent of crews did not return, it is easy to see what the chances were of survival.

At the time 304 Bomber Wing was attached to the 'Coastal Command,' as intensive operations of the German U-boats were observed. The anti U-boats activities of the Coastal Command was so successful that the Germans formed a special long-range Air Force Fighter Unit to combat the activities of British Bomber Wings. Flights over the Ocean were by necessity conducted during the day, by single aircraft for the location of U-boats on the surface. This increased the danger from German fighters operating mainly in trios. During these flights I had no occasion to meet enemy U-boats but one situation I remember well when I was attacked by four long range JU88s. This flight was widely commented on by the Air Force in Great Britain. The flight started on the 9 February 1943 from Dale airfield in Wales. The first pilot at the time was Commander of Wellington's Squadron Captain Pilot Edmund Ladro. I was 2nd Pilot.

We were sent to combat German U-boats; these very long flights lasted up to ten hours. To be shot down over the Atlantic during such flights was certain death, for the chances to be picked up in a small dinghy from the vast ocean was very remote. We flew over the Bay of Biscay right of the shores of Spain. Flying out nothing happened. On the return flight, four long-range JU88s fighters unexpectedly attacked our Wellington with a crew of six. We descended instantly to just above the water in order to avoid being attacked from below. A battle commenced in which we had no reasonable chance. At a certain moment, one of the fighters parted from his company. Apparently, we must have hit him. With more fury, the remaining three attacked us. Our front gunner was severely wounded, the rear gunner had his target visor damaged. I was also wounded. I feel we cannot last much longer in this uneven fight. Then I was overcome by some sort of passion, an extreme feeling of anger. If we die, at least one of the Germans will have to die with us. Just then, one of the enemy aircraft descended for the next attack. I forced the machine up and flew in his direction. The distance between us diminished rapidly. At the last minute, the German lost his cool and turned. Whenever one of the enemy aircraft neared us, instantly I directed the Wellington against him. The battle lasted fifty-nine minutes. For nearly one hour, the Germans attacked furiously and we replied with the same kind. At last, the Germans had enough of the 'game'.

In the German's bulletin, the destruction of a single Wellington over the Bay of Biscay, which as usual was a lie. We were directed to land at an airfield near Cornwall, the name I do not remember. An ambulance was already waiting for the seriously wounded gunner. The airfield was also a long-range fighter base but without Polish units.

After leaving the Wellington, we were approached by their Squadron Leader D.L.Cartridge. Squeezing my hand he said, 'We succeeded in catching your Jerrys, when we met them we delivered them into the sea.'

The British Air Ministry organised a press conference with the participation of Captain Ladro, Squadron Leader Cartridge, as an example and myself of harmonious co-operation of Allies. The Daily Herald called me the oldest operational pilot of the Air Force (I was forty-five years old at the time). They called me 'Anton' for fear of reprisals against my family, I did not allow them to mention my name. It was astonishing to see so many holes in our plane without damage to the engines, fuel tanks and radio. As they say, 'we shoot and God carries the bullets.' Considering the supremacy in speed, armament and numbers of Germans, it still seems that apart from our manoeuvring, luck and God's providence was on our side.

During my service as a pilot with the 304 Bomber Wing, I learnt that my dear friend and colleague Major Jurek Iszkowski had volunteered to continue army service in Poland in the ranks of the AK Home Army (Underground Army). It comes to my mind that if I had completed my Operational Tour, I could have had a rest in Great Britain until the end of the war. But these prospects did not satisfy me. I thought that perhaps my duty is to continue the fight actively against the Germans. In this connection, I volunteered for service in the AK.

Perhaps I was motivated by the desire to help my wife, who according to information received, gave birth to our son in November 1939. I was aware of the risks involved but was not prepared to change my mind.

I later learnt in Poland about my wife. My wife lived at Miechówie near Kraków. After the Germans deported her, she stayed with cousin Pomianowski's family. My wife started to sell and buy in order to provide for her and our son Janusz. She also helped young volunteers to leave the country by illegal means in order to join the Polish Army in the west. Having been under suspicion, she was arrested by the German 'Gestapo' and after a few hours interrogation at Kraków ul. Montelupich. Later my wife was released. Perhaps my son, who smiled at the interrogators and played with their uniform buttons, evoked some sympathy for his mother.

Reverting to my petition to volunteer for service in the AK, the Polish Inspectorate agreed, in the end, to accept me on their 'secret' list of 'AK' volunteers.

Before sending me to Poland by air as a parachutist, I had to undergo special training in Great Britain in conspiracy action. The main training was conducted in Scotland, with strict exclusion of everybody not connected with training.

Training was theoretical and practical. Officers of the Intelligence and Diversion Services held lectures relating to the organisation and preparation of subversive action. Exercises were conducted in the art of parachuting, landing, concealment, approaches, masking of own movements, observation etc.

Physical training was hard, conducted in so-called 'Apes Forests'. Practical lessons were also provided for the construction of tools for demolition of objects and survival techniques. We were also trained in starting and driving railway engines and enemy aircraft Heinkel and Messerschmitts.

In April 1944, I was parachuted into Poland near Lublin. In the AK, I was assigned to organise Air Force Technical Services. Before the Uprising, I was nominated Commander of the Base 'Okęcie' (Air Force unit intended to occupy the airfield in the second phase).

After the collapse of Okęcie offensive, being in the region of dispersed units, I managed to get through to Szczęśliwie, where I finished the war.

The following is a short account of the history of my nearest family — the war did not pass us by.

From my early days, I remember the cordial and sincere family atmosphere. We were brought up in the spirit of patriotism, deeply believing that Poland will be reborn.

My mother comes from a teacher's family; her father was a freedom fighter during the 1863 Revolution.

My nearest family was numerous but for those days, not too big. There were seven of us — myself, my five brothers, and one sister. Only three of us survived the war, my sister Halina, brother, Sobiesław and I.

Władysław, the eldest, was killed in the Legion in 1916. Tadeusz was also in the Legion during the First World War but he survived. After that, he worked as a chief accountant in Częstochowa.

During the Second World War, Tadeusz belonged to the AK Home Army, he took an active part in the Warsaw Uprising. Later he contracted tuberculosis and died in 1945.

Younger than me, Eugeniusz was imprisoned, ill-treated in a concentration camp and died in Warsaw after escaping from the concentration camp. The fifth brother, Miscisław was taken prisoner in 1939 by the Russians and was murdered at Katyń. My youngest brother, Sobiesław, after finishing at Textile College worked for a big textile firm at Częstochowa.

During the Second World War, Sobiesław was an active member of the AK for which he was prosecuted by the Security Police (S.B.) of the PRL. My sister Halina's daughter married Captain Eugeniusz Dyaszynski after the First World War. Her husband was imprisoned by the Russians after the 1939 campaign and died in prison in doubtful circumstances. Their only son Jozef belonged to the AK and was killed during the occupation in the battle against Hitler's Germany. He was aged not fully twenty years. During the occupation, my sister Halina was arrested by the German Gestapo and spent a long time in a concentration camp. After the war, she worked in a state company.

After the war ended, I remained in Poland and was reunited with my wife and young son Janusz. I worked for many years for a mining industry, until my retirement.

Tragically for my wife and I, our son Janusz who had qualified as a doctor died in 1966, aged only twenty-seven years.

On 2 October 1984, Wing Commander Jan Biały passed away aged eighty-seven years.

Flight Lieutenant Bernard Buchwald

I was born in Poland on 15 May 1917. Since a young child, I had dreamed of flying.

My first flight was at the age of seventeen in a Wrona glider (wrona means a grey and black bird — a crow).

This was a very flimsy built glider. Before the flight, four men held it on each side of its wings with rubber ropes attached. Then as they ran down the hillside they would let go of the ropes at the appropriate time. At this point, the glider glided on the air. I felt like a bird in flight, as near to a bird as one could get. It was exhilarating. My trousers acted as flaps. The training took place over a pine-wooded area; warm pockets of air rose from the pine forest here and there as the glider, glided gracefully from one pocket to another.

After glider training, I became a Cadet at Dęblin. I qualified just before the outbreak of war.

After being ordered to leave Poland for Romania, I then travelled by ship to Great Britain.

In England, I was sent to Blackpool for training. In Blackpool, I was billeted with eleven other Polish airmen in a large boarding house along the promenade. The boarding house had two young boys living there, both insisted they were going to teach me English. In fact, my two young teachers were so determined that they made excellent teachers and taught their pupil very well in such a short time.

After training was completed came a posting to 316 Fighter Squadron on convoy patrol, taking off from Porth Reef the West Coast of Wales. Our squadron flew up to four sorties a morning, then up to four sorties the following afternoon. Sometimes we had a weekend off.

On one such weekend off, I remember the occasion very well. At seven pm feeling rather hungry, my friends and I from 316 Squadron wanted to go somewhere nice to eat. As I spoke the best English, I asked one of the British Officers if he could recommend somewhere.

He answered. 'Leave it to me I will organise something.'

Of he went returning a while later and announced. 'Everything is arranged.'

After a journey of about half an hour, we arrived at a large country house in very large well-kept grounds.

This cannot be the right place we all thought. The British Officer informed us it was. He told us it was an RAF Convalescent Home, that guests were permitted at weekends. Still unsure of whether we were in the right place or not we followed him in. The Flight Sergeant on duty showed us towards a large room.

The large room was a ballroom, which through a long hallway opened into a large circle at the end that had been turned into a dining hall. An RAF band was playing. Everywhere were ladies in fine evening gowns and gentlemen in dinner jackets. An Air Commodore was among the many people.

The food laid out on the tables was absolutely mouth watering. We looked at each other in our battledress, then towards the British Officer. He was still assuring us it was all right to enter. By this time, the sight of all the food was making us quite hungry. I asked my Commanding Officer if we should go in uninvited, he decided we should have a vote on it. All of us in the squadron decided yes. I think the food swayed the vote as our tummies were rumbling.

Our Commanding Officer Watchet Wilcheski led us in. As we entered the large room all eyes were upon us. We started to walk slowly towards the end of the room and sat down. The room was silent except for the band playing quietly. We all felt uneasy except for the British Officer who was enjoying tucking into the delicious looking food.

Wacek said to me, 'You must say something, you speak the best English.'

I got up and walked towards the Air Commodore, introduced myself, my Commanding Officer and the squadron, then asked for permission to stay. After a few seconds, he shook my hand and then announced out loud.

'These courageous Polish airmen are fighting alongside our British boys, it would be an honour for us if you would stay and enjoy the evening with us.'

The party went on until one-thirty am, an enjoyable evening was had by all.

On many occasions with 316 Squadron, as my English was so good, I acted as an interpreter. I had a small book with all my friend's British girlfriend's names and addresses in. Being a gentleman I never took advantage of the books contents, besides I had met a girl in Coventry I was very fond of.

Shot Down

On 12 April 1942 while flying on a sortie from RAF Northolt I was shot down.

Firing my Spitfire's guns at a Focke Wulf and hitting their target the enemy aircraft exploded into a mass of flames, I was enjoying the victory and for a second not fully concentrating on all around me. Then 'bang'. My Spitfire was becoming hotter and hotter in the cockpit, the indicator showing the red emergency. The next minute my aircraft started to shake, sweat pouring forth as I was becoming very hot indeed. My Spitfire was trailing lots of smoke and flames were appearing, with my engine on fire, I decided to bale out. This proved very difficult. As I tried to bale out I was thrown from one side in my cockpit and my Spitfire went into a flat spin. The centrifugal force prevented me from using my arms, legs, head, in fact, I could not move at all. My life began to flash before me, thoughts of my parents, my sister, my brothers entered my head. This is it, I thought. Then suddenly the centrifugal force eased my aircraft and it stopped spinning.

'Oh Lord, thank you.' I shouted out loud. Strangely, when faced with the worse, I just felt calm.

As my Spitfire hit the water it seemed to bounce as it landed on the sand, then hit a large concrete block in front of the German artillery on the French coast.

Hitting the concrete block, I was thrown forwards and sideways. The seat belts were unfastened. I had done that when up high when I had thought of baling out. I undid the parachute and jumped out of the cockpit. At that point I did not feel any pain. My poor faithful Spit 'E' for 'Eve' was smouldering with an occasional tongue of flames licking the side of her engine. Fire might shoot up at any moment.

'Run' I hesitated. Then thought again, 'run away'. Some twenty yards away on the edge of the beach the ground was rising and covered with thicket. Then about to run for it, I did a step or two forwards, when suddenly a wooden slab on a stake sprang up in my way. 'Achtung Minen' with a skull and crossbones on it. I halted. What a painful silence but for the delicate hissing of my dying Spitfire, a distant farewell, a burst of machine gun fire and engines, high revs in the sky. The soft murmur of the sea seemed to soothe and comfort me. Then the Germans appeared.

The Germans ran out of the thicket brandishing their rifles and shouting 'Hunde Hock.' Another party of them armed with short handled spades in their hands, they started to throw sand on the engine part of my smouldering Spitfire. They soon made her disappear under a mound of sand.

'Where are the mines?' I thought to myself.

A Major walked up to me, saluted, and in not bad English said,

'I am sorry to inform you that at this moment you are a prisoner of war of the German Wehrmacht.'

I did not quite grasp the idea why, then as the stress I had been under faded away and I was immediately seized with pain. Then, I noticed big gun barrels protruding from the thicket, a sea coast heavy artillery unit. Then they all saw my POLAND badge on my tunic shoulders. Some spiteful remarks must have started to raise as the Major's sharp words in German, thence put an immediate silence to them.

The German Major was smart and polite; he spoke good English and not bad French. He was the Commander of that stronghold built deep into the ground. Maybe parts of Atlantic wall? He took me down there and ordered his MD Officer to attend to me.

I was not in the best of shape. My left hip was aching with occasional shots of pain flashing down to my left knee that was swollen to the size of a football and blood was dripping down my chin. Then I remembered hitting the concrete anti-tank block. I had been thrown forward and sideways. In the former case my face had come in contact with the gun sight a bit too forcibly. My left knee had hit the compass in the latter case, the side force must have injured my back. After an hour or so, when I felt a little better, I was then sent over to the Calais Garrison Orderly Officer of the sector.

I had crashed some five miles off Calais. Imagine me flying over the place only an hour before!

They led me, or rather carried me, into the Orderly Officer's room, Clicking of heels and Hitler-Heil-Hitler shouting, and guttural words followed.

A Prussian looking monocled Hauptman listened to the Feldfebel motionless and wordless. Eventually he waved them away. After they had left, a movement of his hand invited me to sit down in an armchair near the wall. A huge portrait of Hitler was hanging above it. When I saw it, I hesitated and looked at the Hauptman. Something like a feeble smile ran through his face and he waved me to sit on the chair by the desk. Then he spoke, 'Ven did yuu eet yuuur last meal?'

I told him at once I felt hungry (I had my breakfast at seven am at Northolt and now it was past noon, of course, I did not tell him these details, only that I felt hungry).

He lifted the receiver of his field telephone and short gutturals followed. My body ached all over and I longed for something to lie down on. A knock at the door drew my attention off my body.

A soldier marched in. 'Heil Hitler.' He carried a kind of picnic basket covered with a white serviette and another one was hanging over his left arm. A waiter I thought, maybe from their Officers' Mess.

The movements of the Hauptman's hand made the soldier lay the serviette on the desk and unload the contents of the basket. He must have been a waiter in his civilian life as he laid the table professionally. When he had finished he stood to attention as if expecting to wait on me.

Hauptman's hand waved him out of the room. A click of the heels, 'Hitler' and he was gone.

The Hauptman then told me I had forty minutes to enjoy my last-before-the-end-of-the-war-Officer-becoming-meal. It was an excellent French déjeuner, a kind of brunch and I did enjoy it.

When I had finished he called the Officers' Mess. In no time, the same soldier marched in and the ceremony repeated. He cleared the table, picked up the basket, 'Hitlered' and vanished.

Hauptman looked at his watch and a hardly detectable smile ran over his lips.

Some five minutes later the door flung open and two black uniformed criminal-like individuals stormed into the room. 'Hitlering' repeated. Some words were exchanged and a harsh 'Raus' to me accompanied with a blow like push that sent me down to the floor. Then the Hauptman said something and one of the criminals helped me up and led me outside to the waiting black limousine.

I was taken to St. Omer Gestapo quarters. Decency and fairness finished. No good, no nonsense like medical care or a wash and shave. Interrogation, yes!

All through the evening and night I was dragged out of my cell and in again, out again, in again, every hour until the morning. Every time there were the same questions shouted out:

'Name, date of birth, place of birth, service number, where and when shot down?' The intimidating yells were unbearable. Also, I had a problem caused by the little book I always carried with me that had the names of my friend's girlfriends. Because of this book, the Germans at first thought I was a spy. I explained repeatedly about the book contents, fortunately in the end, they believed my story.

At noon on the second day, a piece of 'wurst,' a lump of black bread and a cup of some lukewarm liquid were shoved in. My hip and back were aching, my face and knee very swollen, I could hardly move.

Early morning on the third day, shouts and door slamming woke me up. 'Alle raus!'

The door flung open and a blow with a rifle butt sent me flying into the corridor right into the arms of a red-haired and red-bearded Squadron Leader. 'Biggin Hill,' he whispered, 'Northolt.' I reciprocated.

I was the only Pole among the lot of twelve British RAF Officers.

On foot we were then taken to the railway station, we were guarded by fierce dogs, machine guns and by what were supposed to be soldiers. Packed in one of the compartments of a third class passenger train with wooden benches and heavily guarded, we arrived at Cologne at night. We waited there on the platform for three and half-hours for another train for an unknown destination. Metal pillars were supporting the roof structures and the platform was lit by scarce blue painted bulbs. The redheaded Squadron Leader put his shirt down on the platform concrete and made me sit on it and leant me against one of the pillars.

I dozed off. It seemed to me then that I was dreaming again the same dream I had dreamt a month before.

I was somewhere in a dark place dimly illuminated by bluish-green light, and hard measured steps approaching from the darkness could be heard. Out emerged two strange looking knights, clad in armour with glittering breastplates in the shape of a crescent. Marching heavily past me, they looked sternly down on me and slowly disappeared. But the sound of their steps remained — it was even growing into a strange staccato and approaching.

I woke up with a painful jerk. There they were! No knights though clad in armour but a patrol of two stalwart German soldiers in helmets, with Tommy-guns in their hands hitting the concrete hard with their nailed boots. With crescents on their breasts! They were 'Field Gendarmerie' of which I had no idea. Another dream of mine that had come true.

A train arrived, stopped at the platform and we were yelled at to get in.

Our train journey's destination was Frankfurt-on-Main. To be precise, the Dulag Luft in the outskirts of town.

Prisoner of War

Prisoner of War! By Jove! I had never dreamed of anything of the kind. Nobody had, war was on and I was always fully aware that I might get killed in action or die of war wounds — but the knowledge was rather subconscious. For thinking about it was to any operational airmen the beginning of the end when he would sooner or later become unfit for flying. His reason would get unbalanced and fear would overpower him hampering his action and mind. It did not mean that he had never been scared — I had been. But the fear was more like uneasiness in the face of the unknown rather than panic. I vividly remember my first encounter with German fighters, Messerschmitt 109s.

The air was full of warnings from other pilots like 'four Messerschmitts five o'clock.' 'About twelve bandits some five thousand feet above — nine o'clock', etc. I kept screwing my head all around and saw nothing but Hurricanes. I felt more than uneasy. Although it was all gone the moment I spotted them. Besides the best remedy to overcome that kind of feeling was to understand, to get deep into the whole 'ego', the full conviction that the opponent was only the same, a human and was probably more scared than myself. That was a good help and philosophy to begin with.

Later I became devoid of any sense of that feeling, which on the one hand, was a positive state of mind but on the other hand it could lead to fatal imprudence. And here I was maybe a victim of lack of common sense or of that imprudence!

Well, man proposes but God disposes!

Dulag Luft II

Dulag Luft II was a German Air Force transit camp for prisoners of war. A reception and transition camp for most of the RAF flying personnel. Quite a neat place to look at although not every member of the Royal Airforce flying personnel shot down over Germany and German occupied territories had been directed to the place. Most of them, however, that were captured in France or in the Rhineland had.

The camp was well run, thanks to the British Senior Officer Squadron Leader Elliot, who was nearly a resident. His clever and tactful, though firm and diplomatic attitude towards the Germans did marvels. He had his ways and means to make the Germans carry into effect all the rights due to a prisoner of war on the grounds of international covenants. The camp was divided into two parts: the German Komendantur with the confinement- interrogation building for the newcomers and the general compound.

Immediately after our party arrived, Squadron Leader Elliot convinced the Germans that I should be sent to a hospital. They kept me there in a separate well-guarded room. After my experience with the St.Omer Gestapo functionaries and with the hardship of the journey, the hospital days seemed to me as paradise.

I could wash, shave and sleep, sleep all day and night. The food was excellent, ninety percent of it came from the International Red Cross parcels. I was moderately attended to.

When brought back to the Dulag, I fell at once into the hands of the Interrogation Officer. A Hauptman doubled faced boorish but pretending to be polite. He was beaming as if most delighted to see me, he entered my cell a meagre ten by five-foot den. A tin of fifty 'Players', a bar of 'Cadburys' chocolate and a box of matches were put down on the tiny table with a smile.

'It's for you Lieutenant Buchwald as a welcome gift on your return from the hospital. A few formalities and you will join your friends in the general compound.' He spoke perfect English.

He sat down on the only stool and I got on the bed. He presented an International Red Cross form pushed it towards me, then handed me a fountain pen and asked me to answer all the questions and sign the form.

Name, all right; surname, all right; date and place of birth, all right; the airfield you took off from, number of Squadron, the CO's name — I struck those off.

'Oh no, no, Herr Lieutenant. This must be filled in for the Red Cross purposes,' he put in hastily.

'Sorry Hauptman. I'm sure the Red Cross is not as much interested in military data as you are,' I retorted.

I signed and returned the form to him. 'Is this your final answer?' he asked. 'Yes, it is,' I replied.

'Alright,' he snarled. 'Maybe you will change your mind later.'

He snatched the form, the cigarettes, the chocolate, and the matches and went briskly up to the door.

'Guard,' he yelled. He slammed the quickly opened door and was off.

Yes, I thought that was genuinely like the haughty Germans.

Half an hour had not elapsed when I heard a hissing sound. Steam was getting into a huge radiator that ran from the small window up near the ceiling down to the floor, some ten foot by four. Soon I had to start taking off my garments one by one. Eventually, I lay on the board-bed dressed only in my skids.

Later, towards the evening, a pail was pushed in, this meant no outings to the lavatory. No food, or water for several days. 'Maybe you will change your mind later', I recalled the words of the so-called Master Race Representative.

I did not know how long I lay there swimming in my own sweat — first dozing then unconscious. I don't know what would have happened to me if not for a German sentry 'A Watchman' of Polish nationality. While on duty in the corridor, on the fourth day after the softening up started he entered my cell. He brought me back to consciousness and gave me some 'ersatz' coffee and fed me with some black dried bread. He kept doing this for the two following nights. He wouldn't tell me his name, he only said he was from Silesia.

When Hitler annexed Polish territories to his Reich, all their inhabitants, then German subjects were liable to the German military service. One of Poland's tragedies in that war was that on many a sector of the European front lines, Poles from one side fired at their brothers on the other side. Many such cases were known to happen at Monte Cassino. The Silesian advised me and insisted on that I should sham dead in front of 'that confounded Hauptman' as he called the Interrogation Officer

So when one day some time later, I knew the 'Hauptman' was standing over me, I heard him yell 'Arzt!'

I did not move and even tried not to breathe. A stir at the door and a cold metallic touch upon my chest, then a lift of my left eyelid and some gutturals. 'Alle raus' — the amiable 'Hauptman' let everybody know who was the Master there. The door slammed. I did not dare move. Some minutes later the door opened and someone entered. The stool shifted by a hand rapping on the board-bed. Something was laid on the stool then somebody sat on the edge of the board-bed and started shaking me. I continued shamming dead. Finally after some three or four minutes, I sighed and opened my eyes to narrow slits. A jar of 'ersatz' coffee, a cup what a luxury! A plate with slices of bread and butter — quite a royal banquet.

All that on the stool and a Wehrmacht corporal — what an honour — bending over me.

'You must drink and eat,' he said in German, which I more guessed than understood.

He started feeding me and I did my best to let some coffee pour down my chin and show the difficulty in eating the morsels of bread he cut for me with his clasp knife. He was very patient and fair to say, solicitous.

He kept coming every hour or so and looked quite happy to see me coming to life and improving. Every time he would bring a tray with some food on he would feed me.

Later in the evening the 'Artz' paid me a visit. He saluted me, looked into my eyes, saw my tongue, pressed my belly and started looking at me suspiciously. He did not say a word, however, and left the cell.

The next morning I was given quite a substantial meal and my battledress was returned to me. The same corporal supplied me with a piece of soap, a towel, and a safety razor and led me to the washroom. He stayed there all the time through my shower and shave, which took quite a long time, as my face was still sore. He then led me back to the cell and told me to dress. That really was an effort. I could hardly bend my swollen knee, my back was stiff and the hip was aching. The worst thing of all was trying to lace up my shoes; I couldn't and had to give up.

In the afternoon, I was purged to the general compound. The redheaded Squadron Leader greeted me heartily and took me to Squadron Leader Elliot right away. He had heard about me from the redhead and being worried kept asking the 'Hauptman' about me. The blinking German had assured him that as soon as my true identity had been checked I would join the others. Identity checking! A very peculiar way to do it. He then told me that my so-called 'checking' had taken nine days altogether. One day of interrogation, six days of softening up and two days of growing back in strength. Not bad!

I stayed in the Dulag for another fifteen days. I recovered entirely except for my back and hip those were still aching with occasional shooting pains and I was limping.

One evening Squadron Leader Elliot informed us that we would be given some Red Cross extra food, as on the following day we would be taken by train to Stalag Luft III, a prisoner of war camp in Sagan which was south-east of Berlin. Quite a journey. Again surrounded by dogs and soldiers with an armoured car in front and another one in the back of our column of fifty airmen, we were marched off to the railway station, packed into a carriage and whisked off. Destination Stalag Luft III, Sagan.

Stalag Luft III Sagan

Sagan has been a place of prisoner of war camps by tradition. In the time of the Napoleonic Wars, in the Prussian-French War and in the First World War there were camps.

As early as in September 1939, the so-called Mannschafts-Stammlager-Stalag VIII C was formed for private soldiers only. By 1941, there were over forty-five thousand French, Belgium, British, Yugoslavian, Italian and Russian soldiers. There were 'Branch Officers' of the Stalag VIII C in the nearby Kunau and Neuhammer which later took the name of Stalag 308 and then of Stalag VIII E with just below twenty thousand prisoners of war — mostly Russians. The youngest 'Branch Office' was Kriegsgefangenen Lager de Luftwaffe Nr III — called Stalag Luft III. It was founded in late autumn of 1941 and early spring of 1942. The compound was situated between Sagan and Carlswalde, a small settlement.

Sagan a small town between Berlin and Breslau on one of the railway lines supplying the eastern front.

'Ost Front' — a sinister phrase to any German soldier. To be sent there

was regarded as the heaviest punishment. Stalag Luft III was meant by the Germans to be a representative POW camp. They boasted about it and used it to show to any International Red Cross team visiting camps of that kind in the Reich. The standard of Stalag Luft III was purposely put much above the usual level. Consequently, the German administration behaved in a more civilised way and tried to observe International covenants. Thus, the 'kriegies' — colloquial from German 'Kriegsgefangenen', prisoner of war — in Stalag Luft III were much more privileged than in any other Stammlager. The camp was for the allied Air Force personnel only and was divided into two separate compounds, one for Officers and one for NCO's. The so-called privileges were nothing else but the rightful allowances due to a prisoner of war in accordance with International covenants. Hitler's Third Reich treated their prisoners of war in the way of graduation.

American and British Air Force were treated the best; Soviet Russians prisoners of war, the worst of all services.

Compounds for the Russian soldiers were very often open fields enclosed by barbed wire and guarded by wooden turrets with searchlights and machine guns. They were dying there in the thousands of cold, hunger, diseases and bullets.

The general attitude of Hitler's Reich towards prisoners of war was to limit their rights which had been guaranteed by international conventions. With the progress, however, of the Second World War and its results of the European fronts, which were bad prognostic of the Nazis fate. They not only tried to diminish the authority of the conventions but to ignore them as well. This often led to committing crimes of which Hitler's personal order the Sagan-Befehl was one of the heaviest. It concerned the RAF Officers who escaped from Stalag Luft III on the 24th March 1944, of whom fifty were murdered.

In Captivity Stalag Luft III

I joined the allied Air Force community in Stalag Luft III in the middle of May 1942.

In the inside of the compound behind the main entrance gate, there was a small crowd in RAF uniforms cheering the 'newcomers' up and welcoming them. When a friend was spotted the cheering was louder. Then I heard my name called out. I looked up and saw Tolo Łokuciewski of No. 303 Fighter Squadron, a Battle of Britain pilot. We were flying in the same Northolt Polish Wing when he was shot down on the 13 of March, a month earlier than I was.

'How good of you to come here, we badly need a fourth to play bridge,' he exclaimed.

I thought him a very lucky man to be behind the barbed wire and beyond the reach of my fists.

Stalag Luft III was staffed and controlled by the Luftwaffe being separate from the Army camps.

Everyone made his entrance to the inside compound in a manner peculiar to himself, more from a psychological than a materialistic point of view. New arrivals were sure to meet a friend or friends who had the misfortune to have flown too close to the German fighters or anti-aircraft artillery.

The arrival at Stalag Luft III permanent camp after the temporary stay at Dulag Luft was an amazing revelation in many ways. The newcomers always found friendliness, understanding and a helpful arm in their first dark days. 'All in the same boat' was the attitude, which became a tower of strength during many days of prison life. Everybody was helpful to everybody.

When I arrived at the camp it was called the east compound. The new compound, a larger one was under construction and about to be finished shortly, it was to be called the north compound.

All the RAF Officers from the east compound were moved to the north one in June and July 1942.

A year later an additional compound was built being the south compound, this was soon packed with the airmen of the United States of America Air Force only. It soon outnumbered the north compound.

At its northern side, there was the 'vorlager' kind of antechamber to the main camp. It was separated from the main compound with barbed wire of the same height, width and thickness as at the other sides. Heavily guarded fences also barred it from the outside world. The whole site was situated just below two miles from the centre of Sagan and it was surrounded with pinewoods. The trees were stubbed for security reasons. The site of the south and north compounds and the 'vorlager' covered about seventy acres. Along the northern side of the 'vorlager' ran a road.

'Vorlager' was the place of the German's guardroom, the hospital or rather a sick bay, prison and a coat store.

The RAF north compound had fifteen barrack blocks/wooden huts.

Each was about sixty yards long and twelve wide. A corridor ran through the middle and there were nine rooms each side of the corridor. The rooms were about fifteen by fifteen feet each and were supposed to room eight, but they usually roomed twelve. They were equipped with four two-tier bunks, later three-tier, a large wooden table, wooden stools, narrow cupboards-military type and a small stove set on a brick concrete flooring about three by three feet. At one end of each hut, there were two small single rooms for the seniors of the hut — RAF Officers.

There was also a washroom, a small kitchen and a primitive WC that was open for the night only.

There were also separate huts containing the camp kitchen, theatre, an education block, latrines and a fire pool.

At the southern end of the compound, there was the parade ground where the roll-calls took place at least twice a day. The ground was also used as a sports field. All the sides of the compound were equipped with sentry towers with machine guns, searchlights, a siren, and a telephone set connected with the Guardroom. Along with the main barbed wire fence, from the inside of the compound there ran a fifteen feet 'warning land' — a flat cleanly raked stretch of land guarded by a low warning wire. Anyone who would cross the wire could have been shot at without warning.

The RAF prisoners of war were the reflection of all the nationalities that made the allies then; British, Canadians, Australians, South Africans, New Zealanders, Polish, French, Belgians, Norwegians, Dutch, Czechoslovakians, Greeks and a Lithuanian. Airmen of the USA Air Force were at first with the RAF in the same compound and later in the south compound that was built especially for them.

New arrivals were usually split up into pairs and put into rooms with older prisoners. That was done by the inside-the-camp administration of the POWs. As the Polish airmen made quite a considerable number, the largest after the British Empire personnel, they occupied No. 107 hut all by themselves. This, of course, was consented to by the Senior British Officer — the SBO, who in the years 1942-1944 was Group Captain H. Massey. As a matter of fact, he lived in the end room of No. 107 Polish just behind the wall of the room I lived in.

Polish airmen at Stalag Luft III in 1943. Standing left to right - Bronisław Mickiewicz, Władysław Szczęśniewski, Zbigniew Gutowski, Stefan Kolodynski, Zbigniew Kustrzyński, Witold Łokuciewski, Eugeniusz Nowakiewicz, Wacław Wilczewski, Stefan Janus, Lech Xiezopolski, Stanisław Pietraszkiewicz, Roman Pentz, Emil Landsman and Czesław Daszuta. Sitting left to right - Bernard Buchwald, Stanisław Król, Jerzy Abierzchowski, and Stefan Maciewjewski. Photo: Permission of Bernard Buchwald.

On my first day in Stalag Luft III, I was directed to the Polish hut led by Tolo Łokuciewski. He took me to his room where there was an available bunk. The first man to meet me there was Squadron Leader Wacek Wilczewski, my Commanding Officer when in No.316 Squadron. He was shot down in November 1941. My other roommates at that time were Squadron Leader A. Kiewnarski*, Flight Lieutenant Z. Kustrzyński, Flying Officer W. Rekszczyc, Flying Officer C. Daszuta and Flying Officer H. Skalski (he was no relation to Stanisław Skalski the fighter ace).

Late afternoon on the same day, I met Squadron Leader Petro Pietraszkiewicz, the Commanding Officer of the Versailles Group in France that I was in. He was the Commanding Officer of No. 315 Polish Fighter Squadron when he was shot down in September 1941.

In a few days, I learned who was who and the dos and do nots of prison camp life.

Life was well-organised both by the Germans and much better by ourselves.

Twice sometimes four times a day, the camp was put on parade and counted by the Germans. After the morning parade, it was usual practice to read the notice boards. Here was posted the latest on the parcel situation, lists of parcels to be collected, lists of banned books to dampen the spirits of those who had been waiting to enjoy their favourite author. Sports fans had their lists of various leagues, cricket, soccer, and softball. In winter, some played ice hockey. Many studied various subjects, played in bands and orchestras or were involved with the theatre.

Everybody was interested in the news. We had two sources of the news, one was German and the other English. A wire broadcasting system, which was best received by the general kitchen, broadcast the German news. The German speaking part of our population gathered in front of the kitchen with notebooks and pencils at readiness to take down the news. The German radio was not the only means of getting the news, for tucked away in the walls there were three radio sets in operation. The sets were designed and built in the camp, every component was made by hand with available materials. Variable condensers were made from old biscuit tins cut to shape and insulated by melting down gramophone records; paper formers held coils wound to match the condensers, while a piece of paper with a pencil line acted as a resistor. The valve was the only component of a complete receiving station that was not manufactured in the camp without tools or special appliances. The news received on these sets was top secret and it was read to small groups throughout the camp under cover of every possible security measure. Duty pilots, lookouts were posted all over the compound and a system of signals allowed the paper containing the BBC news to circulate, or to be hidden, or destroyed should capture threaten. The German news, however, was openly discussed and a room set aside in the education block, where a large-scale map supplied by the Germans completely covering one wall, carried all the latest information as received via the German wireless and newspapers. This was known as the 'ops map' and very few prisoners failed to visit it daily and discuss the ever-changing fronts and compare them with the other 'true' news.

The story of Red Cross parcels had been a long one and anyone who had the misfortune of being without them has since realised that he owed his life and health to this meagre ten-pound parcel.

Without the Red Cross parcel the prisoner would have received from the Germans daily: four slices of black bread approximately a quarter of an inch thick, enough margarine to smear on two of them, enough jam to cover one slice, enough cheese to cover half a slice. Three or four potatoes of egg size, one dish of greasy vegetable soup at midday, as much nut coffee as he could drink.

His food parcel then was the food that kept him alive. When for six weeks in the summer of 1943 parcel supplies stopped the time was long enough to make every POW so weak that walking to the latrine was an effort that caused black and starry spots dancing in the eyes.

The parcels varied only slightly in content, although there was quite a difference between the parcels of different countries. There were British, Canadian and American food parcels. No prisoner would say that the Canadian parcel was better than the American was, or that either of these topped the British parcel but rather that the three together gave a greater variety of food. The food, however, became very tiresome and after many moths of bully beef and Spam, one longed for something else. That was why the prisoners were very active in having their small gardens with vegetables of which tomatoes and onions were the most cultivated ones for content of vitamins.

After some time of getting used to camp life, I went into the swing of certain activities that I thought were worth my time. I continued studying English. I became friendly with Tony Gordon, an Australian whose

English was very good his dialectic ability was high. We spent hundreds of hours together talking and discussing. I spent thousands of hours doing the English exercises he advised me to do. I did a lot of reading English books and a lot of writing. I think the teacher was satisfied with his pupil.

Another thing I became busy with was sport. I knew I had to keep fit and sports was also entertaining and kept you out of silly thoughts and ideas. I used to play soccer and softball in the spring, summer and autumn and in the winter, ice hockey. The kit was supplied by the International Red Cross and sometimes by the national organisation for aiding prisoners of war. The last hockey game I played at Sagan was the day before we were moved to exit in January 1945 when the Russian artillery pounding Breslau was heard.

Escape from Stalag Luft III Sagan

The X for escape organisation was something that had emerged from man's natural desire for freedom and liberty. A soldier's internal command when taken prisoner of war had always been to escape. Whether he did or not, whether he was successful or failed depended on many things and circumstances, of the individuality of the given man and luck.

Since my arrival in Stalag Luft III, there had been many escape attempts that involved hundreds of 'kriegies'. Only one of them was successful. Three English Officers: R. Codner, O. Philpot, and Eric Williams were those who managed to get out of the camp and reach Great Britain via Sweden.

It was in early autumn of 1942. One evening in their hut there was a discussion about ancient wars and when the topic was the Trojan War, one of them was struck by an idea. The Trojan horse a huge wooden horse had been built to get into Troy. Inside the horse, had hidden an armed party.

'Why not get out with the use of something like that?' was the suggestion. Soon an idea had been formed.

A vaulting horse had been built in sections and the sides were covered with pieces of plywood taken from packing cases in which the Red Cross parcels had been supplied. The structure was over four feet high and its base covered an area five by three feet. Each narrower side of the horse had two holes through which long bars of wood had been pushed to carry the whole thing out and in by four men. The men had to be quite hefty ones. When the horse was being carried out one of the prisoners would be inside it equipped with a short handle spade or rather something doing the job of a spade. He had a set of bags to put the sand in and section or two of wooden shafts, these were necessary to prevent sand collapsing during digging the tunnel. The shafts looked like a box without a top or bottom. Two pieces of wood were pressed into the ground to mark the corners of the horse and help the vaulters to place it always exactly in the same spot. While gymnastics were going on, the man inside was doing the digging, first the vertical shaft and then the tunnel itself. Although the horse was placed as close to the warning wire as possible to shorten the distance, the whole business was an exhausting job. The dug out sand was put into the bags and together with the digger carried inside the hut. Then the sand was distributed and hidden in various places around the compound. They all had been lucky enough that the guards did not get suspicious, instead, they seemed to be enjoying the gym. After several weeks of very hard work the tunnel was ready, and one night under cover of complete darkness the three got out of the camp. After quite a number of adventures, they managed to get to Sweden and then to Great Britain. After the escape, the Germans installed microphones under the line of the barbed wire fence some twelve feet deep.

All other attempts had been a failure and there were some cases of prisoners being shot. There were also prisoners who could not stand the captivity any longer and a number of total breakdowns had been observed. There were also some people who tried to escape without any notice on their own. This often collided with another organised scheme. To avoid that kind of situation to get the business organised, to build the morale of the prisoners of war to give hope and to keep them busy the X organisation was founded. Squadron Leader George Bushell was proclaimed its 'Big X' and Major George Harsh USAAF its 'Big S' for security. That was in March of 1943.

A great escape of about two hundred officers was planned by means of a great — the greatest tunnel in the history of prisoners of war camps. Although the main duty of the new Committee was to organise and co-ordinate works connected with digging tunnels, permission was sometimes granted to individuals or certain groups of prisoners of war to try to escape. This usually happened when circumstances were partially favourable. The aim was to keep the Germans on the alert. This, however, turned against the plans of the X Organisation; the Germans were too much on their guard. So all escaped were declared forbidden as work got concentrated on building tunnels. The plan was to build three simultaneously; they were coded 'Tom', 'Dick' and 'Harry'. The depth of digging should be sufficient to secure the work from being detected by the installed microphones. 'Tom' and 'Dick' were to run west and 'Harry' north. Consequently, 'Tom' was to be about fifty yards long, 'Dick' about seventy, and 'Harry' about a hundred and twenty yards long.

'Harry' then was the most ambitious enterprise and the work on it was calculated to last a year.

It all had to be top secret. Hundreds of people amounting to nearly a thousand were engaged in the job of the tunnels and everything was usually well run. Although there were some hard nuts to crack, they were all overcome. The hardest three were entrances to the vertical shafts, airing of the tunnels and the distribution and hiding of huge amounts of the dug out sand.

The prisoner of war's experience taught that most tunnels had been discovered because their entrances were neither properly situated nor camouflaged. Our barracks were built on short supporting stakes of wood or brick high enough for a man to crawl under and inspect. Under the washrooms however and also under each stove, there were fundaments of concrete or brick or both. So it was decided that all the entrances to the shafts should be made in the area of brick and concrete. Thus, 'Tom' would have its entrance just by the chimney of the barrack kitchen, 'Dick' in the flooring of the washroom and 'Harry' under the stove in one of the rooms.

The job and work that had been done in connection with the tunnels spread the fame of many a 'kriegie' in Stalag Luft III Sagan out.

Polish prisoners of war had their share too. Flight Lieutenant Bronek Mickiewicz (Mick) of my No. 316 Squadron of the Pembrey time, became an expert in making and camouflaging the entrances. Flying Officer Stanisław Z. Król* of No. 315 Polish Fighter Squadron was one of the skilled diggers. Flying Officer Włodzimierz Kolanowski (Kola)* of No .301 Polish Bomber Squadron was the first hand in Desmond Plunkett's map copying business.

Flying Officer Paweł Tobolski* of No. 301 Polish Bomber Squadron whose perfect knowledge of German was used to converse with the guards and to get out of them as much information as possible on the one hand and to spread false news on the other hand.

Airing of the tunnels was another important item. The longer the tunnel was the less air it contained and stuffier it became. 'Necessity is the mother of invention' goes the proverb.

Airmen kit bags or rather the canvas they were made from, properly impregnated with hot oil (margarine) was made into a longish tube strengthened by wooden ribs. Each end of it was shut with a plate of wood in which two valves were mounted inlet and outlet. A special handle allowed the operator to compress or decompress the tube and thus suck the air in or let it out. The pipelines ran along the sides of the tunnel covered with a ten-inch layer of sand. The pipeline was made from tins joined with straps of impregnated paper.

Distribution and hiding of the dug out sand was done by at least a hundred strong party of 'penguins'. Sleeves of shirts and pyjama jackets were cut off and made into cone shaped bags, a pair of them was joined with a five-foot long strap at the wider opening and had a pin at the other cone end. The pin had a string attached that reached the trouser pocket. When a 'penguin' was given at the distribution place allotted to him the pair of bags containing the sand, he put the strap around his neck and let the bags into his trouser legs. His trouser pockets had their bottoms cut open so he was able to put his hands inside then hold the pin strings, which he would pull at the right moment at the right place and let the sand out.

Each of them knew very well when and where to do it. He would empty the bags among a group of other prisoners who would immediately shuffle it and stamp it into the soil. He would carry the bags to a place like the small gardens where the sand would be dug in. Or he could also go inside the theatre building where the sand would be put under the flooring at once. There were various places, ways and means to hide the sand. Circumstances governed their choice. Sometimes the whole business had to be stopped because of some unfavourable conditions, like sudden searches or prolonged roll-calls done by the Germans. Those who carried the bags developed a special kind of walk which some called a 'penguins' walk the name stuck to them.

To organise an escape on such a large scale required more than just to build a tunnel. Clothes had to be altered and coloured also the type and style of them. Escapees-to-be had to be supplied with documents, passes, maps, compasses and especially nutritious food rations packed in small containers. It required the work of hundreds of men.

Original documents were either stolen or bartered. A party of men who called themselves 'Dean & Dawson' did copying, they named themselves after the well-known English travel office.

The Sagan 'D&D' had been organised by G. Wallen, A. Cassie, and H. Picard.

Compasses were manufactured under the supervision of Flight Lieutenant Albert Hake.

Flight Lieutenant C. Hall ran photo atelier. The camera and other necessary materials were supplied by cunningly roping in a German NCO.

Flight Lieutenant Gordon Brettell was the chief producer of stamps made out of rubber shoe heels.

A thousand people were engaged in the preparation of the 'Great Escape' for a year.

'Tom' was well under way in the middle of 1943, when it was decided to quicken work on it. By the time the Germans were about to finish the south compound where they meant to put the entire American airmen.

Many of the Americans were deeply engaged in the X Organisation and wanted to get out by 'Tom' before they should be moved. So work on the other tunnels was suspended and totally concentrated on 'Tom'.

The Germans, however, were suspicious and had a feeling that there was something in the wind. Search after search took place. Their stubbornness and persistence were unbelievable and unfortunately, led to success.

One day during another special search, one of the guards who was hitting the sides of the chimney with a crowbar heard a changed sound. He hit it again harder and a piece of concrete broke off being a part of 'Tom's' trap appeared under it. After the entrance was eventually opened, German Officers and NCOs went down the tunnel one by one to 'visit' the 'marvel' of 'Kriegies' technique.

German Officers, NCOs, and security personnel from other Stalags were arriving in their dozens to see and to know how. Finally, they blew 'Tom' up.

Having found 'Tom', the Germans were for the time being convinced that there was no other tunnel under construction.

The X organisation took advantage of the German's belief and pushed forward the work on 'Harry' only. 'Dick' was set aside as a reserve if needed.

'Harry' soon became even a much higher 'marvel' of 'Kriegies' technique than 'Tom'.

The diggers required air and light. I have already described the former and now for the latter. At the beginning, light in the tunnels was supplied from primitive oil lamps being a tin filled with melted margarine and thread. While burning they consumed quite a lot of oxygen and emitted unpleasant fumes. Germans themselves helped to solve the problem. They had decided to enlighten the 'Kriegsgefangenen' about the wonderful successes of their Wehrmacht. To do so they installed a wire broadcasting system in the compound. To appropriate a sufficient length of wire and some useful materials on the occasion was an easy job for the X people. The German electricians were almost stunned to death when they found two drums of electric cable some eight hundred yards long had simply 'evaporated'. They must have guessed what had happened but were afraid to report to their seniors. No doubt in fear of being sent to the Eastern Front, for neglect of duty.

To get the bulbs and to connect the whole thing to the camps electric system was a piece of cake. Electric light in the tunnel was a great help to those working inside it. Flight Lieutenant McIntosh, a Scotsman; Flying Officer Muller, a Norwegian; and Flight Lieutenant Travis, a Rhodesian, were the brains of all the mining business, planning, designing and manufacturing of a variety of tools and devices.

'Harry' was getting on nicely and in the middle of March 1944, it was 356 feet long that the 'brains' declared sufficient. The escape was scheduled for the night of 24-25 March. Two hundred officers were supposed to get out. By unfortunate or fortunate coincidences, only seventy-six managed to escape.

Out of that number, there were only three officers, whose escape was a success. Two Norwegians, Flying Officer Jens Muller and Pilot Officer Per Bergsland, who while in Stalag Luft III was known under the name of Rockland; and Flight Lieutenant Bram van der Stok, a Dutchman. All the rest were captured by the German Gestapo and fifty were shot in cold, treacherous, murderous bandit-like-blood.

The fifty were twenty-two British, six Polish, six Canadian, four Australian, three South Africain, two New Zealanders, two Norwegians, one Lithuanian, one French, one Czech, one Greek, and one Belgian.

Their ashes are buried in separate graves in Poznań Citadel Cemetery where they had been transferred to from the Sagan Vault. Designed by

Flight Lieutenant Todd by the perseverance of Mr Joe Walker, a British Consul in Poland in the fifties.

The murders, the criminals in uniform claimed and tried to explain was that the captured fifty prisoners put up a resistance and tried to escape again. Trails after the war proved the German Gestapo's crime entirely.

The cold-blooded murder of the fifty POWs of Stalag Luft III was one of the worst crimes committed by the fighting forces in the Second World War. The worst one was the shooting/murder of several thousand Polish Officers by the Soviets at Katyń in 1940.

Liberation — Return to Great Britain

First day back in Britain after being a prisoner of war. As the Lancasters left Germany, flying over Holland and across the Channel, the prisoners of war of Stalag Luft III left forever, they hoped, the ravages of war and their wired bound world. I was aboard a Lancaster that touched down on English soil one thousand one hundred and twenty days and eight hours after those in my Spitfire had left it.

The first day back in Britain after being liberated from Sagan is not a day I shall forget. The sight that was to greet me is one I will always remember as I arrived at the reception camp. A WAAF greeted each man with a hug and a welcoming kiss. The hangars had been decorated so beautifully with flowers everywhere, the hangars had been turned into large dining areas. The tables were covered with pure white table clothes with each place setting laid out correctly. On each man's plate was a telegram from King George VI welcoming us back to Britain. The meal was grand. After our meal we were taken by buses to a prisoner of war reception camp, we arrived there around midnight. Most of us were still wearing our pyjamas that we had left the prisoner of war camp in. We were then asked to remove our personal objects before taking showers and to hand over all clothes we had at the prisoner of war camp. Our pyjamas were taken away and burnt.

The following morning after breakfast we were shown along narrow wooden tunnels. The Intelligence Officers asked us many questions. When they were sure you were who you said you were, they would let you pass. More arrows followed, which lead to the clothing section. Each man was redressed in battle uniform, any alterations were made on the spot by machinists. Everyone's photo was taken.

Each man was given a spare set of clothes and shoes. After which, each man was given £50 cash, one months' ration card, a railway and bus ticket for wherever one wished to go in Britain. A leave pass for twenty-eight days, after which leave was up for each man and you had to report back to Blackpool.

All the above procedure took place in just two hours in which time about four hundred of us passed through.

In June 1945, I married the girl I had met in Coventry and fallen in love with during the war.

I remained in the RAF in the Polish Resettlement Corps, at the same time studying English at Cambridge proficiency level.

During the war in Poland, my sister and one of my brothers died. One of my brothers, who was in the AK Home Army, survived. My parents survived although, my father had a very narrow escape after being arrested by the Germans whereupon he faced a firing squad. Making a bid for freedom at the last minute my father ran off, escaping the bullets and was not recaptured.

By 1947, my wife and I had two young daughters. I returned to Poland in June 1947 to look for work and somewhere for my family to live. I planned to fetch my wife and children from England to Poland once settled. The Consul of the Polish Consulate General in London assured me that there would be no difficulty in getting a passport from Poland. I naively believed him. Instead, I was refused the passport, put under arrest and later under the rough vigilance of the security services in Poland held for a while.

I had to report to the security people every week, not sure whether of being released after five minutes, five hours, five days, five weeks, many months, even years or, if ever.

I could not finish my studies that I had started in England, as the Department of English at Poznań University was closed by the authority for imaginary political reasons.

Unable to find work, I was regarded as a dangerously suspected person (contra-revolutionary). Automatically, my family became split, my wife and two daughters in England. I unable to get out of Poland. My wife refused to come to live in Poland where there was no democratic freedom. I could not join her in England as I was watched and guarded by security and had no passport. It broke my heart to be separated, I believed at the time, forever from my wife and two young daughters. As a father, never would I be able to have the joy of watching my children grow and living with them as part of their lives.

For two years I had no work, earning just enough money by giving English lessons in secret.

In 1949, I managed to get a job at the Foreign Department of Poznań International Fair.

Three years later a security man joined and I was fired. Managers at that time were asked not to employ 'dangerous' men like myself. Very few were honest enough to ignore the instructions.

After a while a friend of mine found me a job in a state-run engineering firm, I remained there for sixteen years. At that time running English classes in my spare hours.

Later, I was asked to join the teaching staff at the newly restored Department of English at Poznań University.

My dream to become an English teacher was to come true. After a three-year course, I completed my studies gaining my MA in 1970 and PhD in 1976. I was promoted to a Lecturer.

I had remarried during my later life. In 1979, I retired for three years due to ill health. When recovered, I went back to work part-time until I fully retired.

Two of the happiest days in my later life were when Poland gained her independence fifty years after the Second World War had begun, at last, a chance for Polish people to begin to live free.

The other joyous occasion was when I came to England and was reunited with my two daughters after so many years apart. I have since become a grandfather.

In my retirement, I have written about my war-time experiences and had a book published on Squadron No. 316 that I flew in. My wife and I have a little place in the countryside in Poland, where we often visit in the summer. It is very quiet in our little summerhouse; we grow a few vegetables and soft fruits. We enjoy watching the birds and wildlife in our retirement.

Bernard Buchwald died 31 December 2013 and is buried in Poznań, Poland.

During the escape from Stalag Luft III, immortalised in the film The 'Great Escape', seventy-six men escaped — three got away, twenty-three were returned to other camps. The remaining fifty were captured and executed in cold blood by the Gestapo. Six of the fifty were Polish pilots, of which three are mentioned in Bernard Buchwald's memoir and are shown by an asterisk* by their name (see page 191).

Flight Lieutenant Kazimierz Karaszewski

At the beginning of the 20th century my parents, who came from Suwalki a region of Poland bordering with Lithuania, found themselves in Russia.

Just before the Great War my father was serving as an Officer on a Russian Tsarist warship of the Black Sea Fleet. My mother was staying in Russia in Moscow, where I was born on 26th April 1918.

Poland, at last, became a free state and my father served in the 28th Regiment of the Light Artillery in Dęblin, where also he was an Officer at the flying School later called the 'School of Young Eagles'.

When a young boy, I often observed strange machines overhead and from those times a great desire to try such an adventure came into my mind.

Soon my father was posted in 1927 to Ostrołęka where he was to be in charge of a battery of the 12th Light Horse Artillery Unit.

I graduated to Grammar School and began lessons at a local secondary school named King Stanisław Leszczynski Memorial. In May 1938, I passed with success the 'Maturity Examination' and not without difficulties, joined the beloved Dęblin Air Force School.

During my time spent at secondary school besides my normal education programme, I never forgot my souvenirs from my childhood. I started my 'flying' from organising a model aircraft circle with my school mates. We were producing all kinds of 'flying wonders' with rubber propulsion.

During the years of 1935 to 1937, I was lucky enough to join a special glider course in the Polish lower mountains near a place called Ustianowa. It was there that I gained in succession, a glider pilot's classes 'A' and 'B', after which I proudly wore a special badge of three seagulls. From those times, I remember to this day my first real flight on a glider 'Wrona' a

Crow. My first flight in a 'Wrona' was over an area of high spruce forest. Up to that event, our group had its training over open lawns where a glider went with its pilot up into the air a few metres. We were safe all the time being able to land immediately, practically at any given time. These jumps were no longer than some fifty to one hundred metres. Each take off was performed with the help of long strong rubber lines pulled by eight or ten other pilots and later running sideways/ forward at an angle of some thirty degrees.

An instructor leading our team up the mountain arranged the flight over the woods. To our surprise higher and higher, bypassing a large belt of the woods. That was really a first fear and first victory! After when landing safely down the hill on the large grass field, I could not stop looking into the clouds where in my young imagination I saw the smiling face of Our Lady, who must lead me safely through all the approaching war storms — I could not resist saying a prayer of thanks.

In 1938, I was lucky again to join a motor course on RWD-8 light aircraft, where an additional sensation came, a smell of petrol fumes! Yes, at last there was a real 'aeroplane', real flying. Take off, landings, various manoeuvres in the air, also cross-country flying at different heights. To say one word to describe it all is 'delight'! My enjoyment of the smell of petrol fumes comes from in the early thirties when I was also engaged in thinking of working with machine driven vehicles but planes were always my first choice. I used to follow the clouds of smoke that came from passing cars in order to enjoy the smell of petrol.

Turning back to my early childhood, I must confess that a great influence on me as a young boy was the movies in Ostrołęka. The cinema in Ostrołęka showed often, films on the First World War's events. Many times the dogfights over France between the RFC pilots; French and Germans were exposed. Such air duels and battles at the cinema were accompanied by music specially chosen to underline the awe of air clashes! The view of a German Albatross or Fokker going down in flames was 'amazing'!'

It is unbelievable but from those times one melody would always accompany me in my head in future flights over the English Channel, North Sea or Germany and that was Franz von Suppe's overture, 'Light Cavalry'. One detail from those film performances was the beautiful two-wing RAF pilot badge often presented to British pilots wearing it proudly over their upper uniform pocket. In my life, I was lucky to wear one too.

My life of numerous adventures was often accompanied by sports events especially when younger and many situations loaded with humour. Perhaps I was one of those lucky boys in between the war period because my father being a professional Artillery Officer, I was sufficiently endowed for him to let his son 'use the world'.

Before I joined the Air Force I enjoyed many sports, playing tennis with my schoolmates and also elderly people, often I went hunting for hares, foxes, ducks, partridge etc., using my Belgian FN 16 bore two barrel gun. I made many interesting water excursions down Polish rivers and lakes in my own canoe. Lengthy bicycle trips. In the wintertime sledge rides, ice-skating and skiing.

Another detail of my young life 'added fire to oil', in joining the modern army was an accident with a horse. My father's Artillery Unit in those times was, of course, full of horses. All officers and artillerymen were riding horses; it took six horses to pull one of those 75mm guns. Obviously, I often used to ride a horse accompanied by my father. On one occasion he asked me to do my training by myself on a horse not far from the stables. Sitting on the horse at first it moved slowly, then to a sort of trot and then a gallop. Near the stables a horse gave a type of loud voice, maybe well understandable for my 'wee' horse because it replied in a some different way, pricking up its ears and rising on its hind legs almost on its tail. In a second, it smashed its head forward landing me on the ground, 'on three points' it rushed galloping towards its companion that was still neighing. I lifted my sore body from the ground and swore loudly 'never again to mount that savage living brute!'

To the Air Force

After theoretical exams at Dęblin, all future Cadets had to be examined thoroughly by numerous specialists at Warsaw Medical Examinee board for Flying Personnel. In Polish it was in short called 'CBLL' — in the Polish language almost similar word was 'cebula' which is onion! So everybody who passed with success all the tests we were saying: 'Oh, he has had huge luck with 'Cebula'! When I found myself there, some five or seven candidates like me were going from one room to another to see different doctors.

We were dressed as Adam with white gowns only, we were sent into the

X-ray room. At that time, the X-ray room was very dark. The doctor could see everyone clearly but once we got inside it felt almost as if being blind. One of my colleagues, unfortunately, hooked a bunch of cables on the floor with his leg and fell down like a tree trunk. The doctor shouted angrily. 'Where are you going you ram?'

Poor fellow sprang up from the floor to attention and replied, 'To the Air Force, Sir.' His answer made the physician laugh and, of course, all us sky heroes laughed too.

In the autumn of 1938, all who were lucky enough to join the pilot's ranks in Dęblin had to undertake heavy infantry training with one of the infantry regiments during October, November and December.

After such an unpleasant period in infantry regiments training as mentioned before, horses and I did not mix. I was then finally posted to Dęblin in January 1939.

To graduate from the Officers' Pilot School for Eaglets in normal conditions took three years. Each Cadet after three years of training was obtaining the rank of a Pilot Officer of fighter or bomber speciality and joined one of the six Polish Air Force Regiments as it was called then.

The year of 1939 was unusual. From March onwards the German threat against Poland was increasing day after day. Our Command, in order to prepare more pilots to be ready to fight the probable invaders, changed the training programme; the two first year study squadrons were reorganised this way.

I found myself amongst those who had something to do with flying before going to Dęblin. Our squadron, then in March 1939, started intensive training flying PWS-26 bi-twin winged aerobatic aircraft, instead of attending many lectures inside school premises and lengthy learning of theory.

In the summer of 1939, our School Squadron No. 2 was divided into two parts: fighters and bombers.

I got the order to join the first group and we started the quick training on PWS-10 aircraft, then the famous all metal P-7, until the day when Hitlerite hordes invaded Poland.

Although we were all ready to go immediately to meet the invaders, the tears were in our eyes — this was only because there were not enough planes for all of us.

Continuing the Fight
From Poland to Romania to France

As it is known from later revelations some air force cadets from Dęblin in the year 1939, in order to reinforce six Polish Air Force Regiments, were evacuated to Romania. In Bucharest, they were to be trained on English fighter aircraft, Hurricanes; and the French planes, Moranes.

Evacuation was carried out rarely by travelling on coach or trains mainly on foot or upon horse driven carts. Flying Officer Witold Urbanowicz led our group of fifty cadets; later he was to become the famous Polish leader of No. 303 Polish Fighter Squadron in the Battle of Britain. Armed with light infantry rifles, we were approaching our southern border under constant attacks by the Luftwaffe. Making our way through burning villages, people crying in despair against Hitlerite bandits — holding on their stupid belts their stupid inscription 'Gott Mit Uns'! We saw low flying Messerschmitts 109s machine gunning civilians, passing columns of refugees, single animals in fields Ostrołęka — everything that Hitler's heroes saw moving or not moving, they fired at.

We reached the Romanian border on 17 September 1939, on the day the Soviet Army invaded Poland from the east. We were very lucky not to join the Katyń disaster. The border we passed was called Kuty.

Because before 1939 a Military Alliance tied Poland and Romania, our Air Force Command did not know whether we had to pass as military units or civilians.

During the night we received an order to change our uniforms into civilian jackets, this action was practically undertaken by changing the buttons only. The latest order received after this was to change back to uniforms; hence, we crossed the border as soldiers, throwing our rifles on a big pile.

Almost everyone was crying/weeping realising the Polish-Romanian alliance was only a theatrical farce, not a reality. We were pushed in railway goods wagons and sent to an internment camp in a place called Slatina by the Danube River. For the first time, we were located in dark ugly barracks room with primitive beds, where straw mattresses were richly loaded with bed bugs and different insects.

Our Government in exile had already started arranging the strategy of how to move the flying and technical personnel from Romania to France in order to join General Sikorski's forces.

I found myself in charge of a group of ten pilot-cadets. We were given false documents stating that we were students from different high schools. We received some 'lei' Romanian currency and were told to try to escape heading for Constanţa, a big Black Sea Port.

In Romania, the bribery and corruption were 'a tradition'; one of our colleagues offered a cigarette to a guard by the camp's gate and the nine others of our group passed freely by with our modest bundles.

Outside, we took a horse cab, when in town we threw our military caps over some garden fences of houses. By a railway station shop, we made an exchange deal with our military equipment to dress as civilians.

We were lucky enough to buy without any trouble railway tickets to Constanţa. We had to take another train from Bucharest, Romania's capital. While walking about the station hall our shoes, which were affixed with special flat nails for the protection of the leather, produced such a noise. This noise was very noticeable to other passengers awaiting trains. But fortunately, we avoided arrest not being discovered by the numerous 'fifth column' agents looking for escaped soldiers.

We got onto the right train and after a long journey along the Danube, arrived at Constanţa Railway Station.

A man met us, he was a Polish Air Force officer in civilian clothing. Without hesitating, he ordered us immediately not to be long upon the platform but to go outside, to take a taxi to the nearby seaside-bathing centre of Eforie. It was October 1939 and the water in the Black Sea was so warm that we enjoyed our first good bath after quite a while since leaving Dęblin.

Under the command of Mr Waltera who was a captain in the Polish Air Force, we were located in different villas as students where we were able to rest.

A few days later, we were told to move southwards until we reached a little seaside port in the town of Balchik. Balchik seemed a very interesting place situated on picturesque hills that were mainly inhabited by Turks.

We were told that from Balchik we would later embark on a ship that would take us on 'Sikorski's Way'. Thus, it happened on 15 October 1939. The evacuation of Romania for some of us in the Polish Air Force was carried out on a goods ship named 'Nicolaos' of Greek origin and of a very mixed crew of 'pirates' appearance. The Polish Government in exile in Bucharest paid off the ship.

Usually, the ship carried coal; it was reshaped to take many hundreds of passengers. Of these, practically seven hundred were airmen, flying personnel and mechanics; there were also some soldiers from technical units, tanks and artillery units etc. From our horrors of the Polish Campaign, this was a pleasure trip through the Black Sea, Dardanelles, Bosphorus, Sea Marmara, and the Mediterranean Sea to Beyrouth [Beirut] at that time a French colony of Syria, where we were taken over by French Colonial Forces Artillery Regiment.

When I mentioned this was a pleasure trip aboard the 'Nicolaos', there was one rather unpleasant side to the journey — the food. While sailing, we were offered by the crew some goats cheese of doubtful origin and quality, very dirty water and a little amount of dry bread. The goat's cheese and dirty water caused me quite a bad stomach at the time (later in 1943 led to a trip to Ely Hospital in England).

In Beyrouth, after being welcomed at the pier by some French Red Cross ladies with a glass of beer and a packet of French 'Gauloises' cigarettes, we were taken by lorries to the French Colonial Artillery barracks in town. At the gate an orchestra met us playing the French quick military march, their smiling faces and eyes twinkling made us feel welcome. The meal prepared in Beyrouth barracks for the whole transport was consumed at lightning speed by one-third of the newcomers from Poland.

The next day was a solemn open-air R.C Mass that was conducted by our forces Chief Chaplain Rev. Bishop X.B. Gawlina after which we all embarked on the French liner 'Ville de Strasbourg' throughout the Mediterranean Sea to Marseilles.

After a short stay at Istres Airfield, we went by train to Lyon by Rhône where most of us were located at Bron Air Force airfield and in the quarters of the late Lyon's International Fair area by Rhône.

During my time in France, I was proud to assist others in the design of the Polish Air Force Standard.

Training and Flying in Great Britain

In England, along with many other Polish airmen, I found myself sent to Blackpool in Lancashire.

We were billeted in various boarding houses or homes, mostly along the famous 'promenade'. During that time, we felt completely isolated from the war. The British hospitality and friendship shown to us were wonderful. Of course, the language had difficulties but the hands of the English were *always there to help. Many of us attended the wonderful dances, some of which were a marvellous scene for us when the orchestra would stop playing. Then complete darkness upon the dance floor, after which would appear searchlights showing the organ emerging from the ground. Then fashionable melodies were played at that time Tangos, Lambeth Walks, Foxtrots a slow Foxtrot and Waltzes. It seemed as a different world from the hell we had witnessed in Poland and France; a hell that was to arrive soon to many towns and cities in Great Britain.*

Identity card issued by the Royal Air Force to Kazimierz Karaszewski, dated 14 Sep 1940. Photo: Permission of Kazimierz Karaszewski.

Day after day the new organisation of our flying personnel and mechanics were being formed into new units, squadrons, sections, services etc.

On the 9 November 1940 according to my Pilot's Flying Log Book, I left English soil for the first time.

I flew in a double seater Magister R.1922 for a dual type! This took place flying from RAF Station Kingstown, Carlisle; after two hours flying I was back in Blackpool.

No more vacation time in Blackpool. For two months I trained happily and qualified for further training with the RAF at Hucknall near Nottingham. On 15 January 1941, I flew this time in a Magister R.1921 with Flying Officer Anderson. After a few days, I flew duals on type, landings, circuits, and aerobatics as a second pilot.

On the 10 of February 1941, I flew in a true aircraft where I flew duals on type this was in a Fairey Battle. That was something. It had a retractable carriage, changeable airscrew pitch, flaps, trim and speed nothing to compare with any other plane I had the pleasure to fly in.

At first, some Polish pilots had some difficulty to get friendly with these modern aircraft devices, but soon it was all accepted with great approval.

An interesting detail of flying training, which was a great help to all of us, was the rule to memorise a most important prayer the mysterious word; 'PUAFT'!

I still have such a great admiration to the English instructors of introducing this 'prayer' to flying training. Training is a necessity, which was most helpful, I am certain, to many pilots who had trained during the war. Our 'professors' often examined us. If we remembered this mysterious word 'PUAFT' and most importantly, the meaning of the five letters that made the word it could save a pilot's life. Well, with great regret I must admit that in spite of reading many pilots relations and other publications, have never noticed this very simple and yet so important factor among others.

The meaning of the word was so simple — P = Petrol; U = Undercarriage; A = Airscrew; F = Flaps; T = Trim.

I am certain this 'prayer' saved many RAF and PAF pilots from avoiding making flying mistakes during the difficult and often so nervous years of the war.

Each machine had so many indicators, different instruments panels, handles, buttons to press etc and to look at them almost all the time during flying was obviously difficult.

Most important actions were hidden in the magic words of 'PUAFT.'

1. *Petrol — all manipulations concerned with the fuel ignition, tanks capacity etc.*
2. *Undercarriage — up during flight and remember when approaching the land, otherwise you've had it.*
3. *Airscrew — start and landing fine and in the air course pitch or as the instructions were.*

4. *Flaps — for start Fairey Battle for instance 15 down and on landing, of course, all down.*

5. *Trim — this was to correct the flight direction precisely using the control stick and elevator just by a delicate touch.*

Whoever invented the 'PUAFT' word should have some kind of monument built and named after them.

We Poles all knew of the British sense of humour but what some of us experienced while at RAF Hucknall, passed all our expectations. One evening seven of us pilot cadets went to Nottingham for an evening out. We came back to RAF Hucknall airfield at about 11pm. We were all stopped at the main gate by an RAF regiment guard with his rifle ready for action. Seeing us in the foggy air he shouted loudly, as if on parade. 'Halt who goes there, friend or foe?'

All of us like something out of a scene from the theatre all replied. 'Friend.' His next words were, 'Advance to be recognised.' We advanced slowly, just in case he stood at the firing position.

At that moment, a murmur between us could be heard as we spoke to each other in whispers.

'My God, what is tonight's password?' Nobody knew it but one of us, a joker, Tomek Rzyski said, 'Be calm, I'll make one up.' So he approached the guard as near as it was safe to do so.

Politely spoken we again heard the word. 'Password.' Without any hesitation, Tomek replied to the Regiment Guard in genuine Polish. 'Szczotka,' pronounced shchot-ka, which in Polish means brush.

The poor soldier hesitated for a moment then obviously disappointed shouted again, 'Password.'

Our colleague Tomek repeated his 'brush' but in Polish and to our great amusement and astonishment the Guard exclaimed, 'No, no, it's "Tobruk".'

'Oh yes, of course, it is Tobruk,' we all shouted and seconds later passed happily through the gate.

After training on Battles, some of us including myself were posted to RAF Station Unsworth. The airfield was situated between the towns of Newcastle-On-Tyne and Sunderland. At last an Operational Training Unit, being No 55. My first solo flight was on Master 8013 on 28 March 1941.

On the previous day, I was a passenger of the Instructor Sergeant

Prhal's, a Czech pilot, aircraft. (This pilot was later the pilot who crashed his Liberator with General Sikorski on board in Gibraltar in 1943. In the mysterious so-called flying accident.)

My first real success was a real flight on a Hurricane I No. 1889.

Very intensive training started with various air duties, circuits and landings, pin-point flights, high flying formation flying, attacks, instruments, cross-country, aerobatics, firing on the ground, target flying, cloud flying, dogfights, formation attacks, individual low flying, 25,000 feet flying.

During one of these exercises, of formation flying (three machines), it was Hurricane 2321 on the 18 of April 1942, flying as the Leader's left, I was to witness a horrible accident. As a result of this accident one of my closest friends Jerzy (George) Niżyński was killed. Jerzy was flying in formation (close distance), during one of a quick 180-turns, he being on the right side of the leading RAF Officer, acted so hastily that he passed under the Leader's machine too fast forward. His aircraft's tail was completely smashed and cut off in the moment by the Leader's plane. Niżyński's aircraft went down in a frantic dive and crashed into the field. All that was left of Jerzy and the plane was many bits scattered over a 200 yards diameter area from the centre of the disaster. So, as in the Polish Air Force military march words, 'No matter that one of our stars had fallen, our Air Force sign will still more be red'.

That was the worst Air Force crashes among so many, I was unlucky enough to witness.

The Usworth airfield was somehow 'on front line' in spite of the great distance of the British Channel. During the intensive Hurricane training, the nights spent there were not pastoral ones.

The Luftwaffe boys raided the Newcastle Docklands and nearby almost every night at the time I was there.

The British anti-aircraft fire was so intensive that many of the shell's splinters were whistling over the RAF station and many dropped down upon the runways and our huts. At first, many flying heroes could not sleep and luckily at that time none were hurt. These splinter's play was not welcomed on our airfield runways, it caused dangerous damage to our tyres.

To end my short story of flight training Britain, I cannot hide a little mention towards the inhabitants of the British Isles. At that time, they *were so hospitable and hearty to Polish airmen. At first, the English people were very reserved, partially about our flying abilities. During the Battle of Britain, No. 302, No. 303 Squadrons and many Polish airmen flying in RAF squadrons proved themselves and this reserve soon disappeared.*

We Poles found British people extremely cheerful and optimistic nation, with a great sense of humour in most situations. A special bow, however, must be paid to British girls; their companionship during the war was just wonderful. I was once invited to a 'Black Rink' dancing establishment in Newcastle or Sunderland, where I forgot the war was still on while dancing the unforgettable English Waltz, The Fascination.

My desire to face the Knights of the Luftwaffe at last, was near as I ended my Hurricane course at No. 55 OTU. On 28 of April 1941, I was posted from RAF Unsworth to Polish Wilno No. 317 Fighter Squadron at RAF Ouston.

Flying in Britain to War's End

In 1941, at last my dreams of when I was a boy came true. As a youth, I often dreamed that one day I would wear as well as Polish Wings, the RAF Wings. Maybe my dreams were some sort of premonitions — the dreams were so clear to me. I was now a pilot of the famous and much loved Hurricane aircraft.

Flying with No. 317 Squadron, I flew from Fairwood Common in Wales and RAF station at Exeter.

When I flew on sorties, I always hummed the music from Franz V Suppe 'Light Cavalry Overture' as I went into battle.

In 1941, much to my annoyance, my flying was interrupted by illness. I was quite ill with stomach problems and had to go into Ely Hospital.

After recovering from my illness, I was sent to No. 41 OTU in 1943, to train on American Mustangs I.

I joined No. 309 Squadron Polish Army Co-operation Squadron. I flew off the Dutch coast searching for Nazi Navy Convoys, flying to Germany from Belgium, France and Holland. While with No. 309 Squadron flying American Mustangs II, along with other squadrons I took part in long distance flying cover to Lancaster Bombers over Germany until near the end of the war.

Flying over the North Sea towards the Dutch coast in search of Nazi sea convoys. A special camera was mounted behind the pilot's seat to take photographs of enemy ships. When a ship was sighted a message was sent to base using the code word 'Big Fish'. The operation was called Jim Crow. Photo: Permission of Kazimierz Karaszewski.

Polish mechanics working hard at fixing a Mustang I for No.309 Squadron.
Photo: Permission of Kazimierz Karaszewski/author's collection.

In 1945, I was honoured to take part in the escort to the King George VI and Queen Elizabeth. I flew a Dakota over the British Isles, Jersey and Guernsey.

At war's end and the tragic outcome for Poland and her people, after much soul-searching, I returned to Poland mainly for family reasons. I later married and had two daughters. During the war my wife, Janina saw many terrible sights and was very lucky to survive being held in Ravensbrück concentration camp.

Flying had been my whole world, back in Poland I wasn't even allowed to touch a control stick. I was a person of nongrata! Only in my sleepy dreams do I fly again.

I later learnt the Hurricane I flew in 1944, 1V LF 363 is still alive and was used in the film 'Battle of Britain.' She is probably in a museum in England and with her, my dreams of when I proudly flew her. I am glad she survived the war.

Flight Lieutenant Kazimierz Karaszewski with his Mustang III, Andrews Field 1945.
Photo: Permission of Kazimierz Karaszewski.

Squadron Leader Francišzek Kornicki

First Flight

As a Flight Lieutenant with No. 317 Squadron, I flew on my first operational sortie from RAF Northolt to France on 23 July 1941. This was as a guest of No. 308 Squadron and by way of an introduction to the shooting war.

I was told to stick to my section leader come what may, to keep my eyes open, watch my tail and my neighbours in the sky. Also, not to do anything silly, they wouldn't like to lose me on my first flight.

Flight Lieutenant Kornicki (centre) with his two mechanics. Photo: Permission of Františšek Kornicki.

We took off and met several other squadrons over a pre-arranged point, together with a handful of light bombers for bait. We flew to a target in the French coastal area, there were well over one hundred of us.

Fighter squadrons positioned themselves around the bombers and above, one lot on top of another.

We were over 20,000 feet with France glittering in the sunshine below us when I heard on the R/T that enemy aircraft were approaching. Later there were some reports of attacks, orders, warnings, and shouts that somebody was fighting somewhere.

I thought we were moving about a bit nervously when I remembered the golden rule: never fly straight and level for any length of time, so I too weaved behind my energetic leader.

I was trying desperately not to collide with anybody and not lose my leader. I managed but didn't see much else except him and my immediate neighbours.

Our squadron was not engaged in the battle and we all came back home safely.

I landed drenched with perspiration, jumped out of my aircraft, lit a cigarette and inhaled deeply.

Fate decreed that one year and seven months later, I would take over command of this squadron, alas for a very brief period.

Squadron Leader Franciszek Kornicki flew many sorties from 1941, flying with Polish Fighter Squadrons No 303, No. 308, No. 315 and No. 317.

The most precious possessions Squadron Leader Kornicki flew with were two crucifixes made by two mechanics for him when he left No. 315 squadron. The crucifixes were wired into his Spitfire, and he never flew without them after this. Like all Polish airmen, Squadron Leader Kornicki thought most highly of the mechanics and ground crew.

'The mechanics worked so long and hard to make sure their charges were safe to fly, often working all through the night and day with little rest, they celebrated our victories and felt the pain of our losses.'

After the war ended, Squadron Leader Kornicki remained in England, married and had two sons.

Flight Lieutenant Jan Maliński

Upon the Wing

I was born on 1 March 1917. Since a small child, I lived in Ostrzeszów about 120 kilometres south of Poznań.

I wanted to be a civil engineer when I was fifteen and would have to go to High School. As my sister Sally, five years my senior was already studying economics, there was no money for my parents to send me to High School. Instead, my parents sent me to Teachers' College which was run by the state and did not cost much. To be eligible for university exams that would allow me to pursue my final aim, I was privately taking lessons in Latin and French, but something strange happened that changed my mind — 'Poznań Airclub'.

In Ostrzeszów was Poznań Airclub, a gliding school. Every day on my summer vacations, I would spend at the flying club. Watching the flying and listening to the instructors on whatever they had to say to their students, not missing anything and memorising it all. Unfortunately, I was only fifteen and although the Poznań Airclub authorities would have me, I had to wait two long and seemingly endless years until I was seventeen.

In the meantime, I was dreaming of flying aircraft, of roaming the skies; in short, the aeroplane obscured the sun.

When the time came for me to learn to fly, everything was easy except for peddling my bike those 120km to Poznań once a week on Saturdays to attend evening classes given by the airclub instructors.

I completed my soaring course as one of the best trainees and became eligible to then continue on real aircraft the following year.

After my matriculation, needless to say, I barely managed to pass. My Principal Mr. Karaskiewicz said,

'I'll let you go, because I know you'll never make a teacher. The birds — that's what is in your head, but if you fail me and do not become a good pilot, I do not want to know or see you ever again.'

'Thank you, thank you, Sir. I promise I'll be the best, on my word of honour,' I replied enthusiastically.

'All your papers are here and let me know how you are doing,' he said.

To Dęblin

After a few formalities at the club and passing the medical examination in Warsaw, I joined the flying School at Lublinek near Łódź City. It was great.

During my solo cross-countries, I visited some school friends of mine, just to show them 'who is up there now.' I was quite sure what I wanted — to be a Polish Air Force Officer and pilot at Dęblin.

There were more obstacles to conquer the entry examination at the Officer Air Academy in Dęblin.

I knew that my written part of the exam didn't come up to expectation but what probably saved me was the final interview by the board. The Board of Officers had to assess candidate's qualifications among others, their up to date achievements, and a deep desire to serve in the Air Force. Also, to prove that he is joining the school for love of flying and serving the country. Overall presentation and behaviour had probably a great influence on their final decision.

Thankfully, I was accepted in for three years intensive training. We were busy all the time.

From September until May in the Department of Sciences with one day a week flying. Then, flying from May until August, flying every day.

Our group's promotion to Pilot Officers was due on 1 September 1939. Two months before that date we were sent to our respective units. I had chosen No. 3 PAF Regiment Poznań. I was assigned to 132 Fighter flight equipped with P-IIcs under the command of Flight Lieutenant Jastrzębski; he used to say to us:

'A fighter pilot never flies steady (unless in clouds), always looks for something, attacks what he sees, and recognises his prey shortly before pressing the tit.'

During exercises with bomber formations, sometimes we had to attack head on to defend some of the mock up targets missing their wings with ours by a few feet.

'Bunch of irresponsible idiots.' The bomber leader shouted on the general debriefing after not scoring a single hit.

'Who is going to attack like that in real combat conditions?'

Flight Lieutenant Jastrzębski motioned to us to get up and calmly said, 'We will.'

Poland Outbreak of War — 1 September 1939

When the war started our squadron was already at a satellite airfield, with the exception of one section.

That first morning Pilot Officer Kóstecki and Sergeant Jasiński shot down a Heinkel bomber and an Me109 over Poznań. They could not land safely at Poznań, as their airfield was full of craters, so they joined us.

'Nothing to it, a piece of cake, a baby's smile,' they said as we greeted them.

Pilot Officer Kóstecki had only a couple of bullet holes in the aircraft's fuselage. We were happy for them and wondered when we were going to score. There were lots of pilots since the reserve officers started to arrive.

My turn came on the 3 of September on that day late in the afternoon.

Our section took off flying against three Heinkels, flying W.E. along the railway line Poznań Kutno. We were too late to gain height, then we noticed another formation of four sections formatted upwards, flying from the same direction and practically at the same height of about 6,000 feet. Our section leader, Paul Luczyński very wisely kept slightly below us so that we were not seen to clearly against the multicoloured background of the ground below. At a distance of approximately a mile, we pulled slightly upwards and there they were, nice and steady in our sights growing bigger and bigger every second.

Mine, the left wing of their section couldn't stand it any longer and started an away turn and then — I let him have it.

With a slight correction, seeing in the corner of my left eye that Luczyński is doing the same to the formation leader. Their formation leader pulled up just before the would be head on collision.

My tracers were showing a narrow slightly curved line to the huge glass dome of the nose and fuselage until we missed each other by what appeared like a few inches. I pulled to a half loop to attack again from the rear at the last section way above. At that moment, all hell let loose. All air gunners appeared to fire in my direction, they were also using tracer ammo but it didn't look dangerous, rather like rockets fired at the June St. John night celebration; all beautifully curved and meeting somewhere behind me. At the top of my loop, I straightened out to make a half roll and look for my next victim. At that moment, something very strange happened as if somebody from below threw a handful of gravel in my face (we didn't wear oxygen masks). Black spots also began to appear before my eyes. Would that be my soul running away? I thought in a flash, 'wait a minute I can still see, I am holding firmly the control stick and throttle lever.' There was a moment of hesitation when I finished the half roll to get myself straight and level. I could then see a rather disorderly and confused group of Heinkels and our two P-IIs on the right of them trying to do something at a distance almost a mile ahead. Without hesitation, I opened full throttle to give a chance to chase and catch them.

The distance didn't seem to decrease much but after a while, I can see the last three bombers turning left and forming a line astern. What a fantastic opportunity, I thought, coming voluntarily under my guns.

Three lengths correction fire, I switched over to the last one in line. I can see clearly the Ace of Diamonds painted on the fuselage, just behind the glass panelling of the nose. Little sparks that appear on the broad wing, these are my bullets. White smoke is showing coming out of the left wing.

He is straightening out and pulling slightly upwards, probably giving the top gunner a chance to fire at me. But he then makes no attempt to fire he must be out of ammunition; my ammunition is now all gone.

Following him for quite a while, I see the left propellers just turning, that means something.

His engine is packing up and then passing from one side to the other. Suddenly, I get a strong whiff of fuel.

God help me, I must be losing fuel, but no there is still almost half a tank left.

'Let's go home, baby,' I said out loud, looking lovingly around my aircraft's cockpit and wings.

Turning eastwards, looking through my armoured glass windscreen, I see wedged in the corner, the steel link of an ammunition belt.

'What the hell are you doing there?' I said.

Then it struck my mind and I looked at the cockpit floor that should have been covered with those black spent ammo links, hardly any.

'So that was you, you black little devils who scared the hell out of me.' I shouted aloud.

Yes, yes, we were scared too you know little voices seemed to almost squeak in answer.

Smiling and happy, I landed back at base twenty minutes later.

A group of airmen gathered around my aircraft counting.

'Thirteen, fourteen, fifteen, sixteen holes in your aircraft and the radio is kaput.'

The radio in my aircraft was mounted just behind the pilot's back and it now presented a heap of junk.

'Alright, patch me up very gently,' I asked.

'Paul tells me you shot one down. What took you so long get lost or something,' laughed Flight Lieutenant Jastrzębski.

'No, I just wanted to find out what he was going to do. He seemed to be flying on one engine, losing height and leaking fuel and I spent up all my Ammo.' I replied.

'Do you mean to say you got another one?' Flight Lieutenant Jastrzębski said.

'I do not say anything, just glad to be back, Sir.' I replied.

'You may call me Frank.'

'Yes, Sir, yes Frank.' I replied sheepishly.

The next morning after our first patrol, the Liaison Officer, Colonel Lieutenant Kurowski to the Army Poznań HQ arrived; in his hand, he carried a German steel helmet.

'Who was flying near Kostrzyn?' He asked Major Mümler, our Squadron Commander.

'There is a badly shot up Heinkel in the field, this is what is left of the crew.' The Colonel showed Major Mümler the helmet.

'They have probably been taken to a hospital if anybody survived at all,' said Colonel Lieutenant Kurowski.

'None of our aircraft was fighting in that direction but it's worth finding out,' said Major Mümler.

'The Army claims him but I told them to go to hell, all the shots had been fired from above,' said Colonel Lieutenant Kurowski.

As I stood nearby them I thought that most probably it was my Heinkel. Taking courage I stepped up and asked,

'Do you remember the unit or Squadron badge on the fuselage, Sir? Because the one I was firing at had a nice Ace of Diamonds painted on the cockpit wall and was heading for that direction.'

'By Jove, that's it,' exclaimed Colonel Lieutenant Kurowski.

'Congratulations young man, tell me how it happened. Here, that's yours.' He handed me the helmet.

'No thank you, Sir, I don't collect souvenirs; besides I wouldn't know where to carry it, it's bulky.'

'Modesty won't get you anywhere,' he said as he handed it back to me.

I took it and passed it on to Major Mümler as a Squadron trophy.

It was getting dark when we were taken to our quarters. A quite well-dressed farmer greeted us.

'Pleased to have you, Fiszers the name.'

Lucyński, Jasiński, and I answered him. We were taken into a small room with three beds and a small table in the middle. After a while, Mr Fiszer brought a plate of fish, another with bread and a bottle of what looked like cherry brandy, plus three glasses. Paul started eating immediately, loading his plate with fish.

'I wouldn't do that,' I said.

'Why not, it looks good,' he replied.

'Maybe did you hear what his name was.' They both looked at me.

'I bet you anything he spells his name not with a 'sz' but 'sch', Fischer.'

'So what, many Poles bear German names, take for example our Commanding Officer, Mümler.' Paul replied.

'Jan is right, you may not realise that because you come from central Poland, but we know them. All the Nazis are likely to stab you in the back at the nearest opportunity,' said Adam.

'It may not poison us but could make us bloody sick, unfit for flying. Of course, one little swig of that booze should not hurt us. So here's to our victories,' I said as I proposed our toast.

'All of us here are now seasoned fighter pilots, Adam shot down one enemy aircraft over Poznań, you Paul have seen one hit the ground and I have the one with the Ace of Diamonds.'

'But that was yours that hit the ground,' said Paul.

'It wasn't mine, I don't know anything about it and since we are such a wonderful team and you are a wonderful a wise leader, we all share our achievements equally. So cheers.' I said.

Before sunrise, the driver woke us up and we had a hearty breakfast at the field kitchen.

On 7 of September a few minutes after ten we were taking off and immediately turning south, climbing gently saving the engines and fuel for the patrol.

After about half an hour my section leader Flight Lieutenant Luczyński calls, 'Stay here between near two and three (this means the towns of Września and Koło). We will go further west but report immediately when you spot something.'

I acknowledged the message and they left me going west towards Konin and Koło. As I was on my own, I reduced my height to 1500 feet in order to see better against the background of the sky. In spite of the fact that there wasn't any danger about, I did not feel happy. I felt lonely and strange, as a fighter pilot this isn't right I thought. 'If we were supposed to be fighters we should always fight together and now I am alone. Now I must see everything and if I see anything of the enemy attack immediately as I am alone.'

After about fifteen minutes, I see something far on the northern horizon. Straining my eyes, I thought that could not be birds, they are not birds, they are aircraft. Pushing the transmitter lever, I send the message 'Number one, this is number two, are you receiving?'

I am hearing something but completely distorted. He must hear me, otherwise, he would not answer immediately. I continue to push the little microphone cushions against my throat repeating each word twice.

'I am half way between one and two group of aircraft far north flying in my direction, over.'

At last, I can hear a word, 'understand' repeated three times but nothing else.

'What do I do?' I ask myself. 'Wait for them? Meet that bunch singulary?'

After having made another circle, I can already distinguish one aircraft from the others, there are six of them. I realise that I am in a favourable position, the sun well behind me. Adding more power I am gaining height and sending a message to Luczyński, 'Flying towards Mogilno to meet six bombers over.'

What did I say, Mogilno? But it is there where my Father was born and also Grandpa Wojiech; if your spirit dwells in this country, please help your Grandson Janek add courage to win this fight!

A strange thing happened quite unreasonable, although my heart started to beat faster, I began to feel calm and everything seemed to become clear and straightforward. I'll not attack the leader because if he pulls up, just as he did on Paul Luczyński I'll have to pull even steeper to apply a correction. The same as if he dives down. I decided then to shoot at the left winger all he can do is turn away from the formation and if he does that *he's mine. After taking the split decision I concentrated on what I had to do. Even the feelings of uncertainty had gone. There are only two miles separating us — not quite a minute. I'm slightly to the right of the enemy bombers, six of them all Heinkels III; I did not have any difficulties with Heinkels yesterday.*

I thought the pilot must have been feeling bloody stupid and helpless seeing a fighter straight-ahead and flying straight at him. With only his glass copula for protection, I couldn't stand it. Now I'm coming down from the sun to their level turning slightly to the left to have the leader and his right winger in line. It is too far for a burst and I have to turn already to the right by about 30 yards to get the winger in my sight. The aircraft is still a bit wobbly, but I manage to fire for a second straight away into the nose, he is turning valiantly to the right away from his formation. I am turning left to find myself about 300 yards behind his tail.

The Jerry lost quite a bit of altitude. I am trying to get a little closer, opening a long burst of fire, at the same time he is craftily turning back seeking protection under his formation. Suddenly, I find myself surrounded with tracer bullets, it appears that every lower air gunner of the whole formation is firing at me.

This is where I chicken out and break away to 360-turn to the right. After completing my turn I look for my victim, he is not there, he doesn't seem to be anywhere. Way ahead there are only five of them but there were six, so where is he? Frantically checking the sky, then a large forest and lake but I cannot find him.

My aircraft's engine vibrates a little so I return towards our line of patrol to meet my friends.

They were quite high above me. I told them what my problem was. Since only twenty minutes remained of patrol time Flight Lieutenant Luczyński decided we should return to our airfield.

After landing, Luczyński and Jasiński confirmed seeing only five twin-engine aircraft flying in a south-easterly direction but it was much too far to engage in a chase.

The damage to my aircraft was seven holes in the airframe and a damaged propeller that most likely caused the vibrations. I didn't claim any shooting down or damaging any enemy aircraft. How could I as I did not see any apparent damage while shooting at him. Besides I completely lost him not even knowing how!

There should be, however, some witnesses from the ground and I intended to find out what they had seen. Nobody, I believed could miss all that firing which was going on above. I ought to see, if possible, where that damned enemy aircraft went or crashed.

The three of us flew to Dzierżnica, our base. After sunset, Major Mümler led us east.

We are airborne quite a long time. Changing our base was dictated by a suspicion that we were discovered. At the end of the flight, it was quite dark and this was where, for the first time, I gained a great respect for Major Mümler for leading us to quite a new place in the dark.

The following day, the Commanding Officer decided that the landing field was not suitable for a larger number of our PZ IIs. Also, it could be easy to detect. As our aircraft were parked at the edge of a young fir-tree forest in a straight line, they could not easily be camouflaged.

We only flew once that day to a new place Osiek, we were to mainly fly on patrols in the region of Turek, Uniejów (on the Warta River) and Kono.

So far we had not suffered too many losses. Cadet Officer Lorek Kortus and Captain Zaramba, the Commanding Officer of 131 flight, had both been wounded. They went to one of the Poznań hospitals and managed to get out and joined us in Dzierżnica.

With all the reserves at that moment, we had more pilots than was necessary. Before our departure from Osiek, there was a pilot meeting where Major Mümler explained amongst other things that:

'From now on we will be very strictly co-operating with the Army during their crossing over the Warta river, so for this purpose, two sections will patrol one at 3,000 metres and the other at 1,500.'

It looked as if we were going to be much busier than before. The day we got that news was a very busy day.

The patrol composed of Lieutenant Giedymin, Officer Cadet Nowak, Major Mümler and Lieutenant Grzybowski who shot down three Heinkel IIIs west of Konin. Lieutenant Giedymin was badly wounded in his leg but managed to land his badly damaged aircraft safely.

Tragically, my friend Lieutenant Paul Luczyński was presumed killed that day. While chasing a Dornier 17 to the ground that he had shot down, his aircraft hit a tree during the chase and crashed, Officer Cadet Pudelwicz and Cor. Mazur were to witness the terrible sight; a very sad day indeed.

To Krośniewice and Baling Out

After the patrol everybody in our squadron was to return to yet another new base Krośniewice, where we landed and refuelled.

For Lieutenant Wiśniewski it was his first operational flight in the September Campaign. So far, he was acting Adjutant and Intelligence Officer to Major Mümler but being a full-blooded fighter pilot, he persuaded the CO he wanted to do something worthwhile.

At 07.15 hours, we were airborne flying in a south-easterly direction to our patrol region and climbing all the time. Our formation was loose so that everybody could look around without concentrating too much on flying itself, except of course, for enemy aircraft. We were flying around a triangle of Turek, Uniejów and Podbębice; the time was passing quickly being engaged in observation.

While near Turek, Lieutenant Wiśniewski suddenly turned right and flew down. We can now see a section of twin engine aircraft below, which opened fire before we could get close to an effective shooting range. Evidently they saw us sooner. I turned a little to the right with an intention to attack from the right and below. They were Junkers with sticking out air gunners positioned on top of the fuselage and below. Strangely enough, they were quite slow. After the attack, I pulled up on the other side with the aim to repeat shooting from the left side. Before doing that I looked around to see if by any chance I am in anybody's way and what do I see? Another three bombers but with much thinner silhouettes following from about two miles behind. I reported this on my radio. 'Three Dornier 17s behind us.'

At the same time, I am turning towards them for a head-on interception, I am preparing myself to do battle again. Before I pressed the firing lever on the control column, I see little flashes from the leading enemy aircraft coming out of the nose. Pushing down my aircraft to avoid any hits, I am bringing it back to a closer range with reasonable correction and opened fire. Something happened. I could see a kind of explosion and a bit of metal sheeting falling off. As I pass the leader, turning to the left to check the results of my shooting, my cockpit lights up because of a big hole on the left side. I am trying to decide what to do when my aircraft engine dies suddenly and my aircraft goes into a spin. Trying hard to control it, looking outside I can see a great portion of my left wing is without metal sheeting.

Except for the regular swish of the turning aircraft, there is silence. I cannot do anything here. I must get out.

Now my thoughts are like flashes and I am dictated by something or somebody, what to do?

First safety belts, second push the map under the parachute harness, and now think. I am pretty high, plenty of time, aircraft in a spin. Somebody seems to tell me in my head 'don't open the parachute too soon, wait at least ten seconds, the wings won't cut you down everything will be all right.'

I am rising from my seat and feel some sort of numbness in my legs. 'That's nothing, everybody must get soft in the legs in a situation of danger,' I thought to myself. Now I am hanging in the air and counting to myself. One, it seems as if I am a ghost; two, the ground is turning round and round; three, pulling out my arms to grab something to stop this; four, it helps a bit. Then five, the silhouette of my P-II flashed above not very far; six, must be about 100 metres or so. Seven, the earth is getting closer and closer; eight, now I am nice and even like an eagle. Nine, where is the parachute handle, I cannot find it? Ten, it's here under the map blown by the wind.

'Hey now,' I screamed out loud and grabbed the handle.

The sudden shock was painful but otherwise, nothing worse than in my exercise jumps at school. I am hanging as if I am on a swing. Looking towards the ground below and what do I see?

A big forest, but at the same time, I feel wet in my pants.

'Nonsense, I couldn't wet myself.' I thought.

As I look down at my legs, I see blood and a lot of it. I am over the forest area; instinctively, I pull the left belt of my parachute canopy to make a slide towards the field. I knew under no condition must I land in the trees, only landing in the field can I save myself from excessive blood loss. Better not to think of what will happen after.

The trees are shooting up on the horizon as I hit the stubble field. Releasing the parachute harness as I am in a lying position, I look about me. Not far away is a house; it is the last one in the village, behind the fence two men crouching down looking at me.

'Hey, you there.' I call out, but they don't move.

I better call out a few more sentences; maybe they are taking me for a German? Calling out a few more sentences helps as the two elderly men jump up from behind the fence, one of them has a stick.

Nothing hurts but I cannot get up.

The two elderly men came over to help me. Hanging onto their shoulders, I am taken towards the house. In the meantime, quite a few people came around, they were the children of the farmer and two teenage boys, who I asked to go into the house to find something to bandage my leg with.

Once in the house, they were trying to undress me from my flying suit and pants. I had many wounds but they were quite small.

'Why can't I move my legs?'

'Maybe the nerves are cut,' somebody suggested.

I began to worry, hearing machine gun fire, short and frequent bursts.

'Listen, I don't want to be shot like some dog by some crazy Hitlerite. Can you drive me to the main road? Our Army is there; maybe I could get some medical attention.'

I waited but nobody volunteered while my legs were being wrapped in clean bed sheets torn into strips.

An elderly woman shouted to one of my helpers, 'Ignatius, you go.'

'What if they take my horse away,' he replied.

'This isn't a horse, it's an old mare and they will not want you either,' the old women said.

The man went out into the yard and started to prepare the horse and cart putting some straw in the back.

Having done that and harnessing the animal, I was laid gently in the back. The farmer then fired his whip as if he recalled his days in the Field Artillery and went through the fields the way known only to him.

Time was passing very slowly. I thought that the main road was much closer. I began to feel pain increasing with every mile we travelled, especially in my right knee.

Finally, we reached a long village road along the main road. I can see a few soldiers at the edge of the road in shallow trenches a few others are resting against a house. A little further on, two machine guns and an ammunition cart with a horse munching hay. We stop at the house.

'Where the hell do you think you are going, don't you know there's a war on?' shouted a Corporal coming out of the house.

'I know mister, but I've brought a wounded Polish airman, he wants to get back to his unit,' said the farmer.

'Is that the one about an hour ago who jumped with a parachute?' The

Corporal asked.

'Yes, yes that's the one.'

Turning to the soldiers sitting by the house the Corporal said, 'Come here boys, we'll pull him off the cart and, you farmer, go back as fast as you can, the Jerrys are quite close.'

I had found two zloty pieces in my battle dress blouse and wanted to give them to the farmer but he refused, wished me a speedy recovery and a meeting after the war.

Sergeant Cadet Maliński,' I introduced myself.

'Hi, Sir, Corporal Kluziak of the 60th Foot,' was the reply with a voice that he was at least the company Commanding Officer.

'My platoon commander went for further instructions to the HQ but should be back in a few minutes and will take you and your leg wounds to the field ambulance. Right now, we hold the position and shoot the bastards when they come close. We are the last rear guard; everybody else is already over the river I think.'

After ten minutes or so, the 2nd Lieutenant arrived, issued the orders and told the wounded to get into the jeep. Seeing that I cannot bend my leg, with one blow of his carbine he removed the front seat, then put his rucksack under my knee.

Half an hour later, we were loaded into a bus and driven to Koło, where there was a small hospital.

The other injured soldiers that I had travelled with were given anti-tetanus injections.

The hospital was not equipped for major operations and in the evening the worst cases were selected to be taken to Kutno. I was one of them. The pain in my right knee was increasing and nothing could be done about it.

We arrived in Kutno hospital in the morning. The going was very slow on account of the road being packed with refugees. It seemed as if the whole of Western Poland was on the move east, where we men, women and children would stand on the Vistula against the German invaders.

In the small house in front of the hospital was an X-ray department, where I was first taken.

'There are four pieces of metal of a bullet shape in your right leg and one in the left leg, plus many smaller all over. Nothing serious apart from splitting the bone under the right knee,' the young female doctor declared.

'You are lucky that the bullets went first through the aircraft sheeting

and entered at a reduced speed into the body, otherwise, there would be a nasty wound on the other side that's very difficult to heal. We won't do anything now, but should you feel in the future any sensation in that particular zone it will be easier to find the source of the problem,' said the doctor.

After that, I was taken to the main building. The long spacious hall was filled with straw mattresses. Some of those unoccupied were stained with blood. Many of the patients were women and children, who were lying quietly. It was quite upsetting to see the little children. I was told they were brought from the local railway station that was recently bombed.

A girl student with a red shield on her sleeve, also wearing a Red Cross band, brought clean sheets and I was given a pillow and then laid gently on the bed. I could feel I was getting preferential treatment and this made me feel quite embarrassed. The girl left with a friendly smile on her face.

After a while they brought a German flyer, a NCO who was also wounded in the leg, they laid him down next to me. His name was Ernst Ostdorfer.

They brought us little sausages to eat; he wouldn't have any of them.

'Who shot you down?' I enquired.

'English pilot,' he retorted shortly. He lied as if it was an infamy to be shot down by a Pole.

My little knowledge of German helped me because, in my brief encounter, I learned he was an air gunner in an Me110 and baled out after an explosion on board. The pilot of the Me110 was dead and not giving any sign of life, he had said.

After an hour, the girl came over again with a beautiful red rose which she pinned in one of the buttonholes of my torn battle dress. While doing so she bent down, so I could feel the full ardour of this young lady.

'I will look after you upstairs, as soon as somebody dies. I'll get you a comfortable bed,' the girl said.

'How horrible,' I thought, 'I would rather stay here if that should happen? If that happens I must live through all this to payback for all the suffering around.' I let the German know what I thought and he didn't say anything but understood who actually had shot him down — Poles.

Another hour passed and I was taken upstairs. Occupying the first bed to the left of the entrance to a large room where there was about twenty beds. Having found myself on the first floor, I have almost forgotten about *the excruciating pain in my knee during the transfer.*

From the many wounded, questions were addressed to the Sister in charge.

'Who is he? What unit, where did he get it?'

The Sister was not keen to give answers and was trying to keep everybody happy.

I fell asleep. The whole night had left its mark.

I woke up after a series of bomb explosions, after which I could not return to sleep. Now feeling quite comfortable, I started to glance around with interest at the rest of the company.

On my left, I recognised from the dark green uniform a Frontier Guardsman, a man about forty. Both his arms were bandaged and held high with some stiffeners. I asked him what had happened.

'I wish I knew, I was with the army and while we were in an attack a single bullet went through both my arms. The bones are all right but the biceps are badly mutilated,' he replied.

'What about the one behind you?' I asked.

I tried to lift myself a little to see him. A very young face almost as a kid and so pale, his eyes closed. He seemed to be breathing twice as fast as he should be, then shorter.

'That's 2nd Lieutenant of the 7th Fusiliers. They brought him in last night. He's been shot fifteen times in the lungs. They are doing everything to save the boy but he has lost a lot of blood. I don't know how long he is going to last,' whispered my neighbour.

In another few days, I am hoping I will be well enough to join my squadron.

I have noticed next to my bed that someone had left some oranges on the table and a few packets of cigarettes. I opened a packet and went to offer one to my neighbour; instantly realising that he cannot use his hands.

'Forgive me I forgot, I'll light it and let you inhale.' I move myself nearer to the edge of the bed to do this.

'Wonderful, I didn't have a cigarette since this happened and these are superb. Thank you,' he said.

I felt so embarrassed having all these goodies on my bedside table and would like to share them with everyone but how to do so without telling the generous giver?

The Guardsman as if he read my mind says, 'That was the girl student who brought it, the one with the number on her sleeve. She also took your blouse, she said, "it is crumpled, it has to be pressed and cleaned, after a while I will bring it back." The girl also asked what could it mean that there is a Sergeant Cadet on one side of your shoulder straps and on the other, the 2nd Lieutenant star? I could not answer her.'

'Oh, that's simple. Before we left the school in July to our various units we were given part of our Officers' trousseau. Given our battle dress, pants, leather coats and underclothing. The promotion to Officer was supposed to take place on the 1 of September. It never happened. The war started and nobody told us officially to turn the straps around. That's all.'

'Allow me then to call you, Lieutenant,' my neighbour smiled.

'Nothing of the kind. Jan's the name.' I replied.

'All right, It's Jurek. I must say you pilots and airmen have all the luck, although in your case, partially bad luck. To be three years at school to become an Officer and on the first day of becoming such, go to war. That's bad luck in the full meaning of the word.'

'My bad luck is based on the fact that I am lying here doing nothing while my friends are collecting laurels.' I said.

'Nevertheless, you must admit the girls are crazy about you.'

'I don't know, I have never had the chance to experience this. We have very short leaves, there wasn't any time for that sort of thing.' I replied.

'Don't you think that this one, who is pressing your battle dress at this moment; who brought you all these goodies, leaving them on the table when you were half asleep is not half way in love with you, if not completely?'

'Jurek, forgive me, you must be crazy; who I ask you is thinking about love in a situation like this?'

'Who — the women, the greater the danger, the more they cling to a man. You'll recall my words in the future, remember that.'

'Nonsense, Jurek I don't believe a word you have said.' Jurek just looked at me and laughed.

My guardian Angel did not show up that day. The night approached and time for my dressings to be changed, which was done by a professional nurse assisted by a doctor. After that was dinner.

Dinner of bread sausages and a mug of coffee with milk. Then there was a big stir when a Jewish patient opposite refused the sausages and demanded two or three eggs instead. All around the patients passed their remarks:'How can anybody make such demands here?'

'Eat it if you want to get better and live,' someone shouted. The Jewish patient took the sausage in his hand took a bite then another bite and said, 'hmm, quite good, garlicky.'

Everyone relaxed and soon the whole atmosphere of harmony and satisfaction prevailed once more. The night passed quietly.

In the morning, a conversation seemed to wake me up. Somebody was taken out on a stretcher, I turned to my companion Jurek, and he was deeply engrossed in prayer, 'Our Father, please accept him in thy Kingdom.'

The bed of the cavalry Lieutenant was sadly empty.

An hour later, the girls brought us breakfast of two rolls and a mug of cocoa.

My guardian, with a big smile on her face, appeared with the blouse and pants beautifully pressed. They had been dirty covered in blood and full of holes. Now to my surprise! I didn't now what to say. Maybe I said something I don't remember but now I take a closer look at her, listen to her chatter. Jurek's words came into my mind and I turned to his direction. In reply, I received a long indecent blink of one eye.

I asked her to sit down on the edge of my bed and she did. I admired her long beautiful hair resting on the snow-white blouse. Her delicate little hand rested in mine.

'Thank you, thank you for everything.' I mumbled helplessly. Then I felt the tickle of her hair upon my face.

Everything went dark and remained only the ecstasy of a long kiss.

'I must go now, I'll come tomorrow or later,' she whispered, throwing back her long black hair.

My eyes managed to register the goddess shape of an Egyptian beauty disappearing in the doorway and in my mind remained dreams, wonderful dreams. In the room there maintained complete silence.

No commentaries, bloody discreet crowd, I thought and yet everyone saw it.

Jurek was the first to open his mouth.

'I can't understand it, just cannot understand it what you flyers have got that we haven't?'

I didn't answer the remarks, I didn't understand it myself. What can a twenty-two-year-old young boy know; to whom the only love so far was an aeroplane?

A few days later I was able to leave hospital and back to the war.

Onwards to Romania-France and Great Britain

I managed to make my way safely to Romania. After being interned with many other Polish airmen and ground crew, we escaped from Romania to France via Hungary and Yugoslavia.

I often thought of what became of my beautiful guardian, which had cared for me so well and shown me such kindness when in hospital.

In France, thanks to Jastrzębski, who had been my Flight Lieutenant in Poland, I was drafted instantly into 1/145 Squadron in Lyon. I did not get the chance to train fully, as I had to leave France to continue the fight from Great Britain.

I left France sailing on the Arandora Star from St. Jean de Luz to Liverpool.

In England after refresher training, rules and regulations of the RAF and some English lessons, I was posted to No. 302 Squadron.

I flew with No. 302 Squadron during the Battle of Britain. My Commanding Officer was Major Mümler, who had been my Commanding Officer in Poland, so I knew I was in good hands.

After the height of the Battle of Britain, No. 303 Squadron who had been in the thick of the battle were moved to Leconfield and we No. 302 to Northolt. What an exciting time we had at RAF Northolt in the air and on the ground. Our favourite place to visit on our time off in the evenings was The Orchard Pub/Hotel in Ruislip.

The Orchard always seemed to be packed with Polish airmen. Remembering the words of my neighbour, Jurek in the hospital back in Poland about the females. 'The greater the danger, the more they cling to a man, you'll recall my words in the future.' Yes, Jurek was right. I had a most wonderful girlfriend while I was there. The Orchestra often played 'In the mood' or 'Don't fence me in.'

The female waitresses, most of them WAAFs, were very nice too.

'What would you like, sir?' They would ask.

'Your lips, darling,' would often be the reply.

We were always a happy bunch of rascals but never out of line.

From Northolt, we moved to Tangmere's satellite airfield near Chichester and in the spring of 1941 to Kenley.

In June 1941 when the Ruskies were finally attacked, I volunteered for Night Fighters hoping to score something the easy way. I was posted to No. 307 Polish Squadron flying Defiants.

Our Defiants were without radar and without guns for the pilot while the Beaufighter boys such as John Cunningham of No. 604 Squadron at Middle Wallop were shooting Jerrys down every night. (At a Battle of Britain reunion years later, I told John how jealous I was of their luck to fly Beaus).

Finally, we got our beautiful Beaus IIs in the autumn, but it was too late. There wasn't much activity in our Exeter Sector.

For our second Squadron's anniversary, together with Jul Baykowski, we wrote our squadron's song and music. Father Greenstock, who I was friendly with at the time, helped with the English version.

'You are too bloodthirsty.' Father Greenstock said.

'We have a good reason for that, you don't yet. You, Father, will be of great service if you keep on praying for us an absolution 'in articulo mortis' of our committed and likely to be committed sins so that we'll walk without interruption straight into Heaven.' I said.

He promised he will and this is perhaps why we never feared anything.

At Exeter, we were flying practically every night but not against the enemy. We were exercising inexperienced GCI controller (Ground Controlled Interception).

At over fifty hours engine time on some of the aircraft equipped with Merlins, assembled at new Rolls-Royce Crewe factory, they should be kept on the ground but in the case of 'war', they will be used.

A Senior Polish Liaison Officer arrived from Fighter Command and told me that a good pilot is able to fly through a barn door. I showed him a barn in a field and asked if he would kindly demonstrate.

He considered it a personal insult and suggested a rest from operations that I gladly accepted, having arms sore from carrying coffins to the local cemetery.

Life in the Air Force wasn't fun all the time. We had to cope with some important but ignorant ground lubbers, who knew very little of what is going on. They wanted to impose upon us young enthusiasts, their authority to justify their existence and salaries. I was one of their victims, another was Marcel Nayder, also a fine pilot. He simply left the squadron and joined No. 23 Squadron at Luqa in Malta and later disappeared during a patrol and intruder flight to Pantelaria Island. Dear Marcel, a good friend we were both in the same squadron, he was 'B' flight. We were both told to fly Hurricanes at night, that we did with pleasure.

We were both too young to become Squadron Leaders by rank; we had to be replaced by somebody outside, the bomber pilots. One of them was appointed the Squadron Commander after our Antonowicz died in one of those Beaus.

'I want to be treated as just another pilot in your flight,' he said. 'I know little about your work.' What was I supposed to say, especially after he pranged one of our precious Beaus, with engines made in Derby, on landing — a simple landing!

I loved my flying, I felt professional in my job. I wish someone would write about us pilots, what a certain General said in Italy. In his memoirs he said that:

'A good and very good soldier is the one who not only believes and possesses full knowledge of the aim he is fighting for, but also a sufficient will and moral power to be ready for supreme risk in the name of duty. Further, the better training and knowledge of the trade, the better self-ascertain the speedier the decision and effectiveness of his action. Battles are won by soldiers who feel happy fighting and are able to grasp others more passive to decisive actions.' I think they were General Bobiński's words.

I left the squadron then, sixteen months later, I was back with No. 307 Squadron.

Stan Andrzejewski became our Squadron Leader (Commander). He was my contemporary; we had been at the Academy together. The squadron was already flying Mosquitoes.

'Come with me, I'll show you what she can do,' said Stan. I was impressed.

'I won't have to go through a refresher course?' I asked.

'Hell no, I'll give you a week's training and report that I have a new fully qualified pilot, that's all,' he smiled.

I was flying for intruder patrols during moonlit nights, sometimes as far as Munich, to keep German night fighters on the ground while our bombers were blasting to pieces German targets; or escorting on either side of bomber streams so that they could deliver their loads.

I continued flying until war's end. What next?

Second World War Ends

At the end of the war, we were not free. Poland lived under Stalin's evil. In London there was a big Victory parade but without the Poles. Why?

Because Mr Mayski, the Russian Ambassador didn't like that and said, 'The Poles can parade in Warsaw'.

Mr Bevin obediently agreed to that but the British people did not, but nothing could be done.

We didn't celebrate the victory because we did not win what we were fighting for all these years. We were simply sold out to the Soviets.

I decided that now I should go and see the world at His Majesty's expense.

I volunteered for Ferry Command. No. 36 Staging Post in Allahabad, India was my next destination. Nowadays, seeing all these countries from Egypt right down to Australia would cost a lot of money. I saw it all for free.

After my return in 1947, I joined the School of Navigation near Southampton, where I studied for all possible Civil Licences. 'If I don't get a job,' I thought, 'I will blame myself but at least I have a clear conscience that I have done everything to utilise my experience.'

When the Soviets blockaded Berlin, the British and Americans organised the big airlift. I got my first civil flying job with Lancashire Aircraft Corporation, delivering diesel oil to the city. That was in February 1949. After that was finished, I was flying Rapids and DC3 in the UK.

In 1952, there was another Berlin airlift but this time flying out goods to the west. Air Charter Ltd flying Yorks and Bristol Freighters engaged me.

I had also flown a few charters to the Far East and quite a lot to the Canal Zone in Egypt. Flying old clapped out aircraft didn't satisfy me and when a friend of mine found a job in Canada for me, I went.

Mr Freddie Laker my boss said, 'You will be sorry, leaving Air Charter.'

He was right, everything depended on the seasons of the year. In summer, we could work twenty-four hours a day but in winter, everything was at a standstill.

When I lived in England, I had got married. I left flying and worked on fabricating boats from fibreglass and other items in my garage. Making boats and flying collided, because both were requiring most of the work undertaken in the summer months. Life wasn't easy especially with two young children. My daughter Vanda was born in 1957 and my son Konrad was born in 1959.

Another friend of mine moved to Freepost in the Bahamas and suggested *that I come over to fly their Lockheed 14, a pre-war model. The job lasted only six months because of lack of spares for the aircraft.*

Due to a building boom it wasn't a bad place to live. Later, I joined Bahamas Airways.

My wife and I divorced and I kept the children with me.

Life seemed to be going well until in 1968 when I lost my pilot's licence due to some heart trouble. With my insurance money I built a duplex, living in one-half and renting out the other.

When the Bahamas obtained independence, the white population was told to teach the black people our respective trades or leave the Islands. At that time, I was engaged in the construction of a hydroponic farm for an American Corporation. Since they decided to leave and abandon the development, the only thing for me to do was to sell up and leave before I was forced to do so.

I took my children to Poland and, if after a year they liked it there, I would join them. They both stayed in the care of my relatives.

After selling my duplex that I lost a lot of money on, I joined my children in 1973.

I live with my children who give me great happiness, in the town Ostrzeszów where I spent my young and happy childhood.

In 1989 things are improving a little in Poland. I am hoping maybe after a while, which could be a few years, after the free elections we will live as normal human beings.

Everything we did in the war years sprung from love — love of our country, love of somebody who wanted to win and to prove we were worthy of it, and love of freedom.

Flight Lieutenant Jan Maliński passed away in 2006 in Poland at at the age of eighty-nine years old.

The Eagles Owl song with music. Music by J. Maliński and lyrics by J. Baykowski. Reproduced with permission of Jan Maliński.

THE EAGLE OWLS

LWOWSKIE PUHACZE

WORDS BY
J. BAYKOWSKI

MUSIC BY
J. MALIŃSKI

Harmonized by JADWIGA SZYMONOWICZ

First Officer Stefania Wojtulanis

Into the Air

I was born in Warsaw Poland and lived there until the outbreak of The Second World War in 1939.

The Polish Air Force was the apple of the eye of the Polish nation. It was the youngest branch of the Polish Armed Forces. To be a member of the Polish Air Force was a great honour, a privilege. Only men with great physical and spiritual stamina were chosen and, of course, to fly one had to have a lot of fantasy.

The eagle is the emblem which pilots wear on their uniforms.

As a schoolgirl, I dreamed to have wings and conquer the sky. During my vacation in the countryside, I liked to lay in the grass or on a haystack and watch clouds go by and the speedy swallows.

Before my final examination in high school, I went secretly without my parent's knowledge with my friends to the airfield. For a few zlotys (Polish money), we could have a ride in a small commercial aeroplane over the capital of Warsaw. That day was pretty gloomy and the ten-minute flight made little impression on me; my friend and I were very disappointed. In spite of it, I did not give up on my dreams.

I blamed the weather. As soon as I finished high school, I joined the University to study mechanics.

I joined the aero club of Warsaw. Being a member, I had lots of chances to fly as a passenger with the already accomplished aero club pilots. I was not the only woman there, there were three other women pilots. I looked at them with some envy and tried to become a pilot as soon as possible, which was not an easy task. At that time, men still looked at women in an aeroplane cockpit in an unfriendly manner but this did not last for long.

In the early spring of 1935, I started to learn to fly gliders at the gliding school near Warsaw on the beginners course. Soon, I went to a more advanced gliding school near Warsaw, in the hilly countryside and got a 'C' category. I felt like a bird.

I will never forget an event when I was at the advanced gliding school in Bezmiechowa in south-east Poland, which was internationally known, many foreigners went there to train. Before they gave me a real glider to fly, they tested my ability on the beginner's glider. The beginner's glider has, of course, wings; a few strong wires and a chair; no cockpit; no instruments, it was called a Crow. I buckled myself to the seat, the hill was over 2,000 feet high, and I looked into the valley below. My gliders tail was hooked. Also, to the front of the glider were hooked two elastic ropes in the shape of a 'V', on each side six men held onto the rope. On the command 'run' they ran down the hill pulling both ropes while the glider was still hooked to the ground.

In a split second on the command 'release the tail', I found myself high in the sky simply in a chair, gasping for air from my first impression. I was gliding along the slope and a few minutes later landed well below the hill, I then walked up the hill and the horses pulled the glider up.

Now having some flying experience on gliders, I had more of a chance to get into flying school in Warsaw to fly aeroplanes.

Thanks to God, in May 1936 I finished with good results at my flying school and after I accomplished certain conditions got my licence. My licence was called a 'Tourist Pilot Licence' which meant flying for only pleasure and sport. At the same time, I was the first woman in Poland to get a 'Balloon Licence'.

The Balloon Licence allowed me to fly balloons and take passengers with me. Ballooning was quite a different sport but wonderful and completely noiseless.

There are two flights which I will never forget. The first one of these flights, which was related to the conditions of getting one's licence, was that one flight must be done solo of a night. You could choose to take off at night and land in daylight or vice versa. I chose to take off at night, it was a very beautiful moonlit night. The balloon was small, the basket would hold only two people standing; it was really meant for only one person. It took two hours to prepare the balloon for flight. We mostly flew on cooking gas.

The take off was very smooth with the wind almost nil — ideal conditions for a 'freshman.'

It was a magnificent view, millions of lights from Warsaw below me; I was around 200 feet. I was floating over the city for at least four hours before the wind started to blow very gently. On the horizon, I saw the sun rising it was an unforgettable sight. The balloon had a little gas left so it started to go down, I prepared myself for landing. I pulled the string that opens the valve on the top of the balloon, letting out slowly the remainder *of the gas and immediately another string that opened the balloon on the side.*

I landed gently on a footpath between two wheatfields with the basket standing upright. My speed coming down was very slow so I was able to make an excellent landing thanks to good weather conditions.

The second balloon flight that I will never forget, for things were quite different on this flight.

I had three passengers in a much larger balloon and extremely good luck. The wind was blowing from the north to the south, then what happened in Poland as it is said: 'A once in a million.' We had winds mostly south-east and west or south-west.

We were flying during the night, since midnight and well after sunrise as we approached the mountains.

All of us were very tense, especially myself as I was responsible for the flight. I did not have experience of landing in the mountains. Fortunately, the weather was beautiful and the wind moderate. Before landing all had some tasks to do, the speed to earth seemed to be too fast so we regulated this with sand.

Finally, when gas was released from the balloon, we touched the ground pretty roughly and seemed to feel our bones shake. We were very happy indeed. We got back to the capital by train with our balloon packet into the basket. It was the first flight by a balloon of the Aero club of Warsaw to land in the mountains; also one of the longest in duration and distance. I also had the honour to open 'Gordon Bennett Balloons Competition' in Warsaw just before the outbreak of war. So much for my balloon flying.

I also felt great satisfaction and pleasure to learn aerobatics and parachute jumping.

I did some aerobatics and parachute jumping at the Air show. Parachute jumping was not my piece of cake, I did it in case I should need to one day to maybe save my life; fortunately, I never needed to.

In the aero club they called me Barbara 'a universal pilot'. Barbara was my nickname.

I was proud of my achievements in such a short time but at the same time I was humble because I had yet a lot to learn, I was not afraid. My colleagues were joking that the Government is wasting money on women. The Government subsidised the aero clubs and we could get a certain amount of free hours. If we wanted to fly more hours then we had to pay.

I must say it was expensive. The relations between the men and women in the aero club were very cordial.

My fairytale after a few years came to the end.

Outbreak of War

September 1939 the Second World War started by the Germans against Poland.

During the war in my country, four women including myself were Liaison pilots. Flying aero club planes, wearing aero club uniforms that we wore before on special festive occasions.

As is well known, Poland was not able to survive under the crash from the west and east; the Russians near the end of September joining Germany against Poland. Anyway, Poland was fighting longer than most of the Frenchmen who were supposed to be well prepared for war.

I did quite a few interesting flights during the start of the war. On the fourth day of the war I received a message to deliver to the main central base for Polish Air Force, Dęblin. Before the war, I had landed a couple of times at Dęblin, it was a beautiful place.

I took a RWD8 with the open cockpit and remarkable landing qualities because I did not know what conditions the airfield would be in. The weather was simply a dream, not a single cloud in the sky, the visibility limitless. I did not feel the war was on until I got to my destination. It took me about an hour to fly there. During the flight to Dęblin I did not see any aeroplanes in the sky, not the enemies or ours.

Around an hour after I took off, I started to look for the airfield, I knew I was very close to it but still could not see it. Suddenly, I spotted something that looked like an airfield, it was Dęblin. I could not believe my eyes. Here I understood what is 'Blitzkrieg'. Down below, I saw all the hangers destroyed, buildings too, a few burnt out aeroplanes scattered all over, bomb craters covered almost the whole airfield.

I looked around and could not find a safe place to land. Flying a few circuits I finally decided to land on a strip close to a perimeter track which seemed to me to be full of holes.

My aeroplane had no brakes so I approached with power on very slow speed as possible and touched down praying not to wreck the plane. I stopped just in time in front of me was a big crater. I was not able to taxi amongst the craters, so I secured the throttle on 'idling' and left the cockpit.

There was no sign of life around; I started to walk, bypassing burnt out planes, towards the Officers' Casono (Mess). I had a very weird feeling. Some smoke was coming out of the ruined buildings, the smell was awful. The once beautiful Officers' Mess was a skeleton, only a couple of walls were left standing.

I still kept walking, was no one around? Then I heard a voice but could not see anyone.

'Did you land just now?'

In that moment, I saw an officer coming out of the shelter that I knew previously. He told me the Germans had bombed the aerodrome four times that day. He also informed me that the whole base had already been evacuated to another place, only he and a few other young men had been waiting behind for the transport.

I gave him the message, he opened the envelope and quickly read the contents and said, -

'Impossible, all gasoline depots totally destroyed. You are extremely lucky, do you wish to go back to Warsaw?'

'Certainly at once.' I replied.

He wrote me an answer on the envelope and went with the other men and I to my plane.

They helped me to taxi to a point from which I was able to take off. My aeroplane was airborne just in time. My eyes were wet with tears, is it true what I saw?

I reached Warsaw airfield safely and delivered the answer to the General Staff.

The war situation was becoming hopeless. At the end of September 1939, the Polish Air Force was ordered to proceed to Romania by any means possible.

Romania to France

I flew to Romania with another pilot. As we crossed at dawn, the Polish-Romanian border, our hearts stopped for a moment and we said 'goodbye' to our country. But for how long? No one knew at that time.

In Romania, all Polish aeroplanes were confiscated and the personnel were sent to various detention camps, waiting for the unknown future.

The Polish Air Force authority at the Polish Embassy, Bucharest engaged me for over three months as a courier between camps in Bucharest. With the secret agreement with the Romanian authority, we started to organise the escape for the Polish Air Force personnel to France. It was quite interesting work, but very hard.

I delivered false civilian passports and money. Men were escaping to France by private cars, train, but mostly by sea route from the Black Sea.

At the end of 1939, the Romanians began to follow me suspecting me of doing some illegal work. I had to leave the country.

I took a train from Bucharest to Paris by myself, alone and a little frightened I started my journey to France. I had to stop in Milan and Venice to change trains. I used this occasion to mail some postcards home to Warsaw to my parents and sister. My family had no knowledge of what had happened to me after I left Warsaw. I hoped somehow that my mail would reach them.

Exhausted, I arrived in the French capital on Christmas Eve, going straight away to the Polish Air Force HQ.

Here, I got the news that the new Commander of the Polish Armed Forces General Sikorski had promoted three women and I to the rank of Second Lieutenants. I wore proudly my Polish Air Force uniform with one star on my epaulettes. In France until our evacuation, I did only clerical work in the Polish Air Force HQ.

Great Britain – Ferry Pilot

In England women were not allowed to fly in the war in combat. Many women started work on the ground in various jobs in the WAAFs. The jobs included mechanics, meteorologists, plotters telephone operators and many more to help the war effort.

Meantime a paramilitary organisation was formed. It was called ATA (Air Transport Auxiliary).

The ATA's task was to deliver all types of aeroplanes from factories, airfields or maintenance units to fighter squadrons, to flying schools and training schools. At first men could be employed by the ATA but very soon the best English women pilots joined them.

Originally there were only eight women pilots, later on they increased to well over a hundred, not all at once of course but gradually.

In June 1940, the first women pilots of ATA went to the Central Flying School for conversion courses. Flying Masters and Oxfords, these were trainers for fighters and twin engine bombers. The average time taken was two hours dual on Master and two and half-hours on the Oxford. This was followed by a couple of hours solo on each aeroplane. After ferrying fighter and bombers trainers for a couple of months, the women pilots were allowed to ferry operational types. This started with Hawker Hurricane and by the end of the war everything, including four engine bombers.

There were about a dozen ferry pools in Great Britain, some with a few pilots some with about fifty; it all depended on location. Each pool had its Commander, mostly a very experienced pilot assisted by some staff. The pilots were graded from those who flew single engine aircraft to those who flew all types of aeroplanes. Their ranks ranged from Third Officer to Flight Captain.

First Officer Stephanie Wojtulanis 1941. Photo: Permission of Stephanie Karpińska and the Polish Institute and Sikorski Museum.

The daily life of a ferry pool pilot in brief included: In the morning Operational Officer prepared through the Central Ferry Control the program of the day and to taxi aeroplane to serve pilot. He had a list of available pilots and the weather report. Every pilot had a written chit that gave full particulars of its type and mark, its present position also its destination. Embodied in this chit was an authority for collection of the aircraft and equipment, a form of receipt and signal for delivery. Also, a report sheet on the state of the aircraft whilst in the pilots hands. Pilots generally came back to base the same day, although in winter, the return to base the same day was not always possible.

Taxi planes delivered ferry pilots to a place of pick up and then the taxi followed the pilots and collected them one by one bringing them back to base.

It was very difficult to arrange the programme of the day in such a way that minimum time was lost.

Maps and the signal rooms gave us details about restricted areas and the positions of the barrage balloons.

Sometimes there were only very narrow corridors to fly to the airfields.

After six months of great efforts, I joined another Polish girl in ATA on the 1 of January 1941.

At first, we flew only light types of aeroplanes, then after a few months we flew Masters and Oxfords.

Then the beautiful Hurricanes and Spitfires. Later, American Mustangs.

At the end of the year in ATA we flew all types of single and twin engine fighter and bomber aircraft.

We reached the rank of First Officer (after, of course, Third and Second Officer).

In 1942, another Polish girl joined as did quite a few American women pilots. It was really an international society in ATA.

The Polish girls being Anna Leşka, Jadwiga Piłsudska and I were the first foreign women to join ATA.

We wore the navy blue uniform, with the golden wings in the middle of which was the letters ATA. The First Officer had two golden strips on the shoulder.

I was in Hatfield Ferry Pool and Hamble, both were women only and White Waltham and Leicester that were mixed.

I found the flying in Great Britain was often difficult due to the weather conditions. Someone told me: 'If you can fly in England, one can fly safely all over the world.' If this is true, I do not know.

After flying for four and a half years in the ATA in England, I had the map of the country in my head 'little finger'. When the weather was good, I could fly almost without a map.

My greatest joy was to deliver aeroplanes to Polish Squadrons, when they saw me for the first time they did not believe I could fly the same aircraft as they.

The Polish airmen flew in their respective squadron's fighters and bombers and as ferry pilots, we were so fortunate to fly both. My favourite aircraft of the fighters that I flew was the Spitfire. I simply loved it as I did the twin engine Wellington bomber.

I had flown forty-four types of aircraft and logged well over a thousand hours in my flying life.

My flying was not without accidents as a ferry pilot.

One day, while ferrying a Tiger Moth that is a very light type of aircraft, I went too far in bad weather, which forced me to land in a small field on the way to my destination. As soon as I touched down without wrecking the plane, the engine stopped.

There was not a drop of gasoline left in the tank and dense fog encircled me. Thanks to God who guides me, I had landed just in time.

At another time, I nearly killed myself. It was at ATA School on a conversion course, I had not at that time known the aircraft I was flying that well. I practised the take off and landed solo in a Wellington bomber. The airfield was situated on a pretty high hill. I was approaching the landing strip with undercarriage down and flaps down. I was already low when suddenly I saw before me a small aeroplane touching the runway on which I was supposed to land. I had no choice but to go up. I moved my undercarriage and started to climb with flaps down; this was because I needed more height to do so. In one moment I was terrified, my Wellington started to roll with its nose down and the earth was approaching with great speed. I felt terrific pressure on my steering wheel. 'What should I do, what should I do?' My brain worked with lightning speed

A voice from somewhere said to me. 'You fool, flaps up.'

I pushed the lever up and the Wellington did something that is impossible for me to describe.

My hands went off the steering wheel my feet went off the rudders. The aircraft somehow straightened up while still diving. I pulled the wheel towards me and I was safe, the height beyond the airfield had helped me too. My whole body was trembling. Now I knew what was wrong.

During the climb, due to a malfunction one of the flaps went up, while another was still down.

I circled the airfield for a few minutes to steady my nerves, then landed safely without using the flaps. Another day while flying one of my beloved Spitfires, I had to land on a very soggy grass airfield.

I touched down very smoothly and I thought, 'What a beautiful landing I have made.' Then, suddenly at the end of the run my beautiful Spitfire stood on its nose. There was a little hole in the ground that had caused the trouble, I nearly cried.

I am very proud of my small achievements and taking part in the war efforts.

Unfortunately, when the Second World War ended it did not bring independence for Poland. Many Poles did not return to an enslaved country by Russia to be vivid witness of the terrible injustice that was done to Poland.

In 1946, I married General Stanisław Karpiński* while in England. We would not return to live in Poland while under Russian rule. We remained in England until 1958, after which we made our home in the USA.

I am happy to know that there is someone after many years after the war ended, who pays tribute to the Polish airmen and women. When I look back, it seems to me that the Second World War and my part in it is a dream — a terrible dream (not without beautiful and moving moments); not reality.

First Officer Stefania Wojtulanis-Karpińska passed away in America in 2005 at ninety-two years old.

*General Stanisław Karpiński was the last Commander in Chief of the Polish Air Force while in Great Britain.

SOE in the Warsaw Uprising 1944
Stanisław Sroka

In the spring of 1942, the Armia Krajowa (AK Home Army) Command of Air Force department was informed that the Commanding Officer was Lieutenant Colonel Pilot Bernard Adamecki. During the September Campaign, he was Chief of Staff of Modlin Army's Air Force.

The AK Headquarters would organise and prepare reinforcements for the Polish Air Force squadrons that were flying in combat alongside the Royal Air Force. It was presumed that when the Warsaw Uprising started, squadrons from England would arrive in Poland to participate in the uprising operations.

Preparations anticipated the support for the uprising by the Polish Air Force and RAF, who would supply the Home Army with arms ammunition, battledress, medical supplies and other needed materials.

The Conspiratorial Plan was submitted to the Supreme Commanding Officer of the Polish Armed Forces in London, at that time being General Sikorski, but in its original version, it was not approved at that time.

In the letter received by the AK HQ from the Chief Commission was, among others, a statement. In the statement was that Operational Air Force support for the AK operations would only be contemplated if Allied bases were less than 600-700 kilometres from the centre of Poland.

The Air Force Department in Poland was formed from some of the men from the Polish Air Force and ground crew, who were unable to escape in September 1939 so joined the AK in conspiratory actions against the enemy.

At the time, the Air Force Department organised Regional Air Force detachments, whose task was for the organisation of airfields. The most important Air Force bases were Okęcie, Dęblin, and Kraków. The organised Air Force units were supposed to take care of German airfields captured by the AK and prepare for servicing of Polish Air Force squadrons arriving from allied bases.

With great assistance from a specialist unit, the KGL, Polish airmen were trained in England and parachuted into Poland. In 1942, four specialist trained pilots arrived in Poland.

In January 1943, parachutists with Colonel Pilot Roman Rudnicki (pseudonym 'Rudy') reinforced the KGL Units.

The next substantial group arrived in April of that year; half of them were Air Force Signals specialist. At the AK Command, the KGL consisted of several sections — operational, organisational, signals, supplies and Meteorological — their leaders co-operating with regional AK Home Army units regarding co-operation and parachute supplies. Parachute supplies were the responsibility of Department V of the HQ, Commanded by Colonel Dipl. Pluto Czechowski (pseudonym 'Koczuba').

A special acknowledgement was due to the Signals section of Warsaw and London for serving two superb two-way Radio Stations. Thanks to their outstanding work, three actions were realised under the code 'MOST', consisting of the landing on Polish airfields of three RAF transport aircraft flying from airfields in the south of Italy. In these actions the Air Force Officer Lieutenant W. Wojcieszak (pseudonym 'Sum') earned special merit. He supervised the landing of the Dakota DC3 at Bełżyce airfield, Lublin, on the night of the 14-15 April 1944.

Captain Pilot Włodzimierz Gedynicz (pseudonym 'Wlodek') twice received aircraft DC3 at Torun on the night of 29-30 May and 25-26 July 1944.

Colonel Pilot Rudkowski, responsible for Air Force affairs on Polish occupied territory at the AK HQ, had good relations with the English. He was a Commanding Officer of No. 301 Polish Bomber Squadron during 1940-41.

Corrected relevant plans of the AK HQ illuminated the possibilities for the RAF to assist the country. The British considered assistance for the action of Resistance on occupied territory as secondary importance. The allies at that time prepared the opening of the Second Western Front in Western Europe.

In England the organisation 'Special Operations Executive' (SOE) was actively engaged in the co-operation with Resistance Movements in occupied countries.

The 'SOE' had at its disposition Air Force units equipped for long-range flights dropping war materials and parachutists.

The 138 Special Duties Squadron operated from 1943 with one Polish squadron being part of it. (Heavy losses earlier on in the war for No. 301 Polish Bomber Squadron saw it disbanded for a while. Early in 1943 a Squadron was organised as part of 138 RAF Squadron in its place.)

In December 1943, the Polish squadron was made independent, named '1586 Polish Duties Flight' and transferred to Italy's airfield Campo Casale near Brindisi. It was composed of ten complete crews, and Halifax and Liberator aircraft. Its Commander was Major Navigator Stanisław Król and formed part of the British 334 Special Duties Wing. In the Halifax aircraft, the 148 RAF Squadron crews performed flights to Poland and occupied countries. It should be mentioned that British crews flew as well to Poland.

The AK HQ under General Tadeusz Komorowski (pseudonym 'Bór') prepared the Nationwide Uprising, which was given the name 'Burza'. Plans were worked out and sent to the Commander of the Polish Force in London, General Kazimierz Sosnkowski. The task of the AK Headquarters staff regarding Air Force assistance grew from month to month.

Messages were received at the Polish Air Force Inspectorate with requests above the capabilities of the Polish Air Force, which was completely dependent on British authority.

In addition, the intensive demand for operational flights placed on Polish Bomber squadrons No. 300, No. 304 and No. 305, as well as on 1586 Squadron put them through a difficult and critical period as far as crews were concerned.

The Supreme Command's request that the extension of the 1586 Squadron was established to the full complement of a Wing and to restore its name to No. 301 Wing Squadron was not approved by the RAF authorities.

In the first half of July 1944, the General Command and the Inspectorate of the Polish Air Force suggested that four Wings (Squadrons) equipped with Mustangs be transferred to Polish territory liberated by the Russians. This plan was submitted to the Allies and Russia but was rejected.

The Home Army Commander General Komorowski, 'Bór' sent a message on the 25 July 1944 to the Supreme Polish Commander in London informing him of the readiness to start the Battle of Warsaw at that time. He requested the dispatch of a Parachute Brigade as a political and tactical move. He demanded also the bombardment of the airfields near Warsaw by request.

The order to start the Warsaw Uprising was given by General Komorowski, 'Bór' on the 1 of August 1944 at 17:00 hours.

The AK Headquarters assumed Warsaw could easily be captured and held before the arrival of the Russian Army, which would have created *a situation for open discussions by authorities answering to the Polish Government in London. This included the Delegation of the Polish Government in Poland facilitating the taking over of the administration by the left wing concentrated around (The Polish Citizens' National Freedoms Committee).*

The date of the start of the Uprising was not communicated to the Allies or the Russians; even the Supreme Polish Command in London was not informed. In consequence, General Komorowski, 'Bór' was also not informed of the refused request regarding the Air Force and Parachute Brigade.

The Air Force base in Italy was 1,300 kilometers away, and the British Isles was 1,500 kilometres. There was no possibility of bombing targets depicted by the AK Conspirators, as there was no chance of transporting the Polish Parachute Brigade by huge gliders and transport planes. They would have been an easy target for German fighters and AA guns. We were previously notified by RAF authorities that substantial support for the uprising would only be possible after reaching the Rhine by Allied forces.

The supply of arms and war materials was restrained by air for the AK. The English organised flights to Poland but previously promised help was not fulfilled.

During 1941-42, promised were thirty flights, completed were eleven. During 1942-43, 100 flights were planned, executed were forty-six flights. During 1943-44, planned were 300 flights, completed were 172. Materials dropped over Poland for the AK during these periods was minimal in comparison with demands for diversions (sabotage). They amounted to 580 hand-grenades, 281 standard pistols, 255 machine pistols, 23 hand machine guns, 9 anti-tank rifles, and 550 mines, five mortars and 118 kilograms of plastics.

During this period sent to Poland were over 300 parachutists. Well-trained and fearless, they contributed towards the consolidation of the AK ranks. Despite the prevalent situation during the Warsaw Uprising flights, crews were maintained in order to assist the fighting conspirators.

Major Navigator Eugeniusz Arciszewski commanded the base, Campo Casale airfield in Southern Italy in 1944, where 1586 Squadron was based for Special Duties in July 1944. It consisted of twelve crews, nine

Handley Halifax, and three Liberator aircraft. They carried out flights with drops for Resistance Movements in occupied countries in Europe. The frequency of flights in June and July was very great, with the result that on 1 August 1944 (the start of the Warsaw Uprising), the squadron was left with only six crews and three operational aircraft.

The start of the Warsaw Uprising took the Commander of the Mediterranean Air Force Marshal J. Slessor by surprise. He declared to the 1586 Squadron Commander that until clarification of the situation, he was suspending all flights to Poland.

On 4 August 1944, Marshal Slessor allowed flights to Poland but not Warsaw. Despite the order, four Polish crews flew as volunteers to Warsaw. Two Polish Liberators and one Halifax, who dropped supplies to the 'Plac Krasinskich', 'Ogrod Saski' and the Jewish Cemetery, reached the target area. The fourth Liberator was damaged by German AA defences and was forced to return to base from Bochnia, near Kraków. The damage was so serious that the plane crashed during landing at Campo Casale airfield. During the night, seven British Halifax bombers from 148 Group flew to Poland. Tragically, five crews did not return.

On 8 August 1944, Marshal Slessor gave permission for flights to Warsaw. Three Polish crews flew to carry out drops they were successful and returned without losses to their base. Four more Polish crews were successful on 9 August, reporting that 'the whole of Warsaw is burning'. Marshal Slessor authorised more flights to Warsaw; also for the 148 Wing of the RAF.

On 12-13 August, six crews flew towards Warsaw from 148 RAF and five from Polish squadrons. The operation was completed without loss.

For the support of fighting, Warsaw Marshal Slessor included 205 South African Group of bombers with 31 Squadron SAAF (South African Air Force) and 178 Squadron RAF, together with twenty-four Liberators.

During the night of 13-14 August, a large operation with drops into Warsaw was recorded. In action were twenty-two crews, Liberators from the 205 Bomber Group, four Halifax from 148 RAF and five aircraft from Polish squadrons — a total of thirty-one aircraft. Heavy losses befell the Allies with eight crews lost.

The following night a large operation was organised and once more heavy losses.

On 17 August, Marshal Slessor stopped flights to Warsaw.

On the intervention of the Polish Government in London, the Air Force Ministry authorised flights of Polish crews, as mentioned in a despatch by Marshal Slessor, for volunteer flights to Warsaw. All Polish crews of the 1586 squadron expressed their readiness to support Warsaw Combatants by flying in drops.

RAF crews also flew to designated places in Poland. During the period from 1 August to 17 August 1944, the Group's losses were heavy.

The 31 SAAF bombers lost six crew, the 178 RAF lost five crews, the 148 Wing lost six crews, and the Polish 1586 Squadron lost three crews. In total, twenty crews lost 140 airmen's young lives.

Flights to Warsaw were difficult and exceptionally dangerous for Halifax as well as Liberator crews. The flights lasted from ten to twelve hours. They demanded great sacrifice and courage. Flying in the regions of Nowy Targ, Kraków, Nowy Sasz and Tarnow. In the south of Poland, on the routes from bases in the south of Italy, the Germans concentrated powerful anti aircraft defences. These defences the bomber crews had to fly across twice on the way to and from the targets. Burning Warsaw often prevented the identification of marked places for drops during the night.

The approach for drops had to be made at low altitude from 130 to 200 metres. A low flying four-engine bomber was an easy target for the heavy German Anti-Aircraft defences. In the case of a shot down aircraft, the crew had no chance of escape.

Tragically, the 1586 Polish Squadron lost over Warsaw in August and September 1944 fifteen crews, which constituted 150 percent of its establishment. Of the drops, only 45 percent landed in the hands of the AK Home Army.

During the Warsaw Uprising from 1 August until 2 October 1944, the Polish and British Air Force started their flights from Italy's southern airfields. The 1596 Polish squadron completed ninety-seven flights with losses of fifteen crews. The 205 South African Group Wings, 178 Royal Air Force, 31 South Africa Air Force and British 148 and 334 of the Royal Air Force Groups completed 116 flights with heavy losses of nineteen crews. All those who took part in these hazardous operations showed great heroism while trying to aid the fighting people of Warsaw.

At the beginning, the British authorities were against the continuation of help for the Uprising. They maintained that it had nothing in common with operational actions and that the whole of Poland, including the Capital Warsaw, was in the sphere of the Russian Army. This understanding prevented them from any action without the consent of the ZSSR (the Union of Soviet Socialist Republics). Marshal Slessor stated that the Warsaw Uprising was 'madness' without any connection to the war effort.

Immediately after the start of the Warsaw Uprising, the Polish authorities in London were strongly intervening at the British Command for drops of supplies from low altitude by groups of bombers in order to prevent damage to containers. (This was probably not granted because of the danger to bomber crews flying at such a low altitude making them an easy target.) The British authorities rejected these propositions.

The Polish Command presented the propositions to the American Air Force. The Americans agreed under the condition for permission to be obtained from the Russians for landing and refuelling facilities to be provided on their airfields after drops for the return back to base. Discussions with the ZSSR were very protracted. Finally, on the 18 September 1944, a large group of B17s Flying Fortresses flew in from the north-east. When parachutes opened, German artillery and small gunfire was directed against the containers and not the planes, as the Germans assumed a landing of parachutists was taking place. Some of the containers shot down by the Germans fell to partisans. The remainder landed in regions outside of the partisan's reach. The Americans were satisfied with having completed their mission, and in accordance with Russian orders landed at an airfield near Poltava. After refuelling they returned to England via Italy.

Some of the crews of the Polish airmen and their allies who did not return from their operations are laid to rest in graves in Warsaw. Monuments were erected years later to commemorate their sacrifice and heroic deeds while flying to help the men, women and children of Warsaw during the uprising. Their graves are tenderly cared for by Polish people who have never forgotten the bomber crew's ultimate sacrifice.

Many of those who fought in the Warsaw Uprising were family members of Polish airmen fighting alongside the RAF and their Allies.

Near the end of the Warsaw Uprising, the Polish Command negotiated the AK's surrender with the Germans. It was agreed that those who surrendered would be treated as a regular army and subject to the Geneva Convention and treated as prisoners of war. This became meaningless *when the Soviets took over, as thousands of members of the AK were later deported deep within Russia. Many were never heard from again.*

After the collapse of the uprising, I escaped together with civilians through sewers in the old part of the town to the centre. From Warsaw, I was taken to a camp at Pruszków organised by the Germans. From there I managed with the help of Doctor Suchaczka, to leave the camp for my family home in the region of Radomsk and Częspochowa. In mid-1945, I joined the Polish Army, taking part in battles against the Germans from the Oder to the River Lada. I served in the army until 1947.

Stanisław Sroka was involved with the AK Home Army in Warsaw during the uprising and witnessed it first hand. His father was many miles away at the time, serving in Bomber Command with the Polish No. 305 Bomber Squadron, then No. 307 — the night fighter squadron.

Stanisław Sroka remained in Poland after the war and married a Polish girl, Helena. They had three sons.

Sources: Polish Air Force Association. The Polish Institute and Sikorski Museum, London. Interviews: I am indebted to Stanisław Sroka for his account of the SOE involvement with the Warsaw Uprising. The words are his own, but I have reordered sections of those words to put them in chronological order. The interview dates are 25 March 1988 and 2 April 1989. I am also indebted to the many people I met who took part in the Warsaw Uprising but wish to remain nameless. Also, Captain Eric Nanke of the Polish Signals section, and the gentleman who worked for SOE, who wished to remain in the shadows.

PART III

BATTLE OF BRITAIN COMBAT REPORTS FOR No.303 KOŚCIUSZKO SQUADRON
The Eagles Take To The Sky

30 August 1940

At 16.15 hours, six Hawker Hurricane aircraft from No. 303 Kościuszko Squadron 'B' Flight took off on a training exercise towards St. Albans on interception practice with six Bristol Blenheim aircraft. At 16.35 hours, Flying Officer Paszkiewicz sighted approximately 130 German Dornier bombers and Messerschmitt fighters.

'Apany leader, bandits 10 o'clock.' Flying Officer Paszkiewicz said over the radio transmitter, but Squadron Leader Kellett did not reply. Flying Officer Paszkiewicz signalled by 'waggling' his Hurricane wings and moved towards the enemy. He spotted an enemy aircraft banking towards him.

> *'When he was almost head on, he saw me and went into a steep dive. I followed and as he pulled out, I fired from directly behind, a burst at 250 yards at the fuselage. Overtaking him, I fired a long burst at 100 to 20 yards at the starboard engine from underneath. The engine stopped and burst into flames.'*

One of the German airmen managed to bale out, and the enemy aircraft dived towards the ground. With great pleasure, he watched his chosen quarry crash in flames and explode.

Flying back to RAF Northolt, Flying Officer Paszkiewicz was relieved. He had been able to attack the enemy over Britain after months of frustration and waiting. The Polish pilots had arrived in Britain to fight and destroy the enemy; to avenge the ongoing destruction in their homeland. Yet, the RAF had been reluctant to send the Polish pilots into battle even though there was a shortage of pilots. Without realising it, Flying Officer Paszkiewicz had achieved what all the Polish pilots had hoped for in No. 303 Kościuszko Squadron: to prove to the RAF that they could do what fighter pilots do best — fight.

After landing, Flying Officer Paszkiewicz received a strong 'ticking off' for breaking formation. He was also congratulated by Group Captain Vincent for his skill in the sky. Squadron Leader Kellett made a telephone call to Fighter Command that evening. Thus, the following day, No. 303 Kościuszko Squadron became operational.

31 August 1940. First official sortie.

At 18.05 hours, six Hurricanes from No. 303 Kościuszko Squadron 'A' Flight led by Squadron Leader Kellett were scrambled.

Sergeant Karubin sighted approximately sixty German Dornier Do17 bombers flying at approximately 15,000 feet near Biggin Hill in southeast London. He reported the sighting to Squadron Leader Kellett immediately. Three Me109s appeared a few hundred yards in front of them but were not aware of the Hurricanes, which were hidden below the wings of the Me109 fighters. Squadron Leader Kellett gave the order to attack and fired a few short bursts at one of the Me109s.

> *'The enemy aircraft swerved from side to side and pulled up his nose in a steep climb endeavouring to escape, but I saw my ammo going into the enemy aircraft, which finally burst into flames and turning fell over perpendicularly.'*

Sergeant Karubin pursued an Me109 and fired at a distance of 200 yards and hit the aircraft. He dived after the enemy aircraft and fired another burst. He watched his first kill over Britain crash to earth in a trail of smoke.

Sergeant Szaposznikow pursued the other Me109, taking the pilot by surprise.

> *'I fired at him before he saw me. He rolled and dived with me, copying my movements. I fired again as he straightened up. He rolled to his back and fell vertically, trailing clouds of smoke.'*

While Squadron Leader Kellett and the two Sergeants had been busy attacking the three fighters, another three Me109s had flown in to defend those under attack, Sergeant Wünsche, and Pilot Officer Ferić, who had both been guarding the rear, attacked before the Me109s had the chance to fire back. One of the Me109s crashed in flames, the other fell to earth smouldering. Both of the enemy pilots managed to bale out, narrowly avoiding death.

Flying Officer Henneberg sighted another four Me109s in the distance. Waggling his Hurricane's wings for others in 'A' Flight to follow, he flew in pursuit of the enemy fighters. At that point, he was unaware that 'A' Flight was engaging the Luftwaffe fighters already.

Flying Officer Henneberg neared the four Me109s and realised the odds were against him. He flew after them over Kent, but it was as if the enemy fighters had no wish to engage him. He followed, waiting for his chance. When an enemy aircraft broke formation, Flying Officer Henneberg seized his chance. He fired at 300 yards and followed on the tail of the enemy fighter across the English Channel. After another burst from Henneberg's guns, the Me109 crashed into the sea, and Flying Officer Henneberg turned back towards RAF Northolt.

The rest of 'A' Flight had returned to RAF Northolt, the excitement about their victories held at bay while they waited for the return of Flying Officer Henneberg. The wait seemed endless. To the relief of the pilots and ground crew, a lone Hurricane came into view in the distance. Flying Officer Henneberg flew over the airfield and celebrated with a victory roll. All six pilots had returned safely with one victory each.

It was obvious to Squadron Leader Kellett that he and other RAF officers had been wrong to doubt the Polish pilots. The Polish Air Force's rapid destruction at the hand of the Luftwaffe during the first few weeks of the war was not a reflection of the Polish pilots' skill. In the heat of battle, the Polish pilots were handling themselves excellently and were an asset to the RAF, not a hindrance. He dismissed his earlier concerns that the pilots would let their burning hatred for the Germans lead to reckless acts. Squadron Leader Kellett was proud of his Polish squadron. The drinks would be on him that night.

2 September 1940

At 17.30 hours, twelve Hurricanes from 'A' and 'B' Flight, led by Flight Lieutenant Kent, took off from RAF Northolt. At Manston, near Dover, nine Me109s flew out of the sun at 19,000 feet. The twelve Hurricanes of No. 303 Squadron avoided disaster by turning to attack the Me109s and pursued the enemy fighters towards France.

Flying Officer Henneberg approached an Me109 from above, then dived towards the enemy aircraft.

'I fired from about 150 yards, smoke and fire appeared on the starboard engine. He dived and I again attacked, now 8 miles into France.'

Flying Officer Henneberg pursued the damaged enemy but abandoned the chase at 3,000 feet to avoid the machine gun fire and heavy flak.

Sergeant František destroyed an Me109 but was forced to break off the pursuit of another enemy fighter due to heavy flak along the French coast.

Sergeant Rogowski also pursued the Me109s fleeing towards the safety of their airfield in France. He selected his target and fired at the enemy aircraft.

'I followed one and after four bursts, his engine caught fire and he crashed into the sea about 10 miles from France. Then I saw Pilot Officer Ferić in trouble, smoking and gliding...'

Something terrifying happened to Pilot Officer Ferić after he had hit an Me109 during a pursuit towards France. Oil spread across the Hurricane's windscreen, leaving Pilot Officer Ferić to fly blind. Smoke began to pour from his aircraft's exhaust. He had to make a decision — stay in the aircraft and try for home, or bale out into the grey shifting graveyard of the English Channel knowing it had already claimed many other airmen.

Pilot Officer Ferić set off for land, switching off the petrol when his aircraft began to shake. The British coastline was still a few miles away, but Flying Officer Paszkiewicz and Pilot Officer Łokuciewski flew to protect the gliding Hurricane against Luftwaffe pilots looking for an easy target.

With land finally in sight, Pilot Officer Ferić sighted another aircraft in the distance. Was it friend or foe? Thankfully a friend — Sergeant Rogowski. Pilot Officer Łokuciewski and Flying Officer Paszkiewicz returned to RAF Northolt leaving the Sergeant as his protector. Suddenly, two Me109s appeared and advanced towards the two Hurricanes. Sergeant Rogowski circled Pilot Officer Ferić's aircraft defensively. The pilots of the Me109s seemed to realise that the damaged Hurricane was not going to be abandoned and flew off towards France.

Pilot Officer Ferić landed his damaged aircraft in a field a few miles northwest of Dover. He could see Sergeant Rogowski's aircraft flying nearby, waiting for a signal before leaving. Standing near his Hurricane, Pilot Officer Ferić waved to his friend, signalling that all was well.

All eleven of the other pilots from No. 303 Kościuszko Squadron, who had flown in that afternoon's sortie had landed back at Northolt by 18.50 hours and were tucked up in bed when Pilot Officer Ferić arrived at midnight. He knew that Flying Officer Paszkiewicz, Pilot Officer Łokuciewski and Sergeant Rogowski had saved his life. No man could ask for more from another.

After the sortie, RAF Northolt Station Commander Group Captain Stanley Vincent informed Squadron Leader Kellett of a message from Air Vice-Marshal Keith Park, No.11 Group. The message implied that the pilots of No. 303 Kościuszko Squadron should not pursue the enemy over France. In the heat of battle, it was tempting to pursue a damaged enemy aircraft fleeing towards France and finish it off. But if the pilot flew for too long, the depleted fuel levels could mean disaster during the return flight over the English Channel. Squadron Leader Kellett smiled to himself — he knew exactly how the Polish pilots would react to the message.

3 September 1940

At 10.28 hours six Hurricanes from 'A' Flight and six from 'B' Flight of No. 303 Kościuszko Squadron, led by Flight Lieutenant Kent, took off to patrol near Dungeness. Suddenly, two Me109s appeared, one of which nearly collided with Flight Lieutenant Kent's aircraft while the other attacked him from behind.

Pilot Officer Zumbach responded quickly by firing a couple of bursts of gunfire to keep the enemy fighter off Flight Lieutenant Kent's tail. The Me109 broke off the attack.

Sergeant Wójtowicz attacked the other Me109 at close range. The enemy fighter returned fire, his bullets hitting Sergeant Wójtowicz's propeller and engine. The Hurricane caught fire, forcing the young Sergeant to break off the attack. He abandoned any thought of baling out after recalling the tragic fate of Polish pilots who had been shot in the air after baling out of their aircraft in Poland. He made an emergency landing in an orchard in Woodchurch, Kent. The flames died away, and Sergeant Wójtowicz escaped from the aircraft with slight injuries.

Flying Officer Henneberg became separated from his flight and came under attack from four Me109s after his blood. He fired at all four enemy aircraft until bullets hit the fuselage and wings of his aircraft, forcing him to break off the engagement and return to RAF Northolt.

While flying alone in search of the enemy, Sergeant František came under a surprise attack from a Spitfire. He managed to evade further bullets without firing back and returned safely to RAF Northolt.

3 September 1940 – second sortie
At 14.15 hours, nine Hurricanes of No. 303 Kościuszko Squadron took off to patrol over Maidstone and towards Dover. The pilots saw many friendly aircraft in the air.

Sergeant František sighted a lone enemy aircraft at about 8,000 feet and dived towards it to take a closer look. Seeing the black crosses of the enemy, he fired without hesitation at a distance of 100 yards.

'I must have killed the pilot. The enemy aircraft dived into the sea and disappeared.'

Before returning to RAF Northolt, the Czechoslovakian Sergeant came under attack but managed to avoid damage. It made Sergeant František laugh — a Spitfire had attacked him during the morning, and he had escaped a mid-afternoon attack by a Hurricane. He had a good tale to tell upon his return to RAF Northolt.

5 September 1940
Nine Hurricanes from No. 303 Squadron, led by Squadron Leader

Kellett took off from RAF Northolt at 14.53 hours. At around 22,000 feet over the Thames Estuary, they encountered thirty-five Junker Ju88 bombers with a fighter escort of Me109s to protect the bombers from all sides.

Some of No. 303 Kościuszko Squadron attacked, drawing the German fighters away and enabling the rest of the squadron to attack the bombers. Part of the pursuit took place over the coast of Kent.

Squadron Leader Kellett, Sergeant Karubin and Sergeant Wünsche were among those who attacked the fighters. Squadron Leader Kellett fired at an Me109 from below and behind. It caught fire and fell to earth. He hit another Me109, which began to smoke heavily and fall into a dive. At the same time, another enemy fighter, unseen by Squadron Leader Kellett, flew into attack him but the vigilant Sergeant Wünsche saw the danger and fired at a distance of sixty yards.

'I was at 60-70 yards and I fired all my ammo at it (the enemy aircraft) as I was so afraid it would hit the other Hurricane, Squadron Leader Kellett. It turned on its back in a mass of flames and fell into the sea.'

Sergeant Karubin also had a good days' shooting. He succeeded in destroying two Me109s during two brief attacks.

With the German fighters under attack, Flight Lieutenant Forbes, Sergeant František and Flying Officer Łapkowski of 'B' Flight attacked the bombers and the remaining fighter escort over the Thames Estuary.

Flight Lieutenant Forbes fired into a bomber's starboard engines from close range. He was so close that oil from the enemy aircraft covered part of his Hurricane. The bomber fell to earth, trailing great clouds of smoke.

'Blue-2 Flying Officer Łapkowski broke from the section to settle some Me109s. Blue-3 Sergeant František saw an Me109 attacking a pilot, who had just baled out of a Spitfire. He shot the Me109 down. He then caught up and followed me to attack the bombers.'

At first, Flying Officer Łapkowski was having a successful sortie. He had fired on a Ju88 Bomber from close range and watched it fall to earth in a mass of flames.

'I saw the aircraft which Flight Lieutenant Forbes had fired at

falling in such a great cloud of smoke that the aircraft became invisible. I am certain this aircraft was destroyed.'

While enjoying the sight, Flying Officer Łapkowski's Hurricane was hit by a cannon shell. Flames erupted around him, and he knew he had to bale out. The flames began to creep uncomfortably closer. He tried to open his canopy and felt a terrible pain grip his left shoulder. He struggled to get out of his doomed aircraft and realised that the flames had scorched through his trousers and the flesh on his left leg and parts of his face were burning. The horror of burning alive filled Flying Officer Łapkowski's mind. Using all his willpower and remaining strength, he baled out but was in so much pain that he struggled to pull his rip cord. To his immense relief, his parachute opened, and he floated down to land near Rochford.

Later that afternoon, help arrived to take Flying Officer Łapkowski to a hospital to be treated for a fractured shoulder and the burns to his face and leg. After treatment in various hospitals, he returned to RAF Northolt to convalesce.

6 September 1940

At 08.40 hours, nine Hurricanes from 'A' Flight and 'B' Flight, led by Squadron Leader Kellett, took off from RAF Northolt. Flying over Kent, the pilots sighted a formation of over ninety Dornier and Heinkel He111 bombers flying at 20,000 feet. Approximately 200 Me109 and Me110 fighters flew as escort above the German bombers. It was the largest Luftwaffe formation the pilots of No. 303 Kościuszko Squadron had seen fly over Britain.

The spread of enemy aircraft over Kent covered an area of approximately nineteen miles by five miles. One of the Luftwaffe's targets that morning was the airfields of No.11 Group. The airfield had taken a battering over the previous few weeks and couldn't take much more punishment. Fortunately, the airfield at RAF Northolt had not received any such attacks and was on hand to defend any vulnerable airfield.

The nine Hurricanes of No. 303 Kościuszko Squadron flew into battle with other RAF squadrons of Hurricanes and Spitfires. They were vastly outnumbered by the Luftwaffe. Many Hurricane and Spitfire pilots engaged the enemy in dogfights to draw the fighters away and expose the enemy bombers to attack.

Squadron Leader Kellett selected a Dornier Do17 bomber, and once it came into range, he fired a long burst into its port engine. Smoke poured from the enemy aircraft, and after another burst from Squadron Leader Kellett's guns, the stricken bomber caught fire. He was about to break off from the attack when he heard a series of explosions in his aircraft. He realised there was a gaping hole in his starboard wing and he had no elevator control and little rudder action. Squadron Leader Kellett tried to bale out but found he was trapped with no option but to try to land his aircraft.

'I managed to get the aircraft down at 140mph and keep it under control with the stick hard back and over to port. Finding Biggin Hill close, I made a landing with the undercarriage down but without flaps.'

Mechanics managed to cut off his canopy. Squadron Leader Kellett believed he was *'bloody lucky to be alive.'* He escaped with minor injuries but had he been in a Spitfire, it may have been a different story. He felt lucky that his trusty old Hurricane war horse could take more punishment.

At the same time, Sergeant Karubin was in the air attacking two Messerschmitts and wasted little time in shooting them both down in flames. Moments later, the Sergeant's aircraft was hit by a cannon shell, which set his Hurricane alight. Flames began to flicker and move uncomfortably close to his skin. He tried to land his Hurricane while the flames began to burn his skin but he crash-landed near Pembury. Sergeant Karubin was rescued and taken to Pembury Hospital to get treatment for burns and shock. Fortunately, his burns were not severe but very painful. The 'little Sergeant' rejoined No. 303 Kościuszko Squadron a few weeks later.

The enemy fighters were attacking Pilot Officer Ferić from all sides. He fired a burst at about 200 yards and hit an Me109 head on. The enemy aircraft was painted white from its nose to the end of its cockpit.

'I caught him head on and fired three short bursts at 200-250 yards. He burst into flames and fell to the ground.'

Pilot Officer Ferić managed to evade the other enemy fighters and returned to RAF Northolt.

Another of the many dogfights taking place in the fast and furious battle was fought by Sergeant Wünsche. He flew to the aid of a Hurricane under attack. He fired a few bursts, but the enemy fighter had already hit its target. Sergeant Wünsche fired at the Me109, but he came under attack from another Me109. He dived, and the Me109 dived after him. Sergeant Wünsche flew up to meet the enemy fighter and fired a couple of bursts. The enemy fighter's engine caught fire, but the other Me109 he had damaged moments before had vanished. Sergeant Wünsche then flew towards the Hurricane that had been damaged by the Me109.

'I circled around the British pilot who had baled out and saw him land safely. Then went home.'

Sergeant Rogowski came under heavy attack and was burned. He was taken to a hospital to recover from his painful injuries.

Sergeant František fired upon an Me109 at a distance of 150 yards. The enemy aircraft's engine burst into flames and the Me109 crashed to the ground. Two Me109s, attacking from the rear, fired and hit the tail of Sergeant František's Hurricane, forcing him to return to RAF Northolt.

Flying Officer Urbanowicz continued to fight with the enemy.

'I was attacked by an Me109 from behind. We had a short dogfight. I fired from 200 yards. His engine caught fire and fell to earth.'

He then turned his attention to a nearby enemy bomber but came up against three Me109s that flew to defend the bomber eager for Flying Officer's Urbanowicz blood. An order crackled over the radio transmitter, *'All apany pancake.'* Flying over the balloons, Flying Officer Urbanowicz returned to RAF Northolt.

Squadron Leader Krasnodębski was about to open fire on the enemy when, without warning, a shell hit his Hurricane. Bullets riddled his petrol tank with holes, and the petrol began to flow into Squadron Leader Krasnodębski's cockpit. A fire began to spread rapidly throughout his aircraft. The Squadron Leader felt the fire burn his flesh and knew his only chance of survival was to bale out and take his chance as an unprotected target in the battle raging around him. He had been in this situation in September 1939, but that time a Polish pilot had flown to his aid after he had baled out and saved his life.

With his uniform on fire, Squadron Leader Krasnodębski baled out and fell approximately 10,000 feet, waiting for the force of the fall to extinguish the flames before opening his parachute. Landing upon the ground, Squadron Leader Krasnodębski lay in agony, his smouldering uniform and burned flesh melted together. Rescue arrived quickly, but there was confusion at first as it was thought he was German. Once the Home Guard realised he was Polish, he was taken to a hospital for treatment and spent nearly a year recovering from his horrific burns. Squadron Leader Krasnodębski's absence was felt by all in No. 303 Kościuszko Squadron; he was very highly respected. Flying Officer Urbanowicz took over as acting Polish Commanding Officer.

Flight Lieutenant Forbes was another pilot to experience the agony of being burned during one of the day's dogfights.

'I was Blue-1. I heard very little on the R/T and I could not get in touch with Squadron Leader Kellett. There was heavy interference. When over Sevenoaks, at 22,000ft I saw a large number of Bombers to the east. We went over towards them and were engaged by many Me109s.'

Flight Lieutenant Forbes flew among the many Me109s, firing at an enemy fighter from a distance of 200 yards and hitting its engine, which caught fire. Before Flight Lieutenant Forbes could engage the enemy fighter further, he became aware of an Me109 on his tail. Breaking away to evade his attacker, Flight Lieutenant Forbes sighted a Hurricane under attack and flew to its aid by firing at the attacking Me109 and sending it crashing to earth. Moments later, his aircraft was hit by Luftwaffe bullets. Petrol poured into his cockpit, splashing his face and burning his eyes. He instinctively broke away and dived, hoping the Luftwaffe fighter was not following him. The petrol had momentarily blinded him, and he was helpless to defend himself for he could see only darkness. He began to feel sick and faint from the fumes in the cockpit but as his vision began to return — blurred at first — he battled to try to stay conscious. He turned on his oxygen to help him breathe and looked for a nearby field to land in.

On landing, his aircraft hit a grass bank, but Flight Lieutenant Forbes escaped with only a small cut to his nose and neck, some minor burns, and very sore eyes.

6 September 1940. Second Sortie

At 13.10 hours, the remaining nine Hurricanes of No. 303 Kościuszko Squadron led by Flight Lieutenant Kent took off on patrol over western Kent. The squadron was on high alert, but whereas the morning sky had been full of enemy aircraft, there was not a single enemy aircraft to be seen in the afternoon. But that didn't mean danger wasn't far away.

Flight Lieutenant Kent was flying at 11,000 feet when his Hurricane's engine suddenly blew up. Quickly turning off the petrol, he turned on his oxygen. His aircraft was on fire and losing height, but as he was flying over London, he abandoned any thoughts of baling out. As he approached South Ruislip and the welcome sight of RAF Northolt, Flight Lieutenant Kent saw fire engines driving at full speed to where he was about to land. He felt very relieved when his wheels touched down safely. The fire engines sprayed both him and his Hurricane in white foam. He was amused to see he looked like a snowman.

Early evening Flying Officer Januszewicz took off with No. 1 Royal Canadian Squadron. In a short dogfight, he damaged an Me109 fighter, but his aircraft was then shot by a Heinkel He111 bomber, forcing him to land his Hurricane in haste. He escaped without injury; the Hurricane was not so fortunate.

During the combat that day, none of the pilots of No. 303 Kościuszko Squadron lost their lives, although many received injuries and burns. Three Hurricanes had been damaged – two of them were complete write-offs. Also, with two of the British Officers injured, it was decided that only one British Officer would lead the squadron on sorties from that day forward.

The following message was received by General Sikorski and sent to No. 303 Kościuszko Squadron.

London 6th September 1940

I congratulate Squadron 303 on its splendid days' fighting.

This message has been sent to me by the Air Minister Sir Archibald Sinclair. After the words of His Majesty King George VI, in his answer to the President of Poland this is his second message of appreciation for the valour of the Polish Airmen. Fighting for some days side by side with their famous British Colleagues, they have already achieved important success. Their deeds are the only worthy reply that a Pole can give to the infamous lies of German propaganda.

The squadron's mechanics volunteered to work through the night, supported by the prompt supply of parts delivered by the Air Transport Auxiliary. By morning, the mechanics had performed miracles on the damaged Hurricanes.

7 September 1940

At 16.25 hours, eleven Hurricanes were scrambled and flew to meet up with No. 1 RAF Squadron north-east of London. The previous day's sortie played heavily on Flight Lieutenant Forbes' mind as he led the squadron into position at 24,000 feet; approximately 4,000 feet above No. 1 RAF Squadron.

'I led the Squadron up to 24,000ft determined after my experiences yesterday not to be caught napping at too low an altitude. It is easier to get down to the enemy and impossible to attack climbing when the slow speed makes one easy prey to the Me109s.'

They intercepted enemy bombers with a fighter escort flying close by. British Spitfires kept the German fighter escort busy, with No. 1 RAF Squadron drawing away most of the remaining Me109 fighters and leaving the enemy bombers at the mercy of No. 303 Kościuszko Squadron.

'We reformed towards them and launched the attack at vics abreast. Striking the formation a little to the rear of the centre they were easy meat. We came to them particularly up sun and at great speed as they turned away from us.'

Flight Lieutenant Forbes fired a couple of bursts, and his bullets tore into the engine of an enemy bomber. Large pieces of the Dornier's engine and wing began to fall off, and within moments, the bomber with its crew fell to their final resting place beneath the waves.

After watching his kill sink into the sea, Flight Lieutenant Forbes' Hurricane was hit by a cannon shell. Feeling a sharp pain in his leg and seeing blood, an annoyed Flight Lieutenant Forbes had no choice but to head back to RAF Northolt.

Flying Officer Urbanowicz targeted one of the enemy bombers trying to make its escape. Firing at 300 yards, then giving the Dornier another quick burst from his Browning guns, Flying Officer

Urbanowicz watched as the stricken bomber fell crashing in flames. Sighting a nearby enemy fighter, he fired and hit the Me109. Flying Officer Urbanowicz suddenly found himself under attack by a group of enemy fighters and unable to finish off the Me109, which was trying to escape in a trail of smoke. Flying Officer Urbanowicz managed to evade his attackers but was forced to land his Hurricane at a small nearby airfield to refuel before returning to RAF Northolt.

Pilot Officer Zumbach fired two bursts at a Dornier Do17 as it flew nearby, the second burst hitting the bomber. He had secured his first kill for Britain and was determined more would follow.

'I climbed, found another, fired from 30 yards. It caught fire and fell to earth.'

The force from hitting his target at close range caused Pilot Officer Zumbach's Hurricane to plummet to earth in a dive. He began to lose consciousness. With only seconds to spare, the young pilot regained consciousness and pulled the aircraft out of the fall. That evening he celebrated his lucky escape with a whisky down The Orchard Pub.

Pilot Officer Pisarek experienced his own narrow escape in the combat. After successfully destroying an enemy fighter, his Hurricane was severely damaged by a cannon shell, leaving Pilot Officer Pisarek with no choice but to bale out. This was not to prove easy, as one foot became trapped. He struggled to free his foot from his shoe as the earth became uncomfortably close. If he left it any longer to get out, there wouldn't be time to open his parachute. Finally, his foot became free. He baled out, and his aircraft crashed to the ground. Pilot Officer Pisarek floated safely down, landing near Loughton.

Pilot Officer Łokuciewski attacked one of the Luftwaffe Dornier bombers whose bombs could cause so much death and destruction over Great Britain. He fired several bursts of bullets, which hit their target and sent it crashing to the ground in flames. His bullets hit another Dornier, but as the enemy aircraft flew behind a defensive wall of approaching Me109s, Pilot Officer Łokuciewski had to break off the attack to evade enemy bullets. He landed back at RAF Northolt and celebrated his first kill with the squadron.

Pilot Officer Daszewski was another pilot to enjoy his first kill over England. After destroying a Dornier, Pilot Officer Daszewski fired and hit another bomber, but as he was about to finish the Dornier off, enemy fighters flew to the bomber's defence. He was outnumbered but fired back looking for a chance to evade the onslaught of bullets. Suddenly, enemy shells hit the cockpit and he felt the excruciating pain of the shells tearing the flesh from his body. Reacting with speed, he broke away and slipped through an opening between the Me109s. Hot glycol coolant splashed against his face causing it to burn. Trailing smoke, Pilot Officer Daszewski's Hurricane began to dive towards the earth. To survive he had to bale out, but the shrapnel had caused severe damage to his body. Blood poured from his wounds. The pain in his body was indescribable and his face felt as if it was on fire. He became weaker with every attempt to get out of his falling aircraft. With one last surge of strength and courage, he tumbled out of his cockpit into the sky. Spinning as he fell, he began to lose consciousness. He tried to pull the handle on his parachute's ripcord, but his hand was so badly injured that he could not grasp it and had to stretch across his body with his other hand to pull the cord. He hit the ground and lay in agony. People ran over to him, thinking he was German and began pulling at him. *'Polish, not German,'* he shouted. *'I am Polish.'* Thankfully, they understood and changed from being an angry mob to gentle rescuers.

Pilot Officer Daszewski spent many months in a hospital recovering from his horrific injuries. With excellent medical care, the support of visiting pilots and personal determination, Pilot Officer Daszewski made a full recovery.

Sergeant Wójtowicz enjoyed destroying two enemy aircraft on his sortie that afternoon.

> *'I attacked a group of Dornier 215s. One of them caught fire then the whole machine blew up and fell to earth.'*

Bullets from his Hurricane's Browning machine guns then ripped through the wings of another Dornier bomber, setting it alight and crashing to earth.

Sergeant Szaposznikow fired a burst of bullets at an enemy bomber within a large formation. Smiling to himself, he watched as his bullet hit their intended target and the Dornier crashed to earth in a mass of flames. He engaged an Me109 flying at him head on. Sergeant

Szaposznikow destroyed the Me109 and watched it fall in flames. He celebrated his kills over Northolt with a victory roll before he landed.

Flying Officer Paszkiewicz, the first pilot of No. 303 Kościuszko Squadron to destroy an enemy aircraft over England, was another pilot to exact some revenge that day by shooting down two Dornier bombers in quick succession.

During the combat, Flying Officer Henneberg fired and hit one of the many bombers, and badly damaged an Me109 fighter.

The 7 September 1940 had been a very successful day for No. 303 Kościuszko Squadron in terms of destroying enemy aircraft — fourteen enemy aircraft destroyed and five probables. The success came at a price, as many of the pilots from the squadron had been injured and the enemy had left its mark on the landscape.

Over 300 civilians lay dead, and approximately 1,000 had been injured that day when the Luftwaffe dropped their bombs on the people of London. Flying over the destruction, Flight Lieutenant Kent began to feel a surge of anger that he could never have imagined. The country was experiencing the destructive capabilities of the enemy, and the hatred for Hitler reached new heights. The Polish airmen and ground crews empathised — they knew only too well what their English Allies were going through. In turn, the British pilots had a greater understanding of the Polish airmen's consuming hatred. United in their determination to repel the enemy in the sky, those at RAF Northolt watched the burning glow of London night after night.

9 September 1940

Flight Lieutenant Kent led twelve Hurricanes on Wing patrol from RAF Northolt at 17.19 hours and met up with No. 1 Canadian Squadron near Guildford. As the squadrons approached Beachy Head, approximately forty enemy bombers with a large fighter escort flew out of the sun and attacked.

Pilot Officer Zumbach came under attack from every direction. Returning the fire, he destroyed an enemy Me109 and weaved into the safety of the clouds to evade fire. He emerged from the clouds with his eight-gun Browning machine guns blazing. His strategy paid off; he damaged another Me109.

Flight Lieutenant Kent fired at a Junkers Ju88 at about 20,000 feet. An Me109 flew to the bomber's aid. Determined that the enemy bomber was not going to escape, Flight Lieutenant Kent chased the Ju88 across the sky while Flying Officer Henneberg fired at the Me109. Five more Me109s flew to the rear of Flight Lieutenant Kent's aircraft, ready to attack. Seeing the immediate danger, Flying Officer Henneberg flew towards them and drew their fire away. He weaved in and out of the enemy aircraft, doing all he could to keep the Me109s at bay while Flight Lieutenant Kent pursued his target.

Flight Lieutenant Kent continued to fire on the Ju88 until the enemy aircraft caught fire and disappeared into cloud cover. Losing sight of the bomber, he attacked an Me110 as it flew near. Damaged and on fire, the enemy aircraft plummeted through the sky towards the sea with both pilots still inside and exploded on impact.

Turning for home, Flight Lieutenant Kent came under attack when an Me109 fighter emerged from the cover of cloud. His return fire hit the attacker and forcing it to flee towards France.

Flight Lieutenant Kent was pleased with his contribution to the tally of enemy aircraft shot down by his squadron. After landing safely at RAF Northolt, he sought out Flying Officer Henneberg and thanked him for keeping the two Me109s off his tail.

'Not two, but six,' said Flying Officer Henneberg, who wanted no thanks — he was just pleased that Flight Lieutenant Kent had landed without injury.

Two Me109s attacked and caused severe damage to Sergeant Wünsche's Hurricane. He baled out but not before the flames spreading through his aircraft had burnt his skin. After landing, he waited in agony until he was taken to Hove Hospital to treat his burns and other injuries. During his recovery, he received letters from school children wishing him a speedy recovery. He was so touched by their thoughtfulness that he kept the letters.

Seeing a Hurricane under attack Sergeant František flew to attack the enemy fighter. He fired at the Me109 from a distance of 100 yards, hitting his target. As the enemy pilot tried to bale out, Sergeant František fired another burst, killing the pilot. Sergeant František had no intention of leaving an enemy pilot alive to inflict damage on another day. He had seen German fighters shoot unprotected Polish pilots in their parachutes and fire upon civilians as they fled from attack in Poland. He had no problem returning the favour.

Flying alone, as he so often, he hunted over the English Channel for enemy aircraft to attack. He sighted a Junkers Ju88, but before he could go into the attack, two Me109 fighters flew to protect the bomber. Sergeant František flew into the cover of the clouds.

> *'During a right turn, I came out of the clouds and saw 10 yds away a Heinkel 111. I very nearly collided with it. I fired at its fuselage at an angle of 45 degrees from above and behind. The front of the enemy aircraft fell to pieces, the cockpit, and both engines were in flames. Owing to the clouds I did not know where it fell on land or sea.'*

There was little time to celebrate the two kills as two more Me109s flew into avenge the bomber's destruction. Once more, Sergeant František used the clouds as a white veil of protection. Realising he had flown a long way over the English Channel, he checked his fuel and saw it was low. Leaving the safety of the clouds to return to RAF Northolt, Sergeant František came under attack. Enemy bullets hit his aircraft's port wing radiator and its left tank. Sergeant František was thankful for the armour plate behind him in his cockpit. He was convinced that he would have been killed had it not been there. The enemy aircraft attacked again, but two British Spitfires flew in and wasted little time in shooting the enemy fighter down. For the second time that day the Czech pilot had luck on his side.

Flying back to England. Sergeant František looked for a safe place to land. His Hurricane's wheels touched the English soil in, of all places, a field of cabbages. The police were prompt to arrive and help the pilot. The aircraft was anchored, and a policeman was posted to keep guard. The police took Sergeant František to Brighton Police Station, where they offered him every assistance and kindness. Later, he was driven to Brighton Railway Station to wait for a train back to London.

> *'I took my parachute back with me, Sergeant Wünsche left his at the station. At the railway station, people were very kind to me and some girls gave me some chocolate and people photographed me. I am very grateful for their kindness to me, which was shown by everyone.'*

11 September 1940

At 15.45 hours, Flight Lieutenant Forbes led 'A' and 'B' Flight on

Wing Patrol to meet up with No. 229 RAF Squadron. Vectored towards the enemy over the Horsham area, pilots sighted around fifty Heinkel bombers and forty Dornier Do17 bombers with a large fighter escort, numbering nearly a hundred aircraft.

At around 18,000 feet, six Hurricanes of No. 303 Kościuszko Squadron flew in to attack the enemy bombers, which were targeting London. The manoeuvre was a tricky one, as the six Hurricanes had to fly under the mass of enemy fighters to attack and draw the fighters away from the bombers.

As Pilot Officer Łokuciewski flew into the attack, two of the Me109 fighters prepared to engage him head on. As bullets whizzed back and forth, Pilot Officer Łokuciewski targeted an enemy aircraft flying past him and fired. The enemy fighter caught fire as it dived towards the sea.

Glancing about him, Pilot Officer Łokuciewski saw aeroplanes with black crosses seemingly fill the sky. An enemy bomber broke away from the formation to return to France with Pilot Officer Łokuciewski in pursuit.

'I attacked three-quarters from the rear and after the fifth burst the enemy aircraft was set on fire and one of the crew jumped out.'

Firing, Sergeant František sent an Me110 fighter crashing to the ground in a ball of flames, then he flew into the safety of the clouds for cover. Moments later, he re-emerged to attack a nearby Heinkel He111 bomber. Bullets flew from his Browning guns, hitting the enemy bomber and sending the aircraft and its crew crashing in flames to a watery grave. Being low on fuel, Sergeant František turned for home but came under attack when an Me109 flashed past him. Firing quickly at the enemy fighter, Sergeant František's bullets hit the target, giving him his third kill of the afternoon.

Pilot Officer Zumbach noticed an Me109 in difficulty and flew into attack it at close range. The enemy fighter burst into flames, and Pilot Officer Zumbach flew to join other pilots in combat against five enemy fighters. Realising he was low on fuel, he had to break off from the engagement and flew to RAF Biggin Hill to refuel.

In a short dogfight, Flying Officer Paszkiewicz took only a short time to destroy an Me110, and Sergeant Szaposznikow attacked two Me110s that were at the rear of the formation. With pleasure, the Sergeant fired upon one of the enemy aircraft.

'The right hand enemy aircraft soon went into a spin. The rest of my ammunition I emptied into the right engine of the remaining enemy aircraft at very close range and he also fell in flames.'

Sergeant Szaposznikow became a Fighter Ace that day with a tally of five enemy aircraft destroyed over Great Britain so far. Whenever he downed an enemy aircraft he thought of what might have been. *'If only the Polish Air Force had Hurricanes to fly in September 1939.'*

That afternoon, many of the Luftwaffe bombers jettisoned their loads in sheer panic before reaching London. Despite their small number compared to the huge formation of German fighters, the six Hurricanes had caused confusion by turning and attacking the enemy. But the tactics and courage of No. 303 Kościuszko Squadron proved very successful, paving the way for No. 229 Squadron and other squadrons to join the attack shortly after the first attack.

Flight Lieutenant Forbes had just destroyed two German bombers when a squadron of Spitfires joined in the attack on the large enemy formation. He watched with pleasure as the German bombers scattered in all directions in their panic to escape. Suddenly, Flight Lieutenant Forbes felt the impact of the bullets hitting his Hurricane during the chaos. Low on fuel and feeling dizzy from his injured leg, he decided to land at RAF Heston to refuel.

Following Flight Lieutenant Forbes' section, Flying Officer Henneberg led his section into the attack, firing on the scattering bombers. He was attacked by Me109s, but other fighters of No. 303 Kościuszko Squadron drew the fighters away. Flying Officer Henneberg managed to fire a quick burst and hit one of the Me109s as it pursued another Hurricane, then he flew after a lone He111 he had sighted in the distance. Catching up with the enemy bomber, Flying Officer Henneberg fired a couple of bursts at it from close range, hitting his target. The Heinkel crew were fortunate to make a forced landing near to the sea. The prisoner of war camp that awaited them for the remainder of the war was better than a watery grave.

Other members of No. 303 Kościuszko Squadron were also doing their utmost to destroy the enemy aircraft that day.

Twenty-year-old Sergeant Brzezowski fired at a Heinkel at close range, destroyed it and making his first kill in Great Britain. Seconds later, he found himself under attack by another Heinkel. Returning fire he destroyed the enemy bomber. The young Sergeant's second kill that afternoon crashed in flames before any of its crew had time to bale out. In the encounter, Sergeant Brzezowski's Hurricane was hit, smoke began to pour forth as his aeroplane began to labour. Near to Sergeant Brzezowski someone was in more trouble. It was another pilot about to bale out of his burning Hurricane. Sergeant Brzezowski was on full alert for enemy aircraft; he knew only to well from his time in combat in Poland that Germans often fired on the helpless airmen after they baled out. As the Hurricane pilot jumped and his parachute opened, Sergeant Brzezowski flew close by to guard the pilot while he floated down.

Sergeant Brzezowski had considered baling out of his own damaged aircraft, but as it was not on fire, he decided against it. The decision allowed him to help another Hurricane pilot landed safely. Sergeant Brzezowski landed at Croydon unable to make it back to RAF Northolt.

Sergeant Wójtowicz became separated from his flight that afternoon and found he was surrounded by six Messerschmitts. Heroically, he fired at the enemy.

Many local people watched while holding their breath as the young Sergeant fought valiantly. The fight took place over the Kent countryside and at one point, was fought at very low altitude. People watched feeling helpless as Sergeant Wójtowicz shot down two of the enemy fighters in the fight for his life. Seconds later, the enemy shot Sergeant Wójtowicz, killing him instantly. His Hurricane crashed in flames near a chalkpit in Westerham. Sergeant Wójtowicz had flown in defence of Poland and in France before losing his life while fighting in the sky over England.

Flying Officer Cebrzyński came under heavy attack by many enemy fighters. He fought back bravely until his Hurricane was hit and crashed in a field near a farm in Sandhill, Pembury. When the local farmer and others found him, there was nothing that could be done. Flying Officer Cebrzyński had flown, as Sergeant Wójtowicz and many others of No. 303 Kościuszko Squadron, in defence of Poland and France, and had given his life in the fight for freedom.

Growing up in Poland, Flying Officer Cebrzyński's young son knew of his heroic father only through the stories told to him.

For No. 303 Kościuszko Squadron it was a successful afternoon in terms of destroying enemy aircraft, but it came at a price and everyone at RAF Northolt, from the pilots to the ground crew, felt the loss of the two airmen who gave their lives that day.

Forever, Flying Officer Cebrzyński's and Sergeant Wójtowicz's names are written in golden letters; sadly more of the squadron were soon to join them.

15 September 1940

This day, more than any other in the Battle of Britain, is believed by many to be the turning point in the air battle. By 11.30 hours, the sky over southern England was filled with a mass of German bombers and fighter escort flying towards London with the aim of destroying the RAF.

In theory, once the Luftwaffe had won the battle for air supremacy, and Hitler's divisions had sailed across the English Channel, the gates to Great Britain would be open to the German invasion. All that stood in the way of Hitler's invasion plan, codenamed Operation Sealion, was the RAF with her Allies, who the Luftwaffe outnumbered by four to one.

One squadron from No. 10 Group; five squadrons from No. 12 Group flying as a large wing; eleven squadrons from No. 11 Group, of which ten flew as pairs, flew in the first combat of the day. There were losses on both sides, with seven RAF pilots paying the ultimate sacrifice.

The Commander in Chief Hugh Dowding stood looking down at the operations room table at Group Headquarters, Uxbridge. He knew more than anyone what lay ahead for the few courageous Hurricane and Spitfire pilots. Even with the aid of radar, it seemed they stood little chance against a vast number of enemy aircraft.

The sky over the London soon filled with individual dogfights as the pilots fought to shoot each other down. The brave Hurricane and Spitfire pilots fighting to save a free way of life from Hitler's tyranny, held the fate of Great Britain in their hands that day.

At 11.20 hours, twelve Hurricanes of No. 303 Kościuszko Sqaudron led by Flight Lieutenant Kent were scrambled with No. 229 RAF Squadron from RAF Northolt to engage the enemy south of London. The German bombers dropped their loads along the Thames Estuary while the fighter escort flew close by to protect the bombers.

Pilot Officer Zumbach was flying near to Flying Officer Henneberg, as an Me109 fired at Flying Officer Henneberg, but Pilot Officer Zumbach, who had been flying nearby flew to his aid and attacked the enemy fighter.

'I fired a burst at it. It smoked and drew away. I followed firing at 50-100 yards and set him on fire.'

After his narrow escape, Flying Officer Henneberg fired upon a Do17 at a range of 150 yards. Ablaze, the doomed bomber went into a dive. At the same time, three enemy fighters flew in to avenge the Dornier's destruction. Their guns fired at Flying Officer Henneberg, but he managed to evade their bullets. Shortly after, Flying Officer Henneberg saw three other Me109s heading for France. Flying after them, he managed to catch up and fired his eight-gun Browning at his chosen target. He watched in delight as the enemy fighter dived into the sea. With his tally at six enemy aircraft destroyed, Flying Officer Henneberg became a Fighter Ace.

Sergeant František fired as an enemy aircraft came within his sights and, as his bullets hit their target, he watched the enemy fall from the sky in flames.

Attacking some of the Me109s that had been escorting the bombers over London was keeping Pilot Officer Łokuciewski very busy. At the same time, he came under attack from the rear. Evading the enemy Me109 fighters, he sighted another formation of enemy bombers with a fighter escort heading towards London. As Pilot Officer Łokuciewski flew into the attack, another Hurricane pilot joined him. Pilot Officer Łokuciewski fired at the Me109, hitting his target which fell in flames. Seconds later, he found himself under attack again. This time a cannon shell hit his aircraft. With his Hurricane badly damaged and injured leg, he had no choice but to return to RAF Northolt. On landing, he was taken to a hospital.

Sergeant Wojciechowski fired a couple of bursts from his guns while pursuing two Me109 fighters. His bullets hit one target, causing the Me109 to explode in flames. Sighting an enemy bomber, he flew into the attack and was joined by another Hurricane pilot, whom he recognised as Sergeant Andruszków of No. 303 Kościuszko Squadron.

'I attacked an Me109 with Sergeant Andruszków. We fired at it and it burst into flames and crashed to earth.'

Both pilots were pleased with their shared kill.

Pilot Officer Ferić came under fire while chasing enemy fighters over Dungeness. He returned the fire and watched as the Me109 blew up in flames, then turned his attention to another enemy fighter. He fired, damaging the enemy fighter but as his own aircraft had been hit, he was forced to break away and return to RAF Northolt leaving Flight Lieutenant Kent to attack the damaged enemy fighter and send it into the sea. The Messerschmitt pilot managed to bale out but plummeted to his death when his parachute failed to open.

Flying Officer Paszkiewicz and Pilot Officer Pisarek each downed an Me109 bringing the squadron's tally that morning to ten enemy aircraft destroyed, and the day was not over yet for No. 303 Kościuszko Squadron.

During the early afternoon, the Luftwaffe launched another full-scale aerial attack on London. The RAF had at their disposal five squadrons from No. 12 Group, three squadrons from No. 10 Group, and all squadrons from No. 11 Group were airborne with no reserves. Freedom hung in the balance once more for Great Britain.

At approximately 14.20 hours, nine Hurricanes of No. 303 Kościuszko Squadron, led by Squadron Leader Kellett were vectored over Gravesend. A massive formation of over 400 enemy aeroplanes filled the sky. The majority of the Luftwaffe's force consisted of Dornier Do17 German bombers, supported by the usual Me109 and Me110 fighter escort for protection. The enemy aircraft stretched across the English sky for several miles and were flying in the direction of the Polish squadron. The German airmen believed victory would be theirs that day.

Hitting cloud up high, some of the windscreens of No. 303 Kościuszko Squadron began to ice up. Fortunately, the sun began to shine through the cloud, melting the ice. Squadron Leader Kellett and three Hurricanes flew into attack the enemy while the other four Hurricanes led by Flying Officer Urbanowicz joined them.

The airmen of the Luftwaffe must have been quite shocked at the bravado of nine lone Hurricanes flying to attack them, but the Hurricanes were not alone for long and soon other friendly fighters joined No. 303 Kościuszko Squadron. The sky was full of aircraft as the German formation began to scatter.

Squadron Leader Kellett fired at close range at a Dornier bomber, causing severe damage.

'I fired at Dornier 215. I saw pieces fly off both engines and the front of the fuselage. I could not stay to see what happened and I was immediately attacked by 4 yellow-nosed Me110s from all sides and had to dive to get out of it.'

Acting quickly, the Squadron Leader flew into the cover of cloud, where he stayed until all seemed clear. He was attacked once more after leaving the cover of the clouds but manoeuvred with haste behind the attacking Me110 fighter. He fired a couple of bursts from his guns, sending the enemy fighter down in flames with its two airmen inside.

At approximately 15,000 feet, Flying Officer Urbanowicz selected an enemy bomber to fire at. The German bomber fled for cover in the cloud but as soon it emerged, it met the bullets of Flying Officer Urbanowicz's Browning machine guns.

'I attacked another Dornier from the rear. I attacked it again at a distance of 150yds, saw it burst into flames into the sea.'

Flying Officer Żak enjoyed his first kill over England that day by sending a Dornier bomber to its end. His Hurricane was damaged forcing him to return to RAF Northolt, but he had at least experienced his first taste of revenge upon the enemy that was the cause of so much death and destruction in his homeland.

From the vast Luftwaffe formation that afternoon, Sergeant Wojciechowski shot at an enemy fighter and watched it dive into the sea.

'The pilot jumped and I saw him arrested as he landed.'

With one shared kill and one enemy aircraft destroyed, it brought the Sergeant's total for the day to two and a half kills.

Pilot Officer Ferić was attacking an enemy bomber when an Me109 and an Me110 flew to the aid of their bomber. Evading the Germans bullets and turning quickly, Pilot Officer Ferić fired at the Me110 at a range of 90 yards. The enemy fighter became a mass of flames as it crashed. It was his second kill of the day, having successfully destroyed another Me109 in the first sortie of the morning. But he had used up all his ammunition and was forced into the safety of the clouds to avoid attack from a German fighter. With all his ammo used up Pilot Officer Ferić knew he would make an easy target, so waited patiently before emerging from his haven of safety. Shortly after, he landed safely at RAF Gravesend, as he did not have enough fuel left to land at RAF Northolt.

No. 303 Kościuszko Squadron claimed sixteen enemy aircraft destroyed that day, setting a squadron record in the Battle of Britain.

Sergeant Brzezowski, who had narrowly escaped death on 11 September when his Hurricane had been badly shot up, was again under attack. This time the Luftwaffe bullets were to prove fatal and his aircraft was last seen diving towards the Thames Estuary. Sergeant Brzezowski had flown in defence of Poland and lost his life defending Great Britain. His loss was felt by all at RAF Northolt.

Sergeant Brzezowski was one of the four pilots killed that afternoon. The other Polish pilot who lost his life that day was Flight Lieutenant Chłopik of No. 302 Polish Squadron flying from RAF Duxford. His Hurricane was badly damaged in combat forcing Flight Lieutenant Chłopik to bale out. Sadly, he was found dead on landing. In total, the RAF lost thirty aircraft that day with over half the pilots saved.

As the sky finally fell silent over England that Sunday evening, the people of Great Britain awaited the wireless broadcast announcing that *'the RAF had destroyed 185 enemy aircraft'.* **

People all over Great Britain celebrated, unaware at that time just how much was owed to 'The Few'.

Commander in Chief Hugh Dowding was very proud of his fighter boys. He knew, as did the Prime Minister Winston Churchill, what defeat could have meant that September day. Hugh Dowding had done more than anyone to aid the fighter pilots, he would never forget them nor they he.

The courage shown by the Hurricane and Spitfire pilots that day, and throughout the Battle of Britain, saved thousands of lives in Great Britain. Against all the odds, the RAF and her Allies had caused Hitler's Operation Sealion to be postponed indefinitely.

**The claim of 185 enemy aircraft destroyed on 15 September 1940 was exaggerated; fifty-six enemy aircraft were destroyed with many others badly damaged. This number was a magnificent achievement for the RAF. Of the fifty-six enemy aircraft shot down that crucial day twenty-six of them were destroyed by Polish pilots in No. 302 Polish Squadron, No. 303 Kościuszko Squadron, and Polish airmen in various RAF squadrons.

17 September 1940

At 15.05 hours, Flight Lieutenant Kent led No. 303 Kościuszko Squadron to patrol north of Biggin Hill. Sighting a large formation in the distance, the squadron flew to investigate but found the aircraft to be RAF. After an hour, the enemy were seen in the distance but they were too far away for the squadron to have any chance of catching up.

Sergeant Wojciechowski sighted a lone Hurricane under attack from an Me109 fighter and flew to its aid while keeping watch for other enemy fighters drawn to the chance of an easy target.

'I went into the attack, I hit it and it went towards the earth.'

Minutes later, another Me109 came into Sergeant Wojciechowski's sights. He fired, hitting one of its wings as the enemy fighter returned fire. Before he could pursue the Messerschmitt further, he heard a message over the radio transmitter ordering No. 303 Kościuszko Squadron back to RAF Northolt.

Earlier in the day, the funerals of Flying Officer Cebrzyński and Sergeant Wójtowicz had taken place at Northwood Cemetery.

18 September 1940

At 12.20 hours, twelve Hurricanes of No. 303 Kościuszko Squadron led by Squadron Leader Kellett were sent to patrol over West Malling.

A lone Dornier Do17 with a single fighter escort was sighted. Within seconds, eight Hurricanes circled the enemy bomber, trapping it in a hail of bullets. Three of the bomber's crew managed to bale out just minutes before the aircraft exploded.

The lone Me109 fighter escorting the bomber managed to escape with slight damage, but as the pilot turned for France, he flew straight into the path of Sergeant František. The Sergeant had been flying a short distance behind the squadron. After a couple of bursts from his guns, Sergeant František watched with pleasure as the Me109 crashed, taking the pilot with it.

'I think this Me109 may have already been fighting with 303

Squadron. I returned to base, found Flying Officer Ferić, we flew back together.'

23 September 1940

At 09.30 hours, 'A' and 'B' Flight of No. 303 Kościuszko Squadron led by Flight Lieutenant Kent were scrambled from RAF Northolt along with No. 229 Squadron and No. 1 Royal Canadian Squadron. At 23,000 feet approximately thirty Me109s were sighted over the Thames Estuary. Various dogfights took place that morning.

Pursuing an Me109 fighter across the English Channel as it headed for the safety of France, Flight Lieutenant Kent awaited his moment. Once he got the enemy aircraft in his sights, Flight Lieutenant Kent fired and sent the Me109 to its last resting place beneath the waves.

Sergeant Szaposznikow flew to the defence of a Hurricane pilot who was under attack by many Me109s. The Hurricane was returning fire in a desperate attempt to defend itself. Sergeant Szaposznikow fired, destroying one of the Messerschmitts, but while firing at another, he was annoyed to find he had emptied his guns. With no choice but to break away, he returned to RAF Northolt and carried out a victory roll before landing.

26 September 1940

RAF Northolt was honoured by a visit from King George VI, who was given a guided tour of RAF Northolt and taken to the Sector Operations Room to watch the squadrons in action. The Polish pilots were very proud to be introduced to the King. There was little doubt that the King's visit was a success — he overstayed his scheduled time by nearly two hours.

At 12.03 hours, twelve Hurricanes from No. 303 Kościuszko Squadron led by Squadron Leader Kellett took off on Wing patrol over Guildford with No. 229 Squadron. Shortly after take off, they were vectored towards Portsmouth. At approximately 18,000 feet, fifty Heinkel He111 bombers with their fighter escorts were sighted. The enemy fighters flew above and below the Heinkels while the bombers dropped their bomb loads over the east side of Southampton. Unfortunately, the Heinkels were too far ahead for No. 303 Kościuszko Squadron to reach them. With their operation nearly completed, the enemy bombers headed towards the French coast.

No. 303 Kościuszko Squadron set off in pursuit. Once the Heinkel He111s were in range of the squadron's Browning machine guns, the pilots targeted the Luftwaffe fighter escort guarding the bombers and attacked from the rear at approximately 15,000 feet.

Squadron Leader Kellett pursued an enemy fighter, firing a couple of bursts from his guns into the Me109. As the enemy aircraft fell towards the sea, Squadron Leader Kellett found the throttle of his Hurricane had become stuck, and he was unable to control the aircraft. Much to his relief, Squadron Leader Kellett's aircraft became controllable before he had to bale out. Seconds later, he came under attack from two friendly Hurricanes but managed to evade their fire. *'If I am to be shot down,'* he thought to himself, *'it's not going to be by my own side but a bloody Jerry.'*

Flying to attack one of the enemy bombers Sergeant Kowalski came under attack by an Me109.

> *'I broke away from the bombers and attacked the Me109, firing 2 long bursts after which the enemy aircraft dived in smoke to the earth.'*

Sergeant Kowalski had shot down his first enemy aircraft over England that afternoon and *'he felt elated'*.

Flying Officer Urbanowicz was successful that afternoon also, having destroyed a Heinkel He111; and Flying Officer Żak shot down his second enemy aircraft in two days.

Flying Officer Paszkiewicz's eagle-eyes sighted a formation of Heinkels with fighter escort and informed Flight Lieutenant Forbes over the radio transmitter.

Firing at one of the enemy bombers at 250 yards and closing into 50 yards, Flying Officer Paszkiewicz hit the Heinkel, which burst into flames.

Flying to the rear of the enemy bomber formation, Flight Lieutenant Forbes fired at three-quarters astern; his bullets hitting their target. The Heinkel's starboard engine began to fall to pieces and trail smoke. As the Flight Lieutenant's aircraft began to climb, his Hurricane nearly collided with the enemy bomber's wing. The slipstream threw over Flight Lieutenant Forbes' aircraft, and it began to trail smoke from its tail end.

'I saw a trail of white smoke apparently coming from my machine. Thinking I might be on fire I prepared to bale out but as no flames appeared I did a right turn and found the smoke had ceased.'

Turning for home, Flight Lieutenant Forbes' aircraft was attacked by two Spitfires. He was thankful as he managed to evade their bullets and return safely to RAF Northolt.

Sergeant František, who had been flying near to Flight Lieutenant Forbes, fired a couple of bursts at an enemy bomber. Within seconds, it fell in a ball of flames, and Sergeant František turned his attention to another Heinkel He111. He had to pursue the enemy bomber over the English Channel towards France for quite a distance before it came within the Sergeant's sights. Firing, he destroyed it and watched it fall on French soil. Turning for home, Sergeant František celebrated with a victory roll over RAF Northolt before landing.

Sergeant Andruszków attacked, as did many of the squadron that day, from three-quarters astern.

'I then climbed, saw a Dornier 215 to my left which I attacked. The enemy aircraft dived and I followed and fired several bursts at a very short distance. The enemy aircraft continued to dive and crashed into the sea.'

As he watched the enemy bomber sink to its doom, he was attacked by an Me109. Returning fire, he pursued the enemy fighter but lost him.

Pilot Officer Zumbach attacked the enemy formation. It took very little time for his Browning machine guns to send an enemy bomber to earth in flames. He then turned his attention to the fighter escort.

'I attacked another aircraft, this time an Me109. I fired, the pilot must have been killed as the Me109 dived into the sea without any visible sign of damage. No ammo left so I returned to Northolt.'

Flying Officer Grzeszczak fired two long bursts towards an enemy bomber and watched as the Heinkel sank beneath the waves. This was Flying Officer Grzeszczak's first kill with No. 303 Kościuszko Squadron. Moments later, his Hurricane was lifted by a cannon shell exploding underneath his aircraft. Fortunately for the Flying Officer, he was unhurt but a little shaken and he managed to land his damaged aircraft back at RAF Northolt. Another job for the airfield's mechanics, who were kept busy most days and nights repairing the Hurricanes.

Pilot Officer Januszewicz came under heavy attack from the enemy but he managed to escape injury and land his damaged Hurricane on farmland near Farnham.

Sergeant Bełc fired his Browning machine guns at two Me109s, sending one of the enemy fighters crashing to the ground.

'I chased the 2nd Me109 over the coast of France, so returned.'

The flight towards France had depleted Sergeant Bełc's fuel supply, requiring him to refuel at RAF Biggin Hill before returning to RAF Northolt.

27 September 1940. First Sortie

At 08.05 hours, Flight Lieutenant Forbes led eleven Hurricanes of No. 303 Kościuszko Squadron on Wing patrol with No. 1 Royal Canadian Squadron. Approximately seventy Heinkel He111 bombers and a large fighter escort were sighted at around 15,000 feet over the Horsham area.

When Flight Lieutenant Forbes flew to attack the enemy, he came uncomfortably close to being hit by anti-aircraft fire. Glancing around him, he could not see the rest of the squadron and flew off in search of them. He sighted and pursued a lone Heinkel heading back towards the coast. He tracked and fired upon the Heinkel as it began to dive to escape him. Some of the enemy crew managed to bale out of the damaged bomber moments before it crashed in flames.

Flying Officer Urbanowicz came under attack from an enemy fighter escorting German bombers en route to London. Other squadrons were attacking the German aircraft furiously, trying to prevent them from reaching the capital. Flying Officer Urbanowicz managed to evade the Me109's bullets and flew into attack the enemy bombers.

'One broke away I attacked him, he avoided me by zigzagging, finally, I hit him at about 50 yds away. It crashed about 35 miles south of London by some railway lines. One of the crew parachuted out.'

Almost immediately the Polish Flying Officer came under attack by another Me109. After a short dogfight, the enemy fighter crashed in flames. With empty guns, Flying Officer Urbanowicz had no choice but to return to RAF Northolt.

Pilot Officer Ferić fired his guns towards a Messerschmitt in the fighter escort. His bullets hit their target, and the enemy aircraft burst into flames. He targeted a Heinkel bomber next, knowing that it was vital to destroy as many as possible before they could cause so much death and destruction to the people below. Firing a couple of bursts, Pilot Officer Ferić killed the bomber's pilot and the Heinkel was no more. As Pilot Officer Ferić's Hurricane had been damaged by enemy fire, he returned to RAF Northolt.

While attacking the German bombers, Flying Officer Henneberg sighted two Me109s out of the corner of his eye. He fired a couple of short bursts from his position at the rear and sent one of the enemy fighters to the ground in flames. Before Flying Officer Henneberg had time to engage another Me109, a number of explosions took place in his aircraft caused by a cannon shell. Smoke began to fill his cockpit, and the thought crossed his mind to bale out. As his Hurricane was not on fire, he could just about manage to see where he was flying and chose to fly back to RAF Northolt. After the wheels of Flying Officer Henneberg's Hurricane touched down at RAF Northolt, a very relieved pilot climbed out of the cockpit.

'On examining my aircraft I found out it had been hit by 3 cannon shells, one of which had punctured the radiator.'

Flying Officer Grzeszczak was busy engaging the enemy when he noticed a nearby Hurricane was under attack from four enemy fighters. He flew into help, but the damage had been done, and all he could do was watch as the Hurricane crashed with the pilot inside. Avenging the pilot, Flying Officer Grzeszczak fired at one of the Me109s as it came into range and successfully destroyed it.

'I was attacked by 2 Me109s but I was out of ammo, I evaded them and returned to Northolt.'

Sergeant Kowalski fired on a Heinkel He111 bomber, causing the enemy bomber's engine to stop, but Sergeant Kowalski was disappointed to find he had only enough bullets for a few more bursts.

After emptying his guns towards the enemy, Sergeant Kowalski had no choice but to leave the stricken bomber and return to RAF Northolt. Sergeant Kowalski swore to himself; he knew that one more burst of gunfire would have finished off the enemy bomber.

Sergeant Bełc pursued an Me109 and shot it down. Meanwhile, Flying Officer Żak came under heavy fire from enemy aircraft. Flames began to engulf his cockpit forcing Flying Officer Żak to bale out. His face and hands were burning but despite the excruciating pain Flying Officer Żak managed to put out the flames and pull the handle of his ripcord.

After landing on farmland in the Leatherhead area, Flying Officer Żak was rushed to the nearby hospital to be treated for shock, severe burns to his face, and other burns to his body.

Flying to the rescue of a Hurricane pilot who was being attacked by an Me109, Pilot Officer Zumbach succeeded in shooting the enemy fighter down in flames. He turned towards an enemy bomber, firing a couple of bursts into his intended target. Three other Hurricanes joined him, and together they destroyed the bomber in very little time. One of the Germans baled out of the bomber before it crashed on houses a short distance away.

Sergeant Andruszków and Flying Officer Paszkiewicz were both killed that day in the air. It was a sad day for No. 303 Kościuszko Squadron. The loss of two of their own was felt by all in the squadron.

Flying Officer Paszkiewicz's Hurricane was shot down and crashed on farmland in Borough Green. He had flown in combat in France and destroyed six enemy aircraft during his time with No. 303 Kościuszko Squadron. He had been the first pilot of the squadron to destroy an enemy aircraft in England before it was operational. This first kill on 30 August had helped the Polish pilots of No. 303 Kościuszko Squadron avenge their homeland and demonstrate to the RAF that Polish pilots were skilled fighters in the air.

Sergeant Andruszków at nineteen years old was the youngest pilot in the squadron and had celebrated his first kill the previous day. His Hurricane crashed in flames at Holywych Farm in Cowden, Kent.

27 September 1940. Second Sortie
At 14.52 hours, six Hurricanes from No. 303 Kościuszko Squadron's

'A' Flight led by Flight Lieutenant Kent were scrambled from RAF Northolt and flew towards the east of London. The Hurricanes sighted enemy Junkers Ju88s flying back from the capital at approximately 15,000 feet. The flight pursued the enemy bombers towards the coast of Hastings determined to avenge the destruction the bombs had no doubt caused.

As Flight Lieutenant Kent prepared to fire at a Junkers Ju88 from the rear, the Junker's rear gunner fired. Acting quickly, Flight Lieutenant Kent hid as best he could behind the armour plate in his cockpit canopy while bullets flew all around him. He fired, killing the bomber's rear gunner then fired a couple of bursts into the bomber. Parts began to fall off the bomber and, as it caught fire, clouds of smoke poured forth. The smoke blinded Flight Lieutenant Kent for a few moments but as it cleared, he fired once more. The bomber fell from the sky and crashed a short distance from the shoreline. As Flight Lieutenant Kent watched, it seemed as if one of the Junker's crew had been thrown into the water. Amazingly, the bullets that had hit Flight Lieutenant Kent's aircraft had caused little damage. Luck was with Flight Lieutenant Kent that day.

Busy in combat that afternoon, Flying Officer Urbanowicz destroyed a Junkers Ju88; three of the bomber's crew managed to bale out into the sea. Shortly after, another enemy bomber ended its days beneath the waves as a result of Flying Officer Urbanowicz's Browning machine guns. This time, there was no escape for the crew.

Sergeant Szaposznikow, unable to keep up with the rest of the flight, came under attack from a lone German fighter. Getting behind his opponent, the Sergeant fired from the rear and sent the Me109 tumbling into the sea near to the coast of Brighton.

30 September

At 13.15 hours, twelve Hurricanes of No. 303 Kościuszko Squadron took off to meet up No. 1 Royal Canadian Squadron and No. 229 RAF Squadron on patrol over the Thames Estuary and the south coast where they sighted approximately twenty Dornier Do17 bombers flying over the sea with the usual fighter escort.

Flying Officer Urbanowicz flew into attack an enemy aircraft he was chasing towards France. The bomber's escort of two Me109s flew after Flying Officer Urbanowicz but he quickly dealt with them, leaving the Dornier unprotected as it approached the French coast. Flying Officer Urbanowicz was determined that the enemy bomber was not going to escape him to return another day to cause death and destruction.

'I continued to attack the bomber over France, it went to land, hit its right wing and burst into flames.'

Running low on fuel after a successful sortie, Flying Officer Urbanowicz returned to RAF Northolt; the drinks were on him that night.

Returning to action after being burnt and forced to bale out on the 6 September, Sergeant Karubin was back with No. 303 Kościuszko Squadron. He took no time to destroy an enemy fighter, which was flying at approximately 22,000 feet. Sergeant Karubin's bullets hit their target and the Me109 burst into flames before crashing into the sea. Sergeant Karubin became a Fighter Ace that day.

Pilot Officer Radomski fired his Browning machine guns at one of the Dornier Do17 in the enemy formation. A Spitfire flying nearby joined in the attack, and together they sent the German bomber to a watery grave.

Later that afternoon, as Pilot Officer Radomski turned for home, an explosion took place in his engine. Smoke and flames began to pour from his Hurricane and the cockpit filled with smoke. Pilot Officer Radomski's vision blurred, making his eyes sore. He considered baling out in case fire should break out in his cockpit.

'As I was over the channel at a height of 25,000ft I decided not to jump. The smoke became dense as I tried to see where I was. I closed the throttle, turned off the petrol, switched off the engine and side slipped as smoke was blinding me. I glided and side slipped as far as the coast.'

Flames and smoke were still pouring from his aircraft's exhaust, but Pilot Officer Radomski could see at least enough to land his stricken Hurricane belly down on the shoreline shingles, missing the sea by a few yards. Climbing from his aircraft, he walked along the beach enjoying a deep breath of the welcome English air. He spotted men running towards him in a strange zig-zag fashion. He smiled at them but they did not smile back. Instead, they were very aggressive and began poking him with long sticks. It dawned on Pilot Officer Radomski that the men thought he was German as he still wore part of the dark blue battledress he had worn in France. Still smiling, he spoke to them with the few English words he knew. *'Good afternoon, I am a Polish pilot.'* An Army Officer soon arrived and all was sorted out.

The men who had been poking Pilot Officer Radomski with sticks only moments before began patting him on the back and smiling.

Later that day the Pilot Officer Radomski found the answer to the strange running actions; he had landed in a minefield. He had a good a tale to tell when he returned to RAF Northolt the following day. It had been a lucky day for Pilot Officer Radomski.

30 September 1940. Second Sortie

At approximately 16.50 hours, ten Hurricanes from No. 303 Kościuszko Squadron took off on Wing patrol. Before joining up with other squadrons from RAF Northolt, the squadron sighted a large formation of Luftwaffe Me109 and Me110 fighters flying above. There was a lot of cloud about that afternoon, which was a welcome haven of safety.

Leaving the clouds, Sergeant Bełc flew to help a pilot who was baling out of his damaged aircraft. He circled around the pilot's parachute as it drifted towards the ground and remained on guard until the pilot had landed safely.

Flying Officer Urbanowicz attacked and destroyed an Me109 fighter flying nearby. It had been a successful day for Flying Officer Urbanowicz; he had destroyed four enemy aircraft that day.

Unable to start his aircraft, Sergeant František took off later than the rest of the squadron. Flying alone, which he so often did, he was attacked by six Me109 fighters at approximately 17,000 feet over Brooklands in Surrey. The enemy fighters tried to form a circle to trap Sergeant František, no doubt believing that escape was impossible. Undeterred, Sergeant František fired a couple of bursts from his Browning machine guns, hitting one of the Me109s and sending it to the ground in flames. Seconds later, he returned fire and hit at another attacking Me109. Smoke billowed from the enemy fighter's engine, giving Sergeant František the chance to make his escape through a gap in the circle of enemy fighters and disappear into the cover of cloud. After waiting patiently, Sergeant František left his haven, his eyes ever alert for the German fighters in the clear the sky until he returned safely to RAF Northolt. That day Sergeant František had brought his tally to seventeen kills with No. 303 Kościuszko Squadron.

1 October 1940

Flight Lieutenant Kent led No. 303 Kościuszko Squadron on Wing patrol with No. 1 Royal Canadian Squadron. Large formations of, what appeared to be, enemy bombers flying in groups of three were sighted over the Brooklands area.

As Flight Lieutenant Kent flew into attack the enemy at approximately 22,000 feet, he realised that the aircraft were Messerschmitts not bombers. Seconds later, tracer bullets whizzed past his Hurricane. Flight Lieutenant Kent broke right, which probably saved his life as most enemy pilots would have assumed he would have followed normal practice and gone left when under attack. Looking around him, the Canadian Flight Lieutenant could not see the rest of the wing and realised he was a single Hurricane against nearly forty enemy fighters. Acting quickly, he fired his Browning machine guns and hit the nearest Me109, forcing the enemy fighter to break away while trailing smoke.

Firing another couple of short bursts at a distance of 50 yards, Flight Lieutenant Kent succeeded in sending the Me109 down in flames. The sky seemed full of enemy fighters, and Flight Lieutenant Kent kept close enough to weave between them and fire whenever one came in range. The Me109s had to be cautious; they could easily shoot one another with so many bullets flying past. Finally, the enemy fighters broke off the engagement, much to the relief of Flight Lieutenant Kent. He believed the Me109 fighters were low on fuel and had to make for France. The sky that had been full of German fighters minutes earlier was now empty except for the fading vapour trails and one very fortunate Hurricane. After landing back at RAF Northolt, Flight Lieutenant Kent chatted with the mechanics. To their amazement, they discovered that there was not one bullet hole in his aeroplane. Against all the odds, Flight Lieutenant Kent had survived with an interesting tale to tell.

2 October 1940

No. 303 Kościuszko Squadron and others at RAF Northolt paid their respects to Sergeant Andruszków and Flying Officer Paszkiewicz, who were laid to rest at Northwood Cemetery that day.

5 October 1940

Twelve Hurricanes from No. 303 Kościuszko Squadron flew on Wing patrol with No. 1 Canadian Squadron over the Rochester Channel. Other British squadrons flew nearby. Suddenly, at 18,000 feet enemy aircraft flew out of the cover of clouds and attacked. There were approximately 150 enemy Me109 and Me110 fighters, which swooped down a few at a time out of the cloud.

Squadron Leader Kellett fired a burst, and the damaged Me109 broke away.

'I got in a good burst from in front and on the ¼ wing route. Enemy aircraft turned right and dived under me. I could not follow owing to the big dogfight which had developed involving about 100 aircraft. I had another opportunity for a short burst at another Me109 but could not say if I hit it.'

Trapped by many enemy fighters, Flying Officer Pisarek fired a couple of bursts.

'The Me110s formed a defensive circle. I attacked an Me110 and fired 3 bursts from the front to the left. The result of this attack I did not see, but according to Sergeant Bełc the enemy aircraft began to smoke and broke away probably damaged.'

Flying Officer Pisarek fired again and hit an Me110, sending it and its two airmen beneath the waves. Acting quickly, Flying Officer Pisarek seized his chance to escape when a gap appeared between the enemy fighters.

Sergeant Bełc fired at an Me110 at only 50 yards and sent the enemy fighter crashing out of the sky but not before one of the Luftwaffe airmen had baled out.

While attacking an Me109 fighter, Sergeant Siudak was joined by a nearby Spitfire pilot.

'I attacked an Me109 from the rear and slightly to the left and a Spitfire attacked the same Me109. From the rear and slightly to the

right. I fired 2 bursts. The enemy aircraft burst into flames and fell to earth near Ashford, burning on the ground.'

When another Me109 came within Sergeant Siudak's range, he fired twice into his target and watched it as it fell to pieces before his eyes. A third German fighter fell victim to Sergeant Siudak's Browning machine guns that morning and came to rest in the sea. Being low on fuel, Sergeant Siudak landed near Gravesend to refuel before returning to RAF Northolt.

Sergeant Palak attacked an enemy fighter and hit his chosen target but had to break away with haste when he came under attack from two enemy fighters flying to their comrade's aid. Recovering, Sergeant Palak flew towards his attackers.

'I turned and attacked one enemy aircraft, firing 2 bursts from the rear. The enemy aircraft burst into flames and dived to earth in the neighbourhood of Lympne.'

This was the second Me109 destroyed by Sergeant Palak; his first had been while flying with No. 302 Polish Squadron.

Pilot Officer Ferić chased one of the enemy fighters as it flew for home across the English Channel.

'I chased the enemy aircraft and catching up with him about 7 miles from the coast, fired a burst from a distance of about 20 yards into his cockpit. The enemy aircraft immediately dived into the sea.'

Many enemy fighters were flying around Flying Officer Henneberg, trying to trap him. Firing a couple of bursts, bullets from his Hurricane's guns hit one of the Me110 fighters. Flying Officer Henneberg had to break off the attack to avoid the bullets from another Me109.

'Evading the enemy aircraft I chased the Me110 making towards the coast and began to fire from a distance of 250 yds. After firing 2 bursts into its right engine, enemy aircraft burst into flames and dived straight for the sea.'

Barely having time to enjoy his kill, Flying Officer Henneberg once more came under attack by three Me109 fighters. Managing to evade their fire, the Flying Officer returned to RAF Northolt, where he landed safely. Flying Officer Henneberg was amazed his Hurricane had not received any damage during the combat.

As an Me109 fighter came within Sergeant Karubin's sights, he fired from 150 yards and sent the enemy fighter crashing to earth. Another Me109 flew to attack Sergeant Karubin, and after a short dogfight, the damaged Me109 limped away.

Flying Officer Januszewicz also came under fire during the battle. His Hurricane was hit by bullets from an Me109 fighter and crashed in flames at Stowting in Kent.

The death of Flying Officer Januszewicz was another sad loss for No. 303 Kościuszko Squadron.

6 October 1940

During the early morning, twelve Hurricanes of No. 303 Kościuszko Squadron led by Squadron Leader Kellett took off on patrol duty. Squadron Leader Kellett sighted a lone Junkers Ju88. Each time Squadron Leader Kellett prepared to fire upon the enemy bomber it escaped within the cover of cloud, much to Squadron Leader Kellett's annoyance. As the squadron's Hurricanes were running low on fuel, they returned to RAF Northolt without engaging the enemy. Unfortunately, the Junkers Ju88 bomber had not turned for home as it was thought to have done but was waiting patiently for the chance drop its load.

Back at RAF Northolt, the Hurricanes were back on the ground, and most of the pilots had left their aircraft. Suddenly, the Junkers Ju88 bomber appeared, having followed the squadron while hiding in the clouds. Seeing the danger, the pilots and ground crew scattered as the German bomber attacked. Squadron Leader Kellett dived under a nearby table in the dispersal hut. Seconds later, he and the table was all that was left of the hut. Standing up, he was amazed he had not so much as a scratch on him.

Almost immediately, another bomb landed between the hangers. Sergeant Siudak, whom was still in his Hurricane was tragically killed by the bomb. This terrible sight was witnessed by many of the squadron and the ground crew.

Sergeant Siudak had been at RAF Northolt for a short time, having joined from No. 302 Polish Squadron on the 23 September. He had celebrated his first two and a half victories with No. 303 Kościuszko Squadron the previous day.

In that day's raid on RAF Northolt, two other men lost their lives. The bomb blast had been so powerful that the windows had shattered at the Post Office located half a mile away, along Station Approach in South Ruislip. Before the enemy bomber flew away it machine-gunned the Hurricanes waiting at the dispersal pens.

Two Hurricanes of No. 229 Squadron managed to hit the Junkers Ju88* but it escaped. As the enemy bomber flew away, the air raid siren sounded over South Ruislip but the warning came too late. Many local people witnessed the attack on what was usually a quiet Sunday morning in South Ruislip. The Junkers Ju88 bore yellow marks upon it and was possibly a Wing Leader.

It was the first time RAF Northolt had been bombed, and men had lost their lives in the attack. Until that day, RAF Northolt has been spared the attacks suffered by many other airfields under No. 11 Group during the early days of the Battle of Britain.

*A Junkers Ju88 crashed over France on 6 October 1940. It may have been the one that attacked RAF Northolt that day.

7 October 1940

At 13.23 hours, eleven Hurricanes from No. 303 Kościuszko Squadron were sent to patrol over Brooklands with No. 1 Royal Canadian Squadron. A large formation of approximately fifty Messerschmitts was flying over London. Five Me109 fighters flew into attack both squadrons but almost immediately flew away. Both Northolt squadrons pursued the enemy fighters but were unable to catch up with them.

Later that afternoon, other German fighters flew into attack No. 303 Kościuszko Squadron. Sergeant Bełc fired at a Messerschmitt, sending it crashing to earth.

Selecting an Me109 to target, Sergeant Szaposznikow fired a burst as the enemy fighter flew away across the coast. While flying over the sea, the Sergeant saw two Me109 fighters.

'I fired from a distance of 150 yds but there was no sign of smoke or flames, although the enemy aircraft fell into the sea just off Brighton.'

The other enemy fighter escaped, much to Sergeant Szaposznikow's annoyance.

Flying Officer Pisarek pursued his chosen quarry and fired at a close range of 50 yards. The Me109 fighter fell into the sea and sank beneath the waves.

In just under six weeks of operational sorties flown from RAF Northolt, No. 303 Kościuszko Squadron claimed 126 enemy aircraft destroyed. This magnificent achievement set a Battle of Britain record.

Markings on a Hurricane belonging to No. 303 Kościuszko Squadron to show the number of enemy aircraft claimed as destroyed by pilots of the squadron. Photo: Permission of the Polish Institute and Sikorski Museum.

8 October 1940

At 09.00 hours twelve Hurricanes from No. 303 Kościuszko Squadron led by Flight Lieutenant Kent, took off on a routine patrol. During the patrol, the Luftwaffe were not sighted, but one of the Polish pilots was lost in, what remains to be, an unsolved mystery.

At around 09.30 hours, Sergeant František broke away from the formation. Flight Lieutenant Kent called Sergeant František over the radio transmitter but did not receive a reply. Fifteen minutes later Sergeant František was dead.

People on the ground witnessed Sergeant František's Hurricane trying to make a forced landing. As it touched down at Cuddington

Way, Ewell in Sutton, the Hurricane flipped over onto its back. People nearby rushed to his aid, but there was nothing they could do; Sergeant František's neck had been broken. There were no bullet holes in the Hurricane, and Sergeant František had not signalled with his aeroplane wings to indicate he was in trouble, nor did he try to make contact over the radio transmitter. Some in the squadron believe he may have momentarily blacked out in the air, then tried to land at the last minute after regaining consciousness. Sergeant František's loss was a tragic blow to the squadron. He had flown from Czechoslovakia to Poland when the German forces had invaded his country. He flew in defence of Poland and felt at home with the Polish airmen. He followed his Polish comrades to France and Great Britain to continue the fight. In England he insisted on fighting in a Polish Squadron and joined No. 303 Kościuszko Squadron from its formation in the summer of 1940. He was often a loner and single-minded in his determination to destroy as many Germans as possible. In the five and a half weeks Sergeant František flew in combat with No. 303 Kościuszko Squadron, he destroyed seventeen enemy aircraft and became the top scoring Fighter Ace during the Battle of Britain.

Sergeant František is laid to rest at Northwood Cemetery two days later.

Sergeant Josef František Photo: Permission of the Polish Institute and Sikorski Museum.

11 October 1940

No. 303 Kościuszko Squadron was moved to Leconfield airfield for a rest from frontline duties. No. 302 Polish Squadron flew from RAF Northolt until No. 303 Kościuszko Squadron returned on 3 January 1941.

The Battle of Britain is reported to have taken place between 10 July 1940 and 31 October 1940. During that time, eight members of No. 303 Kościuszko Squadron paid the ultimate sacrifice and lost their young lives. Pilots and ground crew from all squadrons fought with bravery during those crucial weeks, with many losing their lives or sustaining debilitating injury. Their sacrifice to keep Hitler's evil from Great Britain's door was not made in vain. There is little doubt that had the Luftwaffe won the war of the skies, Hitler's troops would have invaded Great Britain and laid waste to many more lives as they had throughout Nazi-occupied countries.

In the famous words spoken by of Sir Winston Churchill:

'Never in the field of human conflict was so much owed by so many to so few.'

In the original Battle of Britain combat reports, the pilots incorrectly identify the bombers as Dornier Do215s when the aircraft were Dornier Do17s. Luftwaffe casualty reports also record that only Do17s flew in the Battle of Britain. Where applicable, the correct aircraft, the Dornier Do17s, are recorded throughout this book.

Sources: Interviews Flight Lieutenant Kowalski, Flight Lieutenant Szaposznikow, Major Urbanowicz, Wing Commander Kellett, Mr D.A. Britton, Mr P. Finch, and Mr B. Stevens. **Permissions:** With thanks to the pilots and their relatives for access to various documents, personal letters and for some Log Books — Flight Lieutenant Cebrzyński, Sergeant Bełc, Flying Officer Ferić, Group Captain Forbes, Squadron Leader Henneberg, Sergeant Karubin, Group Captain Krasnodębski, Squadron Leader Łapkowski, Warrant Officer Palak, Flight Lieutenant Radomski, Sergeant Siudak, Sergeant Wójtowicz and Flight Lieutenant Wünsche. The Polish Institute and Sikorski Museum, London. Mr T. Krystek and Mr W. Wybraniec from the Polish Air Force Association. RAF Northolt for the Operational Record Diaries for No. 303 Kościuszko Squadron. The National Archives for Combat Reports, reference Air 50/117. 'One of the Few' by Johnny Kent, published by William Kimber London 1971.

PART IV

No. I POLISH FIGHTER WING
AT RAF NORTHOLT

On 1 April 1941, No. 1 Polish Fighter Wing (Northolt Wing) was formed. It was the first of three Polish Wings, and it flew on various types of sorties. These operations were given code names such as 'Circus,' where fighters escorted bombers over the English Channel into France to protect them from enemy fighters.

The 'Rhubarb', involved a small number of fighter aircraft in the Wing, usually attacking in pairs, and flying low under radar detection. The purpose was to carry out one quick surprise attack on enemy airfields and other nearby enemy targets such as barracks, hangers, gun posts, various airfield defences, and goods trains. The description for other types of sorties can be found in the Glossary.

This section details a small selection of the operations flown by No. 303 Kościuszko Squadron with No.1 Polish Fighter Wing while based at RAF Northolt and gives an insight into the successes and the losses. So often success came at a price, and there was no higher price than the sacrifice of life.

17 June 1941
At 19.00 hours, No. 303 Kościuszko Squadron took off on a Circus operation with No. 1 Polish Fighter Wing and other squadrons. They were attacked by six yellow-nosed Messerschmitts over Cap Griz Nez in northern France.

Flight Lieutenant Kołaczkowski's cockpit was hit. His Spitfire began to roll onto its back and drop towards the ground. As the temperature of the glycol cooling fluid began to rise, his aircraft began to shake. Flight Lieutenant Kołaczkowski considered ditching into the sea but knew his chances of rescue would be slim. Other Spitfires flew to protect his failing aircraft until it landed safely in a field near Manston, Dover. Pilot Officer Bonder was also fortunate that day. His aircraft was hit but he managed to land near Hawkings.

23 June 1941

No. 303 Kościuszko Squadron took off from RAF Northolt during the late morning with other squadrons on a Circus sortie to escort Blenheim bombers. The squadron weaved in and out of the bombers to protect them against the attacks by the enemy fighters.

Pilot Officer Gładych heard a warning, *'enemy fighter above and behind you'*, over the radio transmitter. Other friendly fighters came to his aid. He sighted an Me109 fighter flying to attack from behind one of the friendly fighters. Pilot Officer Gładych flew behind the Me109 and fired from 20 yards, sending it crashing to the ground. He hit another Me109 but ran out of ammunition and broke off the engagement. The Me109 flew away, trailing smoke. Pilot Officer Gładych returned to Northolt pleased with his tally that morning.

Pilot Officer Gładych's second sortie of the day was very different from the first. He took off from RAF Northolt at 19.37 hours with eleven other Spitfires from No. 303 Kościuszko Squadron. Over Maidstone in Kent, the squadron joined No. 242 Squadron on a Circus operation to escort bombers over France. The target that evening was Desvres airfield.

The squadrons were attacked by a heavy force of enemy fighters. Pilot Officer Gładych fired at an Me109 that was attacking another Spitfire. When astern of the Me109, he fired at a distance of 50 yards and the enemy fighter dived to the ground in flames.

Shortly after, orders came over the radio transmitter for No. 303 Kościuszko Squadron to return to base. Before he had the chance to break away, Pilot Officer Gładych came under attack. Ten other Me109s appeared and circled above the Spitfire like hungry predators. They dived towards the Pilot Officer. His Spitfire's engine was hit, and the aircraft became difficult to control. An Me109 flew down for another attack. Pilot Officer Gładych followed the enemy aircraft, pulled up behind it and fired.

'My guns, however, would not fire. I had got quite close to the enemy aircraft by then, when he suddenly half rolled and my aircraft struck the Me109, cutting off its tail. My cockpit cover was open and a piece of the enemy aircraft flew in and cut across my right eye.'

Blood began to pour down his face, blurring his vision. He was still flying over France, so when he turned towards England, he had a long way to travel with a head injury, limited vision in one eye and an aircraft with severe damage to the engine. He radioed ahead with news of his critical state. Fighting to stay conscious due to heavy blood loss, Pilot Officer Gładych somehow landed near Manston airfield. When he later woke up in a hospital, he had no memory of landing his aircraft; it was nothing short of a miracle.

28 June 1941

Thirteen Spitfires of No. 303 Kościuszko Squadron, twelve Hurricanes from No. 306 Polish Squadron and eleven Spitfires from No. 308 Polish Squadron flew as the Wing to target the power station at Comines, France and enemy airfields.

Pilot Officer Bonder's aircraft was hit by enemy fire and crashed to earth, but no parachute was seen. In the encounter with enemy aircraft, Sergeant Bełc flew close to the ground and fired at an Me109 still on its trestles. Together, Sergeant Bełc and Flying Officer Wieldns destroyed another Me109 fighter. Sergeant Majchrzyk fired, his bullets cut an Me109's cockpit to pieces and sent the enemy crashing to the ground.

After successfully destroying ground targets, Pilot Officer Żulikowski of No. 306 Polish Squadron came under fire. His Hurricane was hit and seen diving, trailing smoke. Failing to return from the sortie, Pilot Officer Żulikowski was reported missing. News got through later that he had been injured in the crash and was interned in École Militaire (Military School) in St-Hippolyte-du-Fort, France. Pilot Officer Żulikowski later escaped and made it back to England with the help of the resistance.

Pilot Officer Drecki was also fortunate that day. While returning from the sortie, he was attacked by six Me109s at approximately 15,000 feet. One of the Messerschmitts was painted silver or white from tip to tail, and another seemed to fly much faster than the rest.

'The all white enemy aircraft made an attack by turning in front of me, he came in my sights and a short burst from my guns sent him straight to the ground.'

The attack took place at approximately 30 feet from the ground, and Pilot Officer Drecki used the low altitude to fly low into a valley, then turned and flew head-on towards one of the other enemy fighters chasing after him. At the last minute, he turned to narrowly miss a head-on collision. The Me109 crashed into the ground leaving Pilot Officer Drecki to fight his way through the other enemy fighters. He tried to avoid the enemy aircraft by flying high over the sea. He contacted the operations room over the radio transmitter with news that his aircraft was damaged and he was too low on fuel to last the twenty-minute flying time needed to get to Worthing. He was told to jump, and Air Sea Rescue would be informed of his position. Although he had no choice, Pilot Officer Drecki was reluctant to bale out because he knew the chances of being picked up in the English Channel were slight.

'I made a successful jump. Inflating my dinghy, I was spotted by two Spitfires and then by a Lysander, which dropped a smoke bomb.'

Pilot Officer Drecki was lucky — he was rescued within the hour.

In June 1941, the No.1 Polish Fighter Wing successfully claimed thirty destroyed enemy aircraft, six probables and five damaged.

2 July 1941

No. 303 Kościuszko Squadron and No. 308 Polish Fighter Squadron took off on a Circus operation at 11.52 hours to escort Blenheim bombers targeting the power station at Lille. The fighter squadrons shot down six enemy aircraft, with two probables. The success came at a high price that day as many in the Wing lost their lives.

Squadron Leader Łapkowski was lost over the English Channel, Flight Lieutenant Kawnik and Sergeant Kowala of No. 308 Polish Squadron were shot down and killed. Sergeant Wojciechowski was severely injured and took many months to recover. When he landed his aircraft, the cockpit and part of a wing were splattered with his blood.

Sergeant Gorecki was forced to bale out over the English Channel, approximately fourteen miles from Dover. He survived the rough seas in his dinghy without food or water for a seemingly endless seventy-two hours.

4 July 1941

During a Circus operation, Sergeant Krzyzagorski from No. 308

Polish Squadron was forced to bale out over the sea. He inflated his dinghy and climbed in. Other pilots from his squadron reported Sergeant Krzyzagorski's position. The following morning eleven pilots from No. 303 Kościuszko Squadron flew in search of him. He was located and picked up by a launch. He returned to RAF Northolt as a cold but happy man.

8 July 1941
At 14.30 hours, Wing Commander Johnny Kent, who had flown with No. Kościuszko Squadron in the Battle of Britain, led No.1 Polish Fighter Wing on a Circus operation. At 15.00 hours, they met with other squadrons over Manston to escort Stirling bombers. Enemy fighters attacked No.1 Polish Fighter Wing, and three pilots were lost. Squadron Leader Arentowicz radioed for help near Dunkirk; Pilot Officer Strzembosz from No. 303 Kościuszko Squadron and Sergeant Beil of No. 308 Polish Squadron were believed to have been shot down over the English Channel. Pilots of No. 303 Kościuszko Squadron carried out many searches to find the pilot without success.

During the sortie, Sergeant Giemer destroyed an enemy fighter. Shortly after, he was hit by a cannon shell causing broken bones in his right elbow and leg injuries. In agony and with only one working arm, Sergeant Giemer was unable to keep his Spitfire high. He was losing a lot of blood but managed to head towards Manston airfield at low altitude, and lower his undercarriage without flaps using his foot and left hand. He landed safely and was taken to a hospital to recover.

11 July 1941
No.1 Polish Fighter Wing with pilots from No. 303 Kościuszko Squadron, No. 306 Polish Squadron, and No. 308 Polish Squadron took off at 14.50 hours on a Circus operation. The Wing escorted Stirling bombers from Martlesham to Lille. Many dogfights took place that afternoon. Sergeant Watolski's Spitfire was damaged in one encounter and crash-landed in Kent. His aircraft hit a tree and was irrevocably damaged, but Sergeant Watolski emerged without injury.

13 July 1941
No. 303 Kościuszko Squadron was posted to Speke, near Liverpool for a short rest. No. 315 Polish Squadron joined No. 306 and No.

308 Polish Squadrons at RAF Northolt. Approximately thirty Circus operations took place during July 1941.

23 July 1941

No. 306 and No. 308 Polish Squadrons took off from Northolt to give wing support to bombers on a Circus operation over France. The Wing encountered approximately twenty-five Messerschmitts soon after arriving in France. Two Me109s were shot down by No. 306 Polish Squadron, and another two were damaged.

Pilot Officer Kosmowski and Pilot Officer Maras were shot down. Flying Officer Pniak made a crash landing in Richmond Park, London, but he escaped with slight injuries. Flight Lieutenant Nowak was less fortunate; he managed to bale out of his damaged aircraft but was very severely burnt.

24 July 1941

At 13.45 hours, the Wing with pilots from No. 306, No. 308 and No. 315 Polish Squadrons and led by Wing Commander Rolski took off on a Circus operation to escort Blenheim bombers. They targeted Hazebrouck in northern France without incident, but enemy fighters attacked the Wing on its return flight. Pilot Officer Chciuk from No. 306 Polish Squadron and Pilot Officer Gzachowski from No. 315 Polish Squadron were believed to be shot down and killed over France.

Later, in October 1941, a letter arrived at RAF Northolt with news that Pilot Officer Chciuk was alive and a prisoner of war. He had been badly burnt on his face hands and leg but had managed to bale out. He landed safely in France with a sprained ankle and was captured. He was later credited for the Me109 he had the satisfaction of shooting down before he had to abandon his own aircraft.

During July 1941, No.1 Polish Fighter Wing successfully destroyed thirty-two enemy aircraft with eight and half probables and five damaged. As always, the success came at a high price; eleven pilots were killed, and five were missing, presumed dead.

20 August 1941

No. 1 Polish Fighter Wing with pilots from No. 306, No. 308 and No. 315 Polish Squadrons took off to escort Blenheim bombers on a Circus operation. The weather began to deteriorate, and the Wing did not meet up with the bombers. Pilots sighted enemy fighters over the French coast, near Marydyck. Wing Commander Rolski gave instructions to the Wing to form a circle around the enemy aircraft. Sergeant Blok, Flying Officer Falkowski, and Flying Officer Nowak, all from No. 315 Polish Squadron, shot down one enemy aircraft apiece.

Sergeant Watolski from No. 306 Polish Squadron managed to bale out of his damaged aircraft and was very fortunate to be picked up by Air Sea Rescue.

Sergeant Pietrsiak from No. 306 Polish Squadron was shot down and presumed dead. In November 1941, news reached England that Sergeant Pietrsiak was safe and in Spain.

During August 1941, No. 1 Polish Fighter Wing destroyed thirty-four enemy aircraft, with seven portables, and thirteen damaged.

21 September 1941

Taking off at 14.30 hours, No. 1 Polish Fighter Wing with pilots from No. 306, No. 308 and No. 315 Polish Squadrons met up with twelve Blenheim bombers near Rye, East Sussex. While flying over France at approximately 28,000 feet, the Wing was attacked by approximately eighteen Me109s.

Squadron Leader Marian Pisarek, Pilot Officer Popławski, Flight Lieutenant Janus and Flight Lieutenant Wesołowski from No. 306 Polish Squadron shot down an enemy fighter apiece.

Squadron Leader Pietraszkiewicz from No. 316 Polish Squadron destroyed an unidentified enemy aircraft. This aircraft was believed to be a Focke-Wulf FW190, a new type of German aircraft at that time. Pilot Officer Blok, Flying Officer Falkowski and Pilot Officer Wandzilek also destroyed an enemy fighter each.

After destroying another unidentified aircraft, Squadron Leader Pietraszkiewicz's aircraft was hit and badly damaged, forcing him to land in France. Squadron Leader Pietraszkiewicz was captured and made a prisoner of war. A week later, he was joined by Flight Lieutenant Mickiewicz of No. 315 Polish Squadron, who had made a forced landing in France and was captured. Both pilots were sent to the prisoner of war camp 'Sagan' Stalag Luft III.

October 1941

No. 1 Polish Fighter Wing claimed twenty enemy aircraft destroyed.

6 November 1941

No. 1 Polish Fighter Wing, led by Wing Commander Rolski, took off from Northolt on Low Ramrod operation. No. 308 Polish Squadron gave top cover, and No. 315 Polish Squadron covered the rear. No. 303 Kościuszko Squadron gave close escort to Hurricane bombers. They encountered heavy flak west of Dunkirk.

Pilots of No. 303 Kościuszko Squadron attacked enemy aircraft, blew up fuel containers, and attacked barges on the canals. During the return flight, Pilot Officer Horbaczewski found his compass was not working. As he flew in and out of the cloud, he found himself back in France with a small formation of enemy fighters poised to attack him. He fired and managed to hit an enemy aircraft, but it escaped, leaving a trail of smoke. In the battle, Pilot Officer Horbaczewski's Spitfire was hit, and he was forced to call for radio help to guide him home. Sergeant Czezowski came to his aid and guided him back to base. After landing safely, Pilot Officer Horbaczewski found his aircraft had only two gallons of fuel left in the tank.

During 1943, Pilot Officer Eugeniusz Horbaczewski flew with No. 145 Squadron, known as Skalski Circus, in North Africa. He shot down many enemy aircraft and was made Commanding Officer of British No. 43 Squadron during the invasion of Italy. He was later made Squadron Leader of No. 315 Polish Squadron. In June 1944, Squadron Leader Horbaczewski risked his life to rescue a comrade in distress who had baled out over enemy held territory. Squadron Leader Horbaczewski landed his aircraft and rescued the airmen, avoiding many bullets along the way. The rescued pilot managed to squeeze into the Squadron Leader's Mustang, and they made their escape. After many successful years of combat, Squadron Leader Horbaczewski was shot down and killed by a Focke-Wulf FW 190 on 18 August 1944.

8 November 1941

Thirty-seven Spitfires from No. 303 Kościuszko Squadron, No. 308 Polish Squadron and No. 315 Polish Squadron led by Squadron Leader Rolski met up over Manston as No. 1 Polish Fighter Wing to escort twelve Blenheim bombers on a Circus operation.

On the return flight, No. 10 Group Wing, which was acting as escort cover, caused some confusion by losing height and diving in front of the No.1 Polish Fighter Wing. Suddenly, eight enemy fighters flew in to attack the bombers. Flight Officer Surma from No. 308 Polish Squadron and Squadron Leader Szczęśzniewski from No. 315 Squadron did not return from the sortie.

News later reached RAF Northolt that Squadron Leader Sczęśzniewski was alive and a prisoner of war in Stalag Luft III.

While flying with No. 1 Polish Fighter Wing during November 1941, Flying Officer Bieńkowski had a very lucky escape. During a Rhubarb operation, pilots in the Wing had attacked ground targets with great success by strafing German troops, destroying storage tanks, ground gun positions, aircraft on the ground and later, a goods train.

As Flying Officer Bieńkowski leaned forward in his cockpit to survey the damage he and the other pilots had inflicted on the enemy, a bullet that went straight through the cockpit where seconds earlier his head had been. Had he not been enjoying looking at the havoc on the ground, he would probably have been killed.

23 November 1941

At midday, No.1 Polish Fighter Wing met up with No. 607 and No. 615 Squadrons over Manston on a Low Ramrod sortie. No. 303 Kościuszko Squadron and No. 308 Polish Squadron from No. 1 Polish Fighter Wing gave rear support near Dunkirk.

A small formation of Focke-Wulf FW190s attacked No. 308 Polish Squadron. No. 315 Polish Squadron encountered heavy ground fire near the coast of France, which is reported to be the cause of the destruction or severe damage of five Spitfires from the squadron. Two Spitfires from the squadron were seen to crash into the English Channel. Sergeant Kosmalski, Sergeant Staliński, Pilot Officer Łukasiewicz, Flying Officer Grudziński and Flying Officer Grzech failed to return from the sortie. It was to be a dark day for No. 315 Polish Squadron.

8 December 1941

At 10.55 hours No. 1 Polish Fighter Wing, made up of No. 303 Kościuszko Squadron, No. 308 and No. 315 Polish Squadrons took off from RAF Northolt to fly as rear support for a patrol covering a five-mile area between Le Touquet and Berck. At around 10,000 feet, Me109s attacked No. 315 Polish Squadron. In the return fire, Squadron Leader Janus and Flight Lieutenant Czajkowski each destroyed an Me109.

Squadron Leader Brunon Janus flew with No. 300 Bomber Squadron. He was flying his Lancaster bomber over Nuremberg on the night of 2 January 1945. He and his crew were lost on the return flight during the early hours of 3 January 1945. It was meant to be his penultimate flight, and he was due to be married a few weeks later. Photo: Author's own collection.

The aircraft of Flight Officer Groszewski, from No. 315 Polish Squadron was hit by enemy fire, forcing him to bale out of the burning aircraft over the English Channel. Even though the sea was very rough, he managed to inflate his dinghy and climb in. Flight Officer Gładych and Sergeant Adamek circled around him to give protection. A Focke-Wulf FW190 attacked Flying Officer Gładych from behind but was chased away by Sergeant Adamek's cannon fire. Flying Officer Gładych turned and fired on the damaged enemy aircraft to finish it off. The enemy crashed into the sea and the two

Polish pilots resumed their guard of Flying Officer Groszewski until their fuel levels dropped so low that they were forced to land at RAF Kenley as neither pilot had enough fuel to make it back to RAF Northolt. Rescue launches sailed out in the worsening weather conditions to search for Flying Officer Groszewski, but they could not locate him in the choppy sea. Flight Officer Groszewski's body was later washed up along the French coast.

Due to bad weather during December 1941, No.1 Polish Fighter Wing flew only a few sorties from RAF Northolt.

12 February 1942

No. 316 Polish Squadron, led by Squadron Leader Gabszewicz, was scrambled from RAF Northolt with orders to fly along the British coast and destroy any small enemy vessels or enemy aircraft. After a lengthy search, the squadron sighted twelve small speedboats. Flying Officer Buchwald and another pilot flew closer to investigate and to identify the craft. Squadron Leader Gabszewicz reported the sighting of unidentified vessels to the operations room. He received an immediate reply over the radio transmitter. *'Destroy them, they are German.'* Squadron Leader Gabszewicz held back from giving the order until he was certain about the vessel's identity.

Flying Officer Buchwald flew towards the vessels. The rest of the squadron was ready to attack if necessary. Three rockets were fired from the boats — two yellow and one green. He and the other pilot recognised the colours as the correct signal for the day. Flying closer, the two Polish pilots saw Royal Navy colours and waving sailors. Flying Officer Buchwald informed Squadron Leader Gabszewicz, who radioed the information to the operations room. Regardless, the operations room repeated the order to attack, *'Destroy them, they are the enemy.'* Squadron Leader Gabszewicz hesitated. How had the enemy learned the correct colours of the day? He sent a message back to the operations room: *'Message understood, we are attacking on your responsibility, over.'*

Moments later a panic-stricken voice spoke over the radio transmitter. *'Do not attack, repeat do not attack, standby.'* New instructions followed a few minutes later. *'They are British speedboats, resume your patrol.'* The squadron's hesitation and diligent checks for correct identification saved many lives that day.

7 March 1942

No.1 Polish Fighter Wing took off from RAF Northolt on a Rodeo operation to escort bombers targeting shipping in Ostend. Pilot Officer Dobrucki was shot down and lost. Flying Officer Górski's Spitfire was hit by flak, and he was forced to ditch into the English Channel. He managed to inflate his dinghy and climb in. An SOS was sent and received by Air Sea Rescue, and pilots of No. 316 Polish Squadron flew above Flying Officer Górski to protect him against enemy fire until their low fuel levels forced them back to base. The Flight Officer waved them away, signalling all was well.

News spread that Flying Officer Górski had not been picked up and the pilots of No. 316 Polish Squadron volunteered the next day to search for him. Permission was granted with the understanding that the pilots were responsible for their own safety. The twelve pilots flew over the area where they had last seen Flying Officer Górski and continued the search through the worsening weather. Through thick fog and with heavy hearts, the pilots flew back to Northolt having done all they could. Flying Officer Górski's body was never found.

4 April 1942

Led by Wing Commander Rolski, No. 303 Kościuszko Squadron, No. 316 and No. 317 Polish Squadrons of the Polish No.1 Fighter Wing took off to meet up with twelve Boston bombers on a Circus operation. Coloured marker shells were fired from Boulogne. Once over Aire, the leading Boston bombers split from the rest of the formation. Enemy aircraft flew into the attack and the pilots from No. 303 Kościuszko Squadron fired to protect the bombers. Another formation of enemy fighters flew in pairs and attacked the rear. While protecting the bombers, Flying Officer Horbaczewski, Flight Sergeant Popek from No. 303 Kościuszko Squadron and Sergeant Szymański of No. 316 Polish Squadron shot down a Focke-Wulf FW190 each. Wing Commander Rolski claimed two probable destroyed. In the encounter, Flight Lieutenant Jan Daszewski, a No. 303 Kościuszko Squadron veteran of the Battle of Britain, was shot down and killed.

While flying to avoid enemy bullets, Flight Lieutenant Kustrzyński from No. 303 Kościuszko Squadron became separated from the rest of the Wing. He shot down an enemy fighter but then came under attack from three Focke-Wulf FW190s. He shot down one enemy aircraft and watched as the pilot baled out. Seconds later, Flight Lieutenant Kustrzyński's Spitfire was hit in the fuselage.

'The glycol temperature was rising, then 140 degrees it seemed impossible to reach the English coast. A puff of black smoke poured from my engine. I reported on the R/T, "hit in glycol, forced to try to land in France. Will try to join later."'

'Good luck and come back soon.' Wing Commander Rolski replied.

As his Spitfire began to lose height, Flight Lieutenant Kustrzyński came under attack from the aircraft that had damaged his wing. Bullets flew through his instrument panel, one of which entered his right temple. He became blinded by the blood pouring into his eyes. Each time he wiped the blood away, more poured down, making it difficult for him to see anything. His engine caught fire. He was about to bale out, but the built up area below made him change his mind. Flying on, he spotted a small strip of land that was ideal for landing. It was now or never. Flight Lieutenant Kustrzyński destroyed his radio and anything else he could. He came into land but it was becoming difficult to see, and his head was in terrible pain.

'I tried to land carefully, I could only see through one eye and there was smoke all around. As I approached the field I noticed a ditch with water. The road had high tension cables. As my speed was already too low to fly over, I decided to dive to fly under the cables. I pulled a little, my engine stalled and I bumped my tail on the ground, crashing. As a result of the bump, I found myself 10 yds in front of my aircraft as the harness broke off. I couldn't move my knee, my back ached terribly but somehow I reached a ditch with water in which I put my Mae West and parachute. I crossed the water and made for the woods. There was not much left of my aircraft and one of the wings lay along the fuselage and the engine was some distance away. I hid in the woods until nightfall. I was passed twice by German patrols, they did not see me.'

After resting, he felt a little stronger and hid in a farmer's small barn. Early the next morning, he propped himself up on the side of the barn door and kept watch for the Germans.

'The next day I woke up in terrible pain. I dragged myself up to look out of the barn door. I noticed a girl and whistled to attract her attention. She came over. As I talked to her I noticed she was Polish. I asked for her help. She brought me food and something to drink. The Germans had already been searching the nearby farms. I bandaged my eye and temple, in which a fragment was still lodged. I went to the woods through the nearest field. Nobody liked to hide me.'

Three days later Flight Lieutenant Kustrzyński reached a cemetery, where he believed he would get help from a Priest.

'I must have fainted when I woke up I saw four German officers.'

Flight Lieutenant Kustrzyński was taken to St. Omer Military Hospital to remove the bullet fragments from his temple. After being x–rayed, he was told he had two broken vertebrae and a bad infection. The infection led to a fever and on his fifth day in a hospital, his temperature was 39.5 degrees Celcius (103 degrees Fahrenheit). The doctors then took a quarter of a pint of his blood for another patient. After recovering from his injuries, Flight Lieutenant Kustrzyński was transferred to Stalag Luft III as a prisoner of war. Through a combination of his unshakeable determination and strength of character, and the help of doctors at St. Omer Hospital, Flight Lieutenant Kustrzyński lived to tell his amazing survival story.

Zbigniew Kustrzyński standing at the back between Stefan Kolodynski (left) and Witold Łokuciewski (right) at Stalag Luft III in 1943. See full photograph on page 186. Photo: Bernard Buchwald.

12 April 1942

During the afternoon, Squadron Leader Kołaczkowski led the No. 1 Polish Fighter Wing as target support A with Tangmere and No. 10 Group Wing on a Circus operation targeting Hazebrouck. On the return flight, they were attacked by a small number of Focke-Wulf FW190s. Three pilots of the Wing failed to return to RAF Northolt. Flying Officer Bieńkowski's Spitfire had been streaming glycol all the way back and crash-landed near Ash in Surrey. Pilot Officer Wojda's aircraft was hit, and his engine stopped near Dunkirk. He was forced to glide back as far as he could, then ditch near Dover. Flying Officer Buchwald's Spitfire was hit and crashed in France, where he was captured and made a prisoner of war in Stalag Luft III.

29 April 1942

No. 1 Polish Fighter Wing took off during the morning on a Circus operation with squadrons from RAF Biggin Hill, RAF Kenley and RAF Heston.

Over Hardelot in France, the Wing split up to attack a superior number of Focke-Wulf FW190s. Wing Commander Marian Pisarek, who had flown with No. 303 Kościuszko Squadron in the Battle of Britain, was shot down and killed. Squadron Leader Ozyra from No. 317 Polish Squadron was also killed. Flying Officer Koc had a narrow escape when he engaged an enemy fighter head on at 50 yards. The Focke-Wulf FW190 exploded, and Flying Officer Koc was forced to fly through the scattering debris.

During April 1942, twenty-two enemy aircraft were destroyed. There were thirteen probables and eleven damaged.

Spring 1942 Shooting Contest

During the spring of 1942, No. 11 Group organised the Royal Air Force shooting contest (Air to Air firing) as light relief during the stress and strain of war.

The contest lasted several days and thirty squadrons from the Wings of No.11 Group took part. The contest was held over the sea. A Spitfire towed a canvas sleeve over the sea by 200 yards of steel rope. Hundreds of attacks took place, and many thousands of ammunition rounds were fired. Everyone who took part thought it great fun and enjoyed the short break from the horrors of war.

1. First place — No. 303 Squadron, 808 points (Polish)
2. Second place — No. 316 Squadron, 432 points (Polish)
3. Third place — No. 315 Squadron, 183 points (Polish)
4. Fourth place — an RAF Squadron, 150 points (British)

Flight Lieutenant Zygmunt Bieńkowski was presented with the cup for No. 303 Kościuszko Squadron. Leigh Mallory, No. 11 Group HQ — R/17 12/4 sent a message to RAF Northolt about the event:

> *Group Air- Firing competition had been won by 303 Squadron with 316 Squadron second and No 315 Squadron third. My heartfelt Congratulations to the Polish squadrons for the thoroughness and keenness with which they have entered the competition. The standard of shooting reflects great credit on the pilots.'*

Spring/Summer 1942
During the spring and summer, operations were often hampered by *'bad visibility'* and while *'awaiting of new Spitfires Mark IX.'* No. 1 Polish Fighter Wing flew sixteen operations in May, thirteen operations in June, and July included eight major operations.

19 August 1942
No. 302, No. 303, No. 306, No. 308 and No. 317 Polish Squadrons of the No. 1 Polish Fighter Wing flew as operational air support for 'Operation Jubilee' with fifty other squadrons.

The objective of the raid was to land Commando Forces at the French port of Dieppe to destroy coastal gun batteries and a Radio Direction Finder (RDF) Station approximately a mile from the beach. Coastal gun batteries and other military targets located approximately three to four miles away to the west of Le Havre were to be destroyed in further landings, and the Dieppe St. Aubin airfield was to be taken along with the German Headquarters at Arques, and other installations.

Fighter squadrons from the RAF flew as escorts to protect the bombers and attacked enemy aircraft to protect ground forces as they landed. Aircraft, laying smoke screens along the beaches, protected Allied shipping from the Luftwaffe's attack. In short, the fighter squadron's objective was to protect, deter and attack to enable as many Allied forces to land and take the German-occupied port.

The No. 1 Polish Fighter Wing flew eight sorties during Operation Jubilee. From the Wing, No. 303 Kościuszko Squadron flew from RAF Redhill, in Surrey; No. 302 and No. 308 Polish Squadrons flew from RAF Heston while No. 306 and No. 317 Polish Squadrons flew from RAF Northolt.

The first sortie took off at 05.00 hours with Squadron Leader Nowierski and Group Captain Powlikowski leading No. 302, No. 306, No. 308 and No. 317 Polish Squadrons on Wing patrol over Dieppe. At approximately 10, 000 feet, Flying Officer Cholewka was badly wounded by a cannon shell in his right arm. Barely able to stay conscious, he managed to fly his aircraft back across the English Channel. Flying Officer Cholewka lowered his Spitfire's undercarriage with his left hand while somehow holding the stick between his knees and locking the undercarriage with his foot to land safely at RAF Lympne in Kent. He was carried semi-conscious from his blood-filled cockpit and taken to a hospital to recover from his injuries.

No. 303 Kościuszko Squadron and No. 317 Polish Squadron led by Wing Commander Janus and Squadron Leader Nowierski, took off on the second sortie of the day at 09.30 hours. They encountered many enemy fighters and bombers. Wing Commander Janus and his second in command split the formation of German bombers, who were just about to attack Allied shipping. The enemy bombers jettisoned their bombs in panic, missing their targets in the process. As the German fighters flew towards the ships, pilots of No. 303 Kościuszko Squadron engaged the enemy fighters.

After receiving a warning over the radio transmitter that more enemy bombers were approaching, Wing Commander Janus gave the order for some in the Wing to continue attacking the enemy fighters while others attacked the German bombers.

No. 317 Polish Squadron, who were flying below the Allied bombers at the time of the warning, gained height, and each Spitfire dived into attack the Luftwaffe aircraft before returning to the Wing, whereupon another Spitfire dived down into the attack then returned to the formation as another Spitfire dived. Due to these excellent tactics, seven enemy aircraft were destroyed with five probables and a further three damaged with no losses to the Polish Fighter Wing in this encounter.

During the third sortie of the day, No. 302 and No. 308 Polish Squadrons escorted six Boston bombers. Many Allied ships were seen on this sortie but no enemy aircraft.

At 10.55 hours on the fourth sortie that day, No. 306 Polish Squadron, took off to escort five Blenheim bombers laying smoke screens. They flew without encountering any enemy aircraft but, while flying over the English Channel, the squadron sighted a pilot in a dinghy awaiting rescue and alerted Air Sea Rescue to the pilot's position.

No. 302, No. 303, No. 308 and No. 317 Polish Squadrons led by Squadron Leader Nowierski, took off at 12.45 hours on the fifth sortie to met up with two RAF squadrons from Biggin Hill.

At 6,000 feet, the Wing sighted German Focke-Wulf FW190s attacking a split-off section of an Allied convoy located approximately ten miles from Dieppe. No. 303 Kościuszko Squadron flew into attack the enemy. Of the three enemy aircraft destroyed, only one German pilot was able to bale out.

On the sixth sortie of the day, twelve Spitfires of No. 306 Polish Squadron took off at 13.50 hours to escort Blenheim bombers while they lay smoke screens but the sortie was cancelled, and the squadron was ordered to return to base.

At 15.30 hours, No.1 Polish Fighter Wing took off on the seventh sortie of the day. Wing Commander Janus, Squadron Leader Nowierski, Wing Commander Rolski and Squadron Leader Kołaczkowski flew with the Wing of sixty-two Spitfires from No. 302, No. 303, No. 306, No. 308 and No. 317 Polish Squadrons.

While patrolling over the Allied convoys in the English Channel, the weather began to deteriorate. As the convoys reached mid-channel, the enemy aircraft flew into attack but were repelled by the Wing and jettisoned their bombs early to aid their retreat. No. 303 Kościuszko Squadron arrived in time to pursue the fleeing enemy bombers with No. 317 Squadron. The two squadrons destroyed eleven German bombers while the other Polish squadrons acted as a protective cover. These tactics had proved to be as successful as they been that morning during the second sortie of the day.

Pilot Officer Damm and Pilot Officer Landsman were presumed lost during the sortie, but news filtered through later that Pilot Officer Landsman was alive and in a prisoner of war camp.

Twelve Spitfires from No. 303 Kościuszko Squadron took off on the eighth and last sortie of the day to carry out an early evening patrol over Selsey Bill in West Sussex. The weather began to deteriorate once more, and no further enemy aircraft were seen.

7 September 1942

No. 302, No. 306 and No. 308 Polish Squadrons led by Wing Commander Janus took off from RAF Northolt with nine Defiant fighters to be the middle wing main diversion on Circus Operation 217.

During the flight over the English Channel, the Wing received a warning over the radio transmitter that enemy fighters had been sighted nine miles east of Manston. No. 302 Polish Squadron was attacked by twelve German Focke-Wulf FW190s, but they were able to return fire and destroy one enemy aircraft, damage another, and one probable.

Two pilots from No. 302 Polish Squadron were injured in the battle. Flying Officer Sdzietowicki was forced to bale out of his stricken Spitfire to save himself. Fortunately, he was picked up by Air Sea Rescue.

Sergeant Czajka's aircraft was badly damaged, and he sustained a severe injury to his right arm from a cannon shell. Although in great pain and feeling very weak from the loss of blood, he managed to make a belly landing in Kent. Rescuers ran to him, and he was quickly taken to a hospital to recover.

18 November 1942

Six Spitfires from No. 306 Polish Squadron took off on a Rhubarb operation to search for shipping at the mouth of the Somme. After attacking ground targets the weather worsened, forcing the squadron to turn for home. Due to the poor visibility over England, Pilot Officer Benoit flew into the barrage balloons near Woolwich and was killed.

Only thirty sorties were flown in November 1942 from RAF Northolt. As winter approached, the weather conditions often made it impossible for flying. South Ruislip was known for often having 'fogs as thick as pea soup'.

31 December 1942

No. 306 Polish Squadron suffered two losses during a Rodeo operation on the last day of the year. Twenty-five Spitfires — twelve from No. 306 Polish Squadron, twelve from No. 315 Polish Squadron and led by Wing Commander Janus — took off as cover for squadrons from RAF Kenley and RAF Tangmere, which were returning from their sortie.

As No. 1 Polish Fighter Wing crossed the French coast, thirteen Focke-Wulf FW190 fighters were sighted over Berck. No. 306 Polish Squadron flew into the attack with No. 315 Polish Squadron providing cover. Two enemy fighters were destroyed, with two probables and two damaged, but it came at a cost to the Wing. Flight Lieutenant Gil and Pilot Officer Kosmowski were lost during the battle.

January 1943

Bad weather grounded No.1 Polish Fighter Wing for the majority of January 1943. Only eight Circus operations, four Rodeo operations, one defensive patrol and Air Sea Rescue flights took off from RAF Northolt.

Towards the end of January No. 306 and No. 315 Polish Squadrons were involved in a terrible mid-air collision during a Circus operation. The Spitfires of Wing Commander Janus and Pilot Officer Jasiński collided, and it was presumed both were killed.

3 February 1943

Eleven Spitfires of No.1 Polish Fighter Wing led by Group Captain Mümler took off from RAF Northolt to meet with two squadrons from RAF Hornchurch and provide cover for twelve Ventura bombers. As the weather deteriorated, the bombing operation was called off, and the Hornchurch fighters were recalled to base leaving No. 308 Polish Squadron to escort the Ventura bombers. On the return to England, thirty enemy Focke-Wulf FW190 fighters flew into attack the bombers. The odds looked good for the Luftwaffe pilots as they pitched their thirty fighters against the Ventura bombers and its small protective escort of Spitfires.

No. 308 Polish Squadron showed the Luftwaffe they were not such an easy target and kept the enemy fighters at bay in various dogfights while protecting the Venturas. The squadron shot down two Focke-

Wulf fighters, and damaged another. One Ventura was lost, another crash-landed back at base, and four pilots of No. 308 Polish Squadron were presumed lost in the fight — Flight Sergeant Koc, Flight Sergeant Okrój, Flying Officer Wiejski and Flying Officer Zbierzchowski.

Just under three weeks later, Flying Officer Koc walked into the Officers' Mess at RAF Northolt to the surprise of everyone. After his Spitfire had been badly damaged, Flying Officer Koc had been forced to bale out over Dunkirk but had evaded capture and made his way home with the help of the resistance. Before baling out, Flying Officer Koc had the satisfaction of shooting down a FW190.

8 March 1943

Twenty-four aircraft from No. 306 and No. 315 Polish Squadrons, led by Wing Commander Kołaczkowski and Squadron Leader Szczęsny, took off as No. 1 Polish Fighter Wing on Ramrod Operation 40. The Wing met up with sixty American B-17 Flying Fortress bombers at Esigny to provide third withdrawal cover while the bombers targeted the railroad marshalling yards at Rennes.

On the return flight, three Focke-Wulf FW190s flew to attack the Flying Fortresses and successfully damaged one. The damaged bomber was forced to ditch into the English Channel approximately forty miles south of Selsey Bill in West Sussex.

A flight of six pilots of No. 306 Squadron landed at RAF Tangmere to refuel before returning to the sea in search of the Flying Fortress crew. The squadron located five of the crew in the dinghy, but with five crew still missing, the pilots feared the worse. Shortly after, two Walrus aircraft landed on the sea, and No. 306 Polish Squadron later escorted the two Walrus aircraft back in case of enemy attack. Sadly, when the men of the Walrus had reached the Flying Fortress, the five members of the crew in the sea were already dead.

11 March 1943

Four Spitfires of No. 308 Polish Squadron took off on a Rhubarb operation. The first pair had to return due to radio transmitter failure. The second pair, Flying Officer Stabrowski and Sergeant Domański, flew half way between Dieppe and Le Tréport in France to attack ground targets. Flying Officer Stabrowski reported over the radio transmitter that his engine was on fire and there was a large hole just below the spinner of his Spitfire. During his attempt to make it back, the damage to his aircraft became worse and white smoke began to trail forth. He was forced to ditch into the English Channel. After a few seconds of ditching, Flying Officer Stabrowski's Spitfire sank beneath the waves.

Even though Flying Officer Stabrowski showed no signs of life in the water, Sergeant Domański radioed for help and continued to fly near to his comrade for over an hour until he was so low on fuel, he had to leave to refuel at RAF Lympne. Sadly, Flying Officer Stabrowski was never found; forever lost with so many other airmen in the English Channel.

4 April 1943

The No. 1 Polish Fighter Wing took off 13.40 hours on a Ramrod operation to provide withdrawal cover for seventy Flying Fortress bombers. The Wing met the bombers over Rouen, covering the last two boxes.

News of a lone Focke-Wulf FW190 was given out over the radio transmitter. It is presumed that while looking for this enemy aircraft, two pilots from No. 315 Polish Squadron collided. Neither Flight Lieutenant Łukaszewicz nor Pilot Officer Panek were seen to bale out.

Shortly after the collision, approximately twenty Focke-Wulf FW190s attacked. Squadron Leader Szczęsny shot down two enemy aircraft before he was shot down. He had been due to be posted to Blackpool the following day.

It was a tragic day for the Wing with Sergeant Ostrowski of No. 315 Polish Squadron and Flying Officer Geca of No. 316 Polish Squadron also losing their lives in the battle.

9 August 1943

No. 1 Polish Fighter Wing took off to provide target support to thirty-six B-26 Marauder bombers but the original operation was cancelled. The Wing swept to the Montreuil area but two pilots of No. 316 Polish Squadron collided while turning.

Pilot Officer Kondracki was killed in the accident, and Flying Officer Maciejowski managed to bale out. He was captured by the Germans and made a prisoner of war.

Spring/Summer 1943

The No. 1 Polish Fighter Wing flew Circus, Ramrod, Rodeo and many defensive patrols: twenty operations in May; nineteen in June; and twenty-eight in July. Often, the hazy summer visibility affected flying.

12 August 1943

At 08.45 hours, No. 303 and No. 316 Polish Squadrons took off from RAF Northolt on a Ramrod operation to meet up with Flying Fortress bombers returning from an operation over West Germany. A strong westerly wind brought the Wing to an early rendezvous ten miles north of Antwerp in Belgium. They flew east to join the Flying Fortresses approximately twenty miles north of Aachen in Germany and escorted the bombers to the coast after turning north to avoid the heavy flak at Antwerp. Thus, the honour fell to No. 1 Polish Fighter Wing to be the first Spitfire Wing to fly over Germany.

No enemy aircraft were encountered on the sortie. Due to depleted fuel supplies, some of the Spitfires landed at RAF Bradwell, while others landed at RAF Manston.

19 August 1943

No. 303 Kościuszko Squadron and No. 316 Polish Squadron from No. 1 Polish Fighter Wing took off on Ramrod sortie to support thirty-six Marauder bombers targeting Amiens and Glisy airfields. The Wing fought in many dogfights while the bombers hit their targets and destroyed six Focke-Wulf fighters with one probable and three damaged.

Flying Officer Próchnicki from No. 316 Polish Squadron was shot down over the English Channel during the battle. The squadron searched to locate him, but without success. During their search, the squadron saved two other lives when they located two pilots in the sea and radioed in their position. Both pilots were later rescued by Air Sea Rescue.

22 August 1943

Twelve Spitfires from No. 303 Kościuszko Squadron and twelve Spitfires from No. 316 Polish Squadron took off during the early evening on a Ramrod operation to provide cover for thirty-six Marauder bombers targeting Beaumont airfield in France.

Shortly before reaching the target, No. 316 Polish Squadron was attacked by fifteen Focke-Wulf FW190 fighters. By remaining above No. 316 Polish Squadron, No. 303 Kościuszko Squadron was able to break up another formation of German fighters and prevent them from attacking the squadron below. In the combat, No. 303 Kościuszko Squadron destroyed one enemy aircraft while No. 316 Polish Squadron destroyed three enemy aircraft and damaged three.

Flight Sergeant Janusz was shot down and lost during the battle. Flying Officer Kuryłłowicz also sustained damage to his Spitfire after destroying an enemy aircraft and was forced to bale out.

Flying Officer Kuryłłowicz floated down in his parachute and landed in the sea about twenty miles west of Fécamp in France. His position was reported over the radio transmitter, but he was not located that day. Many of his colleagues flew in search of him the following day. As he was not found, some presumed he was lost forever.

Through sheer strength of character, willpower and luck, Flying Officer Kuryłłowicz did survive the harsh elements of nature. After baling out, he had managed to inflate his dinghy, then climb in and keep afloat in the choppy water as the rain fell and the fog hid him from view. Soaking wet and cold from the strong wind buffeting the dinghy, Flying Officer Kuryłłowicz endured days with no water or food. His eyes scanned all about him for rescue; he knew only too well the fate that had befallen many airmen who had baled out in the English Channel. But the pilots of No. 316 Polish Squadron had not given up, and they continued to fly in search of their missing friend. After nearly eighty-five hours rescue arrived to find that Flying Officer Kuryłłowicz had survived against all the odds.

24 August 1943

No. 1 Polish Fighter Wing took off at 17.59 hours to meet up with fifty Flying Fortresses at Évreux in France and escort the bombers to Conches-en-Ouche. Robert (Bob) Banta, an American of English and Dutch heritage wrote the following account about that day:

'I, Robert Banta was a radio operator and gunner on a B-17 Flying Fortress.

The 390th Bomber Group was new and ready for combat in August 1943. Our bombers had ten men and twelve fifty calibre machine guns for protection while on missions. I was very eager to start my missions and was full of anger when on the biggest mission yet, our bomber sunk in the concrete and a different plane took our place in the formation. Later, my anger would turn to shame as we learnt that the plane that took our place was the first shot down. They died for us and I had called them names. The mission was deep in Germany and continued past Switzerland and Italy to North Africa.

Eight days later, when our planes were ready to return home, the remaining bombers at our base were assigned to bomb two airfields in France. Just as important was that we were to attract enemy fighters away from our returning bombers from North Africa; we were decoys.

On 24 August 1943, we bombed an airfield at Évreux. Our ball turret gunner, Mike Majka of Polish descent, said it was a fake airfield. It was as we approached the second target Conches, I saw through the bomb bay the anti-aircraft fire.

Out of the whole formation, our plane was the only one hit. Shells tore at us all along its length. One Officer was killed and four others wounded. Two engines were knocked out and many holes tore into our plane. Because of only two engines, we were all alone over enemy territory. We were tending to our wounded and checking damage when someone yelled, "fighters six o'clock low".

Eight enemy aircraft rose up behind us, lined up like a firing squad. What followed was a very violent battle. We shot down two of them. They stopped our third engine and were tearing us up.

With six of them left, our finish was certain in seconds. Suddenly they turned away, we couldn't believe our eyes. They had us and quit. Then the answer came. "Fighters ten o'clock high." We shortly identified them as Spitfires. What a relief. They had saved us from certain death.

We lost altitude steadily with only one engine. Soon a different engine caught fire and I worried it would blow up as the flames lay over the gas tank area. I think I'm sweating some.

As we crossed the coast of France, we were instructed to dump overboard all loose things, including the guns and ammunition, into the English Channel. What we didn't know was that an enemy fighter was sitting in the sun and saw we were an easy kill. As he dived on us and we were about to die, the Spitfires returned and shot it down. Twice in minutes, the Spitfires saved our lives. Forty miles from England we crashed into the English Channel. As we sat in our life rafts watching as our bomber went down, the Spitfires flew over waggling their wings. "What violence we say, yet what wonderful brave pilots saved us."

It was not until later that we found out that those Spitfire pilots were of the famed 303 Kościuszko Polish Fighter Squadron attached to the RAF. You should have seen how proud and puffed up our Polish crewman was. We tried for days to fly to your base to thank you in person, but the weather and missions kept us from it. My letter (written in 1943 and sent to RAF Northolt) proves I have not forgotten. The Polish pilots that day got one enemy fighter who was only a bit compared to their usual tally. They were outstanding warriors. I pray for Polish people and for good people everywhere.'

Robert Banta survived the war and settled in Northern State, Wisconsin, USA. He married, had children and grandchildren. He never forgot the names of the Polish pilots who saved him and his crew.

'The enemy fighter that attacked the Flying Fortress over the English Channel was shot down jointly by Flight Lieutenant Majewski and Flight Sergeant Szymkowski of No. 303 Squadron... I am thankful to Polish courage and determination which kept me alive to start a family and find happiness.'

March 1944
No.1 Polish Fighter Wing (131 Northolt Wing) left RAF Northolt and was based at various airfields until it was disbanded in 1946.

Sources: For Polish Air Force Wing flying from RAF Northolt – Polish Air Force Association. Combat Reports The National Archives Ref. Air 50/117; Air 50/118 Air 50/119; Air 50/120; Air 50/125; Air 50/126; Air 50/127. Operation Record Diaries from RAF Northolt. Interviews Flight Lieutenant Bernard Buchwald, Squadron Leader Gandi Drobiński, Flight Lieutenant Marian Chełmecki, Flight Lieutenant Wojda; and Staff Sergeant Banta.

No. 303 Kościuszko Squadron 1945. Photo: Jan Kowalski, Gandi Drobiński/Authors own collection

PART V

ENEMY AIRCRAFT SHOT DOWN
BY FOUNDER PILOTS OF No. 303
KOŚCIUSZKO SQUADRON
SEPTEMBER 1939 - DECEMBER 1943

Pilot Ranks in the Battle of Britain:	Claimed Destroyed	Shared Kill	Probable Destroyed
Sergeant Tadeusz Andruszków	1	1	
Sergeant Marian Bełc	7		
Sergeant Michał Brzezowski	2	1	
Flying Officer Arsen Cebrzyński	3		
Pilot Officer Jan Daszewski	3		2
Pilot Officer Mirosław Ferić	9	1	
Flight Lieutenant Athol Forbes	7	1	
Sergeant Josef František	17		
Sergeant Paweł Gallus	2		2
Flying Officer Bogdan Grzeszczak	2		
Flying Officer Zdzisław Henneberg	8	1	1
Flying Officer Wojciech Januszewicz	3		1
Sergeant Jozef Kania			
Sergeant Stanisław Karubin	7		
Squadron Leader Ronald Kellett	5		2
Flight Lieutenant John Kent	12		3
Sergeant Jan Kowalski	1		1
Squadron Leader Zdzisław Krasnodębski	1		

Name:	Claimed Destroyed	Shared Kill	Probable Destroyed
Flying Officer Wacław Łapkowski	6		
Pilot Officer Witold Łokuciewski	8		3
Pilot Officer Bogusław Mierzwa			
Sergeant Jan Palak	2		1
Pilot Officer Jerzy Palusiński			
Flying Officer Ludwick Paszkiewicz	6		
Sergeant Edward Paterek	2		
Flying Officer Marian Pisarek	12		1
Pilot Officer Jerzy Radomski	2		
Sergeant Jan Rogowski	2		
Sergeant Antoni Siudak	2	2	
Sergeant Eugeniusz Szaposznikow	8	1	
Flying Officer Witold Urbanowicz	17		
Sergeant Mirosław Wojciechowski	2	1	
Sergeant Stefan Wójtowicz	4		
Sergeant Kazimierz Wünsche	4	1	
Flying Officer Walerian Żak	2		
Pilot Officer Jan Zumbach	12	1	
Total of enemy aircraft destroyed between September 1939 and December 1943	**181**	**11**	**17**

Before cameras were fitted on aircraft to gather photographic evidence, a pilot's claim to have destroyed enemy aircraft was accepted in various ways.

Many of the claims of enemy aircraft claimed as probable or damaged may well have been lost before reaching their airfield. Official records have been researched to substantiate the aircraft mentioned in the Battle of Britain documents and recorded in this book; though not all combat reports have survived.

Destroyed

Enemy aircraft crashing on land or crash landing at sea. To break-up in the air, or crash in flames. Pilot to bale out. One or more eyewitnesses to confirm the kill, which was not easy in the fast pace of air combat or during the general melee of dogfights.

If enemy aircraft crashed over Britain after being claimed as shot down, the pilot would have to report the enemy aircraft and the nearest position of the crash site on landing to the Intelligence Officer. Where possible, the claim would be checked. The airmen were allowed to have their kills painted on the side of their cockpit.

Probable
Aircraft to be so badly damaged that it would probably not be able to return or land safely. The pilot has been killed but was not seen to crash. Aircraft believed to be so badly shot up and seen diving to earth or sea but aircraft not seen to crash.

Damaged
Aircraft very badly damaged. Aircraft on fire, smoking or labouring. A bomber when the crew is seen to bale out.

Fighter Ace
A pilot with five enemy aircraft confirmed as destroyed.

ENEMY AIRCRAFT SHOT DOWN BY POLISH PILOTS IN POLISH & RAF SQUADRONS 1940 -1945

Polish Squadron number or description	Claimed Destroyed
No. 302 Squadron	46
No. 303 Squadron	202
No. 306 Squadron	70
No. 307 Squadron (Night Fighter Squadron)	30
No. 308 Squadron	69
No. 309 Squadron	4
No. 315 Squadron	86
No. 316 Squadron	45
No. 317 Squadron	48
Polish pilots in RAF squadrons	108
Polish pilots flying against the Japanese	12
Polish pilots with No. 145 Squadron during the African campaign	25
Polish pilots with joint kills	12
TOTAL	757

POLISH & BRITISH DECORATIONS AWARDED TO POLISH PILOTS
DURING THE SECOND WORLD WAR

Number of POLISH Decorations Awarded to Polish Pilots:

Virtuti Militari Gold Cross*	7
Virtuti Militari Silver Cross	1125
Krzyż Walecznych (Cross of Valour)	3122
Krzyż Walecznych one Bar	2174
Krzyż Walecznych two Bars	1432
Krzyż Walecznych three Bars	426
Krzyż Zasługi z Mieczami (Gold Silver Bronze)	302
Krzyż Zasługi (Gold Silver Bronze)	418

*equivalent to the British Victoria Cross

General Sikorski decorating Polish airmen (left to right) W/C Marian Pisarek, F/O Jan Falkowski, F/O Feliks Szyszka, and F/O Franciśzek Surma Photo: Františzek Kornicki.

Number of BRITISH Decorations Awarded to Polish Pilots:

Air Force Cross	18
Air Force Medal	8
Conspicuous Gallantry Medal	1
British Empire Medal	6
Distinguished Service Order	8
Distinguished Service Order and Bar	1
Distinguished Flying Cross	186
Distinguished Flying Cross and first Bar	4
DFC and second Bar	1
Distinguished Conduct Medal	1
Distinguished Flying Medal	68
Distinguished Flying Medal and first Bar	1
George Medal	1
Military Cross	2
Military Medal	2
Order of The Bath	2
Order of The British Empire	8

TABLE OF POLISH FIGHTER ACES
DURING THE SECOND WORLD WAR

Name:	Destroyed	Name:	Destroyed
Stanisław Skalski	21	Jozef Jeka *	7
Witold Urbanowicz	17	Bolesław Drobiński	7
Josef František* *	17	Marian Bełc	7
Eugeniusz Horbaczeswki*	16	Stanisław Karubin	7
Bolesław Gładych	14	Karol Pniak	6
Jan Zumbach*	12	Wacław Łapkowski	6
Marian Pisarek	12	Stefan Janus	6
Aleksander Gabszewicz*	9	Ludwick Paszkiewicz	6
Mirosław Ferić*	9	Mieczysław Mümler	6
Henryk Szczęsny*	9	Stefan Witorzeńć	6
Michał Maciejewski *	9	Kazimierz Rutkowski*	5
Wacław Król	9	Czeslaw Głowczynski*	5
Alexander Chudek	9	Michał Cwynar*	5
Jan Falkowski	9	Mieczysław Adamek*	5
Antoni Głowacki *	8	Bolesław Własnowlski*	5
Zdzisław Henneberg *	8	Frančišek Surma	5
Stanisław Brzeski *	8	Stanisław Blok	5
Eugeniusz Szaposznikow*	8	Kazimierz Sporny	5
Witold Łokuciewski	8	Grzegorz Sołogub	5
Adolf Pietrasiak	8	Jakub Bargielowski	5
Henryk Pietrzak*	7	Jerzy Popławski	5

*Also credited with a shared kill.   **Czechoslovakian flying with Polish Air Force.

THE STORY OF THE
POLISH AIR FORCE STANDARD

On the cold evening of 7 December 1939, a group of Dęblin cadet officers gathered in quarters in the Fort-de-Bron in Lyon, France. Captain Pilot Observer Jan Hryniewicz entered and spoke to those present in the room. *'Dear Kotoczki, [kittens] are there any amongst you that can paint?'* Touched by curiosity, Cadet Officers Kazimierz Karaszewski, and Zbigniew Wojda volunteered their services.

The following day Captain Pilot Observer Hryniewicz described his idea to the two cadets:

> *'Kittens, we Polish airmen are fighting under the red and white flag and chessboard banner* but we have no real standard. I have dreamed of such a banner and would like you kittens to get busy and help me draw the patterns. I dreamed of an ornamental pectoral plate. On one side would be located the likeness of Saint Theresa of France** and an inscription of "Love Demands Sacrifice", also the traditional Polish Air Force military emblem red and white chessboard of the pilots and observers flying badges.'*

Cadet Officer Karaszewski volunteered to draw this side of the standard, leaving Zbigniew Wojda to do the other based on Captain Pilot Observer Hryniewicz's vision for it:

> *'Our Lady of Ostra Brama of Wilno, the Polish State emblem of a white eagle and the words "God Honour and Fatherland."'*

Both cadet officers were puzzled about the wording 'Love Demands Sacrifice' so Captain Pilot Observer Hryniewicz explained.

'It is in connection to my mother. When I joined the Polish Air Force my mother gave me a small silver plate with such an inscription upon it. These words in my mind connect with a soldier's love, which encourages him to fight for homeland Poland and freedom. Love which so often demands such high efforts and highest sacrifice of airmen's life.'

Later Cadet Officers Karaszewski and Wojda drew three identical patterns with coloured pencils, and Captain Pilot Observer Hryniewicz drafted three different letters asking for Polish women in Wilno to help make the new Polish Standard. The letters and the drawings along with pictures of the military badge for the Dęblin Officers' School passed over the barbed wire frontiers and were smuggled to friends in the Wilno area. At that time, Lithuanians occupied the town of Wilno yet, miraculously, none of the censors troubled the banner's journey.

One side of the Polish Air Force Standard with the words 'Love Demands Sacrifice'. Photo: Permission of Kaz Karaszewski.

Dr. Zofia Wasilewska Swindowa received one letter, as did his friend Tadeusz Żeligowski. The letter stated that the standard was to be consecrated at Ostra Brama (Gate of Dawn) in Wilno, then sent to Polish fighting men in the west. The letter referred to Roman Catholic Priest and ardent patriot, Jozef Kazimierz Kucharski, who was the Underground Army Chaplain.

With the help of the War Refugees Friendly Benefit Society and money collected by Madam Oskierczyna, women from Wilno and nearby villages made the banner. Archbishop Jalbrzykowski of Wilno fully supported the project, but despite the local support, great care had to be taken as many Lithuanians supported the Germans.

Nuns, artists, and embroiderers were some of those who worked on producing a banner to match exactly the drawn design. The women of Wilno added the date 1940, and nuns from the Benedictine Monastery embroidered the standard with gold and silver thread in a secret place within the monastery.

After the surrender of France, a plan was made to transport the standard to Great Britain. It was a dangerous route for the person or persons undertaking such a journey.

An Officer of the Polish Secret Service in Germany, Captain Jerzy Jakubianiec was working in a fictional post at the Japanese Consulate and offered to take the banner to Berlin in his diplomatic case without the Japanese becoming aware of what he was carrying.

In Berlin, the parcel containing the precious banner was handed over to Major Michał Rybikowski of the Secret Military Service in Germany. Major Rybikowski, using the false name of Peter Iwanow, was under the protection of Japanese Consular Offices as a citizen of the Japanese state of Manchukuo, China. After a close brush with the Gestapo, the banner was smuggled by Major Rybikowski to Stockholm. In Stockholm, he was asked what was in his brown paper wrapped parcel and replied, *second-hand clothing.* With luck on his side, he was believed.

The Polish Air Force Standard arrived safely in Great Britain on 4 March 1941. On 16 July 1941, Captain Pilot Observer Jan Hryniewicz had the honour of the first golden nail with his name at a ceremony at RAF Swinderby. With great pride, he took the standard from the hands of Colonel Kwieciński and handed it to General

Lucjan Żeligowski, a member of the National Council of the Polish Government in London.

During the ceremony, the Polish national anthem was played, and the Chancellor addressed the audience.

'From our mothers, from crucified homeland for victory.' Handing the standard to General Władysław Sikorski, the Chancellor kissed the standard's flag staff. The words echoed forth.

> *'To people's Poland, Poland independent, Poland Slavonic, to give to the heroic Polish nation of Warsaw's ruins with the destination of Eagles School of Dęblin.'*

As the ceremony continued, General Władysław Sikorski handed the standard to Commander in Chief of the Polish Air Force in Great Britain General Stanisław Ujejeski. Then, it was handed to Commanding Officer Colonel Makowski of No. 300 Bomber Squadron. Many airmen at Swinderby witnessed this proud day for the Polish Air Force.

July 1941 - General Władysław Sikorski handing the Polish Air Force Standard to No. 300 Bomber Squadron at RAF Swinderby. Photo: Permission of Kaz Karaszewski.

During the Second World War, the Polish Air Force Standard was taken to all the airfields in Great Britain where Polish squadrons flew, ensuring all squadrons held it for a time.

After the war ended, the Polish Air Force Standard could not be returned to Poland until Poland was free. For many years, it resided in the Polish Institute and Sikorski Museum in London.

In a very moving ceremony in Poland in 1992, the Polish Air Force Standard returned home to a free Poland.

*Eliot Chess designed the red and white chequered squares on Polish aircraft.

**When Captain Jan Hryniewicz came up with his idea for the Polish Air Force Standard design, he believed, as did many others, that the war would end in France.

Sources: Interview Flight Lieutenant Kazimierz Karaszewski, 1988 and 1990.

THE STORY OF RAF NORTHOLT

Over one hundred years ago, South Ruislip didn't exist. It was an unnamed rural area nestled between Northolt to the southeast and Ruislip to the north and consisted of five dairy farms, a scattering of small wooden cottages, and a few brick houses. The local people inhabiting the area spoke with a distinctive country dialect.

In 1914, Major Brancker from the War Office decided on a site of approximately 283 acres in, what later became, South Ruislip for a Royal Flying Corps aerodrome. The aerodrome should have been built where Queensmead School stands today, half a mile east of its current position. But, as local legend has it, the government official sent by Major Brancker held the map upside down while deciding on a location for the site, and no one noticed the error. The plans were approved, and the aerodrome was built alongside West End Lane, known today as the very busy A40 motorway of Western Avenue. The remainder of the aerodrome ran alongside a farm and open countryside at South Ruislip.

The airfield opened in March 1915 and became operational in June 1915 when two British aircraft took off on the first official flight from the airfield to patrol over Kent. During the First World War, Northolt airfield was used as a training station for pilots.

On 1 April 1918, the Royal Air Force was formed from the amalgamation of the Royal Flying Corps and Royal Naval Air Service. In June 1919, RAF Northolt was licensed as a joint Civil and RAF aerodrome. It was named after the nearby Northolt Junction railway station. The station became South Ruislip and Northolt station from 1932 and then became South Ruislip station by dropping Northolt from its name a few years later.

The introduction of a railway station in 1904 had been the start of the residential development in the area. The growth of RAF Northolt led to further residential development in the mid-1930s. During this time, there was an increase in the number of Londoners who travelled the fifteen miles west of the capital to enjoy the day in the beautiful countryside. Since the 1950s, the area of South Ruislip near RAF Northolt has become built up. However, it still retains some rural aspects, and Priors Farm still exists near to the Polish War Memorial.

By 1923, the RAF used the airfield regularly, prompting an extension to the site's borders in 1926. On the civil side, the Fairey Aviation Company of Hayes flew many various aircraft between 1919 and 1930.

The increasingly popular flying school drew high-profile students, including members of the Royal family: the Prince of Wales learnt to fly at RAF Northolt in 1929, followed by the then Prince George in 1930.

Between the mid-1930s and 20 May 1939, a popular annual Empire Air Day was held, drawing many people from London as well as the local area. Pilots in various aircraft excited the crowd with displays of flying aerobatics. One of the highlights included a parachute jump from a biplane.

From 1 May 1939, RAF Northolt came under No. 11 Group Fighter Command. Various RAF squadrons came and went during the months leading up to the start of the Second World War. By 1 July 1939, No 604 - No. 609 RAF Squadrons and No. 1 British Squadron were stationed at RAF Northolt.

The headquarters of No. 11 Group were at Uxbridge, Middlesex where many men and women worked to aid the smooth running of aerial defences over London and southeast England. Three of the many people in No.11 Group who carried a huge responsibility during the Battle of Britain were: Commander In Chief, Sir Hugh Dowding, Air Vice-Marshal Keith Park and Senior Staff Officer Gerald Gibb.

Air Officer Commanding-in-Chief of Fighter Command, Sir Hugh Dowding was fifty-eight years old when Great Britain stood alone during the Summer of 1940. He entered the Royal Military Academy, Woolwich in 1899 and was commissioned as a Second Lieutenant in the Royal Garrison Artillery the following year. He served in Gibraltar, Ceylon, Hong Kong and India then returned to England in 1911. He learnt to fly while at the Staff College, Camberley and was awarded a pilot's certificate in December 1913. During the First World War, he served as a pilot and was promoted to Captain. He served as Commanding Officer of No. 9 Squadron, then No. 16 Squadron in France. After the war he was made Chief Staff Officer.

Sir Hugh Dowding was well respected and was said to be by those who knew him, a calm man of determined nature who cared greatly for the men under his command and would argue with the Air Ministry to protect the pilots.

If Sir Hugh Dowding had not made himself heard when many RAF pilots were being lost in France, there would have been few pilots or aircraft left to fly with during the Battle of Britain. In France, the RAF lost nearly 300 pilots and 500 aircraft. Sir Hugh Dowding also fought the Air Ministry over installing two-inch-thick bulletproof glass in the aircraft's cockpit canopy; this he succeeded in, thus helping to save lives.

After the Battle of Britain, Sir Hugh Dowding implied that the Polish pilots' contribution to the number of enemy aircraft shot down may have made a difference to the outcome of the Battle of Britain.

Born in Thames, New Zealand in 1892, Air Vice Marshal (AVM) Keith Park was the Commander of No. 11 Group. He joined the Union Steam Ship Company shortly before his nineteenth birthday and worked for three and a half years until he was granted war leave in December 1913 to join the New Zealand Army. In early 1914, he sailed to Egypt as Lance-Bombardier in the New Zealand Artillery to join the Gallipoli campaign. He rose through the ranks so that by the time he transferred to the British Army in September 1915, he was a commissioned Second Lieutenant. He was evacuated from Gallipoli in January 1916 and sent to France. In 1917, he transferred to the Royal Flying Corps. In the inter-war period, he rose through the ranks, taking command of his first squadron two years later. He joined Fighter Command under Sir Hugh Dowding in 1938 and was promoted to Air Vice-Marshal in April 1940 and took command of No.11 Group.

In August 1940, AVM Keith Park was taken ill and had to have a short leave of absence. Senior Staff Officer Gerald Gibb of Fighter Command took over the responsibility for the air war over southern England for a couple of weeks. During this time, he proved himself to be an outstanding officer. Senior Air Staff Officer Gerald Gibb had been in the Royal Flying Corps during the First World War. He had lied about his age to enlist in 1914. The following year he was approached to join the Royal Flying Corps, the start of a distinguished career.

During the Battle of Britain in 1940, AVM Keith Park would often take to the sky alone, his Hurricane always at the ready. Often, he made surprise visits to many of the stations under No. 11 Group. AVM Keith Park was known to care for the well-being of the men under his command, he was well respected by the fighter pilots in his group.

No. 11 Group had seven sector stations during the Battle of Britain: RAF Biggin Hill, RAF Debden, RAF Hornchurch, RAF Kenley, RAF Tangmere, RAF North Weald and RAF Northolt, which was the chief sector station for Sector Z in defence of the capital.

After the Battle of Britain and throughout the Second World War, RAF Northolt became known by many Polish fighter pilots as the home of the Polish Air Force in Britain. Throughout the war years, nearly all fighter squadrons that flew from RAF Northolt were Polish. Many people of South Ruislip and other small towns nearby billeted Polish airmen and ground crew and welcomed them warmly into their homes.

On 4 February 1946, RAF Northolt officially became a civil airport on loan from the Ministry of Aviation. From early 1947, British European Airways (BEA) became the main airline operating from Northolt, making it one of the most sort after and used airports in Europe. In 1953, BEA aircraft and staff were transferred and thence operated from Heathrow Airport.

In the later part of 1954, most of Northolt aerodrome was back in the hands of No. 11 Group. Today, RAF Northolt is a large and varied Royal Air Force airfield and carries the major role of air transport for VIPs. In March 2015, RAF Northolt celebrated its centenary.

RAF NORTHOLT circa 1930s
Photo: Author's collection

Station Approach, South Ruislip circa 1930s: Walking from the railway station towards the shops and then to RAF Northolt. After the war, the author's grandfather bought the 'One Hundred Acre Dairy' and turned it into 'Arthur Britton's Cobbler Shop.' For several years, Arthur had unusual customers - the cows herded along the road would pop in thinking it was still the dairy. Photo: Author's collection.

THE STORY OF THE POLISH WAR MEMORIAL

During 1943, many of the Polish airmen and ground crew at RAF Northolt discussed the idea of erecting a monument to those killed while serving with the Polish Air Force. The airmen's determination to pay tribute to the fallen intensified as the number of losses increased throughout the remainder of the Second World War.

A year after the war had ended, an appeal for contributions towards the Polish Air Force Memorial Fund was placed in The Daily Telegraph. Money flowed in, donated in honour of the fallen.

By Christmas 1947 most of the details for the memorial monument were near completion. The Polish sculptor, Mr. M. Lubelski, designed the memorial monument. William Wood and Sons Ltd laid the foundations and cut the huge York stone slabs for the base. The Bath and Portland Stone Ltd built the tall column placed at the centre of the base. At the top of the long high column stands a magnificent lifelike eagle with wings spread out as if in flight, as designed by Mr. Lubelski.

Mr. Ralph engraved the rear face of the monument with the names and ranks of 1,241 Polish airmen killed in the Second World War. The names and numbers of the Polish squadrons were engraved at the front of the memorial on the centre column, with some of the famous battles fought by the Polish Air Force inscribed on the base. Unfortunately, space did not permit at that time for the engraving of the many Polish airmen who died in flying accidents.

The front of the left-hand side of the column was inscribed with, *'To the memory of Fallen Polish Airmen'* as suggested by Group Captain Alexander Gabszewicz. Reverend Gogolinski suggested the words, *'I have fought a good fight. I have finished my course. I have kept the faith,'* which were inscribed on the rear of the memorial.

A large pond was built at the front of the memorial for visitors to walk round to the monument, then descend the steps leading to the back of the monument to the list of names of those who sacrificed their lives for freedom.

Flowerbeds were planted with red and white flowers at the front and each side of the memorial near to the pond. Among the spring bulbs, the aptly planted named forget-me-nots were planted. In more recent years, there are fewer flowerbeds, with a grassed and paved area for seating when ceremonies take place.

The now abolished Ruislip and Northwood Urban District Council managed the upkeep of the memorial (the area is now within the London Borough of Hillingdon). The rent for the memorial was set for 999 years on a peppercorn rent with Middlesex County Council.

The Polish War Memorial's official unveiling ceremony was on 'All Souls Day', 2 November 1948 and was attended by many people.

Many years ago a planning consultation was held in South Ruislip to discuss the plans and proposals for various road changes included a flyover along the Western Avenue. The meeting was attended by representatives from RAF Northolt, the Polish Air Force Association as well as many local people, and ex-combatants who had flown over from Poland to voice their objection to the proposed relocation of the Polish War Memorial. To say there was an uproar is an understatement. It is amazing that the applicants had placed so little value on the significance of the war memorial site and its meaning to think it could so easily be moved. For once people's voice was heard and, thankfully, the memorial remained.

In 1994, the names of over 600 Polish airmen who died in training or non-sortie flying were added to the memorial when restoration work was carried out.

Many people travel from all over the world to visit the memorial. Throughout the year white and red flowers or a single red rose can often be seen at the Polish War Memorial. There is also a special ceremony held each September at the Polish War Memorial to honour those lost. This service is now organised by the Polish Air Force Memorial Committee. A Hurricane or Spitfire usually flies over at this ceremony to pay homage to the Polish airmen and ground crew who gave their lives.

The Polish War Memorial is located a short walk from RAF Northolt, South Ruislip. Photo: Dennis Britton/author's collection.

RECOLLECTIONS ABOUT PILOT WALENTY KREPSKI

Mieczysław Dodo

The author contacted the family of Walenty Krepski in 1988 to inform them that Walenty did not have a known grave. He had been lost at sea off the coast of Yorkshire during the Second World War while flying with No. 54 RAF Squadron.

Like so many of the Polish airmen who lost their lives but were never laid to rest, Walenty Krepski's name is inscribed with others on the Polish War Memorial and other memorials in Great Britain in honour of their sacrifice for the fight for freedom.

My cousin Walenty Krepski was born on 30 July 1917 at Czelabinsk (in the Ural, former Tsarist Russia, today the ZSSR). During his early childhood he was weak and often ill. In the second half of October 1921 his parents with their 4 year old first-born arrived from Czelabinsk in Independent Poland, settling in Wilno.

In 1922 his 35 year old father died leaving his 30 year old wife with her 5 year old son alone. The boy suffered his father's death badly. During the funeral, he contracted a severe cold and was ill for a long time but his young organs did not give in and surrounded by the dedicated care of many members of the Dodo family, Walenty recovered his health.

As a 7 year old he started his elementary schooling. He was not an "Eagle". As a 10 year old he loved ice-skating and in particular skiing. He devoted much time to it, encouraged by the beautiful mountainous Wilno area. I remember well the anxiety of Walik's mother when mostly during the holiday he disappeared with his skis and rucksack regardless of the weather. He roamed about all day. At dusk he appeared fresh, sunburnt (hungry like a wolf) and we saw how he developed his health and spirit. From a poorly boy, he grew up into a man to the satisfaction of his mother and the whole family Dodo, who cared for him, amongst them also myself, Mieczysław Dodo.

During the years 1928–1937 Walenty Krepski attended Wilno Grammar School. During this time he did not neglect his beloved skiing, taking part in many events and competitions in the winter resort capital of Poland, Zakepane. From grammar school days dates his interest in gliding, parachute jumping and aeroplanes. Shortly before matriculation, which he passed in May 1937 at Adam Mickiewicz Grammar School in Wilno, he declared to his mother and protectors that he decided to be a pilot; that he already submitted documents to the Dęblin Pilot School's Command and that he was already accepted. His mother's and family's objections he rejected by a hunger-strike, which he ended after having obtained permission to commence studies at the Dęblin's "Eaglet School".

In the tragic September 1939, the war broke out and contact with my cousin broke off, as it proved ... forever. We learnt that Walenty was promoted to 2nd Lt, left the country together with many airmen and through Rumania and France and had arrived in Great Britain already in December 1939 with the first group of pilots. He fought in the "Battle of Britain" in which Poles contributed to a high degree towards the victory of the Allies over the "Hitler's Beasts".

In 1946, within the repatriation frame, Walenty's mother and my family settled in Olsztyn. Immediately, we started our search through the Red Cross in Warsaw. In December 1948 we received the sad news addressed to his mother from the Red Cross H.Q. in Warsaw that: "The looked for W. Krepski Lt. of the Air Force of the Polish Forces in the west, was killed on the 7 September 1940 and is buried at the Newark Cemetery (Gr. Britain) in grave No. 306."*

Other documents successively received from London confirmed the death of my cousin at the date stated, with the underlining of: "Lt. Pilot Walenty Krepski officer of the 54th RAF Squadron did not return from and operational flight."

He died a pilot's death — young, only 23 years old, Polish Officer (single), away from his Fatherland, in the defence of the English sky, the only son of his mother who cried for him till her death in Olsztyn on the 18 February 1964.

*The author visited Pilot Officer Krepski's recorded grave at Newark Cemetery in Nottinghamshire to lay flowers on behalf of the family but she was unable to find the grave. The Polish Air Force Association and Commonwealth War Graves Commission checked their records and realised that the family had been misinformed. Pilot Officer Krepski has no known grave.

Cadet Officer Walenty Krepski in Poland 1939 with his uncle. He is wearing his Polish dagger with pride. The dagger, inscribed with 'Honour and Fatherland', was awarded to all Polish airmen qualifying from the Dęblin Officers' School.
Photo: Permission of Mieczysław Dodo/author's collection.

Pilot Officer Walenty Krepski in England, September 1940 with the squadron's mascot. The photograph was taken shortly before his death on 7 September 1940.
Photo: Permission of Mieczysław Dodo/author's collection.

SUMMARY OF THE POLISH AIR FORCE
1940 - 1945

In Summer 1940, the RAF incorporated into British squadrons the Polish airmen who had completed refresher training. The Polish pilots began to show the skills they had learned with the Polish Air Force and had put into practice against the Luftwaffe in Poland and France. Despite the language barrier, the Polish pilots earned the respect of the British pilots they flew with in combat.

During the Battle of Britain, Polish pilots flew with RAF squadrons: No. 3, No. 17, No. 32, No. 43, No. 54, No. 56, No. 65, No. 74, No. 79, No. 85, No. 111, No. 145, No. 151, No. 152, No. 213, No. 229, No. 234, No. 238, No. 249, No. 253, No. 257, No. 501, No. 601, No. 603, No. 605, No. 607, No. 609 and No. 615.

On 19 July 1940, Flying Officer Antoni Ostowicz, flying with No. 145 Squadron from RAF Tangmere, was the first Polish pilot in Great Britain to shoot down an enemy aircraft. On 11 August 1940, Flying Officer Ostowicz was shot down and killed over the Isle of Wight. On 14 August 1940, No. 302 Polish Fighter (City of Poznań) Squadron, became the first operational Polish squadron. Flying Hurricanes from RAF Leconfield under No. 12 Group, No. 302 Squadron celebrated its first kill on 20 August 1940 — a Dornier bomber. While on a training flight on 30 August 1940, the No. 303 Polish Fighter Squadron, named the Kościuszko Squadron, celebrated the squadron's first kill. Against orders, Flying Officer Paszkiewicz broke formation and shot down an enemy aircraft. No. 303 Kościuszko Squadron was made fully combat operational the following day. During the Battle of Britain, the squadron flew from RAF Northolt under No. 11 Group.

During the Battle of Britain Hitler made ready his troops of over a hundred German divisions on the shores of France. All Hitler had to do was wait while Reichsmarschall Herman Göring's Luftwaffe destroyed the British RAF.

The German fighters needed to destroy the RAF fighters before sending in German bombers to destroy England's docks and industrial centres. Hitler believed that the invasion would be over in a week.

The lives of everyone in Great Britain hung in the balance; their free way of life was under threat. As the Luftwaffe flew across the English Channel in the summer of 1940, the odds were in Hitler's favour. The mighty Luftwaffe outnumbered the RAF Hurricane and Spitfire aircraft by four to one. Even with the aid of radar, Great Britain needed a miracle. Radar was Great Britain's secret weapon at that time. It could detect enemy fighters up to sixty miles away and detect bombers up to ninety miles before they flew over the English Channel.

Radar could not pick up the German aircraft once they had reached the English Channel so the Observer Corps would take over. Fighter Command knew that the war in the air was vital for the defence of the country to be successful. The RAF and her Allies fought with extraordinary courage against such odds; often six Hurricanes or Spitfires facing ten, twenty, thirty or up to a hundred enemy aircraft in combat.

By the middle of August 1940, the Luftwaffe were consistently bombing many of Fighter Command's airfields. Fighter Command could not take much more of such punishment. German bombs knocked out radar stations and destroyed aircraft before they could even take off. The raids killed many men in the RAF and women in the WAAFs. After the attacks, pilots who had taken off found it dangerous to land at their airfield because of all the bomb craters.

On 24 August 1940, a German bomber that was targeting the aircraft factories on the outskirts of London lost its bearings. At a time when Hitler had forbidden raids on London, the pilot jettisoned the bombs without realising he was over England's capital. In retaliation, the RAF was ordered to bomb Berlin the following day and for several subsequent days. In Hitler's fury, London was bombed from 7 September 1940 onwards. It was the start of the Blitzkrieg — the lightning war.

When many Londoners were sitting down to afternoon tea on 7 September 1940, the enemy's bombs began to rain down on the capital. Reichsmarschall Herman Göring gave orders for the continued bombing of London, and later that evening, the Luftwaffe targeted London once more. Approximately 300 men, women, and children of London lay dead among the burning rubble, and over 1,000 were injured. It had been a year since Polish civilians in Poland's capital had met the same fate. Many in the RAF were beginning to understand the hatred felt by the Polish people.

The London raids gave Fighter Command's airfields precious time to recover and time to find much-needed pilots. After so many young RAF pilots had been lost in France during the earlier days of the Battle of Britain, the RAF recruited men from Allied countries with the largest number of pilots coming from Poland. During the Battle of Britain, 145 Polish airmen flew in combat, some incorporated in various RAF squadrons while others flew with No. 302 and No. 303 Polish Squadrons. Between them, Polish fighter pilots destroyed 215 enemy aircraft during the Battle of Britain. Twenty-nine of the Polish pilots who flew in the Battle of Britain lost their young lives, and seventy-two never survived to see wars' end.

During the vital day of 15 September 1940, when at one point Fighter Command had all its aircraft airborne, Polish fighter pilots shot down twenty-six of the fifty-six enemy aircraft destroyed that day. No. 303 Kościuszko Squadron was the highest scoring squadron in the Battle of Britain with claims of 126 enemy aircraft destroyed in less than six weeks.

With the Battle of Britain won by Great Britain in the greatest air battle of all time, Hitler shelved the invasion indefinitely. The people of Great Britain owed so much to 'The Few'.

On 14–15 September 1940, No. 300 (Land of Mazovia) Polish Bomber Squadron and No. 301 (Land of Pomerania) Polish Bomber Squadron became combat operational. All the Polish crews returned from their first operation. This was not to be as the days weeks, months, and years passed. The Polish bomber pilots started their training with No.18 Operational Unit, then incorporated into No. 6 Bomber Group and became part of No. 1 Bomber Group on 15 September 1940. Refresher training had taken place at RAF Hucknall. Fighter training commenced after two weeks in Fairey Battles, which had a pilot, a navigator, and a wireless operator. The training included navigation practice, night bombing on training targets in Oxford, identification training as well as English lessons.

During April 1941, No. 304 (Land of Silesia) Polish Squadron and No. 305 (Land of Wielkopolska) Polish Squadron became operational. A further seven Polish squadrons were operational by Summer 1941. These were No. 306 (City of Toruń) Squadron; No. 307 (City of Lwów) Squadron, being a night fighter squadron; No. 308 (City of Kraków); No. 309 (Land of Czerwień) Squadron, which was an Army Support Squadron; No. 315 (Dęblin) Squadron, No. 316 (City of Warsaw); and No. 317 (City of Wilno) Squadron.

In April 1941, the first of the Polish fighter wings No.1 Polish Fighter Wing (Northolt Wing) was formed and flew from RAF Northolt. No. 2 Polish Fighter Wing followed in Exeter during August 1941. In 1942 No. 3 Polish Fighter Wing was formed at Perranporth.

Various types of sorties were flown by the Polish fighter wings including 'Circus' operations. During a Circus operation, the fighters met up to escort and protect the bombers flying to France to attack enemy targets.

The 'Mosquito' sortie, which later changed to 'Rhubarb', involved a small number of aircraft in the Wing, usually attacking in pairs.

Rhubarb sorties targeted enemy aircraft on the ground at airfields and other nearby enemy targets such as barracks, hangers, gun posts, various airfield defences and goods trains. The idea of a Rhubarb sortie was to fly low under the radar and use the element of surprise to carry out quick single attacks.

'Sphere' sorties were offensive sweeps flown at high altitude over the cloud in enemy territory to search for enemy shipping and submarines. Pilots did not sight many enemy aircraft on Sphere sorties. Other types of sorties included patrols over the English Channel and Air Sea Rescue operations.

In March 1943, No. 318 (City of Gdańsk) Polish Fighter Reconnaissance Squadron was formed from the Desert Air Force (2nd Army Corps in the Desert Air Force), making No. 318 Squadron the tenth Polish fighter squadron.

During Autumn of 1944, No. 663 Polish Observation Artillery Squadron formed to co-operate with Polish Artillery Units and 8th Army in Italy. Polish bomber squadrons were active in all major battles within Bomber Command, such as Berlin, Bremen, Brest, Essen, Frankfurt, Hamburg, Lorient, Mannheim, Nuremberg, Osnabrück, Rotterdam and the 1,000 bomber raid over Cologne on the evening of 30 May 1942 and returning on 31 May.

In mid-1942, No. 304 Polish Bomber Squadron transferred to Coastal Command until June 1945. The squadron was kept busy over the Bay of Biscay searching for U-boats, of which they destroyed six, and attacking shipping convoys.

Other Polish bomber squadrons were active in the Battle of the Atlantic. These operations were extremely hazardous, as many enemy fighters would attack the bombers to prevent the bombers reaching their target. On 3 November 1943, No. 301 Bomber Squadron became No. 1586 Special Duties Squadron attached to No. 138 British Squadron and stationed in Italy until 1944. The squadron co-operated with underground organisations in occupied Europe and laid approximately 1,800 mines at sea during 1943.

In 1944, No. 305 Bomber Squadron took part in night raids, flown with the aid of flares, to attack targets including railway bridges and advancing enemy troops.

While the courageous Polish fighter and bomber crews were fighting their battles up high, the battle raged on the ground. Many highly skilled Polish mechanics worked with the RAF ground crew who were relentless in their work to keep the aircraft in the air.

In Poland, an air force mechanic trained for two years or more at the Dęblin Officers' Training School or Bydgoszcz Central Aircraft Mechanics' School. Once they had completed their training in Poland, the mechanic was responsible for one aircraft, bearing sole responsibility for it.

As with the pilots, the Polish ground crews had escaped from internment camps in Romania and made their way to France, then England after the surrender of France. The first mechanics arriving from France went to RAF Eastchurch or RAF Manston to train on British aircraft. From August 1940, most of the mechanics trained on British aircraft in RAF Blackpool. Their training was in the hands of the British with the help of interpreters. Later, as the war continued, the Polish mechanics were able to train their own men.

Each mechanic carried a huge responsibility for taking care of the aircraft. Every victory won by the fighter pilot or bomber crew was possible with the assistance of others. Among this support team, the mechanic carried out various repairs and sometimes performed a miracle on an aircraft so shot up that one could believe it would never take to the sky again.

The mechanics worked for long hours, often through the day and night at their own request and barely taking the time to eat. They felt pride and the joy when a pilot returned with a celebratory victory roll; the mechanic knowing he had made the aircraft safe to fly. As the number of casualties rose, the mechanic felt the deep pain of loss when airmen did not return.

On landing, all aircraft would undergo a thorough check — oil levels checked, oxygen tubes checked for blockages, fresh batteries installed, the aircraft refuelled and rearmed. Polish men and women took part in all aspects of the RAF. Polish women were part of the Women's Auxiliary Air Force (WAAF) and carried out important duties as plotters, radio operators, and drivers. Polish women ferry pilots flew with the Air Transport Auxiliary (ATA) to deliver much-needed aircraft to various airfields.

From early September 1940 to the end of the war, the Luftwaffe dropped thousands of tons of bombs on Great Britain. The valiant airmen fought in the air to repel the enemy aircraft and keep the bombs from hitting British soil.

The Germans launched a new terror weapon in June 1944. The V1 flying bomb, nicknamed the doodlebug or buzz-bomb, flew unmanned at a speed of up to 400 miles per hour and at a height of up to 3,000 feet. The V1 was recognisable by a high-pitched whining sound, followed by a terrifying silence as it crashed nearly a ton of high explosive on its target. The first V1 to crash in London hit the suburb of Bethnal Green on 13 June 1944, killing six people.

It was possible to shoot down a V1 flying bomb once it had launched from the mobile sites in occupied Europe. Anti-aircraft guns were able to destroy the V1s during night flights as the light from the bomb's exhaust flames was visible in the darkness. Other V1 flying bombs were destroyed when they hit the barrage balloons over London.

Fighter aircraft could also destroy the flying bombs by a skilful manoeuvre where the aircraft flew, so its wing was close to touching the underneath of the V1's wing. The manoeuvre created a slight slipstream that caused the flying bomb to crash. Another dangerous method of destruction of the so-called wonder weapon was for a fighter aircraft to fire at very close range and shoot it down. Between 1944 and 1945, Polish pilots shot down 190 flying bombs.

In 1943, the French and Polish underground sent details and drawings to the Allies about a small unmanned aircraft the Germans were building in a secret location in Peenemünde. To find out what was going on, Coastal Command flew photo reconnaissance operations over the site. It was the development site for the V1 flying bombs.

On the night of 17 August 1943, 596 RAF bombers took off from Great Britain in an operation codenamed Hydra. Approaching Peenemünde via the North Sea, Denmark and the Baltic, Bomber Command aircraft dropped over 1,650 high explosives and approximately 270 tons of incendiaries, hitting part of the target.

As always the cost to life was high. Bomber Command lost 40 aircraft from the 324 Lancaster bombers, 218 Halifax bombers and 53 Stirling bombers that flew in the operation. The raid killed 180 German technical staff working on the V1 flying bombs. In a tragic mistake, bombs dropped on a nearby camp for forced labour workers killed close to 600 Polish men and women and Soviet prisoners of war. Post-war analysis of the information from Bletchley Park, the Polish Home Army, the French allied underground intelligence, photo reconnaissance from Coastal Command shows that Hydra delayed the launch of further V1 flying bombs by up to two months. Later in the war, the V1s claimed 6,184 lives and injured over 18,000 people. If the Germans had not been delayed from launching, many more thousands would have died.

After the Peenemünde raid, Hitler moved the V-weapon development site to an underground factory in the Harz Mountains, close to Nordhausen, Germany.

In 1944, Germany was ready to launch another unmanned flying weapon, the V2 rocket. Unlike the V1 flying bomb, the V2 rocket could not be destroyed once launched.

Controlled by a gyroscope on graphite vanes behind a radio signal, it had a range of 200-250 miles. The jet deflected the exhaust gasses and steered the rocket. It weighed between eleven and a half and fourteen tons and had a top speed of 4,000 miles per hour. The explosive one-ton warhead made the V2 Rocket a deadly and worrying menace.

In 1944, the Polish Home Army AK, who had been in radio contact with London about the V1 development site, managed to find an V1 bomb intact and were prepared to hand it over to the Allies.

In the darkness of the 25 July 1944, members of the Home Army AK waited with lighted brush handles in a field on the outskirts of Jadowniki Mokre in Poland while George Stanley Guilford landed his Dakota aircraft. The Home Army AK loaded the V1 parts knowing that if caught, the penalty was almost certain death at the hands of the Gestapo. With his precious cargo aboard, George Guilford flew in secret to RAF Northolt. The transfer gave British scientific experts many answers to their questions about the deadly weapon.

Every risk the Home Army AK took to help the Allies was one step closer to winning the war. Many people struggling under the bloody boot of Nazi occupation in Poland fought back. They did not lay down their meagre arms in the hope that one day the Allies would liberate them; they resisted with everything they had.

Hitler wanted to erase Poland and all she stood for from the map of Europe. Many of the atrocities that befell the Polish nation were designed to mentally and physically destroy the Polish people. No amount of words can explain the terror the Polish people endured. Only those who survived to tell the tale can express the true meaning of the hell they lived through.

Historians estimate that close to six million Polish men, women and children were killed during the Second Word War. Polish Jews, those with mental or physical illness, the Polish intelligentsia — artists, priests, scholars, and writers — were all among those murdered. Some were shot, or hanged, or beaten to death. Others were tortured beyond human endurance and killed or deported to labour and concentrations camps. The list of mindless murder is endless.

Along with the individual murders, mass murders took place in Poland's villages, towns, and cities. One of the worst mass murders befell the inhabitants of Bydgoszcz, a city that was part of the

Pomerania Voivodeship in Northern Poland. Before the outbreak of war, the city had been home to many young Polish airmen during their training at the Bydgoszcz School for Non-Commissioned Officers.

The atrocities in Bydgoszcz followed 'Bloody Sunday', the name given by German propaganda ministers to the indiscriminate attack on civilians during 3–4 September 1939. In truth, it was German saboteurs in the city who first fired upon Polish civilians. Some German civilians were killed by Luftwaffe bombs while fleeing from the city. The German Propaganda Ministry inflated the number of ethnic German casualties and used the incident to bolster support for the occupation of Poland. In an act of retaliation, approximately 10,000 Polish residents were executed. This included cavalry officers and veterans of the First World War, officials, priests, professors, workmen, women, and approximately a hundred schoolboys and young scouts as they heroically sang their national hymn, 'God Who Protects Poland'. Another of those executed was Father Szarek, a Catholic clergyman. Before killing him, the Germans gouged out his eyes and broke his nose and jaw.

As the German forces swept through the country, so did the body count. The German aggressor took great delight in destroying Polish churches, monuments to Polish Kings, and heroes' castles. In fact, they ransacked and destroyed anything connected to Polish heritage. Most of the Polish population lost one or more of their family. Many entire families vanished during the horror of war. There are harrowing tales of German soldiers arranging the bodies of each murdered family into the shape of a swastika to terrify other residents.

Soviet Forces in Poland

Not all atrocities in Poland during the Second World War can be laid at the feet of the Germans. In 1939, the Soviets took more than a million Polish people from their homes by force and transported them to labour camps deep within Russia. Many were never seen or heard from again.

During Spring 1940, the NKVD, a Soviet secret police organisation, executed approximately 22,000 prisoners of war in a series of massacres known as the Katyń Massacre. To stop Poland rebuilding another military, Stalin signed an order for the execution of the intelligentsia, police officers and the thousands of Polish military officers who had not escaped at the outbreak of war.

The Katyń Massacre first came to light in 1943, when German troops found the remains of 4,000 bodies in a mass grave in Katyń near Smolensk, Russia. At first, the Soviets blamed the Nazis, but finally admitted to the massacre in 1990 and revealed the location of the two other mass graves associated with the massacre — Mednoye and Piatykhatky.

Despite all German and Soviet efforts to prevent any organised military resistance, many ordinary Polish people joined the Home Army AK. The Home Army was the largest organised underground movement of men and women fighting in Europe. There were other smaller independent Polish resistance groups within Poland, but the Home Army AK was the largest. It had over 300,000 members, and 28,000 of those were armed. Many were the families of Polish airmen and ground crew fighting alongside the RAF in Great Britain.

The Home Army AK organisation was excellent; it printed and distributed newspapers, ran four universities and educated one and a half million children. The penalty for any of these activities was death. The Home Army AK kept in contact with the Polish Government-in-exile in London, assisting with whatever was required for the war effort.

In November 1943, Winston Churchill and Franklin Roosevelt met with Joseph Stalin at the Teheran (Tehran) Conference. Stalin demanded forty-two percent of Polish pre-war territories in the east. In compensation, Poland would receive German territories in the west. The three leaders did not resolve all the territorial details until the Yalta and Potsdam conferences in 1945, but the top secret agreement signed at the Teheran conference sealed the post-war fate of Poland. The Polish Government-in-Exile was not consulted on the agreement; it would never have agreed to Stalin's demands, nor would it have agreed to the stipulation that future Polish Governments would be friendly to the Soviet Union.

Soviet gunfire echoed across the Vistula River as the Soviets advanced towards Warsaw in late July 1944. By 31 July the Polish Underground AK knew that Soviet tanks had broken through German defences to the east of Warsaw and were only ten miles away. The Polish people had information that the Soviets would enter Warsaw and continue to fight the Germans. Instead, the Soviet advance halted. This had catastrophic consequences for the Home Army's planned rebellion, which became known as the Warsaw Uprising.

At precisely five o'clock in the evening on the 1 August 1944 thousands of windows opened in Warsaw and flashes of light seemed to ricochet all around the Poland's capital as guns fired and bullets flew.

Day after day the courageous Polish people fought with outdated and homemade weapons against the tanks and superior military might of the German forces. As the battle raged, the Germans captured many Polish women and children, marching them in front of the German tanks to deter the members of the Home Army AK from firing upon the tanks.

The Germans bombed Warsaw continuously and shelled street after street. Warsaw burned and the streets ran red with Polish blood. People hid in the sewers or waded through the excrement as they moved from one part of the city to another. The Germans threw gas bombs and grenades into many of the sewers to seal the tunnels. The German SS shot the sick and injured where they lay in their hospital beds.

As the Polish people fought on, they waited for their so-called Soviet Allies to enter Warsaw to help. None came. The Soviets waited outside the city and let the Germans and Polish destroy one another.

Stalin even refused to give the British and the Americans access to Soviet-held airfields to stop the Allies from flying in the weapons, food, and medical supplies to the desperate people of Warsaw. Polish pilots asked to fly aid to Warsaw from England even though it would have been a suicide operation as their aircraft would not have held enough fuel for the return flight. Their requests were denied.

The Polish Air Force, RAF and South African Air Force in Brindisi, Italy carried out operations to drop supplies over burning Warsaw. These flights were hazardous, especially as the bombers' return journey was flown during daylight hours. The bombers flew close to 200 flights, of which sixteen Polish Air Force, nineteen RAF and South African Air Force bombers crews made the ultimate sacrifice to aid the people of Warsaw.

On 18 September 1944, Stalin permitted the US Air Force to fly supplies from a Soviet-held airfield. The Americans suffered heavy losses; the brave bomber crews were an easy target for the Luftwaffe's anti-aircraft guns. Despite the Allied flights, the constant smoke above Poland's burning capital affected visibility and few supplies reached their intended target.

The Warsaw Uprising was the biggest mass revolt in occupied Europe during the Second World War. After sixty-three days of heroic fighting against overwhelming odds, 200,000 Polish men, women and children lay dead. Approximately 10,000 Germans died, 7,000 were missing, and 9,000 were wounded.

The Polish Command negotiated that on the surrender of Warsaw the Germans would treat the Home Army AK as a regular army and as prisoners of war. The Germans held approximately 15,000 members of the Home Army AK in the prisoner of war camps but sent many civilians to face the horrors of the Nazi concentration camps. After Warsaw was evacuated, Hitler ordered his troops to raze the city to the ground.

Later, Stalin did not want to risk another hard-fought uprising. So, in 1945, Soviet forces arrested many members of the Home Army and sent them deep within Russia.

Back in England, those serving in the Polish Air Force waited as news of Warsaw's surrender came through. Most had no word from their loved ones; all they could do was pray their families were alive and would one day live in a free Poland. Until that day, they would continue to fight.

On bomber operations, the bomber crews climbed into their metal crates and took to the sky. The pilots were alert at their controls, the navigators aimed to keep on target, and the gunner's scanned the skies for the enemy. Despite their skill, the bomber's journey into enemy territory was a long and perilous one. With gallons of fuel and explosive bombs on board, the bombers were a priority for enemy fighters to destroy before they reached their target.

The risks were no less hazardous after the bombs had been dropped. The bombers had to navigate their way home through the searchlights, flak and again the enemy fighters. The odds against the crews flying their thirty operations and making it home again were slim. Many bomber crews lost their lives over the English Channel on the way home. It must have taken immense courage to repeatedly fly such hazardous operations.

The time off between operations was a chance for the airmen to enjoy themselves. They flew together then shared a joke and a drink down the local pub. They sang, and if they were lucky, they could spend a few hours with a young lady by their side to push aside any thoughts about the next operation. Regular drinking sessions with the same faces were rarely repeated. For the airmen, it was a solemn reminder that they could be next. By wars' end, over 55,000 men in Bomber Command had lost their young lives.

As with bomber crews, the fighter pilots faced overwhelming odds each time they took to the sky. Death could be instant if the pilots' aircraft exploded under enemy fire or enemy bullets tore into their flesh, proving fatal. Some pilots faced an agonising death while trapped or burnt alive in their aircraft as it went down. Others survived with serious life-changing injuries or burns.

But what the pilots feared most was the sea. Pilots only baled out over the English Channel as a last resort. Rather than ditch into the sea, pilots tried to make it home, even if it meant crash landing. For those forced into the sea, the cold water was a lonely place to die. Choppy waters and strong currents claimed many lives.

To survive at sea, a pilot had to get free of his parachute, inflate his dinghy and climb in without the sea pulling it away or dragging it under the waves.

Pilots would often fly protectively over their comrades in the sea to ward off an enemy attack and to mark the position for Air Sea Rescue. But once their aircraft was low on fuel, the pilot had no option but to return to the nearest airfield to refuel.

Some pilots survived in the water against all odds but most drowned or died of hypothermia. Air Sea rescue did their best, but often they could not locate the pilot or compete against the elements of nature. Thousands of pilots in Fighter Command lost their lives during the Second World War.

As with all airmen, the Polish pilots knew that death could await them in combat, but the desire for freedom and the love for their country drove the Polish airmen on until the end of the war.

On 8 May 1945, as the Second World War ended in Europe. Great Britain celebrated, as did many of her Allies, but not Poland. For Poland and her people, there was no celebration, no freedom, just a new oppressor, Joseph Stalin. The people of Poland had fought a long hard and bloody war where over six million of their men women and children had perished in the fight for freedom. The survivors felt betrayed by the British and American governments for their part in the Teheran, Yalta, and Potsdam conferences. Unfortunately, it wasn't the only time the Polish Allies felt betrayed by the British Government.

On a summer's day of 6 June 1946, people lined The Mall in London to watch a victory parade in honour of those who had fought and died during the Second World War. Representatives from most of the Allied countries took part. But there was not a single representative from the Polish forces. The British Government of the day under Clement Attlee did not want to upset Stalin so only invited members of the Soviet-controlled Polish government. Winston Churchill and representatives from the RAF, who knew how much the Polish forces had supported Great Britain objected. Prime Minister Atlee compromised and made a token invitation to a small number of Polish pilots. Insulted by the turn of events, and the lack of recognition for all Polish forces, the pilots declined the invitation.

By 1947, all of the Polish Air Force squadrons in Great Britain had been disbanded. It was a sad day because the Polish Air Force's hope for freedom in Poland had not been realised.

The British Government did their best to persuade the Polish men and women to return to Poland. Only a naive government would fail to realise what waited for those who returned to a Soviet-controlled Poland. Many in the House of Commons and in the Royal Air Force objecting to the plans. For many Polish men and women in Great Britain, returning to Poland was not an option. They felt they could not return to live under a communist dictator even though they had family in Poland. Some had not heard from their family for eight years and did not know if they were alive. Some men in the Polish Air Force had fallen in love and married English women had started families. This led to the Polish Resettlement Act 1947, giving the citizenship to the Polish forces who did not choose to return to Poland. The RAF did what it could and found jobs for close to 500 men.

After a period of intense political intimidation in Poland, a rigged election took place on 19 January 1947, giving full power to the communists. The saying, 'save us God from false friends, against our enemies we will defend ourselves' seems fitting here.

Over 7,500 from the Polish Air Force remained in Great Britain even though their hearts ached for their families. Work was scarce for so many Polish men after wars' end, but they made the best of life away from their homeland. Some experienced discrimination and acts of hate but they would not return to Poland until she was free.

It hurt the Polish men to see the words 'go home Poles' written on walls. Only a few years before the people of Great Britain had welcomed them while they fought to keep Hitler's evil from the shores. Others in Great Britain did not forget that the Polish were among 'The Few' in The Battle of Britain. Nor did they forget the thousands of Polish men and women who had served alongside various British forces throughout the Second World War.

Approximately 3,000 Polish Air Force personnel returned to Poland. The need to find out what had happened to their loved ones was a strong pull. So strong was each airmen's belief in their decision to stay or return to Poland that it fractured some friendships forever.

Once back in Poland, the Iron Curtain closed around the airmen. They were watched for many years. Some were arrested and interrogated by the NKVD. The Second World War had ended but starvation, beatings, torture and deportation to labour camps deep within the Soviet Union still occurred on a regular basis in Poland.

Many of the prisoners had been members of the Home Army AK, and some had taken part in the Warsaw Uprising.

In 1947, the NKVD arrested General Stanisław Skalski shortly after he returned to Poland. He had flown in defence of Poland and flown with an RAF squadron during the Battle of Britain. Among his list of credits, he had shot down twenty-one enemy aircraft, had been the first Polish fighter pilot to lead an RAF squadron into battle, had led the 2nd Polish Fighter Wing, and had flown in the Western Desert attached to No. 145 Squadron (Skalski Circus). In Poland, the Soviets kept him in a filthy cell on suspicion of being a spy for England. General Skalski knew he could be taken out and shot, as some Polish airmen had suffered such a fate. After many years, the Soviets changed General Skalski's sentence to life imprisonment. Eventually, he was released in 1956 at the age of 40 years old. Despite the difficult years that followed, General Skalski lived to witness Poland regain her independence in 1989. It came fifty years after the start of the war in 1939 and millions of lives had been lost, but Poland was free.

Tragically for the Polish forces and the Polish people who fought for freedom in the Second World War, many never lived to see their country free. Held deep within their heart, they took their love for their country, their faith, and freedom to the grave. Only in a higher place were they free.

Sources: Professor Bernard Buchwald, Dennis Arthur Britton, Jadwiga Cebrzyńska, S/L Zdzisław Krasnodębski, F/L Jan Kowalski, F/L Gen Szaposznikow Cpt Eric Nanke, Witold Pietrasiewicz, Helana Radomska and Stanisław Sroka, Tadeusz Krystek, PAF Association for details on Polish bomber and fighter squadrons and RAF Northolt. Members of the Home Army and survivors of labour and concentration camps who wish to remain nameless. The section on The Massacre Of Poles In Bydgoszcz in The German New Order In Poland (known as The Black Book) published 1942 by the Polish Ministry of Information.

APPENDICES

APPENDIX I

Arsen Cebrzyński
French Squadron Mission Order dated 15 April 1940

BASE AERIENNE MIXTE DE LYON   TÉL. P. 93-01

D.I.A.P. – G.I.V. – E.C.

D. I. A. P.

Groupe d'Instruction en Vol

Escadrille de Chasse

ORDRE   DE   MISSION

Il est ordonné au (I) Lieutenant C.EBRZYNSKI

d'exécution la mission aérienne , qui lui a été prescrite sans

sortir de la zône : NEUVILLE–sur–SAONE –AMBERIEU–LA TOURDE PIN–

VIENNE –NEUVILLEsur SAONE .

Altitude : MINIMUM 500 m MAXIMUM 3000 m.

A BRON , le 15/4/1940.

Le Capitaine ROUGEVIN-BAVAILLE
Cdt. L'Escadrille de Chasse

(I)Grade et Nom en capitales

APPENDIX 2

Arsen Cebrzyński
Death Certificate dated 11 September 1940 & Author's Note

Many years ago I visited the grave of Arsen Cebrzyński at Northwood Cemetery. At that time his grave was marked with 19 September 1940 as his date of death. This contradicted the date I had identified during my research.

I wrote to his wife Jadwiga, who confirmed the date of death was 11 September 1940. This is the date recorded on his death certificate.

I felt it was important that the date should be correct for the family and contacted Northwood Cemetery. Records held at the cemetery show that the burial took place on 17 September 1940 — two days before the date of death shown on his grave.

As a result of the evidence, the headstone was amended to the correct date by the Commonwealth War Graves Committee in 2002.

Nina Britton Boyle

APPENDIX 3

Stanisław Karubin
Document detailing his squadrons & medals

Nr ewid: aug: 793420
STANISŁAW KARUBIN

-.KRÓTKI PRZEBIEG SŁUŻBY WOJSKOWEJ 1)

Data wstąpienia do P.W.

W Polsce: 2.11.34r. - 18.9.1939r.   We Francji: 23.1.1940r.   W Anglji: 26.6.1940r.

Pobyt w jednostkach: 2.8.1940r.   303 Dyon Myśliwski.
                        7.3.1941r.   57 O.T.U.w Hawarden.
                        8.4.1941r.   55 O.T.U.w Ustvorth.

Awanse: 2 sierpnia 1940r. awans na sierżanta zawodowego.

Odznaczenia i pochwały: W 1940r.Krzyż Virtuti Militari V.klasy jako pilot.
                          Distinguished Flying Medal / Odznaczenie angiel./
                          Odznaka Honorowa za rany i kontuzję odniesione w obr.
                          Ojczyzny.

Podpis Oficera A.Ú.Ur.Z.

Kn.

Komenda Uzupełnien Nr. 2

APPENDIX 4

Wacław Łapkowski
Letter written by Flying Officer Łapkowski dated 1 December 1940 describing his injuries after his aircraft was shot down during the Battle of Britain.
(See the translation of the letter in Pilot Biographies, page 95)

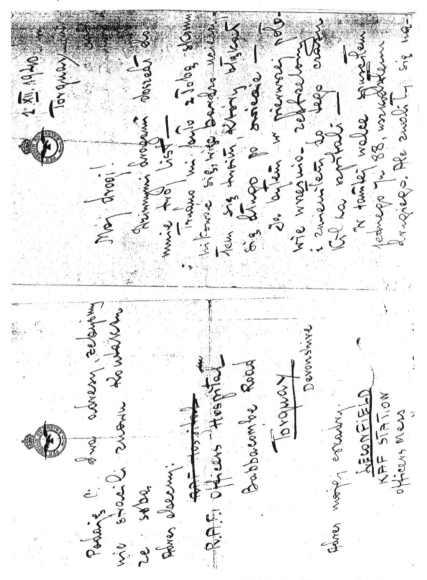

The letter is folded as a booklet - above are pages 1 & 4, the first & last pages of the letter.

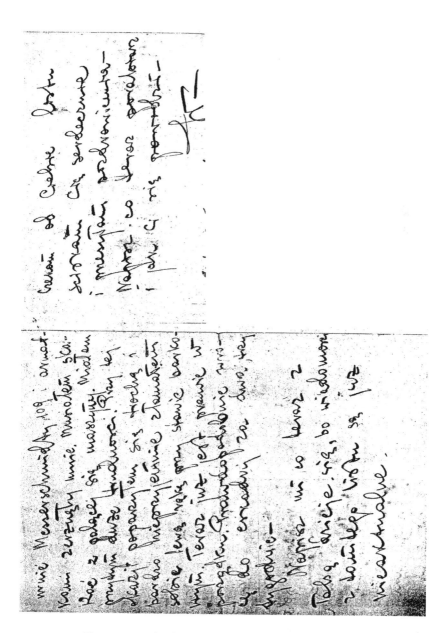

These are pages 2 & 3 (the two internal centre pages) of the letter.

APPENDIX 5

Wacław Łapkowski
Memoir written by Flying Officer Łapkowski describing flying in battle on 22 January 1941.
(See the translation of the memoir in Pilot Biographies, page 96-98)

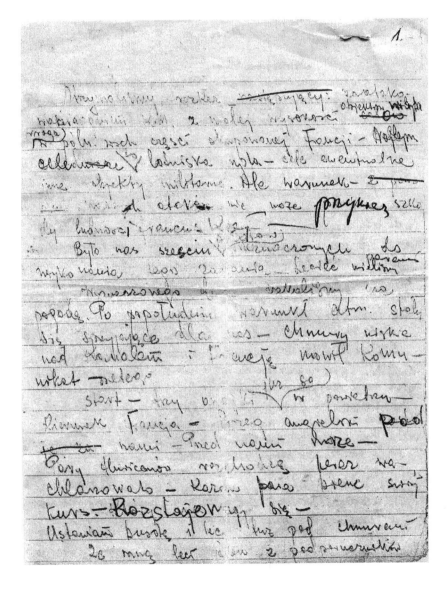

2. 2.

mój ... Kolega z którym należ...
... jednej eskadrze jeszcze w Pols...
... teraz ... ...
... na ... "german Bardyn" —

Zbliżamy się do brzegu Francji — Wcho...
... w chmury — Prowadzą ... ...
... ... minuty — "Wskazówka repa...
... ..., że czas już zejść pod
chmury i szukać celu —

Schodzimy — Chmury ... po chwili
jesteśmy pod ... ... około 200
... —

Staram się zorjentować — ... ...
celu — czy znajdę? Problem ten pochłania
mnie ... w zupełności —

Jest! Widzę ... ...
raus! Dwie maszyny ustawiają się do
startu — To starzy znajomi — Me. 109 —
Jestem w dogodnej pozycji — Skręt w
prawo i atakuję ich sdl ... — Za mną
atakuje ... ... — drugi ...

3

4   4

Celuję w ten Krzyż... Strzelam
maszyna moja szybko rusza się
do wierzchołka w dnem. Chcę, wyk...
... strzelać jeszcze dłużej — Nagle w...
przed maską maszyną, majętem wylontan...
tą się jakieś dziury. Na wszelką
reakcję zapoznu — franzmę się
maszyną strzelać bzyp. — Tylko
Wyskoczyłem już nad ziemią —
Poderwałem maszynę Odwracam głowę
do tyłu — z lewej z prawej górni...
strzeliłem coś zaczaił... dymie —
lepiej spostrzegam co to w co
uderzyłem. Było dwie wyrwzmego
wnętrza — na skrzydłach niet dziu-
strzelić...
                 Mój m. B. W ....
atakował ... mnie. Pamiętam żywić
z Km te dwa moment... —
              Okazały się wtedy sta-
nowiska APL — jeden z ...ów trafił
jego maszyn... ... sam wielem tzyk
przeciwpancernej —

powietrz [...] jest [...] rakieta — [...]
[...] w akcen [...]
[...] do [...] momentu — [...]
się końcem skrzydła [...] walki z
[...] strzelająca [...]
Odpowiedz [...]
[...]
VVV Teraz [...] jednko [...]
w lesie — kilka serii — atak
jego [...] nakierowany — kurs 290 — na
morze — Mr 2 [...] doścignąć [...]
[...] Ale [...] to za trudne
do [...]
Na [...]
skrzydle i sterach [...]
[...]
[...]
i sterach — trudno utrzymać
maszynę — [...] jest nie [...]
martwy V [...] się wejsc
w chmury — [...]
z [...]
[...]

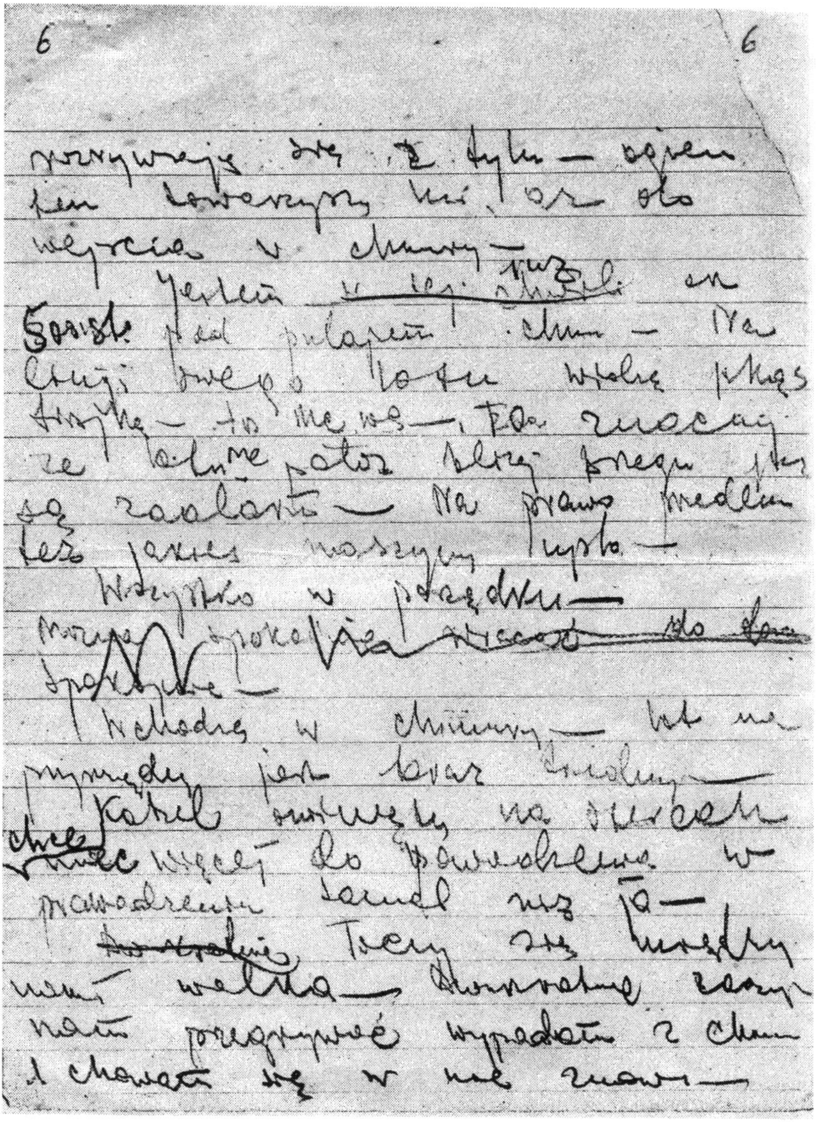

6   6

[handwritten Polish manuscript, largely illegible]

Wszystko w porządku —

o utrzymaniu kursu nowy wikm

W Krucu zwycięstwo jest po mojej
stronie — udaje mi się przebić między
grubą warstwę chmur. Poprzedni kurs po...
... — jestem sam — naokoło płynek wielki
i słońce, Nadeau po wierzchołkach chmur
... mogę tworzyć — sterowność maszyn

Sterowność maszyny jest ograni-
czona — gdyby mi zaplanował
mnie nie mógłbym wykonać
nawet skrętu ani walki — ani w
... również niewiele zrobił

obliczam czas — musi być już
blisko brzegu. Najwyższy czas
po temu. Ilu. wiralb. — To wynosi
na chłodnica —
Zawijam się w chmury —
...
Nikn... Słońce — ... coraz
cieńmierszw warstwy chmur i w...

APPENDIX 6

Bogusław Mierzwa
No. 303 Kościuszko Squadron Identity Card dated 4 July 1941

303 DYON MYŚL. WARSZAWSKI
IM. T. KOŚCIUSZKI.

LEGITYMACJA Nr. 23...

NA MOCY STATUTU KOMISJA 303 DYWIZJONU

NADAŁA W DNIU 4 lipca 194 1 r.

ppor.pilot MIERZWA BOGUSŁAW

BOJOWĄ ODZNAKĘ 303 DYWIZJONU MYŚL. WARSZ.
IM. T. KOŚCIUSZKI.

DOWÓDCA DYONU.

ADJUTANT DYONU

APPENDIX 7

Stefan Wójtowicz
French Identity Card for the Polish Air Force in France 14 May 1940

ARMÉE DE L'AIR

UNITÉS D'AVIATION POLONAISE — POLSKIE JEDNOSTKI LOTNICZE

Nom : *WÓJTOWICZ*
Nazwisko

Prénoms : *Stefan*
Imiona

Grade : *Caporal-Chef*
Stopień

Né le : *19 – VI – 1919* à *Wypnicha (Pologne)*
Ur. dn.

Résidant à : *Bron (Rhône)*
Zamieszk. w.

Profession : *Pilote*
Zawód

Fils de *Stanisława* et de *Weronika née Post*
Syn

Domicilies à *Wypnicha (Pologne)*
Zamieszk. w.

Situation de famille : / Célibataire, ~~Veuf~~, ~~Marié~~. /
Stan   / Kawaler,   Wdowiec. Żonaty. /

Nombre d'enfants : —
Ilość dzieci

Taille : 1 mètre *82* centimètres
Wzrost : 1 metr   centymetrow

Marques particulières : —
Znaki szczególne

Fait à *Bron* , le *14 Mai* 1940
Wystawiona. w :   dn :

EMPREINTES DIGITALES
Odcisk   Palcow
Index gauche   Index droit
Palec wskazujący
Lewy   Prawy

SIGNATURE DU TITULAIRE :
Podpis właściciela dowodu

ATTESTATION DE L'OFFICIER
SUPÉRIEUR POLONAIS DÉLÉGUÉ
Zaświadczenie starszego polskiego
oficera delegowanego :

LE COLONEL COMMANDANT DU DÉPOT D'INSTRUCTION
DE L'AVIATION POLONAISE :
Pułkownik dowodca centrum wyszkolenia
lotnictwa polskiego :

APPENDIX 8

Stefan Wójtowicz
Letter written by Sergeant Wójtowicz 29 August 1940 & translation

Dear Leon,

Thank you very much for your letter. I admit I was very worried about your being silent, but at last. Thank you very much for congratulating me regarding the celebration with alcohol. I know today that I would like to do it very much, I've got the money after all! We celebrate every night.

With regards to sleeping, one sleeps very little, therefore it is not worth going to bed. The Germans pay visits very often and English soil welcomes them nicely with an evil laughter, therefore you can only dream of sleeping.

[personal details about his friend]

I didn't go to Blackpool for my leave despite I was planning to. I was a bit unlucky and was down ill, then I had five days of leave. I was wondering around the neighbourhood, sightseeing in London and other nearby nooks. London is currently empty, there is hardly any life in there for such a big city. I met many Polish men and women but Polish women are not the same as they initially were in Poland. I cannot describe them well but they seem to look like French women. I had a bit of trouble with the girl I met in Blackpool as she writes letters to me quite often and I cannot reply and reading is even worse. I had her as a candidate for a wife but you know what is on my mind…flying.

I apologise for such frivolities and naughtiness that is because I would like to share everything with you and today I have a bit of time so I would like to express what is wrong or stupid.

Leon, I feel similar as the old days in Warsaw, there is a whole bunch of us from Warsaw. Many a time others come to visit and it is so strange that some go away into the unknown — and some come [back]. It is very nice here, hell of different activities to Poland.

[unreadable]

I am sending a sincere hug.

APPENDIX 9

Stefan Wójtowicz
Burned remnants of a RAF Map of Great Britain found with the body of
Sergeant Wójtowicz on 11 September 1940

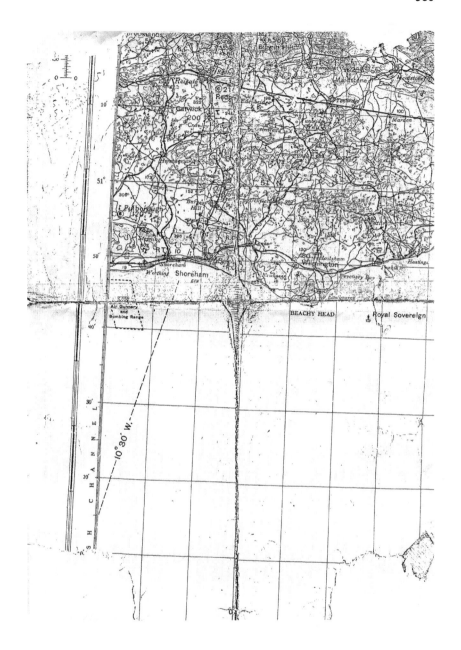

ACKNOWLEDGEMENTS

Often acknowledgements begin with the words. 'How do I begin to thank...' and 'it could not be written without the help of so many'. In my case, this is 100% true. For without the kindness, patience and unlimited time given by others, my book could never have been written.

I give my heartfelt gratitude to all the ex-combatants and ground crew I have interviewed and the relatives of the many men who made the ultimate sacrifice in the fight for freedom. I thank the people who wrote to me, even though the letters had to be smuggled out of Poland because the country was still under Soviet rule. Decades after the Second World War had ended, some of those who wrote to me were still desperate for news of their lost loved ones.

I thank the people who fought in the AK Home Army, the labour camps and concentration camp survivors for the interviews. Some of whom do not wish me to put their names in my book. I am deeply indebted to them and the following:

For their memoirs
Stefania Karpińska (Wojtulanis), Flight Lieutenant Kazimierz Karaszewski and Flight Lieutenant Jan Maliński. Helana Dyaczyńska for allowing me to include the memoirs of her late brother, Wing Commander Jan Biały. Wanda Krasnodębska for memoirs of her late husband, Wing Commander Zdzisław Krasnodębski. General Witold Urbanowicz for sharing a little about himself and writing about his friend, Zdzisław Krasnodębski. I also thank him for his helpful advice. Squadron

Leader Franciśzek Kornicki for writing about his first flight. Stanisław
Sroka for his assistance in writing about SOE and V1-V2.

For their time and research
Tadeusz Krystek and Wacław Wybraniec (Polish Air Force Association)
for their endless help with details about Polish airmen, squadrons,
various statistics, addresses and endless other gems of information.
I thank staff at RAF Northolt, the Polish Institute and Sikorski
Museum, and the Ministry of Defence for all their help. Also, thank
you to Piotr Sikora, Polish Air Force Historian and Researcher for his
expertise.

The National Archives, RAF Hendon Museum, where I researched
through hundreds of documents, and Cabinet Office for various
licenses. The Commonwealth War Graves Commission for all they do
to preserve the resting places of so many. The Polish newspapers 'For
Freedom and People,' 'ZBOWID,' and PRZEKOJ, who placed free of
charge requests on my behalf to trace people; and the paper 'Wings'.
The British Embassy in Warsaw. John Gallehawk for introducing me
to my publisher.

To the many airmen and their families — it was and has been
a true honour: Mieczysław Dodo, Bob Banta, Bernard Bukowicz,
Tadeusz Beresticki, Sergeant M.Bristow, Flight Lieutenant Marian
Chełmecki, Jadwiga Cebrzyńska, Jan Delowicz, Squadron Leader
Gandi Drobiński, Zwonier Ferić, Mrs L. Forbes, Peter Finch, Flying
Officer M. Hardwick, Professor Macej Henneberg, Franciśzek
Jankowski, Flight Lieutenant Jan Kowalski, Flight Lieutenant Julian
Roch Kowalski, Wing Commander Ronald Kellett, Squadron Leader
Wacław Król, Janina Karubin, Major W. Lapinski, Antoni Owczalski,
Mirosław Radomska, Helana Radomska, Zofia Rozycka, Stefanie
Palak, Witold Pietrasiewicz, Squadron Leader Tadeusz Sawicz, Tadeusz
Siudak, Dr Antoni Slupik, Stanisław Szczepaniak, Flight Lieutenant
Gen Szaposznikow, Sergeant Pat Walsh, Mrs Irena Wünsche, Matylda
Wianarska and Flight Lieutenant Zbigniew Wojda. To General
Stanisław Skalski for his prayers and kind advice. I give thanks to
the families for sending copies of their precious photographs to be
included in the book.

Without the help of two very unassuming gentlemen, my book
could never have got started let alone finished: 'Dear Bernie,' or

to be precise Flight Lieutenant Bernard Buchwald, my dear friend who traced so many people in Poland and introduced me to them as someone to be trusted. Thank you for allowing me to use extracts from your book and for your constant encouragement. What would I have done without you?

To my other dear friend Eric, or to be more precise, Captain Eric Nanke who fought in Monte Cassino and later worked for The Polish Government in Exile. Dearest Eric, who undertook the mammoth task of translating into English all the letters sent from Poland. Over the years, there have been hundreds of such letters. How I miss our wonderful chats on Poland.

To Derek Sibson, a most brilliant surgeon who twice saved my life. My friend Susan Summers for her honest comments. My very supportive family — my parents Joan and Dennis Britton, my sisters Carol and Tanya, my wonderful children Charlotte and Carl. Not forgetting my dearest grandchildren Chelsea, Errin Elizabeth, Evelyn, Ethan and Isla.

Special thanks to my publisher Kerry Howard for all her assistance great patience and hard work. I give extra thanks to my son Carl for his patience and commitment to typing my longhand manuscript onto a computer, and his fiancee Marta Kasperek for all her hard work with translating Polish into English and name checking.

Also, my ex-husband John, for looking after our two children when they were young and enabling me to travel and research for my book. Most of all, I thank my father who enlivened my imagination with stories of the Polish pilots during the war. He lived in South Ruislip, close to RAF Northolt and experienced the roar of planes taking off, and the sight of returning aircraft, some of which were badly damaged. His memories about the Polish pilots and the aircraft they flew inspired me as a child and became a lifelong passion. My father has instilled in me a gratitude, respect, and love for the Polish airmen who flew in defence of Britain in the Second World War and their ground crews. Without the knowledge he has shared with me through the years, this book may not have happened.

'All those in the Polish Air Force live on as long as we remember them and in stories told of them. The fighting Eagles.'

Nina Britton Boyle

GLOSSARY

In the earlier stages of the Second World War the Royal Air Force gave some of the Polish airmen a lower rank than they held in the Polish Air Force. Promotions were awarded as the war progressed. Throughout the book the ranks of the Polish airmen while serving alongside the RAF are written as RAF ranks and change to reflect any promotion they received in Great Britain.

SELECTION OF RAF RANKS:

W/O	Warrant Officer
P/O	Pilot Officer
Sgt	Sergeant
F/Sgt	Flight Sergeant
F/O	Flying Officer
F/L	Flight Lieutenant
S/L	Squadron Leader
W/C	Wing Commander
G/Cpt	Group Captain
AVM	Air Vice Marshall
C-in-C	Commander in Chief

SELECTION OF POLISH RANKS:

Cadet	Cadet Officer often referred to in training.	
S/Lt	Second Lieutenant	(equivalent to an RAF Pilot Officer)
Lt	Lieutenant	(equivalent to an RAF Flying Officer)
Cpt	Captain	(equivalent to an RAF Flight Lieutenant)
Mjr	Major	(equivalent to an RAF Squadron Leader)
Lt./Col	Lieutenant Colonel	(equivalent to an RAF Wing Commander)
Col	Colonel	(equivalent to an RAF Group Captain)
C/O	Commanding Officer	(equivalent to an RAF Commanding Officer)

POLISH SQUADRONS AND WINGS IN GREAT BRITAIN:

No. 300 (Land of Mazovia) Bomber
No. 301 (Land of Pomerania) Bomber
No. 302 (City of Poznań) Fighter
No. 303 Kościuszko (City of Warsaw) Fighter
No. 304 (Land of Silesia) Bomber
No. 305 (Land of Wielkopolaska) Bomber
No. 306 (City of Turuń) Fighter
No. 307 (City of Lwów) Night Fighter
No. 308 (City of Kraków) Fighter
No. 309 (Land of Czerwein) Army Support
No. 315 (Dęblin) Fighter
No. 316 (City of Warsaw) Fighter
No. 317 (City of Wilno) Fighter
No. 318 (City of Gdańsk) Reconnaissance
No. 663 (Observation)

No. 1 Polish Fighter Wing (Northolt)
No. 2 Polish Fighter Wing (Exeter)
No. 3 Polish Fighter Wing (Perranporth)

BRIEF SELECTION OF AIRCRAFT:

Bloch MB152	French fighter aircraft
Karaś	Polish bomber used in the September Campaign 1939
PZL-7	Polish Air Force fighter
PZL-11	Polish Air Force fighter
Hurricane	Hawker Hurricane RAF fighter
Spitfire	Supermarine Spitfire RAF fighter
Wellington	Wellington Bomber RAF bomber
Me109	German Messerschmitt fighter with one Pilot
Me110	German Messerschmitt fighter with a pilot and a gunner
Do17	German Dornier bomber
He111	German Heinkel bomber
Ju88	German Junkers bomber
FW 190	German Focke-Wulf fighter

OPERATIONAL STATUS:

Standby	Pilot in the cockpit and ready to take off
Readiness	Pilot is 5 minutes from take off
Available	Pilot is 30 minutes from take off

VARIOUS:

Apany	No. 303 Kościuszko Squadron's radio call sign
AA	Anti-Aircraft
AK	Armia Krajowa, Home Army, the main Polish Resistance group
Des	Destroyed

MG	Machine Guns
NKVD	Narodnyi Komissariat Vnutrennikh Del, Soviet Secret Police
Ops	Operations flown by PAF, RAF and Allies
	(Americans used the term Missions for bomber raids)
ORD	Operational Record Diary
OTU	Operational Training Unit
PAF	Polish Air Force
RAF	Royal Air Force
RCAF	Royal Canadian Air Force
RDF	Radio Direction Finder
R/T	Radio Transmitter
SOE	Special Operations Executive
Sortie	An operational flight
TNA	The National Archives
Wing	A group of Squadrons flying together as a Wing.
	The PAF sometimes referred to a Squadron as a Wing.

Groupe de Chasse French fighter wing
No.111 & No.112 Fighter Flight in Poland Squadron a twin squadron, part of
No. 111/1 Fighter Squadron Wing

TYPES OF SORTIES:

Rhubarb	A small number of fighters, usually attacking in pairs, flying low under radar detection to destroy aircraft on the ground, airfields and other nearby targets on enemy territory.
Circus	An operation to escort bombers with a fighter escort.
Ramrod	Similar to a Circus sortie, escorting or meeting up with bombers over France to draw enemy fighters away from attacking RAF bombers.
Rodeo	A Fighter only sweep over enemy territory
Sphere	An offensive sweep, flown at high altitude over cloud in enemy territory. Not many enemy aircraft were sighted on Sphere sorties.

SELECTION OF MEDALS POLISH:

Krzyż Walecznych	(KW) Cross of Valour (Polish)
Krzyż Zasługi	Cross of Merit (Polish civilian state award)
Krzyż Zasługi z Mieczami	Cross of Merit with Swords (Polish military award)
Virtuti Militari (VM)	Gold Cross (equivalent to the British Victoria Cross)

SELECTION OF MEDALS BRITISH:

AFC	Air Force Cross
DFC	Distinguished Flying Cross
	(additional decorations were added by way of bars e.g. 2 bars)
DFM	Distinguished Flying Medal
DSO	Distinguished Service Order
OBE	Order of The British Empire

INDEX

Printed in Great Britain
by Amazon